DOSTOEVSKY
ON THE THRESHOLD OF OTHER WORLDS

DOSTOEVSKY ON THE THRESHOLD OF OTHER WORLDS

ESSAYS IN HONOUR OF MALCOLM V JONES

Edited by Sarah Young
and Lesley Milne

Bramcote Press
Ilkeston, Derbyshire
2006

© Sarah Young and Lesley Milne and authors of signed contributions 2006

All rights reserved. No reproduction, copy or transmission of the whole or any part of this publication may be made without written permission.

First published 2006 by
BRAMCOTE PRESS,
81 RAYNEHAM ROAD,
ILKESTON,
DERBYSHIRE DE7 8RJ,
UNITED KINGDOM

Printed in Great Britain by
Biddles Ltd., Kings Lynn

ISBN 1 900405 13 X

CONTENTS

Contributors vii

Note on Transliteration and References xii

Acknowledgements xii

Introduction: Dostoevsky Today xiii
    SARAH YOUNG

Part I: Mythos

Genres of Novel and Tale in Dostoevsky's Works 3
    RUDOLF NEUHÄUSER

Raskolnikov's Wardrobe: Dostoevsky's Use of Vestimentary
Markers for Literary Communication in *Crime and Punishment* ... 14
    BORIS CHRISTA

Dostoevsky and Pushkin: Petersburg motifs in *Crime and Punishment* ... 21
    VALENTINA VETLOVSKAIA

Reading *The Gambler* as *Roulettenburg* 40
    ERIK EGEBERG

Finding Form for Chaos: Dostoevsky's *The Adolescent*
and Akhmatova's *Poem Without a Hero* 46
    ALEXANDRA HARRINGTON

Whence Came Ivan Karamazov's Nightmare?
(Correspondence and Literary Creation) 64
    JACQUES CATTEAU

Part II: Dialogue

Apollon Maikov and the Cult of the Leader 75
    RICHARD PEACE

Dostoevsky, 'Bobok', Pierre Bobo and Boborykin 84
    JOHN MCNAIR

Public Education in England in the Pages of *The Citizen*
(1873-1874) during Dostoevsky's Editorship 98
    IRENE ZOHRAB

Dialogues with Dostoevsky in Tolstoy's *Resurrection* SARAH HUSPITH	110
Dostoevsky in the lectures and conversations of Merab Mamardashvili VLADIMIR TUNIMANOV	120
'A More Important Connection than People Think': Dostoevsky and Russian Music ARNOLD MCMILLIN	137

Part III: Text and Reader

The *Siuzhet* of Part I of *Crime and Punishment* ROBERT BELKNAP	153
Of Shame and Human Bondage: Dostoevsky's *Notes from Underground* DEBORAH MARTINSEN	157
Narrative Technique as 'Maieutics': Dostoevsky's *Crime and Punishment* HORST-JÜRGEN GERIGK	170
Crime and Punishment in the Classroom: The Elephant in the Garden ROBIN FEUER MILLER	175

Part IV: Religion

Dostoevsky on Children in the New Testament BORIS TIKHOMIROV	189
Dostoevsky and Music DIANE OENNING THOMPSON	207
Buddhism in Dostoevsky: Prince Myshkin and the True Light of Being SARAH YOUNG	220
'The Hero's Mistake' as a Special Device in Dostoevsky's Works TATIANA KASATKINA	230
Dostoevsky's Fantastic Pages VLADIMIR ZAKHAROV	239
Afterword LESLEY MILNE	255
Bibliography of Malcolm Jones's Publications	259
Index	269

CONTRIBUTORS

Robert L Belknap is Professor Emeritus of Russian at Columbia University in New York. He was educated at Princeton University, The University of Paris, Columbia University, and Leningrad (now St Petersburg) State University. He is the author of *The Structure of The Brothers Karamazov*, *The Genesis of The Brothers Karamazov*, and other studies of Russian literature or of American educational practice.

Jacques Catteau is Professor Emeritus of Russian Literature at Paris-Sorbonne and editor of *La Revue des études slaves*. Translator of Babel, Bely, Pilnyak and Zamyatin, among others, he was also co-editor from 1967 to 2000 of the *Slavica* collections for L'Age d'Homme. The author of numerous studies on Dostoevsky, he edited *Dostoïevski* (Cahier de l'Herne, 1973) and *Dostoïevski* (Verdier, 1983). His book *La Création littéraire chez Dostoïevski* (IES, 1978) was awarded the Grand Prix de la Critique littéraire in 1979, and was translated into English as *Dostoyevsky and the Process of Literary Creation* (Cambridge University Press, 1988), while his edition of Dostoevsky's correspondence (3 vols, Bartillat, 1998-2003) won the Prix Sévigné de la correspondance 1999.

Boris Christa is Emeritus Professor of Russian and Honorary Research Consultant at the University of Queensland, Australia. His publications include a book and many articles on Andrei Bely and Russian symbolism. Recently he has written extensively on aspects of pragmatic semiotics, focusing on the literary use of vestimentary markers especially by Dostoevsky.

Erik Egeberg is Professor of Russian Literature at the University of Tromsø, Norway. His research has focused on both Russian poetry (including Pushkin, Lermontov, Fet and Brodsky), and prose. In addition to writing a book and numerous articles on Dostoevsky, he was from 1989 to 2001 executive secretary of the International Dostoevsky Society, and from 1991 to 2000 was also editor-in-chief of the journal *Scando-Slavica*. He has translated major works of Russian literature, by Lermontov, Gogol, Dostoevsky, Tolstoy, Bely, Platonov and Bulgakov, and poetry from Lomonosov to Aigi.

Horst-Jürgen Gerigk was born in Berlin in 1937, and has been Professor of Russian and Comparative Literature at the University of Heidelberg since 1974. His main fields of study are Russian, German and American Literature. In 1995 his monograph *Die Russen in Amerika* appeared. From 1998 to 2004 he was President of the International Dostoevsky Society, and is Managing Editor of *Dostoevsky Studies*, New Series.

Alexandra Harrington completed her doctoral thesis at the University of Nottingham, and is now Lecturer in Russian in the School of Modern Languages and Cultures at the University of Durham. Her primary research interest is twentieth-century Russian poetry. Her study of Akhmatova, *Living in Different Mirrors: The Modernist and Postmodernist Incarnations of Anna Akhmatova*, is currently in press and due to be published in 2006 by Anthem Press.

Sarah Hudspith is Lecturer in Russian at The University of Leeds. A graduate of the University of Exeter, she received her PhD from the University of Sheffield in September 2000. She specializes in nineteenth-century Russian literature, particularly in the works of Dostoevsky and Tolstoy, and Russian religious thought. She is the author of *Dostoevsky and the Idea of Russianness: A New Perspective on Unity and Brotherhood* (London: RoutledgeCurzon, 2004).

Tatiana Alexandrovna Kasatkina is Professor in the Faculty of the Theory and History of Culture at RGU nefti i gaza im. I M Gubkina, a director of research in the Department of Theory at the Institute of World Literature and chair of IMLI RAN's Commission for the study of the works of F M Dostoevsky. She is the author of *Kharakterologiia Dostoevskogo* (Moscow, 1996) and *O tvoriashchei prirode slova: Ontologichnost' slova v tvorchestve F M Dostoevskogo kak osnova 'realizma v vysshem smysle'* (Moscow, 2004), and around 130 scholarly articles, and compiler, editor and author of the introductory articles and commentaries to the Collected Works of Dostoevsky (9 vols, Moscow 2003-2004).

Arnold McMillin, Professor of Russian Literature in the University of London, has written on Russian literature, Belarusian language and literature, and Russian music. Publications include: *The Vocabulary of the Byelorussian Literary Language in the Nineteenth Century* (London, 1973); *A History of Byelorussian Literature from Its Origins to the Present Day* (Giessen, 1977); *Belarusian Literature in the 1950s and 1960s: Release and Renewal* (Cologne etc., 1999); *Belarusian Literature of the Diaspora* (Birmingham, 2002), the latter two translated into Belarusian in 2001 and 2004 respectively.

John McNair heads the Russian programme in the School of Languages and Comparative Cultural Studies at the University of Queensland in Brisbane. He obtained his PhD in Russian literature at the University of Edinburgh, and held teaching appointments at the University of Ulster and Trinity College, Dublin before moving to Australia in 1983. His publications include *Russia and the Fifth Continent: Aspects of Russian-Australian Relations* (St Lucia: University of Queensland Press, 1992) and *At Home with the Gentry: A Victorian English Lady's Diary of Russian Country Life* (Nottingham: Bramcote Press, 1998), as well as numerous articles on nineteenth-century Russian literature. He is currently completing a literary biography of Boborykin and a critical anthology of Australian travel writing on Soviet Russia.

Deborah A Martinsen, Adjunct Associate Professor of Slavic, is Acting Director of the Core Curriculum at Columbia University and Executive Secretary of the

North American Dostoevsky Society. She is author of *Surprised by Shame: Dostoevsky's Liars and Narrative Exposure* (2003) and editor of *Literary Journals in Imperial Russia* (1997).

Robin Feuer Miller is the author of *Dostoevsky and The Idiot: Author, Narrator and Reader* and *The Brothers Karamazov: Worlds of the Novel*. She has also written on other nineteenth century Russian and European writers and is the editor of *Critical Essays on Dostoevsky*. Her most recent work includes two co-edited volumes, Kathryn B Feuer's *Tolstoy and the Genesis of War and Peace* (with Donna Tussing Orwin) and *The Cambridge Companion to the Classic Russian Novel* (with Malcolm Jones). She is Edytha Macy Gross Professor of Humanities at Brandeis University, where she teaches Russian and Comparative Literature.

Lesley Milne is Head of the School of Modern Languages and Cultures, University of Nottingham. Her publications include the monographs *The Master and Margarita: A Comedy of Victory* (Birmingham Slavonic Monographs, 1977), *Mikhail Bulgakov: A Critical Biography* (Cambridge University Press, 1990), *Zoshchenko and the Ilf-Petrov Partnership: How They Laughed* (Birmingham Slavonic Monographs, 2003). She is editor of the volumes *Bulgakov: The Novelist-Playwright* (Harwood Academic Publishers, 1995) and *Reflective Laughter: Aspects of Humour in Russian Culture* (Anthem Press, 2004).

Rudolf Neuhäuser, Professor Emeritus, completed his PhD at the University of Vienna in 1956. He taught in North America 1961-1975, becoming Full Professor at the University of Western Ontario, Canada. Professor of Slavic Studies at Klagenfurt University, Austria (1975-2001), he was a founder member of the International Dostoevsky Society, President 1989-1995 (Honorary President since 1998), and editor of its publications 1971-1996. He has held guest professorships at the Universities of Alberta, Cologne and Ljubljana. Elected Corresponding Member of the Slovenian Academy of Sciences and the Arts in 1995, until 1996 he was chairman of the Austrian Association of Slavists and Austrian Representative on the International Committee of Slavists. His interests include Russian literature eighteenth-twentieth centuries, South Slavic literatures, comparative literature and literary theory. He has published several books, including *Towards the Romantic Age* (The Hague, 1974), *Das Frühwerk Dostoevskijs* (Heidelberg, 1979), and *F M Dostoevskij: Die Grossen Romane und Erzählungen* (Vienna, 1993), and around 140 articles, including 'Zur Frage des literarischen Biedermeiers in Russland' (1982), 'Cechov und das Kierkegaard'sche Paradigma' (1997), and 'Die Weltsicht Dostojevskijs und das heutige Russland' (2003).

Richard Peace studied at Oxford University before lecturing at the University of Bristol (1963-1975). He was Professor at the University of Hull, 1975-1984 (Dean of Arts 1983-1984), and at Bristol 1984-1994. He has been Professor Emeritus at the University of Bristol since 1994. He was President of BUAS 1977-1980. His major publications are: *Dostoyevsky: An Examination of the Major Novels* (Cambridge University Press, 1971); *The Enigma of Gogol: An*

Examination of the Writings of N V Gogol and Their Place in the Russian Literary Tradition (Cambridge University Press, 1981); *Chekhov: A Study of the Four Major Plays* (Yale University Press, 1983); *'Oblomov': A Critical Examination of Goncharov's Novel* (Birmingham Slavonic Monographs, 1991); *Dostoyevsky's 'Notes from Underground'* (Bristol Classical Press, 1993); and *The Novels of Turgenev: Symbols and Emblems* (On Line: http://eis.bris.ac.uk/~rurap/welcome.htm). He is currently working on a book on *Crime and Punishment*.

Diane Oenning Thompson is an Affiliated Lecturer at the University of Cambridge, and has written and published widely on Dostoevsky. Her book, *'The Brothers Karamazov' and the Poetics of Memory* was published in 1991 (Cambridge University Press), and appeared in Russian translation in St Petersburg in 2000, and she co-edited (with George Pattison) *Dostoevsky and the Christian Tradition* (Cambridge University Press, 2001).

Boris Nikolaevich Tikhomirov, Assistant Director of research at the F M Dostoevsky Literary-Memorial Museum in St Petersburg. Vice-president of the Russian Dostoevsky Society. Member of the editorial board of the almanac *Dostoevskii i mirovaia kul'tura* (Compiler and editor of issues 6, 11, 13, 15, 16, 18-20). Author of around eighty publications in journals including *Russkaia literatura, Russkaia rech'*, collections such as *Dostoevskii: Materialy i issledovaniia, Dostoevskii v kontse XX veka, Stat'i o Dostoevskom: 1971-2001*, the almanac *Dostoevskii i mirovaia kul'tura*, and others.

Vladimir Tunimanov has worked at the Institute of Russian Literature (Pushkinskii dom) since 1968, until 1986 in the Dostoevsky group. He contributed to vols. 12 and 18-28 of the Academy *Complete Works of Dostoevsky*. From 1986-1988 he was deputy Academic Director of the Institute, and has also headed the Goncharov group and the Modern Russian Literature Department. His research focuses on the history of Russian literature and criticism nineteenth-twentieth centuries. He is the author of over two hundred articles, and his major publications include *Tvorchestvo F M Dostoevskogo 1854-1862* (1980), *A I Gertsen i russkaia obshchestvenno-literaturnaia mysl'* (1994), and *Dostoevskii i russkie pisateli XX veka* (2004).

Valentina Evgenievna Vetlovskaia graduated from Leningrad State University in 1962, completed her post graduate studies in 1967, and works at the Institute of Russian Literature (Pushkinskii dom). She is a specialist in modern Russian literature, a renowned researcher on Dostoevsky, as well as Pushkin, Gogol and other classic Russian writers of the nineteenth and twentieth centuries, a member of the Russian writers' union, and author of many articles and books, including: *Poetika romana 'Brat'ia Karamazovy'* (Leningrad, 1977), *Roman F M Dostoevskogo 'Bednye liudi'* (Leningrad, 1988), and *Analiz epicheskogo proizvedeniia. Problemy poetiki* (St Petersburg, 2002).

Sarah Young is Assistant Professor of Russian Literature at the University of Toronto. She was supervised for her doctoral thesis on Dostoevsky by Malcolm Jones, and held a Leverhulme Special Research Fellowship in the Department of Russian and Slavonic Studies at the University of Nottingham (2001-2003). Her book, *Dostoevsky's 'The Idiot' and the Ethical Foundations of Narrative*, was published by Anthem Press in 2004, and she has also written several articles on Dostoevsky. She is currently working on genre and the narrative voice in Russian labour camp prose.

Vladimir Nikolaevich Zakharov is Deputy Director of the Russian Humanities Fund (Moscow) and Professor in the Faculty of Russian Literature at Petrozavodsk University. He is a Vice President of the International Dostoevsky Society and author of the monographs *Problemy izucheniia Dostoevskogo* (1978) and *Sistena zhanrov Dostoevskogo: Tipologiia i poetika* (1985), and more than one hundred and thirty articles on the history and theory of literature. He has published Dostoevsky's Complete Collected Works in the author's orthography and punctuation (1995-present); *Polnoe sobranie sochinenii Dostoevskogo: V 18-ti tomakh* (Moscow, 2003-2005), and the electronic edition of *Polnoe sobranie sochinenii V Dalia*. He is editor of *Problemy istoricheskoi poetiki* (1990 and 1992), *Novye aspekty v izuchenii Dostoevskogo* (1994) and *Evangel'skii tekst v russkoi literature XVIII-XX vekov* (1994, 1998, 2001, 2005), and supervisor of the internet project www.philolog.ru.

Irene Zohrab, Victoria University, Wellington, New Zealand. Honorary Research Fellow, former Associate Professor in the School of European Languages and Literatures and Editor of *New Zealand Slavonic Journal: Journal of the Australia and New Zealand Slavists' Association*. Vice-President of ANZSA. National Representative of the IDS and Associate Editor of *The Dostoevsky Journal: An Independent Review*. Editor of a number of Festschrifts and collections; contributor to numerous books, series and journals on Russian culture and Dostoevsky.

Note on Transliteration and References

IN the bibliographic references for this volume, Russian is transliterated according to the Library of Congress system. In the text of the essays themselves, however, proper names are transliterated according to the standardized versions given in the *Oxford Writers' Dictionary*, changing '-ii' to '-y', '-ia' to '-ya' etc.; thus 'Dostoevsky' rather than 'Dostoevskii', 'Mayakovsky' rather than 'Maiakovskii'. Where anglicized versions and accepted spellings exist, these too have been used: 'Alexander' rather than 'Aleksandr', 'Tchaikovsky' and 'Mussorgsky' rather than 'Chaikovskii' and 'Musorgskii'. In citations from critical works which use an alternative system, that system is retained.

Throughout this book, the abbreviation *PSS* (followed by volume and page numbers) is used to indicate the standard complete edition of Dostoevsky's works: F M Dostoevskii, *Polnoe sobranie sochinenii v tridtsati tomakh* (Leningrad: Nauka, 1972-90). Where the author of a chapter cites other editions, full details are given in the notes.

Acknowledgements

Bramcote Press and the editors gratefully acknowledge the support given for this Festschrift by the University of Nottingham from the following sources, in recognition of the service given by Malcolm Jones to the University throughout his career at all levels: the Vice-Chancellor's Fund; the University Research Committee; the Dean's Fund, Faculty of Arts; the School of Modern Languages and Cultures; and the Department of Russian and Slavonic Studies.

The editors also wish to express their gratitude in particular to James Muckle of Bramcote Press for his careful work on the manuscript, and to Alexandra Harrington for assistance beyond her own essay. Finally, sincere thanks are due to Malcolm Jones himself, for his invaluable advice, support and friendship over many years.

Introduction

DOSTOEVSKY TODAY

Sarah Young

'WHY should we read Dostoevsky today?' is a question many lecturers face from students in one form or another. Does Dostoevsky's world of religious visionaries and cynical revolutionaries, of meek, kind-hearted prostitutes and hysterical *femmes fatales*, of brutal sensualists and sexual innocents, of aspiring Rothschilds and Napoleons, of melodrama, scandal and the grotesque, of hallucinations, devils and doubles, of dialogues with and indictments of the 'progressive' ideas 'in the air' in the mid-nineteenth century and the ever more forceful assertion of the Russian and in particular the Russian Orthodox ideal—a world which at first glance seems in many ways so remote from our own, from which everything 'normal' has apparently been removed, and which frequently, in spite of the all too often overlooked humorous aspects of his work, makes for painful reading—have a relevance today which continues to justify critical attention and his place on university syllabi? While the very question of 'relevance' may occasionally, and not without justification, cause scholars and teachers to throw their hands up in despair, it is not simply the product of a political agenda, or the sign of a utilitarian approach which increasingly dominates in the contemporary world, not least in education, but is a major factor in our work. Would we continue to read and study Dostoevsky in such numbers if he were only of historical interest? If the profound spiritual and ethical dilemmas he dramatizes in his writings, the 'accursed questions' he addresses with such terrifying urgency, did not still exercise us now? If his 'fantastic' evocation of Russian (and not only Russian) reality did not strike a chord today? If the foundations of not only the modern, but also of the postmodern world were not perceptible in his works? If he had not inspired responses in so many later, and great, writers and thinkers?

The multi-faceted and ambiguous nature of Dostoevsky's *oeuvre*—that which has resulted in the author being harnessed in support of the most diverse ideological positions, which meant, for instance, that *The Devils* could be deemed sufficiently reactionary and anti-revolutionary to be stocked in the pre-Revolutionary Tbilisi seminary library, where it was read by the young Stalin as a *blueprint* for revolution and terror[1]—led Mikhail Bakhtin to develop many of his ideas on dialogue, polyphony and carnival, which he later applied to other areas of literature and linguistic theory, initially, to borrow Pyotr Stepanovich

---

[1] See Donald Rayfield, *Stalin and His Hangmen* (London: Penguin Viking, 2004), p. 22.

Verkhovensky's formulation, 'whilst looking at' Dostoevsky. The fact that these ideas played a fundamental role in the development of later theories of narrative, intertextuality and culture shows Dostoevsky's importance not only as an acute commentator on human nature, but also as an experimental writer, and his impact—frequently indirect, for he is often only mentioned by theorists in passing—on literary scholarship as a whole.

While Dostoevsky's continuing presence in and influence on the literary world is evident, for example, in the fiction of Victor Pelevin (in which the post-Soviet world of gangsters and oligarchs proves just as Dostoevskian as the Terror of the 1930s), in the creative responses to the author's life and works of J M Coetzee's novel *The Master of Petersburg* (1994) and Leonid Tsypkin's *Summer in Baden-Baden* (written before 1981, but only now achieving the recognition it deserves), and in new translations of his works in recent years, for example those by David McDuff, and Richard Pevear and Larissa Volokhonsky, which have brought Dostoevsky alive again for a new generation of readers in the English-speaking world, his cultural impact extends far beyond the written word. Theatrical productions, art exhibitions and installations based on Dostoevsky's life and works are a regular feature of cultural life in Russia's two capitals; the Dostoevsky Memorial Museum in St Petersburg is now frequently cited as the most popular literary museum in the city; and Dostoevsky walking tours of Petersburg habitually attract far greater numbers than those dedicated to other writers connected to the city.[2]

Moreover, in addition to the Russian film scores and operatic reworkings of Dostoevsky's texts discussed here in Arnold McMillin's contribution, the wider film community has frequently turned to Dostoevsky. Passing hastily over the 1958 Hollywood version of *The Brothers Karamazov*, directed by Richard Brooks, which now retains mainly curiosity value for the pre-*Star Trek* appearance of William Shatner, the high point of Dostoevsky adaptations perhaps remains Akira Kurasawa's version of *The Idiot* (*Hakuchi*, 1951). More recently we have seen Karoly Makk's *The Gambler* (1997), which intertwines the novella with the perennially fascinating story of Dostoevsky's quasi-Faustian pact—the author as gambler—with the publisher Stellovsky, and his romance with Anna Grigorievna. Rob Schmidt's *Crime and Punishment in Suburbia* (2000) reworked Dostoevsky's novel in a contemporary American setting, while the same novel was given a more traditional treatment in a 2002 BBC production. The merits of turning Dostoevsky into sanitized heritage costume drama may of course be endlessly disputed, but in spite of the inevitable simplification, not to say in many cases bowdlerization, which occurs in such productions, the fact that reading, as Robin Feuer Miller emphasizes in her essay in the current volume, is in decline – and not only in the West but also in Russia—suggests that film

---

[2]My thanks to the historian Timofei Kruglikov, who regularly conducts Dostoevsky and Pushkin tours in St Petersburg, for this information.

and television adaptations now have a significant role to play in introducing classic texts by 'off-putting' writers like Dostoevsky to a new audience, whatever the reservations of (us) purists.[3] Vladimir Bortko's epic adaptation of *The Idiot* for Russian television in 2003, whilst not untypically for Dostoevsky, both in print and on the screen, dividing critics and viewers alike, achieved large audiences and generated a huge amount of press coverage, suggesting that, one way or another, his pre-eminent position within Russian culture is not in doubt.[4]

For much of the twentieth century, Dostoevsky's enduring legacy was perhaps his prophecy of totalitarianism, a perennial topic on which Vladimir Tunimanov's article in this collection sheds new light, but what of today, following the collapse of the Soviet system? Many of the social problems he addresses repeatedly in both his fiction and non-fiction—crime, poverty, gambling, alcoholism, child abuse, the breakdown of the family—remain pressing concerns. His indictment of materialism—most forcefully expressed in *The Idiot*—has perhaps even greater resonance now than it did when he was writing, and it is in the concomitant loss of fundamental values, and in the matrix of faith and its absence which underlies his entire mature *oeuvre*, that Dostoevsky's relevance is most clearly visible today. While for many years, following the Revolution, and during the Cold War for the West in particular, the fundamental, and most prescient, opposition in Dostoevsky's works may have seemed simply to be that between religious belief and atheism/socialism/utilitarianism, now, in the post-9/11 world, the ground has shifted somewhat; the danger arising out of the secularized world's loss of faith today comes not from extreme forms of that loss of faith, but rather from extreme forms of faith itself. However, although Dostoevskian radicalism and revolutionism—and their real-life twentieth-century counterparts—and twenty-first-century religious fundamentalism and terrorism may be far apart in terms of content, reversing the polarities of faith and unbelief to which we have grown accustomed, they pose a threat for the same reason: both are totalizing (monologic) ideologies, which admit neither doubt nor dialogue. In this context, the role of the 'crucible of doubt' in forging Dostoevsky's own religious beliefs and his representation of spiritual questions in his novels, about which Malcolm Jones has spoken and written so eloquently, becomes more central than ever to

---

[3] Indeed, when it comes to teaching Dostoevsky, a topic of great importance for many of us, film adaptations/interpretations can provide a useful starting-point for discussion.

[4] Some time ago, a friend told me of a newspaper report about a monument in Petersburg to hairdressers who had continued to work during the siege of Leningrad; the inscription on the monument was Dostoevsky's immortal line, 'Beauty will save the world'. Subsequent canvassing of friends and colleagues in the city suggests (hardly surprisingly) that the story was apocryphal (?), yet it is somehow entirely fitting: it harnesses Dostoevsky himself to the rumour-mongering with which his novels are filled, and is a supreme example of double-voiced discourse, the use of the quotation in its very inappropriateness participating fully in Dostoevskian poetics; it is also, in its knowingness (whether as a story or as an actual inscription on an actual monument), indicative of his unique place in Russia; it is not only his characters and the atmosphere of his works that have become part of the cultural landscape, but the entirety of his novelistic vision.

our understanding of the author's works. To this we can add questions of torture, imprisonment and political prisoners, raised primarily by *House of the Dead* but also present implicitly in many of his other works, the clash between the Christian and Muslim worlds (as well as that between East and West) he addresses in *Diary of a Writer*, and the eternal question, 'Whither Russia?' In the geo-political, as well as the spiritual and ethical, realities of the early twenty-first century, in other words, reading Dostoevsky has as much to offer as ever. He is, as Robin Feuer Miller says, always a timely writer.

It is for this reason that Dostoevsky not only retains his cultural importance, but also remains such an exciting subject for research. His 'broadness' means that there is always new scope for interpretation, and new angles, going far beyond the confines of literary theory and criticism, from which to approach him,[5] so that there seems little danger of him going out of fashion. However, this certainly does not signify complacency, and in fact, the last two or three decades, and in particular in the last fifteen years, with the greater freedom of Russian scholars to contribute to, and indeed set the agenda for, debate, have seen Dostoevsky studies flourish as never before. The publication of a new *Complete Works*,[6] with excellent notes and essays, edited by Vladimir Zakharov, demonstrates the strength of Dostoevsky scholarship in Russia, while the on-line concordance of Dostoevsky's works,[7] behind which Professor Zakharov was once again the driving force, has become an invaluable resource for many researchers. The development of the resource centre at the Dostoevsky Museum in St Petersburg has been an equally welcome addition.[8] Long-standing annual conferences at that museum and at the Dostoevsky museum in Staraia Russa, and the triennial symposium of the International Dostoevsky Society provide a fascinating forum for discussion and argument (not to say, on occasion, scandal), and have created a world-wide scholarly community which has in itself contributed much to the strength of the subject. Meanwhile, publications dedicated to Dostoevsky, from journals (the International Dostoevsky Society's *Dostoevsky Studies*) and almanacs (*Dostoevskii i mirovaia kul'tura* (*Dostoevsky and World Culture*), published by the Petersburg Dostoevsky Museum), to series (IRLI RAN's *Dostoevskii: Materialy i issledovaniia* (*Dostoevsky: Materials and Research*); IMLI RAN's new series of collections of essays under the editorship of Tatiana Kasatkina), and the

---

[5] Debate on Dostoevsky over the years has been enriched by contributions from scholars in as varied fields as psychoanalysis, neurology, law, criminology and, most significantly, theology.

[6] F M Dostoevskii, *Polnoe sobranie sochinenii: v 18-i tomakh* (Moscow: Voskresen'e, 2004).

[7] See: <http://www.karelia.ru/~Dostoevsky/main_e.htm>.

[8] See the museum's web site, <http://www.md.spb.ru/index.cgi?pg=collection&lg=rus>, for details of books, manuscripts and other materials in the collection. The companion site is a fascinating catalogue of illustrations of Dostoevsky's works: <http://www.dostoevsky.net>. Mention should be made here of the extraordinary achievement of staff at the Dostoevsky Museum, including Natalya Ashimbaeva, Vera Biron, Boris Tikhomirov and Natalya Chernova, in developing the museum.

regular appearance of one-off collections and monographs,[9] both ensure that debate continues to develop and testify to the centrality of the field within Russian literary studies.[10]

While a large range of interpretative and theoretical approaches remains the norm, undoubtedly the most important development in Dostoevsky studies in recent years has been the focus on religious interpretations. Although always an important topic, the study of the religious foundations of Dostoevsky's work has been given fresh life by Russian scholars well versed in Bakhtinian poetics—several of those represented in these pages prominently among them—and embraced by many in the wider Dostoevsky community, leading, among other things, to analysis of his use of biblical and liturgical sources, the role of Christian and more specifically Orthodox motifs such as hesychasm, holy foolishness and kenosis, and the image of Christ in his works.

---

[9] Including, but by no means limited to, the publication in the last five years of: Joseph Frank, *Dostoevsky: The Mantle of the Prophet, 1971-1881* (Princeton: Princeton University Press; London: Robson, 2002); Richard Freeborn, *Dostoevsky* (London: Haus Publishing, 2003); Bruce French, *Dostoevsky's 'Idiot': Dialogue and the Spiritually Good Life* (Evanston, IL: Northwestern University Press, 2001); Sarah Hudspith, *Dostoevsky and the Idea of Russianness* (London: Curzon Routledge, 2004); Robert Louis Jackson, ed., *A New Word on 'The Brothers Karamazov'* (Evanston, IL: Northwestern University Press, 2004); Malcolm Jones, *Dostoevsky and the Dynamics of Religious Experience* (London: Anthem, 2005); T A Kasatkina, *O tvoriashchei prirode slova: Ontologichnost' slova v tvorchestve F M Dostoevskogo kak osnova 'realizma v vysshem smysle'* (Moscow: IMLI RAN, 2004); T A Kasatkina, ed., *Roman F M Dostoevskogo 'Idiot': Sovremennoe sostoianie izucheniia*, Moscow, Nasledie, 2001); Efim Kurganov, *Roman F M Dostoevskogo 'Idiot': Opyt prochteniia* (St Petersburg: Zvezda, 2001); W J Leatherbarrow, *A Devil's Vaudeville: The Demonic in Dostoevsky's Major Fiction* (Evanston, IL: Northwestern University Press, 2005); W J Leatherbarrow, ed., *The Cambridge Companion to Dostoevskii* (Cambridge: Cambridge University Press, 2002); Deborah Martinsen, *Surprised by Shame: Dostoevsky's Liars and Narrative Exposure* (Columbus, OH: The Ohio State University Press, 2003); George Pattison and Diane Oenning Thompson, eds., *Dostoevsky and the Christian Tradition* (Cambridge: Cambridge University Press, 2001); James P Scanlan, *Dostoevsky the Thinker* (Ithaca and London: Cornell University Press, 2002); Sarah Young, *Dostoevsky's 'The Idiot' and the Ethical Foundations of Narrative: Reading, Narrating, Scripting* (London: Anthem, 2004).

[10] It is not, however, all good news; while in Russia and North America Dostoevsky is still a major force in undergraduate and postgraduate studies, as well as among scholars, in British universities the climate is somewhat different. The retirement of a number of prominent nineteenth-century scholars, not least Malcolm Jones and Richard Peace, has left a large gap which seems unlikely to be more than partially filled. Not only are fewer postgraduates in Britain studying nineteenth-century literature, but at undergraduate level as well, the traditional literature syllabus, which for so long formed the backbone of most Russian degree courses, is gradually being supplanted by more 'popular' options—again, the decline of reading comes into play here—such as history, cultural studies and film. Nevertheless, the fact that when Dostoevsky courses are offered to students, they generally prove extremely popular, even among reluctant readers, should give pause for thought. And the presence of the British (by birth or university affiliation) contributors to the current volume, and of several more academics working in Britain who write on Dostoevsky and participate in conferences and symposia on the author, suggests that all is not yet lost.

This is one of several areas to which Malcolm Jones, to whom this volume is dedicated, has made a significant contribution. His long engagement with writings on religious themes, both within Dostoevsky studies and beyond, alongside his extensive knowledge of theology and the Bible,[11] and his sensitivity and alertness to the subtleties of the text, have now resulted in a new monograph, *Dostoevsky and the Dynamics of Religious Experience*,[12] bringing together and developing several years' work on the topic, but the religious context of Dostoevsky's *oeuvre* is also a central theme in *Dostoyevsky after Bakhtin* (1990).[13] In this book, Malcolm demonstrates the possibility of combining different factors—most prominently the Christian, the psychological, the narratological, the intertextual—into an overarching theory which not only elucidates and connects many aspects of Dostoevsky's novels by developing Bakhtin's theories, but has also become a model and starting-point for many subsequent analyses, making it surely one of the most regularly cited monographs on Dostoevsky, particularly since its translation into Russian in 1998.

As the breadth of the frames of reference of *Dostoyevsky after Bakhtin* suggests, religious themes are far from being Malcolm's sole preoccupation, and he has throughout his career addressed many other issues within Dostoevsky studies, in particular relating Dostoevsky to the tradition of European philosophy, be that in the guise of German Idealism, psychoanalysis or deconstruction, as well as writing on numerous other authors, thinkers and cultural figures, including, not infrequently, subjects far beyond Russian literary studies.

It therefore befits both the range of Malcolm's work, and the nature of Dostoevsky studies as a whole, that the essays collected in his honour here cover such a broad spectrum of topics and methodologies, covering not only literary themes and narratological analyses, but also responses to Dostoevsky by other writers and in cultural production more broadly, as well as the author's own intellectual milieu. The scope of interpretative possibilities in Dostoevsky's *oeuvre* is demonstrated by the radically different approaches brought to ostensibly similar themes, encompassing both the familiar, for example, the fantastic (Zakharov and Catteau), and Petersburg (Vetlovskaia and Harrington), and the new, notably music (Thompson and McMillin), and education (Miller and Zohrab). Meanwhile, five very different essays focusing on *Crime and Punishment*, from minute details to the broader picture, from its literary origins to its effect on the reader, indicate the potential for variety in the examination of a

---

[11]Knowledge he is always happy to share; I am particularly indebted to Malcolm for his generosity in respect of this aspect of my work.

[12]See note 9 for full publication details.

[13]Malcolm V Jones, *Dostoyevsky after Bakhtin: Readings in Dostoyevsky's Fantastic Realism* (Cambridge: Cambridge University Press, 1990).

single novel,[14] while other contributions, for example those by Neuhäuser, Thompson, Tikhomirov and Kasatkina, cover multiple texts, elucidating Dostoevsky's artistic, philosophical and theological development, and drawing our attention to some of the many points of contact between his works.

The essays in Part I explore the patterns of symbols and ideas at the basis of Dostoevsky's novelistic world. Rudolf Neuhäuser and Boris Christa concentrate on the encoding of the text on very different levels, the former relating to the differences between Dostoevsky's use of longer and shorter genres, the latter introducing a new means of orientation around *Crime and Punishment* by clarifying an area which is generally opaque for the contemporary reader. Jacques Catteau and Valentina Vetlovskaia both examine the literary substructure of Dostoevsky's novels, demonstrating the development of the author's response to Pushkin. Like Vetlovskaia, Alexandra Harrington and Erik Egeberg emphasize the importance of setting in Dostoevsky; the implications of the Petersburg text are related here not only to his predecessor but also, by Harrington, to one of his most important twentieth-century heirs. In both these essays the impact of the city on the characters is emphasized; this feature, moving to an entirely different location, is seen from a different angle in Egeberg's contribution, which shifts attention from the individual to interpret the significance of the collective in *The Gambler*.

In Part II, Dostoevsky's dialogues come to the forefront. Richard Peace examines the poetry of one of Dostoevsky's close contemporaries, a name we all know but whose work is much less familiar, and indicates the connections between their writings. John McNair, in charting the curious relationship between Dostoevsky and Pyotr Boborykin, and Irene Zohrab, in her exploration of a debate on English public schools, shed further light on the literary atmosphere of the times, taking us into the preoccupations and mores of the nineteenth-century intelligentsia, in one case relating to one of its worthier pursuits, in the other somewhat less so. Arnold McMillin broadens the picture in an essay on musical interpretations and adaptations of Dostoevsky's fiction, while in Sarah Hudspith and Vladimir Tunimanov's contributions, the ethical foundations of the author's work are clarified through the responses of other writers.

Part III focuses on the reader's dialogue with the text, and in particular its ethical implications. Robin Feuer Miller addresses issues of contemporary readership and the role of educators in her discussion of teaching *Crime and Punishment*, while Deborah Martinsen demonstrates how the underground man's strategies for dealing with his 'audience' become part of his (shame-based) relationships with others. Robert Belknap and Horst-Jürgen Gerigk both examine the manipulation of the reader in *Crime and Punishment*, the former in relation

---

[14] The fact that such a sizeable proportion of the contributors to this collection have chosen to address *Crime and Punishment* also suggests that, having been somewhat neglected in comparison with the large volume of scholarly work devoted to *The Idiot* and *The Brothers Karamazov* in recent years, this novel is now returning to the forefront of critical attention.

to the series of oppositions the novel establishes, the latter in relation to the possibility of a new ethic.

The essays in Part IV turn to the religious themes which play such a major part in Dostoevsky studies today. Both Boris Tikhomirov and Tatiana Kasatkina concentrate on Dostoevsky's use of biblical quotations. Tikhomirov's commentary on Dostoevsky's references to children in the New Testament elucidates the process of exegesis in the author's writing, leading to the creation of his unique theology, while Kasatkina examines the reader's role in the reception of these quotations; both she and Diane Thompson, who explores musical motifs in Dostoevsky's final three novels, confirm the importance of the Christian substructure in his narratives. In common with Thompson's essay, the contributions by Vladimir Zakharov and myself show the different forms the religious aspect of Dostoevsky's work can take; Zakharov demonstrates how it is manifested in the key concept of the fantastic, while I focus on the question of religious experience, to suggest a broader search to clarify our understanding of the theological and philosophical underpinnings of Dostoevsky's novelistic world.

PART I

Mythos

GENRES OF NOVEL AND TALE IN DOSTOEVSKY'S WORKS

Rudolf Neuhäuser

IN questions of literary genre, it is usual to establish certain parameters pertaining to form and content with the aim of distinguishing, for instance, the novel from the tale or story. Fundamental questions of this kind are not, however, treated here. It is assumed that these genres functioned in nineteenth-century Russia much as they did in other European literatures.

This essay deals rather with the relationship of genre and content-oriented elements, above all motifs and situations with which the characters of the texts are confronted, and the question of how they react to them on the basis of their psychological and intellectual constitution, the author thereby eventually revealing himself and his intentions in a more or less encoded form. The question posed in this context is whether a clear distinction can be established between the genres of tale or story *(povest'/rasskaz)* and novel *(roman)* in Dostoevsky's work. In the writer's early period, which extends roughly until 1860/1861, this remains as yet ill-defined. Apart from *Poor Folk* (1845), an epistolary novel patterned on the eighteenth-century English model—as well as being his famous first work—the unfinished novel *Netochka Nezvanova* (1846), and *The Insulted and Injured*, Dostoevsky did not write any novels in this period. Furthermore, his early work clearly shows his dependence on literary models, although his originality in the treatment of these models cannot be questioned. The kind of novel that characterises his mature creative period developed only in the course of the 1860s and ultimately included five 'great' novels. The novel *The Gambler* (1866), which appeared at the same time as *Crime and Punishment* and was written by Dostoevsky out of the need to fulfil a contractual obligation, stands apart from the great novels and exhibits rather the characteristics of the smaller genres. We shall classify it as such here.

In the course of the transition from the Romantic Age to Realism, the assumption had developed in Russia since approximately the 1830s that the novel found its central theme in the representation of aspects of Russian society. It can be said, with Lotman, that the realist novel made the transition to a literature that went beyond the fate of the individual, which had been the central problem of romantic literature, turning to the problems of society as such in its very existence. This required formulating the theme and *sujet* (Russian: *siuzhet*) in such a way that, as with myth, a universal meaning would again become possible, in which state and nation in their entirety would be reflected in the relationships (as Lotman puts it) generated by the *sujet*.[1] The realist novel tends therefore, Lotman argues, to a re-mythologization, or to the creation of novelistic 'pseudo-myths'. Lotman thus sees the originality of the Russian realist novel in the development of a Russian *sujet* in the sense of an *'archisujet'*, which forms the basis of more or less all, and in particular Dostoevsky's, novels. Lotman's account of the *archisujet* has three fundamental components: (1) *Rus'* (embodied in a female figure), and the opposing figures of (2) a *pogubitel'/soblaznitel'* ('destroyer' /'seducer') and (3) a *spasitel'/mnimyi spasitel'* ('saviour'/'false saviour') (both embodied in male figures). The *sujet*'s sphere of action extends with regard to *Rus'* between the poles of *byt' pogublennoi* and *byt' spasennoi*. From time to time, a mediator appears between the two opposing figures, who functions as an *uchitel' zhizni* ('teacher of life'). Lotman's general assertions regarding the *archisujet* of the Russian realist novel apply to a considerable extent to Dostoevsky, who, after his own fashion, used this pattern for his novels. His hopes rested with the aristocrat who, purified on the one hand by his experience with the West and on the other by having accepted his Russian heritage *(pochva)*, turns into the saviour *(spasitel')* of his people, bringing about a reconciliation of the two great social strata of the nobility and the people. Dostoevsky found his model character in the figure of Chatsky from Griboedov's drama *Woe from Wit*. We notice this first in *Winter Notes on Summer Impressions*, where we read: 'Chatsky is a quite specific type of our Russian Europe, a pleasant, enthusiastic, suffering type. Appealing to Russia and to our native soil, and yet going back to Europe again all the same [...] Now he is reborn in the youthful generation and, we believe, in youthful vigour, we believe that he will appear once more [...] as a conqueror, proud, mighty, meek and loving'.[2] Chatsky turns up again later in Dostoevsky. In the novel *The Adolescent* this is explicitly made clear in play-acting, with Versilov playing the role of Griboedov's hero. Yet the Dostoevskian saviour of Russia, as a rule, turns out to be a Chatsky manqué, i.e. a *mnimyi spasitel'*.

Horst-Jürgen Gerigk recently extended this pattern fundamentally,[3] replacing the Lotmanian concept of chronotope with the more comprehensive term *Zeitwelt*. The concept of *Zeitwelt* originated with Reiner Wiehl, who calls *Zeitwelten* 'subjective personal worlds'. Wiehl: 'A *Zeitwelt* is in this context an individual: an unrepeatable, unique, indivisible union of world, time and subject. The components of this union belong inseparably together. Outside this totality,

---

[1] Ju M Lotman, 'Die Entstehung des Sujets—typologisch gesehen', in Ju M Lotman, *Kunst als Sprache* (Leipzig: Reclam UB 905, 1981), pp. 175-204. Cf. R Neuhäuser, 'Gončarovs Roman *Obryv* und der russische Roman des Realismus,' in *I A Gončarov. Beiträge zu Werk und Wirkung*, ed. Peter Thiergen (Cologne-Vienna: Boehlau, 1989), pp. 85-106.

[2] *PSS*, V, 4f.

[3] Horst-Jürgen Gerigk, 'Das Russland-Bild in den fünf großen Romanen Dostojewskijs', in *Zeitperspektiven. Studien zu Kultur und Gesellschaft*, ed. Uta Gerhardt (Stuttgart: Franz Steiner Verlag, 2003), pp. 49-79.

none has an independent existence'.[4] All five great novels, so Gerigk argues, reveal a *Zeitwelt* characterized by certain features common to all of them. It is relevant in this context that the events portrayed in these novels are all concerned with one decade, i.e. the years from 1865 to 1875. This period begins with the novel *Crime and Punishment*, set in 1865, and ends with *The Adolescent*, which deals with the years 1873/74. In between lie the events of the other three novels. Gerigk writes: 'Dostoevsky records with these four novels [*The Brothers Karamazov* is not included in this reckoning] the developments in Russian society step by step from 1865 up to the threshold of 1875'. As to *The Brothers Karamazov*, which is set in 1866, Gerigk argues, 'Here Dostoevsky wanted, once more, to write the diagnosis of his decade, this time incorporating the insights he had gathered in the meantime'.[5] As we know, there existed a plan for the continuation of the novel, taking the action up to 1879. However, this was not realized. The *Zeitwelt* of the five novels, in fact, shows an astounding unity. This also applies to the scene of action—Russia—and to the configuration of characters of the novels, who represent a cross-section of contemporary Russian society. The central characters are either depicted in their youth or early maturity. Raskolnikov, Myshkin the 'Idiot', Rogozhin, Stavrogin/Verkhovensky, the Adolescent, and the Karamazovs differ little in age; they are all variations on the archetype *gubitel'/spasitel'*. It is notable in this context that at the beginning of the series of great novels, i.e. the five novels mentioned above, the Chatsky model is still lacking a clear outline—not until the epilogue does Raskolnikov actually appear as a potential *spasitel'*. In later novels, as in *The Devils*, *The Adolescent*, and *The Brothers Karamazov*, this figure becomes split into two or more component parts. In the novels *Crime and Punishment* and *The Idiot*, the main characters may still be classified rather as belonging to the type of *mnimye spasiteli* than the 'saviours' of Russia. The main characters of the next two novels, who once again can clearly be classified as *mnimye spasiteli*, are joined by a second character, who embodies the qualities of an *uchitel' zhizni*. In *The Devils* this is Bishop Tikhon; in *The Adolescent*, Makar Dolgoruky. The latter figure reappears transformed into a veritable ideal as Starets Zosima in *The Brothers Karamazov*. All three characters clearly correspond to the Lotmanian *uchitel' zhizni*. In the beginning, the *mnimyi spasitel'* is drawn barely in outline. Raskolnikov, embodying hope or premonition, is followed by Myshkin, who at the beginning of the novel seems to be conceived as a *spasitel'*, but who finally fails, as his character flaws, caused by an overly romantic and idealistic attitude, lead to fatal consequences. He is the first of the author's characters to be accompanied by an antithesis, embodied in the merchant Rogozhin. The contrast is exploited even more sharply in *The Devils*, where Stavrogin and Verkhovensky

---

[4]Reiner Wiehl, *Zeitwelten. Philosophisches Denken an den Rändern von Natur und Geschichte* (Frankfurt am Main: Suhrkamp, 1998), p. 7.
[5]Horst-Jürgen Gerigk, 'Das Russland-Bild...', p. 59.

junior dominate the action and the *mnimyi spasitel'* Stavrogin is manipulated by the *gubitel'* Verkhovensky. In *The Adolescent* the constellation is altered once again. Dostoevsky confronts the now ageing aristocrat Versilov—who in the past had slipped into the role of Chatsky—with his 'son', the adolescent who desperately wants to decipher his father's role-play. Versilov, as *mnimyi spasitel'*, cannot, however, point the way to salvation. This is undertaken, by Makar, the bearer of Orthodox faith and the adolescent's biological father, the family ties emphasizing this fact. What did not reach fruition in this novel was evidently intended to find fulfilment in Dostoevsky's final novel: Alyosha Karamazov, the spiritual son of Starets Zosima (*uchitel' zhizni*), was now to become the ideal model of a *spasitel'* in the unwritten continuation of the novel. This is as much as indicated by the author's few notes on the novel's continuation.

With respect to plot-structure and the author's manipulation of the reader's expectations, we can observe another pervasive characteristic, as Horst-Jürgen Gerigk has convincingly shown: Dostoevsky constructs his five great novels in accordance with his 'secret machiavellian' poetics (Gerigk), in such a way that he captivates the 'sensation-hungry' reader (meaning the great mass of readers of his time) and thereby ensures the (financial) success of the novels. 'The result is five great novels which are a calculated mixture of crime, disease, sexuality, religion, and politics, presented with an unremitting "joviality of spirit" and a narrative technique that puts everything to the service of a single central situation and constantly makes us crane our necks, for there is simultaneously something shown to us and something withheld'.[6] Yet that is only the author's superficial intention. Behind these five constituent elements lies something entirely different. This superior aim, part of the 'meta-'fictional sphere, is obvious: Dostoevsky wants to present the reader with an exemplary moral world; one that corresponds little, however, to the world around him. He achieves this through the purposely distorted presentation of the latter's negative aspects, above all crime, accompanied, as its preliminary stage or consequence, by disease, the result of an increasingly questionable morality, a false consciousness, a 'diseased', or absent, conscience. This makes the potential or actual criminal recognisable for his environment. Alongside crime and disease the author places unbridled sexuality, libidinous excess, so that in contrast *his* model of a moral world receives clear outlines—a world that, in the view of the author, is anchored in the human conscience and has its origin in God. For the criminal who refuses to atone for his deed, there remains only the possibility of a flight abroad, i.e. the world outside Russia, which is thereby characterised as the location of immorality, or at least indifference in the face of moral law—or suicide, i.e. absolute exclusion from society, eternal damnation.

---

[6]Horst-Jürgen Gerigk, 'Die Gründe für die Wirkung Dostojewskijs', *Dostoevsky Studies*, 2 (1981), 7. Crime, disease, sexuality, religion and politics are discussed here in the sense of 'Wirkungsfaktoren' (H-J Gerigk: 'constituent elements'), meant to ensure the commercial success of the novel.

Belief in God and Christ is the most direct expression of authorial intention; the essence, so to speak, of those aspects of the genre of the Dostoevskian novel that stem from the metafictional sphere. But even here Dostoevsky provokes the reader through the often very direct links between aspects of religiosity and crime and immorality, turning the reader's attention to the precarious nature of religious ideas in an uncertain world, shaken in its morality. Apart from the novel *The Devils*, politics remain in the background, but are associated nevertheless in Dostoevsky's *Zeitwelt* with the remaining constituent elements, in order to achieve the task the author has set himself—to give a diagnosis of his time and society; to outline the place of Russia in Europe and the world, which, according to Dostoevsky, depends on the historical, or providential, mission of Russia, to the realization of which he desired to contribute.

We shall now ask how this compares with Dostoevsky's shorter narrative work from 1860 until the end of the seventies. Eleven tales were written between 1860 and 1877, to which we can add *The Gambler*, which in form and scope corresponds more to the *povest'* than to the novel. We immediately notice the manifold terms of classification employed by the author himself: (1) notes and comments *(zapiski, zametki)*; (2) anecdotes and stories *(anekdoty, istorii)*; (3) stories and tales *(rasskazy, povesti)*; (4) fantastic tales *(fantasticheskie rasskazy)*. Criteria of form and content mingle and little uniformity is to be expected at first glance.

The short narrative works that appeared before Dostoevsky's first great novel *Crime and Punishment* (1866) differ fundamentally from the later texts. These early texts can be seen as a preparation for, or preliminary stage to, the five great novels, insofar as the author worked out his ideological position in them. *Notes from the House of the Dead* are the basis for his understanding of the people, the ordinary Russian as the author came to know him in Siberia. *Winter Notes on Summer Impressions* clarify his position with regard to the West. They are an incisive critique of bourgeois society and the social and political system that predominated in Western Europe. Furthermore, it is here that the figure of Griboedov's Chatsky is first clearly drawn as a model for the 'saviour' of Russia from Western depravity. 'A Nasty Story' and 'The Crocodile', described as an 'anecdote' and an 'occurrence' *(sobytie)* or 'truthful story' *(spravedlivaia povest')*, are polemical texts from the time of Dostoevsky's clash with the 'progressive' intelligentsia. The polemic is in constant danger here of interfering with literary quality. Both still owe much to Dostoevsky's tales of the forties. In both, the theme of the civil servant and Russian bureaucracy is continued, the emphasis being put on hierarchic differences. The former tale was published in 1862, on the eve of the great reforms, and it caricatures the then fashionable liberal attitude of higher-ranking civil servants, which proves finally to be nothing but a role-play. In 'The Crocodile', a first-person narrator describes events from the point of view of a spectator. There are clear references to be found to Dostoevsky's polemic with the Nihilists. Chernyshevsky, Saltykov-Shchedrin, Pisarev, Zaitsev, and others criticized by Dostoevsky form the ideological background to 'The Crocodile'.[7] With one exception, Dostoevsky was to write no similar polemic texts in this genre. Also the situation of the civil servant—apart from the one exception ('Bobok')—remained marginalized.

So much for the five tales that precede the *Zeitwelt* of the great novels. *Notes from Underground*, as has been argued many times, form the 'gateway' to the great novels. Here Dostoevsky defines the starting point, so to speak, of his novels, the situation at the very beginning of the *Zeitwelt* of the great novels. What Dostoevsky once wrote about the 'sceptical and unhappy' consciousness (Hegel) of the Russian intellectual, which he saw realised in the character of Pechorin from Lermontov's *Hero of our Time* (1840), defines the background for the youthful hero of Part II of *Notes from Underground*: 'In Pechorin he achieved a restless, caustic bitterness and experienced the strange, specifically Russian conflict of diverse character elements; an egotism driven to the point of self-apotheosis, accompanied by a furious self-contempt, the same yearning desire for truth and action and the same unremitting and disastrous inactivity...'[8] Sixteen years later, this essentially romantic type, having tried Rationalism, Utilitarianism and Socialism, becomes the irrationally judging and acting voluntarist, the sceptic and cynic of Part I of the *Notes*.[9] Something else should be noted: the first person narrators of the *zapiski/zametki* of the sixties can either clearly be recognized as the author himself, or as his more or less masked double.

With the terms *zapiski* and *zametki*, Dostoevsky had, in the early sixties, taken up genres from the thirties and forties. It is characteristic that *zapiski* appear once more only in a late text of the seventies, and there only in the subtitle of the story. The tale in question is the above-mentioned exception 'Bobok': *Notes of a Certain Person* (1873).[10] 'Bobok' is an exception insofar as Dostoevsky, writing in the seventies, picks up characteristics of his early work: the first-person narrator as a masked double of the author ('This is not me; it is somebody quite different'; *cf. The Double*); and the civil-servant theme of the forties. He published the tale in his *Diary of a Writer*, and in this context it was obvious that the reader would tend to identify the first person narrator with the author. The former combines characteristics of Golyadkin with those of Ivan Petrovich, the writer-hero of the early novel *The Insulted and Injured*, which obviously has an autobiographical character. This is in line with the narrator's polemic in 'Bobok' with publishers, editors and booksellers of the time, which suggests a look back at the beginning of the author's own literary activity—all the more so as the narrator identifies himself as a '*literator*'. The corpses

---

[7]*PSS*, V, 388f.

[8]*PSS*, IX, 94.

[9]Rudolf Neuhäuser, 'Nachwort' in Fjodor M Dostoewskij, *Aufzeichnungen aus dem Untergrund* (Munich: dtv 2154, 1985), p. 157.

[10]In all texts labelled as *zapiski* there is a first-person narrator. In *Winter Impressions...* (1863) which bears the alternative label of *zametki*, this first-person narrator is clearly identified for the reader with the author.

decomposing in their graves, yet still capable of conversations which the narrator overhears, once belonged to the upper classes of society, above all the higher ranks of the civil service and the aristocracy. The moral stench that exudes from them—'the stink we get here is, so to speak, a moral stink—he-he!'[11]— illustrates Dostoevsky's understanding of Russian society as widely dominated by these two groups. Dostoevsky's critique is mitigated only by the author's irony and the obviously absurd circumstances of the macabre scene in the graveyard. One of the deceased succinctly formulates it: 'It's impossible to live on earth and not lie, for life and lies are synonyms'.[12] Two more sketches were published in the *Diary* in 1876 that recall the early work: 'The Little Boy at Christ's Christmas Tree' and 'The Peasant Marei'. Dostoevsky described the former as an *istoriia* and the latter as an *anekdot* and *dalekoe vospominanie* ('distant recollection'). In both the first-person narrator and the author are identical. In 'The Little Boy...' Dostoevsky describes an experience of his own (an encounter with a beggar-child in St Petersburg) which serves as the subject of a story he has 'invented': 'I know very well that I made it up.'[13] His theme is child poverty, at the same time, he refers to Christ as a comforter. In 'The Peasant...' Dostoevsky recounts, again in his own name, what was probably his earliest, deeply moving encounter with a Russian peasant, and himself draws a parallel to his experiences in Siberia. The tales and stories cited so far can be understood either as a continuation of themes from his pre-Siberian work, or as a contribution to the development of his ideological premises. This, however, is not true of the following tales.

The novel *The Gambler*, which could also be described as a tale, was written simultaneously with the first of the great novels, *Crime and Punishment*, and is known to owe its publication to an unfortunate obligation of the author to an unscrupulous publisher. It is devoted to the theme of Russians travelling abroad, primarily those of aristocratic origin, a theme that is of some significance in the author's *Weltanschauung*, and one that can be found again in the great novels. The critique of aristocratic Russians travelling abroad is quite pronounced. In addition this text presents an analysis of a predominant personality type, which characterizes early modernism and did not become manifest in literature until the 1880s, but then became apparent to everyone in the literature of Decadence! Sigmund Freud and Arthur Schnitzler would have appreciated Dostoevsky's text! In the view of the author himself, the hero of *The Gambler* obviously is a variation on and further development of the nameless 'Underground Man'. At the same time, this text signifies a break with the tales that preceded it, insofar as this is the first extended text in which a profound psychological analysis was achieved, something that Dostoevsky had already attempted, though only vaguely,

---

[11]*PSS*, XXI, 51.
[12]*PSS*, XXI, 52.
[13]*PSS*, XX, 14.

in Part II of *Notes from Underground* and had applied more successfully in his first great novel. Viewed in this light, *The Gambler*, together with *Notes from Underground*, can be seen as the threshold leading to the *Zeitwelt* of his late work.

If we now turn aside from the less significant stories and tales, what remains of the shorter narrative work Dostoevsky wrote parallel to his five great novels? The answer is: three of the most interesting and, in many respects, complex narrative texts, of which, characteristically, two were again published in The *Diary of a Writer*. They count among the best that Dostoevsky produced in the genre of tale and story. Only three years after the novel *The Gambler*, Dostoevsky published his longest tale, *The Eternal Husband* (1867). We are faced once again with variations on the complex personality of the 'Underground Man', one of whom, Velchaninov, the 'eternal lover', says to the other, Trusotsky, the 'eternal husband': 'We are both depraved, repulsive, underground people...'[14] It is not only a question of seductions and character flaws, but one of aggressive prejudices and emotional resistance to repressed feelings of guilt; i.e., the author takes up a theme of his early work, when, in a cycle of four only loosely connected stories, he had condemned contemporary marriage in no uncertain terms, in a satirical and ironic vein. In the background the careful reader will notice the influence of Fourierist psychology and the anti-bourgeois reflex of his younger years.[15] Added to this were aspects of the personality of the 'Underground Man'. In his next tale, 'A Gentle Creature', this is taken further and takes on a profoundly tragic form.

The tale 'A Gentle Creature' filled the entire November issue (1876) of the journal, for which the author apologised to the readers. In his Foreword ('Ot avtora') he explained the subtitle 'A Fantastic Story' *(fantasticheskii rasskaz)*, an early anticipation of the stream-of-consciousness style, and made it clear that this text did not belong to the genre of *zapiski*! This made it immediately clear that the first-person narrator had nothing in common with the author! The analysis of human behaviour in extreme situations, which had begun in *The Gambler* and continued three years later in *The Eternal Husband*, is taken further here in a most impressive fashion. This is the story of two people who yearn for love; yet neither can break through the wall that separates their souls. 'Everything is dead, everywhere there are corpses. Solitary people only, and around them silence— that's the Earth',[16] as the pawnbroker precisely summarises, thereby raising his personal situation to the level of a universal situation. After his wife's suicide, the husband meditates, his words anticipating the theme of the next tale, 'The Dream of a Ridiculous Man': 'Paradise was in my soul, I would have planted it all around you. "People, love one another"—who said that? Whose teaching is

---

[14]*PSS*, IX, 87.

[15]Rudolf Neuhäuser, *Das Frühwerk Dostoevskijs* (Heidelberg: Carl Winter, 1979), pp. 104-110.

[16]*PSS*, XXIV, 35.

that?'[17] He has no answer. The 'Ridiculous Man' would find it later in his own way!

The second tale to appear in *The Diary of a Writer* (1877), 'The Dream of a Ridiculous Man' bears the same subtitle as 'A Gentle Creature'. However, Dostoevsky obviously no longer saw a need to explain the fantastic elements in this tale, since it is presented to the reader from the beginning as a dream-experience. Dostoevsky draws a magnificent picture of a potential earthly paradise, of the Fall of Man, the loss of innocence, the victory of evil in society, all however masked by the fact that these events, portrayed as if in a time-lapse, take place in a dream and on another planet. Here too, we find references to other texts. The author further develops the character of the 'Underground Man' and gives an approximate account of the passages in Chapter Ten of Part I of *Notes from Underground* which had been removed by the censor.[18] He takes up Versilov's description of a paradisiacal condition in early Greece (*The Adolescent*) and anticipates Zosima's (*The Brothers Karamazov*) thoughts on the possibility of an earthly paradise. At the same time we see a reflection in this tale of Dostoevsky's interest at that time in spiritualism and in the question, much discussed in philosophy and theology as well as among spiritualists and Dostoevsky's friends, of whether the souls of the deceased continued life on other planets.[19] It is the author's last tale and can be seen as the end of the road covered by the 'Underground Man', i.e. the contemporary Russian intellectual, from the sixties to the end of the seventies, extending from the Crystal Palace of the 'Underground Man' to the earthly paradise of the 'Ridiculous Man'. Whether the latter, however, can break through human isolation (*'krugom molchanie'*) with his message, remains just as much in doubt as the question of whether the message the author desired to communicate to his compatriots, the Russian people, Russian society, his readers, actually arrived as the author wished it to! We can say that the *Zeitwelt* of the novels, which on the level of the small narrative genre had begun with *Notes from Underground* and *The Gambler*, found its conclusion in 'The Dream of a Ridiculous Man' Man.

If we attempt, in conclusion, to bring the shorter narrative work into a meaningful order, the following can be established:

1. The period of preparation: 1860-1863. The stories and tales of these years serve to develop the author's ideology. The main focus is the qualities of the Russian people, depicted with the aid of a cross-section of Russians (*Notes from the House of the Dead*), and the critique of Western society (*Winter Notes...*); both supporting pillars in the edifice of his *Weltanschauung*.

---

[17] F M Dostoevskii, *PSS*, XXIV, 35.
[18] Rudolf Neuhäuser, 'Nachwort', pp. 153-173.
[19] Cf. Rudolf Neuhäuser, 'The Dream of a Ridiculous Man: Topicality as a Literary Device', *Dostoevsky Studies* I, 2 (1993), 175-190.

2. The period of the polemic with the 'progressive' intelligentsia: 1862. Dostoevsky's polemic unfolded in his journal *Time* in the course of this year and is reflected in the tales 'The Crocodile' and 'A Nasty Story'.
3. On the threshold of the *Zeitwelt* of the great novels: 1864-1866: With his first great tale, *Notes from Underground*, Dostoevsky created the prototype of a hero that was to accompany his work from then on. At the same time, this text represented the peak of his polemic with the radicals of the time. In accordance with these main elements, this text is organised into two dissimilar parts. The 'novel' *The Gambler*, which we classify here, as I believe rightly, as belonging to the shorter genre, continues those themes touched upon by the 'Underground Man'. It is Dostoevsky's second great narrative.
4. The short prose of the later years, connected thematically with the early work, partly based on recollections, partly a continuation of the polemical discussions of the early years: 1876-1878. These three texts were all published in *The Diary of a Writer* and have the character of literary sketches, based partly on topical events. 'The Peasant Marei', is most obviously devoted to early recollections, although 'Bobok' and 'The Little Boy at Christ's Christmas Tree' likewise contain elements that recall the early work. 'Bobok' is a polemic aimed at refined aristocratic society, with obvious echoes of the early work.
5. Three great tales: 1869-1877. These three very different texts stand out for the sharpness of their psychological analysis. The 'Underground Man', of whom Dostoevsky is known to have said that he was the first to have recognised and depicted in all his significance, defines the framework for the otherwise very different characters in these texts. They run the gamut from the more amusing and burlesque conflicts of *The Eternal Husband* to the tragic suicide of 'A Gentle Creature' and the dream vision of the 'Ridiculous Man'. In contrast to the novels, the main characters of these texts do not fall strictly within the age limits of the novel-heroes. The latter are all between twenty and thirty years old, the former at times over forty or even fifty—which by no means implies that the 'underground character' does not apply to them. We note that the 'Underground Man' himself had already passed the forty mark in Part I of the text!

If we limit ourselves to the *Zeitwelt* of the five great novels, we see that they have complements in the smaller genre. Including *The Gambler* and *Notes from Underground*, we are left with five texts, of which two form the beginning (the 'threshold'), while the other three mark the peak of the author's creative work in this genre. The *Zeitwelt*, as a framework, is roughly the same for both genres. With respect to plot structure, configuration of characters and themes they differ, however, considerably from the novels, with Dostoevsky setting different emphases. The five constituent elements mentioned earlier recede into the background. No murders take place, although attempted murder is not excluded. Disease plays no great role, although it may also be present. The author, as it were, restrains himself. The above constituent elements lose their ideological and symbolic weight. Ideology as such recedes into the background, although ideological elements never disappear entirely. A good example of this is the depiction of the 'progressive' youth on the country seat of the Zakhlebinins in *The Eternal Husband*. This has, however, almost no bearing on the conflicts played out between the main characters of the story. The same can be said of the other tales. Put another way, Dostoevsky pursues different aims in his tales as compared to those in his novels. His aim is no longer the fundamental conflict embodied in the three central characters, *gubitel'-spasitel'/mnimyi spasitel'-uchitel' zhizni*, but the attempt to provide a profound psychological analysis of the contemporary Russian. Time and again the 'Underground Man' appears as the fundamental pattern, as it were, behind the main characters. This is especially true of the great tales that appeared from 1864 onwards. In these five texts the conflict unfolds mainly around the motif of the problematic relationship between the sexes, whereby Dostoevsky concentrates his interest on the male characters. The last tale about the 'Ridiculous Man' even gets along without a female counterpart to the hero, if we disregard the little care-worn girl who addresses him on the street. As already stated, it has much in common with Dostoevsky's last novel, *The Brothers Karamazov*. Just as this novel enjoys a certain special position among the five novels, 'The Dream of a Ridiculous Man' likewise occupies a special place in the smaller genre! What has been said about the five great tales does not, however, apply to the three sketches that appeared in 1873 and 1876 *(anekdoty, istorii, vospominaniia)*. These are more casual works, 'mechty i grezy' ('dreams and reveries'), connected with reminiscences of the author's early texts.[20]

In the 'architecture' of Dostoevsky's entire creative work, the tales are by no means to be seen simply as texts published at random in breaks between the novels. As we have seen, they are distinguished by a remarkable internal coherence. It is the analysis of the 'underground character' of Russian men of the 1860s and 1870s that stands in the centre of the author's attention, along with themes and recollections of the early period. Central to the tales is a psychological analysis that exposes the deeper layers of consciousness displacing and marginalizing the ideological concerns that dominate throughout the novels. The focal point is the individual and not the total of society. The important issue is not the evolution of Russian Society ('die russische Gesellschaftsentwicklung', H-J Gerigk), but the 'depraved, repulsive, underground people' (*The Eternal Husband*) that inhabit Russia, and their potential for an escape from isolation. The 'Ridiculous Man' was intended to point the way!

Translated by Gareth Roberts

---

[20] An aphorism in the manuscript of the essay 'Mechty i grezy', which was published in *The Diary* three months after 'Bobok', associates it with 'Bobok', where the maxim also appears. The beginning of the story is a reaction by Dostoevsky to a journalistic remark in the journal *The Voice (Golos)*; see *PSS*, XXI, 402.

RASKOLNIKOV'S WARDROBE: DOSTOEVSKY'S USE OF VESTIMENTARY MARKERS FOR LITERARY COMMUNICATION IN *CRIME AND PUNISHMENT*

Boris Christa

DOSTOEVSKY'S literary work has many facets, but there is no evidence that he ever concerned himself with the theory of narratology or semiotics. Yet there is no doubt that he was well aware in practice of the power of semiotic signs. He certainly appreciates fully the value, as a medium for literary communication, of vestimentary markers—images that draw attention to specific aspects of attire. Indeed, in *Crime and Punishment*[1] he justifies their importance by having Raskolnikov quote (p. 36) the Russian proverb 'po odezhke protyagivai nozhki' (stretch your legs in accordance with your clothes), which is much the same as the English 'clothes maketh the man'. Certainly, the characters of his novel constantly and consistently define themselves through the statements made by their vestimentary markers.

Clothes can be seen as a kind of language with its own grammar[2] and the use of this vestimentary language for literary communication is a major feature of Dostoevsky's narrative technique. He taps its resources to the full, and in his novel *Crime and Punishment*, he deploys a wide range both of synchronic vestimentary markers that refer to features of attire that are timeless and universal, and therefore easily understood, and also a large number of diachronic markers, clothing signs the full meaning of which only becomes apparent in the context of the dress-codes of their time and place. These are obviously harder to appreciate fully for the modern general reader, but for the literary critic they can open up significant areas of sub-textual meaning.

The notion that Dostoevsky was a needy author, always writing hastily and carelessly to meet pressing datelines, has long been discarded. His technique in using vestimentary markers certainly shows him as a careful, literary craftsman. The semiotic images he selects are always sharply in focus and attuned to the task of communicating intimately with the reader. They are never arbitrary and they avoid the cliché. Frequently, in fact, they invert completely conventional synchronic, vestimentary values, so that the wearing of fashionable and

---

[1] All page references to *Crime and Punishment* are to *PSS*, VI. Translations are by the author.

[2] Joanne Entwistle, *The Fashioned Body: Fashion, Dress and Modern Social Theory* (Cambridge: Polity Press, 2000), p. 66.

scrupulously clean items of dress, for example, carries pejorative meaning, and clothes that are ragged and worn signal moral integrity and goodness. This technique is employed particularly effectively in the delineation of the two rivals—Razumikhin and Luzhin, but also in the characterization of Marmeladov and Svidrigaylov.

But Dostoevsky is equally adept in the use of diachronic vestimentary markers. Particularly in the depiction of the novel's heroines, Sonya and Dunya, he demonstrates how well-versed he was in the dress-codes of his time. He evokes charisma and appeal while completely avoiding romantic banality. A further noteworthy aspect of Dostoevsky's description of women in *Crime and Punishment* is his technique of using their vestimentary markers to inform the reader about erotic matters that could not be mentioned explicitly in his time of oppressive censorship and wide-ranging sexual taboos.

Dostoevsky's main use of vestimentary language, however, is in characterization. Virtually with every one of his personae he focuses attention on some individual aspect of their attire to distinguish them and make them memorable. His secondary characters acquire vestimentary trade-marks that accompany them through the novel like a Wagnerian 'Leitmotif'. As an example, we might cite Katerina Ivanovna's green, 'drap-de-dames' shawl, or Razumikhin's unshaven chin or Zamyotov's heavy rings and watch-chain. The use of vestimentary markers in the portrayal of the main hero, however, goes a great deal further.

Crime and Punishment is a very hero-centred novel. All in all, it contains some 893 vestimentary markers. No less than 228 of these are devoted to the depiction of Raskolnikov. They bring him visually into focus, but they also provide valuable insight into the recesses of his secretive mind. In Part III of the novel, when the hero has expanded his theory that there are exceptional people to whom everything is permitted, the investigator asks him whether these people should not be identified by some special form of dress or personal trademark so that misunderstandings would be avoided. Raskolnikov replies by congratulating him on the cleverness of his question (p. 201). Porfiry Petrovich's enquiry comes as a jest and yet it is heavy with irony. It spells out directly what was for Dostoevsky a very palpable literary and artistic problem. How could he best use the medium of vestimentary language to make his hero credible and help the reader to understand him? From the well-stocked warehouse of his imagination, what clothes should he put into Raskolnikov's wardrobe?

The term 'Raskolnikov's wardrobe' is, of course, a purely metaphorical one. He certainly does not own such an item of furniture. Indeed, the room where he lives is a tiny, claustrophobic place. We are informed that it is hardly larger than a closet and totally filled by his bed. His accommodation is meagre and so are his clothes. Raskolnikov's resources to give vestimentary expression to his singularity and eccentricity are clearly limited. Moreover, he lives in a part of town where we are told 'it is difficult to surprise anyone with one's clothes' (p. 6).

Dostoevsky meets the challenge of expressing Raskolnikov's exceptional personality in semiotic terms by resorting to a very Russian, maximalist solution. His hero plays the role of the outsider with a special mission by discarding all bourgeois conventions of dress and lifestyle. Raskolnikov ceases to shave or wash and the housemaid stops doing any cleaning in his room. He allows his clothes to become filthy and tattered. He wears them day and night, inside and outside, and we are told that 'no normal person would venture on the streets in such rags' (p. 6). In fact, his complete disregard for all considerations of hygiene or comfort is evocative of the self-denying, monastic traditions of the Russian Orthodox Church. Adopted by a university law student from a culturally middle-class background, such drastic asceticism certainly succeeds in showing him as being dramatically out-of-the-ordinary.

Raskolnikov's wardrobe at this stage consists of worn, torn and sagging pants with a loose hem, decrepit down-at-heel shoes and a baggy, light overall of cotton material, with wide pockets for secreting stolen goods and a loop inside for hiding an axe. Worn by an unkempt, unshaven and dirty young man, this outfit signifies obvious neglect and penury. Raskolnikov's negative synchronic vestimentary markers, however, are sharply at variance with his speech and bearing, and the ambivalent reactions which his appearance produces is a constant leitmotif in the novel. It communicates effectively his waywardness and instability. One police officer thinks he is a vagabond and begins by addressing him with the intimate 'ty', but then changes his mind (p. 76). Another cannot understand how dressed like that he can give away money to a penniless street girl (p. 41). His friend thinks he looks like 'a chimney sweep' (p. 28) and a merchant's wife takes him for a beggar and gives him twenty kopecks (p. 89).

Raskolnikov's clothes are quite exceptionally disreputable. They are referred to no less than fourteen times as 'rags'. The text states explicitly that it would 'be difficult to be more unkempt and slovenly than Raskolnikov' (p. 25). Razumikhin even voices the hypothesis that Raskolnikov's wretched clothes are the cause of his conduct. How could he behave differently, he asks, leading a solitary existence for six months with nothing to wear but rags and shoes without soles? (p. 206). Dostoevsky, however, lets us know that this argument is not valid. He tells us that Raskolnikov in fact enjoys flaunting his rags (p. 25). He has money to improve his appearance but he chooses to give it away. His display of abject poverty and rejection of all vestimentary norms is an act of choice and all reference to dire necessity is camouflage. The exhibitionist display of scarecrow garments, in fact, signals the psychological state of a hero, who at this stage is supremely self-confident and arrogant.

Richard Peace has made the comment that Dostoevsky's heroes need their clothes not for the demands of normal living, but 'to satisfy...their own psychological perverseness'.[3] The case of Raskolnikov strongly supports this statement. His adoption of the vestimentary markers of the down-and-out is really a charade. Psychologically, he has projected himself into the role of the superior, extraordinary being, permitted to reject all human laws and codes of conduct. While planning to break much more fundamental rules, he is rehearsing by flaunting all bourgeois conventions of dress. He is deliberately challenging the accepted standards of a society where the immaculate turnout of a Luzhin, with his elegant lilac gloves and golden lorgnette, hides a mean and grubby soul, and where the exemplary cleanliness of the pawnbroker is a mask for ruthlessness and greed. Raskolnikov sees himself as the champion of revalued values, where rags are a sign of virtue and cleanliness is a dirty word.

The revelation of Raskolnikov's hidden agenda is also greatly furthered by two diachronic vestimentary markers which Dostoevsky puts into his hero's wardrobe. The first is the overcoat which dates from his student days. We learn that this is a quality garment which comes from Sharmer—a well-known St Petersburg tailor patronized by Dostoevsky himself. Overcoats, of course, have special semiotic significance in the Russian vestimentary language, but even to the Russian contemporary reader the signals emitted by Raskolnikov's *shinel'* would not be immediately apparent. Students in slovenly clothes are understandable enough, but university students in prescribed regulation uniforms are almost beyond the modern imagination. Wearing his overcoat would have identified Raskolnikov immediately as an undergraduate of the St Petersburg University. Hardly a vestimentary marker compatible with the status of an aspiring superman. So in the early part of the novel Raskolnikov deliberately chooses not to wear it and just to use it as a blanket.

The second very noteworthy diachronic vestimentary marker in Raskolnikov's wardrobe which he does wear constantly is his hat. Dostoevsky clearly chose it carefully and describes it in detail. It complies with the assertion made elsewhere in the novel that the most significant item in any person's attire is their hat which 'serves as a kind of recommendation' (p. 101). Dostoevsky was, moreover, well aware that diachronic vestimentary markers often have programmatic meaning. He was, for example, very prone to castigating Slavophiles for donning ethnic garments to make their professed ideology a matter of public display. Raskolnikov's hat similarly signals quite specific messages about the Weltanschauung of its wearer. This is substantiated by the reaction to it of other characters in the novel.

Razumikhin sees it as showing Anglophile leanings and calls it a 'Palmerston', a term more usually employed to describe a kind of tweed. Razumikhin evidently associates Raskolnikov's headgear with an English bowler hat. It is certainly described on several occasions as being 'round'. But it is also said to

---

[3]Richard Peace, *Dostoevsky: An Examination of the Major Novels* (Cambridge: Cambridge University Press, 1975), p. 6.

be 'tall'—a feature which distinguishes it from the kind of hat an English gentleman of the time, such as Lord Palmerston, would have worn. Nevertheless, it functions semiotically as an indicator of some cultural orientation towards Britain, which at the time was the world's leading industrial nation and the most rationalistic and technologically progressive.

On the other hand a tipsy gentleman driving by, for no reason at all abuses Raskolnikov loudly for wearing a German hat. This national classification is to some extent endorsed by Dostoevsky. In describing it he uses the adjective 'tsimmermanovsky' identifying it as being a product of the St Petersburg German hat-maker Zimmermann, where he himself had once bought a hat (p. 7).

Whether the styling of Raskolnikov's hat is correctly described as English, or as German, hardly seems very relevant. What does matter is that it is clearly identified as being provocatively western. In a period where overt political activity was banned in Russia and the clash between Slavophiles and Westerners was the main surrogate political issue, a western-style hat clearly became an important symbol, the importance of which could easily be missed by a contemporary western reader. By wearing it, Raskolnikov is demonstrating sympathies for Western cultural and intellectual values.

The political message is, however, only a part of the significance of Raskolnikov's hat. Even more meaningful is its eccentricity. It is not simply unusual, it is totally unlike anybody else's. It is totally dilapidated, full of holes and covered with spots. It is also very tall and round and has no brim. Furthermore, it is red in colour and he wears it tilted outrageously to one side (p. 7). Such is the eye-catching headpiece which Raskolnikov wears to commit his crime and it is a hat far more appropriate for a clown than for a murderer.

The striking incongruity of the hat and the occasion for which it is worn, make it all the more expressive as a vestimentary marker. It draws attention to a side of Raskolnikov that has received little critical comment, namely that he is something of an exhibitionist, a show-off. But even more, it demonstrates graphically and vividly, Dostoevsky's view of his hero as a man possessed by the folly of a Luciferic daydream, which gets out of control. The image of the crazy hat communicates perfectly the psychological make-up of a deluded, irresponsible, experimental killer, who only in retrospect will come to realize the gravity of his actions.

Dostoevsky shows us Raskolnikov as clinging firmly to his bizarre hat, even though he knows how conspicuous and foolish it is. Irresistible forces draw Raskolnikov to his fatal deed. It is as if 'his clothes have got caught in a machine which drags him in', says the narrator (p. 58). So, although he realizes full well that his conspicuous hat is a liability he carries on, blindly following his irrational impulses. It is as if the superstitious Raskolnikov clings to his hat as a kind of talisman, emblematic of his aspirations to superman status or functioning as a 'shapka-nevidimka'—a legendary cap making its wearer invisible. Certainly, on the fatal day, Raskolnikov flaunting his outrageous headgear goes to commit his crime in a kind of trance and returns home totally unobserved. His rude awakening, however, comes very swiftly and the transition from arrogant killer to repentant sinner begins.

Dostoevsky once again makes good use of vestimentary language to communicate the stages in Raskolnikov's metamorphosis. It is heralded by a dramatic change of the hero's clothes. Much of his old get-up is spattered with blood and has to be disposed of urgently and radically. His remarkable hat simply rolls off his head when, exhausted, he flings himself on his bed, and as his aspirations to supermanhood collapse, it gets cast away together with his other outlandish gear. The outsider outfit is replaced by garments that make a very different statement. These are fortuitously provided by Razumikhin, who is determined to make Raskolnikov 'a human being again' (p. 101).

Every item in Raskolnikov's new wardrobe is chosen to enable him to make his way in society. He gets immaculate grey trousers tailored from light-weight woollen material and a monochrome fashionable waistcoat to match; new linen shirts with stylish tops and imported smart shoes. The only item from his previous wardrobe that he is allowed to retain is his overcoat which is assessed as having 'an air of particular quality' (pp. 101-2). When his mother and sister come, he dresses in his new clothes, gets carefully washed and does his hair (p. 170). No more the outsider, his vestimentary markers henceforth signal the presence of a respectable young man with a promising future, studying law at a prestigious institution of higher learning.

Raskolnikov's audacious hat is now replaced by a new and handsome 'furazhka'—a student's peaked cap described playfully by Razumikhin as 'a product of the jeweller's art' (p. 101). Porfiry Petrovich subsequently refers to it as a 'furazhechka'—a nice little cap (p. 258)—emphasising its significance as a vestimentary marker identified with the young and immature. In wearing it, Raskolnikov clearly signals his reversion from the assumed role of the Napoleonic hero to that of the aspiring student. For Dostoevsky it defines the image of Raskolnikov during the process of his rehabilitation—now outwardly respectable, but tormented by hidden guilt. The peak cap features in all of the hero's subsequent appearances and is mentioned specifically no less than fifteen times.

The culminating stage in Raskolnikov's struggle to find redemption is marked by a brief regressive interlude. His mental turmoil before giving himself up, once more, finds expression in negative vestimentary terms. When he comes to say farewell to his mother his clothes are again in a bad state—dirty and torn. He has spent a night alone outside in the rain battling with himself to reach his decision. But then finally resolved on his course of action, he goes to Sonya to receive the vestimentary marker which henceforth will become an indispensable item of his attire. She places around his neck the orthodox cross which is the most unequivocal statement of spiritual commitment available in Dostoevsky's vestimentary vocabulary (p. 403).

But even Sonya's symbolic act does not bring Raskolnikov's regeneration to an immediate positive conclusion. Raskolnikov is still tormented by uncertainties and struggling to find himself, and his looks betray his insecurity. Right to the very end of the novel Dostoevsky continues to deploy vestimentary markers to communicate to the reader this residual ambivalence and the continuing quest of his hero. For example, when Raskolnikov goes to the cross-roads and kisses the ground, his appearance produces very different reactions from the by-standers. One takes him for a pilgrim off to Jerusalem. Another decides that he looks like a real gentleman, but a third is not so sure. 'These days, he says, it is hard to tell who is a gentleman and who isn't.' (p. 405)

Finally, in the *Epilogue*, describing the terminal phase of Raskolnikov's catharsis, Dostoevsky yet again makes good use of the resources of the vestimentary language bringing the depiction of his hero to a dramatic climax. His appearance is now radically transformed as he begins his life in prison. We have him doing penance with shaven head, while his newly found humility and gradual acceptance of Christian brotherhood is semiotically underwritten by the final item in his wardrobe—the striped regulation jacket of the Siberian convict.

In conclusion, we can safely say that *Crime and Punishment* demonstrates very convincingly Dostoevsky's great skill in using vestimentary language for literary communication. This is an aspect of his narrative technique that deserves much wider critical acknowledgment. As a writer of high-tension fiction, he thrives on false trails and mystification. However, amid the swirling mists of his narratory smoke-screens, his vestimentary markers are always reliable beacons of orientation.

DOSTOEVSKY AND PUSHKIN: PETERSBURG MOTIFS IN *CRIME AND PUNISHMENT*

Valentina Vetlovskaia

THIS article is a gift offered with profound respect for the long and fruitful work of Professor Malcolm Jones in the field of Dostoevsky studies. It takes the form of a commentary clarifying certain motifs from the novel *Crime and Punishment* (1866), although what is set forth here is in no way a complete survey of the theme.

Of Pushkin's works reflected in one way or another in *Crime and Punishment*, the most important role is played, as we know very well, by the story *The Queen of Spades* (possibly written in 1833, published 1834) and the long poem *The Bronze Horseman* (1833, published 1837). On the subject of the literary sources of Dostoevsky's novel in the Academy edition of the Complete Works of the author, G M Fridlender noted:

> In nineteenth-century Russian literature the tragic theme of *Crime and Punishment* was to a significant degree prepared by Pushkin's creative work [...] It has been pointed out many times that the fundamental thematic collision of *The Queen of Spades*—the duel between the poor Germann, all but reduced to beggary, [...] and the old countess, who is living out her life needed by no-one—was given new life three decades later by Dostoevsky in the tragic duel between Raskolnikov and another old woman: the moneylender. No less closely connected is the 'rebellion' of Raskolnikov with that of Evgeny in *The Bronze Horseman*.[1]

Indeed, A L Bem also wrote:

> The Pushkinian thematic structure [of *The Queen of Spades*—VV] formed the foundations of *Crime and Punishment*. There can be no doubt about this, if the concrete development of the two coinciding structures are closely compared. In fact, at the basis of both works lies the same plan: *achieving one's aim through crime*.[2]

This scholar goes on to demonstrate thoroughly the textual points of contact, both obvious and less apparent, which unite Dostoevsky's and Pushkin's heroes. Bem

---

[1] *PSS*, VII, 343.

[2] A L Bem, 'U istokov tvorchestva Dostoevskogo: Griboedov, Pushkin, Gogol', Tolstoi i Dostoevskii', in *O Dostoevskom: sbornik statei*, III (Prague: Petropolis, 1936), p. 46 (author's emphasis).

is interested in the very fact of the influence of the one writer on the other: he does not however go beyond the bounds of considering the common features in the psychological delineation of the characters.

Approximately ten years earlier Valery Briusov had discovered that the poem *The Bronze Horseman* was the fundamental influence on Dostoevsky's novel. He wrote, '...the idea of *The Bronze Horseman* lay as a whole at the basis of *Crime and Punishment*: does man have the right, for the sake of aims he considers elevated, to sacrifice the life of another? (Peter the Great here is Raskolnikov, Evgeny the old moneylender)'.[3] If we are to consider such an idea, then besides *The Bronze Horseman* we should also name *Boris Godunov* (1824-1825, published 1831) and (with some reservations) *Evgeny Onegin* (1823-1831, published 1833), which Dostoevsky interpreted precisely from this angle in his Pushkin speech of 1880. (*PSS*, XXVI, 140-143) Besides drawing together Raskolnikov and Peter the Great, Briusov (like Bem, moreover) overlooks the most important feature in the author's description of the hero: Raskolnikov is not only and, perhaps, not so much a hangman as a sacrificial victim. Therefore comparing Raskolnikov with Evgeny from *The Bronze Horseman* is more than justified.

Certain motifs from the novel connect directly with this. For example:

> On Nikolaevsky bridge he [Raskolnikov] had once again to come fully to his senses as a consequence of a quite unpleasant incident which happened to him. He was soundly whipped on the back by the driver of a carriage, because he was on the verge of falling under the horse, even though the coachman had shouted out to him three or four times [...] (for some unknown reason he was walking in the very centre of the bridge, which is used by vehicles, not pedestrians). (*PSS*: VI, 89)[4]

But we do in fact know why he is walking there. We know it from Pushkin, insofar as Raskolnikov, although he cannot pick his footsteps (or even, precisely because he cannot pick them), is following the unsteady route of the poem's insane hero:

> Одежда ветхая на нем
> Рвалась и тлела. Злые дети
> Бросали камни вслед ему.
> Нередко кучерские плети
> Его стегали, потому
> Что он не разбирал дороги
> Уж никогда; казалось—он
> Не примечал. Он оглушен

---

[3] V Briusov, 'Pushkin-Master', in *Pushkin: sbornik*, I, ed. N K Piksanov (Moscow, 1924), p. 114.

[4] Translations of quotations from *Crime and Punishment* are based on Fyodor Dostoevsky, *Crime and Punishment*, trans. David McDuff (London: Penguin, 1991), with some alterations (*Translator's note*).

Был шумом внутренней тревоги.[5]

> his garments, old and fraying,
> Were all in tatters and decaying.
> And the malicious boys would pelt
> The man with stones; and of the felt
> The cabman's whiplash on him flicking;
> for he had lost the skill of picking
> His footsteps—deafened, it may be,
> By fears that clamoured inwardly.[6]

Raskolnikov is deafened by just such 'fears that clamoured inwardly'. Except perhaps that his forgetfulness and ancient clothes arouse in those around him not only malicious taunts, but also pity: 'By his coat and his appearance they [the mother and daughter who have given Raskolnikov alms—VV] could easily have taken him for a beggar [...] and for the presenting of a whole twenty-kopek piece he was, certainly, indebted to the blow of the whip, which had moved them to pity'. (*PSS*: VI, 89) But we shall return to this episode later.

The Queen of Spades and *The Bronze Horseman* enter *Crime and Punishment* on an equal footing because they are united by a single theme—the theme of Petersburg. The subtitle of *The Bronze Horseman* ('A Petersburg Story') could also be applied to *The Queen of Spades*, a minor masterpiece, in Dostoevsky's words, 'the acme of artistic perfection'. (*PSS*: XXIV, 308) From this point of view it is necessary, so it seems, to look at the 'presence' of Pushkin's works in Dostoevsky's novel. It is not a question of 'influence', whatever this might be (more or less profound; understood or unconscious), but that a common problem exercised both writers. This relates to the fate of a huge Slavonic country, abruptly halted in its natural historical development by Peter I and violently,

---

[5] A S Pushkin, *Polnoe sobranie sochinenii v 17-i tomakh* (Moscow and Leningrad: Nauka, 1948), V, 146. Further references to this edition are given in the text (volume and page number), prefixed by the initials 'ASP'. Reference to Pushkin is made by V B Shklovsky in a negative form: 'Raskolnikov stood on the bridge, enduring the blows from the lash. The coach-driver hit him not for the reasons described in relation to Evgeny in *The Bronze Horseman*: "coachmen's lashes/Frequently struck him...", but simply because there are poor people and lashes in the world', *Za i protiv: Zametki o Dostoevskom* (Moscow, 1957), p. 216. See also Dostoevsky's *Peterburgskie snovideniia v stikhakh i proze* (*PSS*: XIX, 71), and the commentary on this by I D Iakubovich (*PSS*: XIX, 269). I L Al'mi writes: 'The idea of the presence of *The Bronze Horseman* in Dostoevsky's 'Petersburg' works is axiomatic amongst literary critics. However, "concrete" observations which would confirm this [...] are rather scanty (most frequently recalling the "coach-driver's lash" raining down on the shoulders of Pushkin's and Dostoevsky's heroes)...', '"Ekho" *Mednogo vsadnika* v tvorchestve F M Dostoevskogo 40-60-x gg. (ot *Slabogo serdtsa k Prestupleniiu i nakazaniiu*)', in I L Al'mi, *O poezii i proze* (St Petersburg, 2002), p. 501.

[6] English translation of *The Bronze Horseman* by Oliver Elton, in Waclaw Lednicki, *Pushkin's 'Bronze Horseman': The Story of a Masterpiece* (Westwood, CT: Greenwood, 1978), pp. 140-151 (p. 148). Further references to this edition are given in the text. (Translator's note.)

without mercy, reformed by him in accordance with the Western European model.

Petersburg is Peter's creation, a realization in life of his autocratic power, the administrative and martial centre of the new Russian state—and the focus of its painful social anomalies, of open and hidden opposition. The Petersburg theme, beginning with Pushkin, which has occupied such a durable position in Russian literature, was created as a result of exactly this turning point.

Apropos of *The Bronze Horseman*, Belinsky wrote: 'Its real hero is Petersburg. This is why it begins with a grandiose picture of Peter, planning the foundation of his new capital, and the vivid portrayal of Petersburg in its present form' (and the critic then reproduces almost in full the author's introduction to the poem).[7] Being located on the Western frontier of Russia, on the border between two worlds, its own and the foreign world, Petersburg became that 'window into Europe' through which Russians were obliged to look whether they wanted to or not, and regardless of the results it would bring for them.

According to Dostoevsky,

> Peter's reforms tore one part of the people from the other, from the main part... The reforms came from the top down, rather than from the bottom up. The reforms did not reach the lowest strata of society [...] Sensing no advantages from the reorganization, seeing no real relief for themselves in the new order, the people felt only terrible oppression, and with pain in their hearts endured the desecration of that which from time immemorial they had been accustomed to considering sacred to them. This is why as a whole the people remained as they had been before the reforms. (*PSS*: XX, 14)

However, Peter's acts cannot be interpreted in only one way. The author continues:

> ...we would in no way wish to deny that Peter's reforms have any significance for the whole of mankind... As Pushkin so beautifully expressed it, they cut a window into Europe for us, they showed us the West, from which we could learn a little. But the problem was that it remained nothing more than a window, from which a select public looked at the West and saw mainly not what they were supposed to see, and learnt altogether not what they should have learnt... (*PSS*: XX, 14)

Everything depended on who was looking.

The vista opened by Pushkin's view was in no sense resplendent. Europe, which had always played an essential role in Russia's history, was at the end of the eighteenth and beginning of the nineteenth century experiencing bloody revolutionary convulsions, which inflicted irreparable damage on the monarchical order. The triumph of the Third Estate, the bourgeoisie, who ended up in power,

---

[7] V G Belinskii, 'Sochineniia Aleksandra Pushkina. Stat'ia odinnadtsataia i posledniaia', in V G Belinskii, *Sobranie sochineniia v 9-i tomakh* (Moscow, 1981), VI, 460.

replaced earlier values, which were one way or another linked to Christian commandments and traditions, with only one thing: the value of money. In accordance with this, personal profit and mercenary calculation prevailed in the hearts of people educated by the new order over all the diversity of other passions and motives. The possibilities of the bourgeois revolution and its inevitable consequences, not only for the West, but also for Russia, did not win Pushkin over. Meanwhile the course of state development chosen by Peter was leading to precisely such a result. After the French revolution of 1830, which reverberated around other European countries, all these reflections became particularly topical.

Both the action of *The Queen of Spades*, the problematics of the story, and its main hero, from amongst the Russified Germans, are closely connected with Petersburg—the Imperial Capital, assimilating and mastering together with European forms of life, at least in the high-level and urban strata of society, its ideals, which are alien to the traditional ideals of old Rus'. For the hero of Dostoevsky's novel *The Adolescent* (1875), Pushkin's Germann is 'a colossal character, an extraordinary, perfect Petersburg type—a type from the Petersburg period' of Russian history. (*PSS*: XIII, 113)

Germann is afflicted by one passion, which becomes in him a form of mania— the passion for rapid enrichment, which he is prepared to achieve by any means, even going as far as committing a crime. In Pushkin's representation the character of this monomaniac, his aims, are an exceptional phenomenon. Hence the non-Russian origins of the hero, his separation from others. Hence the characteristics he is given by Tomsky: 'Germann is a German: he's thrifty, and that's it!' (ASP: VIII: 1, 227), and, 'This Germann [...] his face is truly patrician: he has the profile of Napoleon, and the soul of Mephistopheles. I think he has at least three crimes on his conscience'. (ASP: VIII: 1, 224) In fact there is nothing outstanding in Germann except the frenzied power of his feelings. However, Germann's passion is not lofty, but is of a base, petty and soulless nature:

> He returned to his little corner; for a long time he could not sleep and, when sleep overpowered him, he dreamt of cards, a green table, piles of banknotes, heaps of money. He played card after card, bent the corners decisively, won continually and raked in his gold, and placed the notes in his pocket. When he woke up it was already late; he sighed at the loss of his fantastic wealth, went again for a wander round the town, and again found himself in front of the house of Countess ***. (ASP: VIII: 1, 236)

It is precisely to this countess, as Bem correctly suggested, that Razumikhin's words about Raskolnikov's ravings after he has committed the murder allude: 'Don't worry, you didn't say anything about any countess.' (*PSS*: VI, 98)[8]

---

[8] Bem, p. 56. But for Bem this allusion is simply an example of 'the authentically unconscious process of creation', with which it is impossible to agree.

If Germann could have comprehended how his dream and the reality succeeding his dream would be his fate, he would have sighed all the more deeply. The hero's unrestrained passion justifies any evil in his eyes, hardens his heart, removing all good feelings from him, any manifestation of nobility. Having under the pretext of an assignation with the young ward penetrated into the old countess's bedroom in order to discover from her the secret of the three cards which will give an incontestable win, Germann does not stop half-way: 'In his heart there spoke something like the pangs of conscience, and then they again fell silent. He turned to stone.' (ASP: VIII: 1, 240) Just such a momentary rejection by Raskolnikov of his planned crime is glimpsed fleetingly in his consciousness as a lucky chance to not move on to the act. (*PSS*: VI, 10-11)

Finding himself before the countess, Germann attempts to achieve his aims with truths and falsehoods, with humiliations, solicitations and supplications, with coarse abuse and threats. He says to the old woman, 'Who are you keeping your secret for? Your grandsons? They're rich, and besides, they don't know the value of money. Your three cards won't help a spendthrift [...] I'm not a spendthrift; I know the value of money.' (ASP: VIII: 1, 241)

But Germann is mistaken in his calculations. Instead of an incalculable win, which turns for him in the end to nothing, insofar as he still loses, the hero pays for his treachery and villainy. He pays too high a price for his heaps and piles of money, which by the cruel mockery of fate proves to be the price of emptiness. This is why unforeseen madness is also added to the reckoning of the hero's treachery and villainy. Such a result, it goes without saying, is not worth a kopeck, let alone a whole heap of money: 'Germann went out of his mind. He is in ward 17 of Obukhovsky hospital, will not answer any questions, and mutters incredibly quickly, "Three, seven, ace! Three, seven, queen!.."' (ASP: VIII: 1, 252) Exactly that which, because of his thrift, he believed himself to be insured against, has happened to the hero: 'Gambling interests me a great deal [...] but I'm not in a position to sacrifice what is necessary in the hope of gaining what is superfluous.' (ASP: VIII: 1, 227) However in this very 'hope of gaining what is superfluous', Germann is compelled to lose everything he has: in the final analysis, he loses himself.

Pushkin's Germann is an exceptional character only because he slightly forestalls time. In actuality, his feelings and convictions correspond fully to the spirit of the bourgeois-mercantile era approaching Russia. The hero anticipates those people who were to multiply unbelievably in the near future, for whom calculation and material advantage, such as money, guaranteeing personal comfort, were the primary consideration.[9]

---

[9] '*The Queen of Spades* [...] is distinguished by the fact that its main character, Germann, represents a social force that was only just appearing in Russia but which was already declaring itself in commanding fashion in France, and which brought new, previously unknown moral-psychological and social collisions to Russia', E N Kupreianova, 'A S Pushkin', in *Istoriia Russkoi literatury v 4 tt.* (Leningrad, 1984), II, 298.

Dostoevsky's Raskolnikov is captivated by the same passion for immediate enrichment as Germann. The maid Nastasya asks him (*PSS,* VI, 27):

> 'You said before you used to go and give lessons to children, but now you don't do anything?' [...] 'They only pay you in coppers for teaching children. What can you do with a few kopecks?' he continued reluctantly, as if answering his own thoughts. 'So you want all the capital at once?' He looked at her strangely. 'Yes, all the capital', he replied firmly, after a short silence.

Like Germann, Raskolnikov is thrifty. But his 'arithmetical theory', which gives him the right to commit crimes, represents nothing special. It is available to anyone and everyone; it is in the air. This theory of his, and even in striking detail, Raskolnikov heard from the lips of an unknown student in the very first 'inn' he dropped into by chance (*PSS*: VI, 53):

> Raskolnikov was in a state of extreme excitement. Of course, all this was the most ordinary and frequently-encountered type of conversation and ideas [...] among young people. But why precisely now had he happened to hear precisely such a conversation and such ideas, when... *exactly the same ideas* had only just formed in his own head?' (*PSS*: VI, 55; author's emphasis)

The capital acquired through crime in Raskolnikov's hands also turns to dust, because the empty things which are fit for nothing and in which, however, traces of the murder he had committed could be seen, as possible evidence, unexpectedly prove for the hero to have more value than money or goods to pawn.

> 'No, don't get up', continued Nastasya [...] 'if you're ill, don't go [...] What's that in your hand?' He glanced: in his right hand he was holding the bits he had cut off from the bottom of his trousers, his sock and the scraps he had torn out of his pocket. He had slept with them like that. Later on, thinking about this, he remembered that half waking up in a fever, he had squeezed all these things as tightly as possible in his hand and then fallen asleep again. 'Look at him, he's collected these rags and he's sleeping with them as if they were treasure...' and Nastasya went off into peals of her morbidly nervous laughter. In an instant he pushed the whole lot under his overcoat and fastened his eyes intently on it. (*PSS*: VI, 73)

Thus for this 'rubbish', in Razumikhin's words,[10] for some bits of trouser-leg and rags which remain in his hand instead of any 'capital', Raskolnikov also

---

[10] See also: '"What was I raving about?" "Oh, how you go on! Is it some secret you're afraid of giving away? Don't worry, you didn't say anything about any countess. But you said a lot about [...] some bulldog, and about earrings, and about some chains. Yes, and besides that you were terribly interested in one of your own socks! You were moaning "give it to me" over and over. Zamyotov went round looking in all the corners for your socks, and with his own hands, scented and covered with rings, gave you all this rubbish. Then you calmed down, and held on to that rubbish for days on end; we couldn't get it away from you [...] And then you asked for the ends of your trousers, and you were so tearful about it!"' (*PSS*: VI, 99).

pays an excessively high price. It may not be as drastic as in the case of Germann, but it is all the same highly detrimental to his (and not only his) soul.

Raskolnikov's 'arithmetic', his theory and calculation, were a reversed chimera. Dostoevsky was convinced that such chimeras were natural for Petersburg, where dreams and delirium turn into reality, and reality has the character of a dream (a transparent theme of the novel, also expressed through motifs in the action). This idea resonates in *The Queen of Spades* (Germann's dream), and in both the action of the poem *The Bronze Horseman*, and the thoughts of its poor hero, whose most humble dream, it would seem, also sinks into non-being, is broken up, leading to confusion in his mind and leaving only fragments of his consciousness of himself:

> Там буря выла, там носились
> Обломки... Боже, Боже! Там—
> Увы! близехонько к волнам,
> Почти у самого залива—
> Забор некрашеный, да ива
> И ветхий домик: там оне,
> Вдова и дочь, его Параша,
> Его мечта... Или во сне
> Он это видит? Иль вся наша
> И жизнь ничто, как сон пустой,
> Насмешка неба над землей? (ASP: V, 142)

> Where the storm howled, and round were driven
> Fragments of wreck... There, God in Heaven!
> Hard by the bay should stand, and close,
> Alas, too close to the wild water,
> A painted fence, a willow tree,
> And there a frail old house should be
> Where dwelt a widow, with a daughter
> Parasha—and his dream was she!
> His dream—or was it but a vision,
> All that he saw? Was life also
> An idle dream which in derision
> Fate sends to mock us here below? (p. 145)

We encounter a reference to *The Bronze Horseman* in the very first pages of *Crime and Punishment*, in the scene when Raskolnikov makes the acquaintance of Marmeladov, in which he in the first place suggest that Raskolnikov, like both Pushkin's Evgeny and himself, is a poor clerk who has been deprived of his place: 'Dare I ask whether you have been working in the service?' (*PSS*: VI, 12); and then,

> 'Most gracious sir', he began with almost ceremonial solemnity, 'poverty is not a sin—that's a known truth. And I know that drunkenness is not a virtue either, and that's all the more true. But destitution, gracious sir, destitution is a sin [...] For destitution a man isn't even driven out with a stick, he's swept

out with a broom from human society, so as to make it as insulting as possible; and that's how it should be, for when I'm destitute I'm the first in line to insult myself. Hence the drink! [...] Allow me to ask another question, just out of simple curiosity: have you ever spent the night on the Neva, on the hay barges?' 'No, that's never happened to me', replied Raskolnikov. 'What are you getting at?' (*PSS*: VI, 13)

Marmeladov's question about the barges on the Neva, where the drunken clerk has spent several days and where in his understanding Raskolnikov would also find a place, was not asked out of 'simple curiosity'. It forces us to recall poor Evgeny, who in his very worst destitution was sheltered at night by a landing stage on the Neva:

> [...] Ужасных дум
> Безмолвно полон, он скитался.
> Его терзал какой-то сон.
> Прошла неделя, месяц—он
> К себе домой не возвращался [...]
>   Он скоро свету
> Стал чужд. Весь день бродил пешком,
> А спал на пристани [...]
> И так он свой несчастный век
> Влачил, ни зверь, ни человек,
> Ни то ни се, ни житель света
> Ни призрак мертвый...
>   Раз он спал
> У невской пристани... (ASP: V, 146)

> A host of hideous thoughts attacked him,
> A kind of nightmare rent and racked him,
> And on he wandered silently;
> And as the week, the month, went by,
> Never came home [...]
>   he would roam,
> A stranger to the world [...]
> So, dragging out his days, ill-fated,
> He seemed like something miscreated,
> No beast, nor yet of human birth,
> Neither a denizen of earth
> Nor phantom of the dead.
>   Belated
> One night, on Neva wharf he slept. (p. 148)

Several motifs from this extract (on which we will however not dwell here) relate to both Marmeladov and Raskolnikov.

Later on, telling of the mishaps which had fallen to his lot and that of his family, Marmeladov continues: 'It will soon be a year and a half since we at last found ourselves, after all our wanderings and many tribulations, in this magnificent capital city adorned with its numerous monuments.' (*PSS*: VI, 16)

The first amongst these monuments is, of course, the monument to Peter, the 'miracle-working' builder of the new capital, he:

> [...] чьей волей роковой
> Под морем город основался. (V, 147)

> Whose will was Fate
> Our city by the sea had founded. (p. 149)

But Marmeladov does not mention this. Later, staring straight at this monument, Raskolnikov does not see it either. Stopping on Nikolaevsky bridge, where he 'was on the verge of falling under the horse', Raskolnikov:

> turned his face to the Neva, in the direction of the palace [...] The dome of the cathedral [...] was gleaming, and through the pure air it was possible to make out clearly each one of its adornments. The pain of the knout died away and Raskolnikov forgot about the blow; one uneasy and not entirely clear thought was occupying him exclusively. He stood looking fixedly into the distance for a long time [...] he had often, perhaps a hundred times, stopped at this very same spot, to peer fixedly at this truly magnificent panorama, and each time had been amazed by a certain unclear and insoluble impression it gave him. An inexplicable coldness always drifted towards him from this magnificent panorama; this splendid picture was for him full of a dumb and deaf spirit. (*PSS*: VI, 89-90)

Looking into the distance 'fixedly and for a long time', Raskolnikov can see distinctly every adornment on St Isaac's cathedral, but resolutely does not notice the monument to Peter, which is bigger than any of these adornments, and closer to him.

It must be said that in the preparatory materials for the novel, where the narrative is in the first person (the future Raskolnikov), the Bronze Horseman and the square around it are at the centre of attention: 'I went then to Senate square. There's always a wind there, especially around the monument. It's a sad and painful place. Why in the whole world have I never found anything more miserable and painful than the view of this enormous square?' (*PSS*: VII, 34) In his commentary to these lines, G F Kogan rightly notes that

> Senate square is inextricably linked with the memory of the Decembrists. Both the square and memorial to Peter I by Falconet (The Bronze Horseman) could not but have been associated by Dostoevsky with the theme of Pushkin's *The Bronze Horseman*: the clash between the little man and the autocratic state, his suffering in cruel and autocratic Petersburg. (*PSS*: VII, 401)

In the final text a somewhat different viewpoint is taken: Raskolnikov, standing on the bridge, sees the embankments of the Neva, the imperial (Winter) palace, St Isaac's cathedral and... the very same Bronze Horseman which, although the hero's attention skirts round it, has not, it goes without saying, disappeared. It is in fact the *genius loci* of Petersburg.[11] Here it is all the more noticeable for not being named, for not being there; it is, to use Tacitus's phrase, conspicuous by its absence.

This omission by Dostoevsky is deeply meaningful. It signifies that the main memorial to Peter I is not Falconet's work, but the tsar's palace (the residence of the autocratic heirs of Russia's reformer), St Isaac's cathedral and the whole panorama of the Neva, described by Pushkin in the Introduction to *The Bronze Horseman* in sharp, severe, magnificent verses which correspond so well to the subject at hand. But not only that. Relatively close to the 'sovereign' Neva, and serving as a contrast to the memorial to Peter, we also find the Haymarket, the streets and lanes surrounding it, the inns and taverns 'adorning' them, the corners and rooms being let out, and the refuges of poverty and corruption. In the final analysis the whole of Petersburg is the chief memorial to Peter—not only the splendour of the capital, but also its stench, filth and poverty. Of the novel's hero, scarcely stepping over the threshold of his 'little box', it is said:

> He was so poorly dressed that another man, even one accustomed to such a way of living, would have been ashamed to go out in the daytime in such rags. However, this was the sort of district where it would have been difficult to surprise anybody by the clothes one wore. The proximity of the Haymarket, the abundance of notorious establishments, and the local population, consisting in the most part of tradesmen and artisans, crowded together in these streets and lanes in the centre of Petersburg, rendered the general panorama colourful sometimes with such gaudy subjects that it would have been strange for anybody to be surprised at meeting the occasional odd figure. (*PSS*: VI, 6)

As we can see, here we have quite a different panorama.

Raskolnikov looks at the many beauties of Petersburg with the eyes of a Haymarket man, a man of the world of the destitute and unfortunate; this beauty is as alien to him as he is to it. Therefore the picture of the Neva, full in Pushkin of movement and life:

---

[11] N P Antsiferov writes: 'Almost at the foot of St Isaac's, in the square, enclosed on two sides by the serene, bright, majestic buildings of the Admiralty, the Synod and the Senate, washed by the regal Neva on the third side, stands the monument to Peter I erected by Catherine II: Petro Primo Catharina Secunda'. His further description of the statue confirms once more that in the perceptions of Russians the statue is altogether inextricably linked to Pushkin's verses: 'If somebody happens to be near it on a foul autumn evening, when the sky, transforming into chaos, draws closer to the earth and fills it with its turmoil, when the river, constrained by granite, groans and tosses, when sudden gusts of wind shake the lamp-posts, and their flickering light makes the surrounding buildings stir—let him peer at the Bronze Horseman at that moment, at this fire which has turned into bronze with sharply outlined and mighty forms. What power will he feel, a passionate power, stormy, calling to the unknown, what grand scale, calling forth the disturbing question: what next, what lies ahead? Victory or destruction and death? *The Bronze Horseman* is the *genius loci* of Petersburg', 'Dusha Peterburga', in N P Antsiferov, *'Nepostizhimyi gorod...'* (Leningrad, 1991), p. 35.

Прошло сто лет, и юный град,
Полнощных стран краса и диво,
Из тьмы лесов, из топи блат
Вознесся пышно, горделиво [...]
По оживленным берегам
Громады стройные теснятся
Дворцов и башен; корабли
Толпой со всех концов земли
К богатым пристаням стремятся;
В гранит оделася Нева;
Мосты повисли над водами;
Темнозелеными садами
Ее покрылись острова... (ASP: V, 135-136)[12]

A century—and that city young,
Gem of the Northern world, amazing,
From gloomy wood and swamp upsprung,
Had risen, in pride and splendour blazing. [...]
today, along
Those shores, astir with life and motion,
Vast shapely palaces in throng
And towers are seen: from every ocean,
From the world's end, the ships come fast,
To reach to loaded quays at last.
The Neva now is clad in granite
With many a bridge to overspan it;
The islands lie beneath a screen
Of gardens deep in dusky green. (pp. 140-141)

---

[12] The Introduction, as with all Pushkin's works, is sometimes understood not only as praise for Peter, but also as the poet's conviction of the rightness of the tsar's actions which would sooner or later serve in Russia's prosperity (as, for example, Belinsky thought). Meanwhile, even the final lines of the passionate introduction: 'Красуйся, град Петров, и стой/Неколебимо, как Россия,/Да умирится же с тобой/и побежденная стихия;/Вражду и плен старинный свой/Пусть волны финские забудут/И тщетной злобою не будет/Тревожить вечный сон Петра!' (ASP: V, 137) 'Now, city of Peter, stand thou fast,/Foursquare, like Russia; vaunt thy splendour!/The very elements shall surrender/And make her peace with thee at last./Their ancient bondage and their rancours/The Finnish waves shall bury deep/Nor vex with idle spite that cankers/Our Peter's everlasting sleep!' (p. 142) — express not so much a confident assertion by Pushkin ('It will be thus') but a kind of incantation ('Let it be thus!'). This was also noted in passing by Briusov (*Moi Pushkin: Stat'i, issledovaniia, nabliudeniia* (Moscow, Leningrad, 1929), p. 70; see also N V Izmailov, 'Mednyi vsadnik A S Pushkina', in Pushkin, *Mednyi vsadnik* (Leningrad, 1978), pp. 191-192, 259-260). But the incantation expresses only the desire of the poet, which may or may not be realized. And this is the heart of the matter. The realization of the desire demands particular conditions, and these depend not on the personal will of the poet, but on historical circumstances and the objective course of events. Pushkin points to the problems arising from within state life, but solving these problems is a matter for history. The Introduction to the poem describes one side of the coin, and the reverse, and more important side, is shown in the main body of the poem.

only fills Raskolnikov with the chill of death.

The contrasts of the capital, the dividing of the inhabitants into the rich and indigent, the elect and the outcasts, those who have rights and power and those who have been deprived of both, are witness to the fact that the 'dumb and deaf spirit', indifferent to want and misfortune, is ruler of all here. Exiled to a certain place,[13] this spirit of enmity and separation appeared in another, settled comfortably in 'this magnificent capital city adorned with its numerous monuments', finding for itself, apparently, much better shelter in the first among these: precisely in the 'haughty statue', (ASP: V, 148) the 'idol' sitting on a 'bronze steed'. (ASP: V, 142; see also 147)[14]

The symbolism of the Bronze Horseman in Pushkin's story, as Kupreianova emphasizes, is connected to the symbolism of Falconet's monument, the composition of which, 'embodies the epochs of absolutism, traditional for art, but art was already familiar with the Renaissance comparison of the horseman to the sovereign lord, and his horse as subject to the state or the people'.[15] Pushkin makes such a comparison himself. When for a moment the consciousness of the insane hero, broken by sorrows, returns to him, he realizes:

> И место, где потоп играл [...]
> и того,
> Кто неподвижно возвышался
> Во мраке медною главой [...]
> Ужасен он в окрестной мгле!
> Какая дума на челе!
> Какая сила в нем сокрыта!
> А в сем коне какой огонь!
> Куда ты скачешь, гордый конь,
> И где опустишь ты копыта?
> О мощный властелин судьбы!
> Не так ли ты над самой бездной,
> На высоте, уздой железной
> Россию поднял на дыбы? (ASP: V, 147)

>   for it was here
> The flood had gambolled [...]
>   and Him
> Who, moveless and aloft and dim [...]

---

[13]Cf. Jesus [...] rebuked the foul spirit, saying unto him, Thou dumb and deaf spirit, I charge thee, come out of him, and enter no more into him. And the spirit cried, and rent him sore, and came out of him. Mark 9: 25-26.

[14]Briusov writes, 'The hero of [Pushkin's] story is not the Peter who thought to 'threaten the Swedes' and call 'all flags to visit' him, but the 'Bronze Horseman', the 'haughty statue' and above all the 'idol'. It is precisely an 'idol', that is, an object of worship [...] that Pushkin himself calls Peter's memorial', *Moi Pushkin*, pp. 70-71.

[15]Kupreianova, pp. 300-301.

> Appalling there
> He sat, begirt with mist and air.
> What thoughts engrave his brow! what hidden
> Power and authority He claims!
> What fire in yonder charger flames!
> Proud charger, whither art thou ridden,
> Where leapest thou? and where, on whom,
> Will plant thy hoof?—Ah, lord of doom
> And potentate, 'twas thus, appearing
> Above the void, and in thy hold
> A curb of iron, thou sat'st of old
> O'er Russia, on her haunches rearing. (pp. 149-150)

The 'proud charger' climbing 'on haunches rearing' 'above the void' with the horseman cannot be tranquil. A happy outcome of this movement is possible only if horse and horseman are united by a single feeling, a single idea and will. If matters are otherwise, then any horse (and a 'proud' one all the more) will try to throw his rider in order to save himself over this void.[16]

But the necessary unanimity between the power and the people is absent from the poem. The self-will of Peter, having undertaken the new construction of both a city and a state, knew no bounds, and least of all considered the feelings, desires, understanding and often also the practical resources of the people subject to its authority. Moreover, it from the very beginning accepted their torments and the shedding of their blood. This threatened serious consequences. The sparks of revolt could not but be flickering among the people, the flames extinguished temporarily when they had barely begun to flare up (the Pugachev movement). And they continued to break into the open in one form of protest and rebellion or another:

> Вскипела кровь. Он [Evgenii] мрачен стал
> Пред горделивым истуканом

---

[16] Two verses which correlate to each other serve, possibly, as an allusion to this idea. First: 'В неколебимой вышине,/Над возмущенною Невою/Стоит с простертою рукою/Кумир на бронзовом коне.' (ASP: V, 142) 'With Neva still beneath him churning,/Unshaken, on Evgeny turning/His back, and with an arm flung wide,/Behold the Image sit, and ride/Upon his brazen horse astride!' (pp. 146-147) Inasmuch as Peter is sitting, rather than standing, on the horse, he can stand only by being solidly fused together with it. Later: 'И прямо в темной вышине/Над огражденною скалою/Кумир с простертою рукою/Сидел на бронзовом коне.' (ASP: V, 147) 'Upright and glooming,/Above the stony barrier looming,/The Image, with an arm flung wide,/Sat on his brazen horse astride.' (p. 149) Here horse and rider are separated. In this sense, Pushkin's picture is characteristic, and absolutely linked with his poem, where 'the memorial to Peter I drawn by Falconet's pen is a rock, and on it a horse, trampling a snake. But the rider—Peter himself—is absent, and the saddle nor bridle, neither of which the horse had at first, were both drawn on later; moreover the bridle with reins coming from the bit, and the girth and saddle without stirrups, are composed very carefully (as indeed is the whole picture), giving the entire composition an ironic, almost caricatured appearance' (Izmailov, p. 182). The interpretation by Izmailov of the illustration introduced here does not seem convincing.

> И, зубы стиснув, пальцы сжав,
> Как обуянный силой черной,
> «Добро, строитель чудотворный! —
> Шепнул он, злобно задрожав, —
> Ужо тебе!...» И вдруг стремглав
> Бежать спустился. (ASP: V, 148)

> And in his [Evgeny's] veins the blood was leaping.
> He halted suddenly beneath
> The haughty Image, clenched his teeth
> And clasped his hands, as though some devil
> Possessed him, some dark power of evil,
> And shuddered, whispering angrily,
> 'Ay, architect, with thy creation
> Of marvels... Ah, beware of me!'
> And then, in wild precipitation
> He fled. (p. 150)

He begins to run because the dumb and deaf 'statue', indifferent to the howling of the storm, the frenzy of the raging elements, suddenly catches (from 'the unshakeable heights' and somewhere far below, beneath his feet) this weakened whisper and comes to life. It comes to life in order to throw all of its gigantic might at 'poor Evgeny', to subdue him, return him to 'the old order', after he has shown the weakest glimmer of reason and a barely distinct manifestation of rebellion:[17]

> Показалось
> Ему, что грозного царя,
> Мгновенно гневом возгоря,
> Лицо тихонько обращалось...
> И он по площади пустой
> Бежит и слышит за собой—
> Как будто грома грохотанье—
> Тяжело-звонкое скаканье
> По потрясенной мостовой. (ASP: V, 148)

> For now he seemed to see
> The awful Emperor, quietly,
> With momentary anger burning,
> His visage to Evgeny turning!
> And rushing through the empty square,
> He hears behind him as it were
> Thunders that rattle in a chorus,
> A gallop, ponderous, sonorous,
> That shakes the pavement. (p. 150)

---

[17] See Briusov, *Moi Pushkin*, pp. 80-81.

The dumb and deaf 'statue' hears Evgeny's whisper and even begins to speak to him in the language of thunder, lightning, the ringing of his heavy hoofs, and a more serious means of reprimand:

> И озарен луною бледной,
> Простерши руку в вышине,
> За ним несется Всадник Медный
> На звонко-скачущем коне;
> И во всю ночь безумец бедный,
> Куда стопы ни обращал,
> За ним повсюду Всадник Медный
> С тяжелым топотом скакал. (ASP: V, 148)

> Illuminated by the pale moonlight,
> With arms outflung, behind him riding
> See, the bronze horseman comes, bestriding
> The charger, clanging in his flight.
> All night the madman flees; no matter
> Where he may wander at his will,
> Hard on his track with heavy clatter
> There the bronze horseman gallops still. (p. 150)

The extended hand of the tsar-reformer in the logic of this situation must be wielding a knout. And so he is. So seems to be the case in Adam Mickiewicz's poem 'The Memorial of Peter the Great' ('Pomnik Piotra Wielkiego'), where a detailed interpretation of the monumental sculpture's symbolism is given in the words of a celebrated Russian poet (that is, Pushkin):

> Pielgrzym coś dumał nad Piotra kolosem,
> A wieszcz rosyjski tak rzekł cichym głosem:
> 'Pierwszemu z carów, co te zrobił cuda,
> Druga carowa pamiętnik stawiała.
> Już car odlany w kształcie wielkoluda
> Siadł na brązowym grzbiecie bucefała
> I miejsca czekał, gdzie by wjechał konno.
> Lecz Piotr na własnej ziemi stać nie może,
> W ojczyźnie jemu nie dosyć przestronne,
> Po grunt dla niego posłano za morze.
> Posłano wyrwać z finlandzkich nadbrzeży
> Wzgórek granitu; ten na Pani słowo
> Płynie po morzu i po lądzie bieży,
> I w mieście pada na wznak przed carową.'[18]

> The Pilgrim mused on Peter's awesome mien,
> While gently thus the bard explained, the scene:

---

[18] Adam Mickiewicz, *Dzieła Poetyckie, III: Utwory Dramatyczne* (Warsaw: Czytelnik, 1965), pp. 283-285. Also quoted in A S Pushkin, *Mednyi vsadnik* (Leningrad, 1978), p. 143.

> 'To the first tsar, of mighty fame and deed,
> Great Catherine here a monument decreed.
> So this gigantic image of the tsar
> Bestrides the bronzed back of a mettled steed
> And waited for space where he may ride afar.
> But Peter could not rest on Russian ground;
> His native land was small for such as he:
> His pedestal they sought beyond the sea. [...]
> The mound is ready now, and forth he goes,
> A Roman-toga'd tsar who rules by blows
> His charger gallops up the granite steep
> Rearing its body for a mighty leap'.[19]

In precisely the verses of his own poem which speak of Russia being raised on its hind legs, Pushkin adds a footnote, referring to this poem by Mickiewicz.[20]

Peter drove his people into European civilization by domestic means—the knout and the truncheon.[21] (However, the line-beatings with rods borrowed by him from Prussia and which took root in Russia were no better.)

We do not know where the 'proud steed' will gallop in the future, and where he will put down his hooves, but for now, controlled by the terrible horseman, having torn free of the pedestal, he will chase the poor man so that the horseman can either flog him to death or crush him with the horse's hoofs.[22] See the words of the Russian poet in the penultimate stanza of Mickiewicz's poem:

---

[19]English translation by George Rapall Noyes and Marjorie Beatrice Peacock, in *Adam Mickiewicz, 1798-1855: Selected Poetry and Prose: Centenary Commemorative Edition*, ed. Stanislaw Helsztynski (Warsaw: Polonia, 1955), p. 108.

[20]Pushkin writes: 'Look at the description of the statue in Mickiewicz [the text cited here—VV]. It is borrowed from Ruban—as Mickiewicz himself notes' (ASP: V, 50). In fact, the Polish poet borrows only one line from V G Ruban, a poet (1742-1795) whose name Mickiewicz does not in general mention (see Izmailov's note in Pushkin, *Mednyi vsadnik*, p. 270). Pushkin simply needed to refer to Mickiewicz's poem. Unlike some Pushkin specialists, we do not consider this reference to have only a polemical sense for Pushkin, or that Mickiewicz ascribed his ideas to the Russian poet. Pushkin's attitude to Peter had more than one facet; he could embellish what Mickiewicz had said, but not nullify his words entirely. Some of these words he corrects and elaborates. However, discussion of the polemic between Pushkin and Mickiewicz is a separate topic.

[21]In the preparatory materials for his history of Peter I, Pushkin writes: 'A fitting surprise is the difference between the state institutions of Peter the Great and his provisional decrees. The first are the essence of the fruits of reason, vast, and full of benevolence and wisdom, the second are *not infrequently cruel, wilful, and, it seems, written with a knout*. The first were for eternity, or at least for the future, the second burst forth from an *impatient* despotic landowner' (ASP: X, 256; author's emphasis). And in his notes on eighteenth-century Russian history: 'History around [the time of Peter I] represents universal slavery [...] all positions, shackled indiscriminately, were equal before his *cudgel*. Everything trembled, everything silently obeyed' (ASP: XI, 14; author's emphasis).

[22]'The pursuit of Evgeny by the horseman', writes Briusov, 'is depicted not so much as the delirium of a madman, but rather as a real fact, and in this way an element of the supernatural is introduced into the story', *Moi Pushkin*, pp. 63-64. In our view, everything is united here: a particular event and generalization, delirious reality and symbolism.

Car Piotr wypuścił rumakowi wodze,
Widać, że leciał tratując po drodze,
Od razu wskoczył aż na sam brzeg skały.
Już koń szalony wzniósł w górę kopyta,
Car go nie trzyma, koń wędzidłem zgrzyta,
Zgadniesz, że spadnie i pryśnie w kawały.

His charger's reins Tsar Peter has released;
He has been flying down the road, perchance,
And here the precipice checks his advance.
With hoofs aloft now stands the maddened beast,
Champing its bit unchecked, with slackened rein:
You guess that it will fall and be destroyed.[23]

Pushkin's final lines correct this: Peter sits not on a 'maddened' (wild), but on a 'proud steed'. It is rather the tsar who is 'maddened' (terrible, angry, impetuously cruel), and it is the tsar (or if not he himself, then in his descendants), who therefore, being thrown off, will 'fall and be destroyed'). 'Poor Evgeny' is neither flogged to death nor crushed. He is simply 'driven' by the night-time pursuit into 'the old order' (madness) and only later to death.

The heirs of the tsar-reformer, these countless 'fledglings of Peter's nest' (ASP: V, 57), distributed, according to the *Table of Ranks*, on all the rungs of the state ladder, have in memory of the founder retained the same means in their hands. They have forgotten about love and charity. More than that, guided by the latest economic theories, in the form of the 'light' coming into Russia via that same little 'window', they have turned their hard-heartedness into a principle (as has *Peter Petrovich* Luzhin in *Crime and Punishment*). Therefore, after a hundred years and more, simultaneously with the heightening of the beauty of the Russian capital there was also a heightening of evil, which is hidden from the very beginning behind its imposing façade. From the top to the bottom (and in the very best style), here the 'old order' functions. See the scene with the courier whom Dostoevsky saw in his early youth at a staging-post, and about whom he wrote in *Diary of a Writer* for 1876:

> The coachman started up the horses, but before he could even get them going the courier stood up and silently, without a single word, raised his strong right fist and brought a painful blow down on the very back of the coachman's neck. The coachman shuddered forward, raised his whip and lashed the shaft horse with all his might. The horses darted forward, but this did nothing to appease the courier. He was not irritated; this was his method, something preconceived and tested with many years' experience, and the terrible fist was raised again, and again it struck the coachman's neck [...] Naturally, the coachman, who was barely able to hold on because of the blows, ceaselessly and every second kept lashing the horse as though he had gone mad, and at

---

[23] Polish and English versions as before (see notes 18 and 19).

last landed a blow which made the horses fly off as if possessed. (*PSS*: XXII, 28)

Dostoevsky also recalled this scene in the notebooks for *Crime and Punishment* (*PSS*: VII, 138), as the scene of 'a certain exhausted horse' (*PSS*: VII, 41), which in the final text Raskolnikov sees in his 'shocking dream'. (*PSS*: VI, 46-49)

As a result of this 'order', Katerina Ivanovna Marmeladova, like 'poor Evgeny', is 'driven' to insanity and death ('"They've driven the jade to death! I've overstrai-i-ned myself"', she screamed out in despair and hatred, and crashed her head back down on to the pillow' (*PSS*: VI, 334)); her intoxicated (and also, therefore, insane) husband in the place of 'poor Evgeny' is crushed by horses (*PSS*: VI, 136); and Raskolnikov (who for all his intelligence is also still 'mad' (see *PSS*: VI, 225 and elsewhere)) both 'drives' others and is himself 'driven'; he both crushes, and is crushed. Desiring to break out from the midst of the 'poor' and the 'driven', he dreams of raising money even if it means shedding blood. Money gives him the power (whilst evading official power) to pardon or to crush everyone, one after the other, at his own discretion: 'Oh, how I understand the "prophet" with his sabre, on horseback. Allah orders, and "trembling" mortals obey! The "prophet" is right, he's right, when he places a go-o-od-sized battery somewhere across the street and blows away the righteous and the guilty alike, not even favouring them with an explanation!' (*PSS*: VI, 212)

Insofar as for Dostoevsky this 'accursed dream' (*PSS*: VI, 50) about money is dependent on poverty, on the extent to which the hero has been 'driven', then in his novel *The Queen of Spades* and *The Bronze Horseman* are united not simply as a general theme, but in their internal logic. Later, in *The Adolescent*, they are united again in the reflections of the main character:

> On [...] a Petersburg morning, putrid, damp and foggy, the wild dream of someone like Pushkin's Germann from *The Queen of Spades* [...] must, I think, become even more intense. A hundred times in this fog I've been struck by a strange but persistent reverie: 'and what if, when this fog disperses and lifts, this entire putrid and sleazy city were to rise up with it and disappear like smoke, and all that remained would be the old Finnish swamp and in the middle of it, perhaps, for decoration, a bronze horseman on a snorting, driven steed?' (*PSS*: XIII, 113)[24]

Translated by Sarah Young

---

[24] Translation based on Fyodor Dostoevsky, *An Accidental Family*, trans. Richard Freeborn (Oxford: Oxford University Press, 1994), pp. 144-145, with some modification (*Translator's note*).

READING *THE GAMBLER* AS *ROULETTENBURG*

Erik Egeberg

THE original title of the novel Fyodor Dostoevsky (and his future wife) wrote down in twenty-six days in October 1866 was not *The Gambler* but *Roulettenburg*. This title, however, was not accepted by the publisher Fyodor Stellovsky, who proposed the version which from then on has followed the book: *The Gambler*. Dostoevsky did not set himself against the change, even though the inventor of the new title 'did not understand anything'[1]—maybe because the question did not seem all that important to him. Or maybe the writer did not want another controversy with this unscrupulous speculator.

But what does this change mean? Nothing? The text of the novel remains the same. On the other hand, the title is in fact the first words the prospective reader meets, and everything that happens in the novel is viewed and evaluated in the light of these first words. When the novel is named *The Gambler*, the focus inevitably is on the narrator, who in fact is 'the gambler',—but not the only one. If the novel had retained its original title—*Roulettenburg*, the attention of the reader would have been directed more towards the whole society gathered around the roulette table. However, there is no sharp contrast between these two possibilities; in both cases Aleksei Ivanovich in his capacity as author of the notes, as narrator, will occupy a special place, just as the whole gambling society surrounding him will attract the attention of the reader anyhow. But if we look at the novel as *Roulettenburg*, the society will move from the background to the foreground.

Dostoevsky has a relatively high rate of work titles indicating collectives — from *Poor Folk* to *The Brothers Karamazov*. But *Roulettenburg* and *The Village of Stepanchikovo and its Inhabitants* are the only two containing a place name. Roulettenburg and Stepanchikovo, however, are names of two different types; the last one has no apparent symbolic meaning, while the first one is saturated with it. No real town or city is named Roulettenburg; the name has been invented with an evident intention—to show a community totally dominated by gambling. And in fact we see very little of what is going on in the town outside the precincts of the casino, the spa with the adjacent park, and the hotel.

---

[1] *PSS*, XXVIII: 2, 159. (Letter to Anna Korvin-Krukovskaia, dated 17th June, 1866).

We are not told in what country the town of Roulettenburg is situated, but the ending -burg and several other details point at one or another of the western German states, although the first part of the word is of Romance origin. Thus the name attains a more general Western European colour, indicating that what is happening there is not connected with only one nation or one country. In accordance with this striving towards a general European setting Dostoevsky also chooses characters from various great European nations: France (Mlle Blanche des Cominges, Marquis des Grieux), Great Britain (Mr Astley), Germany (the Prussian baron Wurmerhelm and his spouse) and of course Russia; there are also some Poles, as usual in Dostoevsky's work—very unsympathetic ones. Moreover, these representatives of various countries also bear their nation's typical characteristics according to common cliché (or even prejudice): 'The General is the pathetic Russian cosmopolitan, prey to all the evils Dostoevsky imagines come with rootlessness; de Grieux is the prototypal Frenchman, smooth, well-mannered, and unprincipled; Mr Astley is the quintessential Englishman, laconic, honest, unperturbed on the surface; Mlle Blanche is the beautiful, predatory, superficial French seductress.[2] In fact, Dostoevsky himself explicitly emphasizes the 'Germanness' of the baron's appearance and asserts that des Grieux 'was like all Frenchmen' (p. 58), then listing all the main traits of that variety of mankind.

Then comes the Russian group, by far the largest. It is not homogeneous; several ages and social layers are represented. At the top we find the general, his sister and his children, then comes his stepdaughter Polina, then the family's tutor Aleksei Ivanovich—the narrator; he too is a nobleman, although in a subordinate position. Servants also appear on the scene but play no significant role.

This Russian group is closely affiliated with the French one, which consists of a false marquis, a mademoiselle with a dubious identity, and her pretended mother. The Englishman remains on the periphery of the story, while the Prussian baron and baroness are only episodic figures; one even gets the impression that Dostoevsky introduces them only to expand his list of represented national types.

All these uncertain positions—general but not rich, nobleman but only a tutor, stepdaughter, not daughter, false title, false identity—create a state of general instability which is reflected in the prevailing tense atmosphere; scandal is continually looming on the horizon. As usual both in Dostoevsky and in literature in general, the story gains speed when a new person arrives in this labile milieu. In *The Gambler*, the new person is *la baboulinka* ('Granny'),[3] who also brings

---

[2]Edward Wasiolek, 'Introduction', in Fyodor Dostoevsky, *The Gambler: with Polina Suslova's Diary*, ed. Edward Wasiolek, trans. Victor Terras (Chicago, Ill. & London: University of Chicago Press, 1972), p. xxxii. All quotations are from this edition, pages indicated in brackets in the text.

[3]The Russian word *babushka* with the diminutive *babulin'ka* denotes not only the mother of the father or mother (grandmother), but any elderly female relative.

with her fresh money, the stuff that keeps the story going on. Coming directly from Russia, she gives a new facet to the Russian group, which otherwise consists of people who have lived abroad for quite a long time and have become affected by their absence from home.

The arrival of 'Granny' is the big surprise in the novel. Everybody has been waiting for a message about her demise, but then she suddenly appears 'like a bolt from the blue' (p. 78)—true, in a wheeled chair, but bursting with energy. There is often something wrong with Dostoevsky's generals; their wives and widows, however, are magnificent: 'Granny' is 'alert, perky, and sure of herself as ever before, sitting upright in her chair, shouting in a loud and imperious voice, scolding every one.' (p. 78)

'Granny' has come to Roulettenburg to undergo treatment—and to visit the roulette table. The medical treatment is hardly mentioned any more, for when 'Granny' enters the casino the roulette immediately attracts all her attention. She is totally unprepared, knowing the casino only by hearsay or from literature, and therefore needs a guide or 'tutor'. She chooses Aleksei Ivanovich. He has gambled once before, on behalf of Polina, and he has studied the procedures of the roulette, so he is quite able to act as 'Granny's' adviser. The old lady soon becomes totally absorbed by the gambling, and her excitement also infects Aleksei Ivanovich: 'I was myself a gambler; I felt it at that very moment. My limbs were trembling, and I felt dazed.' (p. 104) But Dostoevsky has composed his novel in a way that does not let us see both of them gamble at one and the same time; only when 'Granny' has finally lost all her money and all of the stocks and bonds she had brought with her from Russia, Aleksei Ivanovich starts gambling, again for Polina's sake, but now with his own money—fifty pieces of gold which he has got from none other than 'Granny'.

Their fates on the whole follow the same curve: first they win an enormous fortune—and then they lose everything. But they end in different ways; 'Granny', having spent her last rouble in the casino, returns to Russia, where she still possesses three villages and two houses; Aleksei Ivanovich, however, seems to be fettered to the roulette for the rest of his life.

There is a multitude of gamblers in the casino of Roulettenburg; especially in chapter one, when Aleksei Ivanovich enters the casino for the first time, we are given a vivid description of the various categories of gamblers. 'Granny' and Aleksei Ivanovich, however, are the only two whom we follow as individuals. We are offered insight into their psychology, we can see how people *become* involved with gambling, while for all the others we only observe how they already *are* gamblers. This makes them by no means uninteresting. First of all they form an impressive background for the development of gambling addiction in the heroine and the hero—'*The Gambler*'. But they are important also in themselves, giving meaning to the whole society's name—'*Roulettenburg*'. The novel is in fact more than the story of one single man, it is the tale of how gambling changes *men in general*. Therefore Aleksei Ivanovich is not alone, his psychological development is paralleled by that of 'Granny', and all the other people around the tables in the casino show traits of the same addiction that befalls these two. When reading the novel as *Roulettenburg*, we interpret the detailed description of Aleksei Ivanovich's development as gambler as a prototypal feature rather than as something singular and only personal.

But what does the roulette do, then, to those who touch it? Let us first have a look at 'Granny'. The imposing old lady has now turned weak and meek: 'Verily, even in our old age God exacts retribution and punishes us for our pride.' (p. 147) Almost all her energy is gone, what is left of it she spends to organize her return by train to Russia. However, she has been taught a lesson in Roulettenburg: 'From now I shall no longer blame young people for doing foolish things' (p. 147)—and probably she will be able to lead a normal life home in Russia for the rest of her days. That will not be twenty-five years, till the age of 100, as supposed by the Russian group when she arrives in Roulettenburg, but only one or two. The reader suspects that the remaining expected years have been devoured by the gambling.

In the novel's last chapter, a couple of years after the events in Roulettenburg, Aleksei Ivanovich again meets Mr Astley, who reproaches him with the following words (among others): 'Yes, you have destroyed yourself. You had some abilities, a lively disposition, and you were not a bad man. In fact, you might have been of service to your country, which needs men so badly. But you are going to stay here, and your life is finished'. (p. 196)

However, the changes that take place in Aleksei Ivanovich's mind are more complex that those in 'Granny', since his involvement with gambling lives side by side with his problematic infatuation for Polina and competes with it. In fact, he starts gambling in order to help his beloved, but what happens? 'A huge pile of bank notes and rolls of gold filled the whole table, and I could not take my eyes off it. There were moments when I completely forgot about Polina.' (p. 160) And further on: 'I swear, I felt sorry for Polina, but strangely enough, from the moment I had touched that gaming table the night before and had begun to scoop up those bundles of money, my love had somehow receded to the background.' (p. 168) Part of the explanation for this may be that 'gambling passion serves as a substitute for eroticism because it keeps one caught in the same sado-masochistic labyrinths.'[4] Aleksei Ivanovich does not get Polina, but he gets another woman—Mlle Blanche. True, there may have been a touch of eroticism in their relationship, but decidedly no love: 'No, as I recall now, I was terribly sad even then, even though I tried to laugh as heartily as that silly goose Blanche.' (p. 172) She, too, is part of the machinery that rules Roulettenburg and robs him of his two hundred thousand francs almost as rapidly as the roulette itself could have done.

What is going on with 'Granny' and Aleksei Ivanovich clearly shows the effect of the roulette: it drains the life energy—including the ability to love and

---

[4]Peter Normann Waage, *Fjodor M. Dostojevskij* (Oslo: Gyldendal, 1997), p. 175.

thereby make life continue in new generations—out of them and the other people gathered around the gaming table. It also supplants the normal common reason with a mind filled with illusions: the gambler seeks power and freedom, but becomes trapped in hopeless determinism.[5] Before he starts gambling, Aleksei Ivanovich is fully aware of 'the mercenary motives and snares upon which the bank is founded and built' (p. 18), just as he clearly understands the immorality of the whole institution of the casino. But being one of Dostoevsky's rebels, revolting against the restrictions set by reason and morality, he confesses: 'But I would like to take notice of one thing: of late I have been finding it somehow extremely repulsive to apply any kind of moral standard to my actions and thoughts. I was guided by something quite different...' (p. 19) These words also show that the future gambler has been infected with the spirit of Roulettenburg even before entering the casino building. We may suppose that he possesses the same knowledge also after this spirit has completely invaded him, but then he has neither the freedom nor the power to make use of his insight.

It should be mentioned that this devastating effect has not only an individual aspect, but also a national one, insofar as the roulette seems to be especially suited for Russians. Thus it becomes an instrument with which wicked Western Europe can tap the more primitive and formless but also more vigorous Russians for their energy.

All in all, the result is a sort of mental death befalling everyone trapped by the roulette, and in accordance with this interpretation of his situation Aleksei Ivanovich claims: 'Tomorrow I may rise from the dead and begin a new life!' (p. 187) Consequently *Roulettenburg* can be viewed as a kind of 'House of the Dead', and in fact, in the early stages of the planning of his novel, Dostoevsky mentions that book as a model for his new enterprise.[6]

The realm of the dead in the Christian tradition is either heaven or hell. And the gambling casino is surely no heaven; Aleksei Ivanovich confesses: 'Yet at the same time I have a feeling that I have grown numb, somehow, as though I were buried in some kind of mire.' (p. 189) Konstantin Mochulsky states: 'The author relied on the effect of the subject's novelty and compared the "hell of roulette" to the hell of the House of Death.'[7]

The interpretation of *Roulettenburg* as a hellish place is strengthened by the occurrence of another place name connected with it: Schlangenberg, that is 'the

---

[5]Regine Nohejl ('"Alles oder nichts." Die Gestalt des Spielers im Werk Dostojewskis', in *F M Dostojewski: Dichter, Denker, Visionär*, ed. Heinz Setzer, Ludolf Müller, Rolf-Dieter Kluge (Tübingen: Attempto, 1998), pp. 63-88) gives a detailed analysis of the gambling addict.

[6]*PSS* XXVIII: 2, 50-51. (Letter to Nikolai Strakhov, dated 18 (30) September, 1863.)

[7]Konstantin Mochulsky, *Dostoevsky: His Life and Work*, trans. and introduced Michael A Minihan (Princeton, NJ: Princeton University Press, 1967), p. 315.

Serpentine Mountain'.[8] Both 'serpent' and 'mountain' are associated with the devil: 'Again the devil taketh him up into an exceeding high mountain, and sheweth him all the kingdoms of the world, and the glory of them; And saith unto him. All these things I give thee, if thou wilt fall down and worship me.' (Matt. 4: 8, 9) In the first chapter of *The Gambler*, Polina says: 'You told me last time at the Schlangenburg [sic] that you were ready at a single word from me to throw yourself down head first, and it's a thousand-foot drop there, I think' (pp. 12-13), which reminds the reader of an adjacent passage from the Holy Scripture: 'Then the devil taketh him up into the holy city, and setteth him on a pinnacle of the temple, And saith unto him, If thou be the Son of God, cast thyself down.' (Matt. 4: 5-6) True, the eventual throwing himself down from the Schlangenberg is here connected with his infatuation for Polina, not his gambling habit; however, there is at this point already a 'metonymic' connection between these two themes insofar as the Schlangenberg promise is mentioned just before Polina urges him to go to the casino and gamble for her. Later on we see this feeling of falling (with its symbolic overtones) more explicitly transferred from Polina to the roulette: 'There was a moment, though, as I was waiting, which may perhaps have resembled the feeling experienced by Mme Blanchard when she was hurtling to the ground from her balloon, in Paris.' (p. 154) Marie Blanchard's life ended in flames.

We may have our forebodings, but Dostoevsky does not tell us whether Aleksei Ivanovich will succeed in 'rising from the dead'. But we have already heard Mr Astley's prediction, and this English gentleman is playing the role of the mysterious omniscient figure in the novel. Aleksei Ivanovich's hope for a 'new life' (p. 187) after the roulette appears as just another illusion.

The Gambler is, together with *Notes from the House of the Dead*, the most autobiographical of all Dostoevsky's novels, and quite naturally it has been extensively used to illustrate the author's own experiences at the roulette, his phantastic liaison with Apollinaria Suslova, the psychology of the gambler etc. Its full meaning, however, can only be brought to the surface if we include the whole gambling community of Roulettenburg in our analysis.

---

[8] Joseph Frank, in *Dostoevsky: The Miraculous Years*, 1865-1871 (London: Robson Books, 1995), pp. 170-183, repeatedly names the town 'Roulettenberg', thus unconsciously (?) emphasizing the ties between it and the mountain (in German: 'Berg'). The very same effect is achieved, although inversely, when Victor Terras in his translation writes 'Schlangenburg'.

FINDING FORM FOR CHAOS

Dostoevsky's *The Adolescent* and Akhmatova's *Poem Without a Hero*

Alexandra K Harrington

> А в книгах я последнюю страницу
> Всегда любила больше всех других.
>
> And in books I always loved last page
> More than all the others.
> *Anna Akhmatova*

AT first sight, Fyodor Dostoevsky's intense, feverish, and lengthy novels appear to have little in common with Anna Akhmatova's elegant, emotionally restrained, and concise poetry. However, the first suggestion that Akhmatova drew upon Dostoevsky was made relatively early in her career by Osip Mandelshtam, her fellow Acmeist and close friend. He asserted:

> Akhmatova introduced all the enormous complexity and wealth of the nineteenth century novel into the Russian lyric. If not for Tolstoi's *Anna Karenina*, Turgenev's *Nest of Gentlefolk* (*Dvorianskoe gnezdo*), all of Dostoevsky and even some Leskov, there would be no Akhmatova. Akhmatova's genesis lies entirely in the realm of Russian prose, not in poetry. She developed her poignant and unique poetic form with a backward glance at psychological prose.[1]

Akhmatova's interest in Dostoevsky's work and extensive knowledge of it are reflected in the memoirs and biographical material about her written by later acquaintances such as Lidia Chukovskaia, Anatoly Naiman, and Sir Isaiah Berlin.

The epigraph is from A A Akhmatova, *Sochineniia*, ed. V A Chernykh, 2 vols (Moscow: Khudozhestvennaia literatura, 1986) I, p. 194. All translations into English are my own unless otherwise indicated.

[1] 'A letter about Russian poetry', in Osip Mandelstam, *The Collected Critical Prose and Letters*, trans. Jane Gary Harris and Constance Link, ed. Jane Gary Harris (London: Collins Harvill, 1991), pp. 156-59 (p. 156). For the Russian text, see 'Otryvok iz neopublikovannoi stat'i o russkoi literature i "Al'manakhe Muz"', in O E Mandel'shtam, *Sobranie sochinenii*, ed. G P Struve and B A Filippov, 2 vols (Washington: Inter-language Literary Associates, 1964-66), II, 487.

The fact that Dostoevsky was a frequent topic of her conversation was well known to contemporaries such as Boris Pasternak, who informed Sir Isaiah that when he visited Akhmatova she 'would surely talk [...] about Dostoevsky and attack Tolstoy'. Sir Isaiah recalls, 'in fact, she did speak to me of Dostoevsky with passionate admiration'.[2]

Mandelshtam's observation was made in 1916, long before Akhmatova wrote 'Northern Elegies' ('Severnye elegii', 1940-64) or *Poem Without a Hero* (*Poema bez geroia*, 1940-66), both of which invoke Dostoevsky as a means of characterizing nineteenth-century Russia. Yet, despite these overt references, surprisingly little critical attention has been paid to the extensive textual connections that exist between the two writers. The majority of scholars who have discussed the issue at any length tend to confine themselves to reproducing Akhmatova's observations about Dostoevsky or outlining areas for further study, usually emphasising the fact that a good deal of research remains to be undertaken.[3]

The most illuminating treatments of the subject to date are L K Dolgopolov's exploration of the roles played by Dostoevsky and Alexander Blok in *Poem Without a Hero*, and Susan Amert's analysis of 'Prehistory' ('Northern Elegies', 1). Dologopolov argues that Dostoevsky and Blok form two poles of *Poem* in terms of its philosophy of history, with Dostoevsky representing the nineteenth-century past, and Blok as contemporary Silver Age hero.[4] Amert, on the other hand, demonstrates that, in 'Prehistory', Akhmatova describes nineteenth-century Petersburg through the prism of Dostoevsky's life and fiction, and in so doing writes a new 'myth of origins' for her later period.[5] The aim of the present article is to contribute further to our understanding of how and why Akhmatova drew upon Dostoevsky's work by focusing on the textual relationship between *Poem Without a Hero* and *The Adolescent* (*Podrostok*, 1875). *The Adolescent* is only one of many intertexts perceptible in *Poema*, but is of considerable significance, as it bears on its conception and structure, as well as on the central themes of Petersburg and the death of poets.

It is likely that *The Adolescent* was used consciously in the composition of *Poem*. Akhmatova 'worked with books' on her poem, studying 'like a scholar', and a careful examination of what she was reading in 1940 as she embarked

---

[2] Isaiah Berlin, 'Meetings with Russian Writers in 1945 and 1956', in *Personal Impressions* (Oxford: Oxford University Press, 1982), pp. 156-211 (p. 188).

[3] For instance, see Ivailo Petrov, 'Dostoevskii i tvorchestvo Anny Akhmatovoi', *Slavica*, 21 (1984), 161-70; and E A Shestakova, 'Akhmatova i Dostoevskii (k postanovke problemy)', in *Novye aspekty v izuchenii Dostoevskogo*, ed. V N Zakharov (Petrozavodsk: Petrozavodskii gosudarstvennyi universitet, 1994), pp. 335-54 (p. 352).

[4] 'Dostoevskii i Blok v "Poeme bez geroia" Anny Akhmatovoi', in *V mire Bloka: sbornik statei*, ed. A Mikhailov and S Lesnevskii (Moscow: Sovetskii pisatel', 1981), pp. 454-502 (p. 455).

[5] Susan Amert, *In a Shattered Mirror: The Later Poetry of Anna Akhmatova* (Stanford, CA: Stanford University Press, 1992), pp. 60-91. See also Susan Amert, '"Predystoriia": Akhmatova's Aetiological Myth', *Anna Akhmatova 1889-1989: Papers from the Akhmatova Centennial Conference, Bellagio, June 1989* (Oakland, CA: Berkeley Slavic Specialties, 1993), pp. 13-28.

upon *Poem* can yield illuminating results.[6] Roman Timenchik, for instance, made the important discovery that Akhmatova based her distinctive stanza form on that of Mikhail Kuzmin's *The Trout Breaks the Ice* (*Forel' razbivaet led*), a poem that Chukovskaia and Akhmatova discussed after the latter read it in 1940.[7] In May of the same year, she informed Chukovskaia that she had recently re-read *The Adolescent*.[8]

Poem Without a Hero is astonishingly capacious. As has long been recognized, its main principle of construction is intertextuality, a single line often containing multiple echoes of previous literary works. Akhmatova consciously draws upon and develops the 'Petersburg text' (*peterburgskii tekst*), using its characteristic language and themes. Some of the most densely allusive passages depict the city of Petersburg, so that the poem becomes 'an encyclopedia of [the Petersburg] mythos' and 'quintessential postmodernist text'.[9] A key point of reference for the representation of Petersburg is Dostoevsky's distinctive vision of the city.

One of the first of several metapoetic statements drawing the reader's attention to the presence of the discourse of other writers in *Poem* contains an indirect allusion to Dostoevsky via Bakhtin's notion of the 'alien word' (*chuzhoe slovo*):

> ... а так как мне бумаги не хватило,
> я на твоем пишу черновике.
> И вит чужое слово проступает.[10]

> ... and since I have run out of paper,
> I write on your rough draft.
> And here an alien word shows through.

The reference is probably deliberate. As Lev Loseff remarks:

> The term was coined by Bakhtin in his famous *Dostoevskii's Poetics* (1929) where the role of *chuzhoe slovo* in a literary text was so thoroughly investigated. It is inconceivable that Akhmatova, with her life-long affection

---

[6] Tat'iana Tsiv'ian, 'The Double Bottom of the Casket; or, Two Hypostases of *Poema bez geroia*', in *The Speech of Unknown Eyes*, ed. Wendy Rosslyn, 2 vols (Nottingham: Astra, 1990), I, pp. 113-20 (p. 119).

[7] R Timenchik, 'K analizu *Poemy bez geroia*', in *Materialy XXII nauchnoi studencheskoi konferentsii* (Tartu: Tartusskii gosudarstvennyi Universitet, 1967), pp. 121-23.

[8] L Chukovskaia, *Zapiski ob Anne Akhmatovoi*, 2 vols (Paris: YMCA-Press, 1976-1980), I, 88.

[9] Solomon Volkov, *St Petersburg: A Cultural History*, trans. Antonina W Bouis (New York: Free Press, 1995), p. 472.

[10] A A Akhmatova, Pervoe posviashchenie. 1. References to *Poema* are to Elisabeth Erdmann-Panžić's, *Poema bez geroja von Anna A Akhmatova: Varientenedition und Interpretation von Symbolstrukturen* (Cologne: Böhlau, 1987).

for Dostoevskii, Akhmatova, who was always surrounded by the university crowd, would not know, at least in outline, the theories of Bakhtin.[11]

It is indeed inconceivable. After the 1946 Communist Party resolution which banned her from publishing, Akhmatova embarked upon an academic study of Pushkin and Dostoevsky, which was destroyed when she burnt her archive following the arrest of her son in 1949.[12] Moreover, *Poem* contains other indications of familiarity with Bakhtin:

> No consideration of genres as they affect the meaning of *Poèma bez geroia* can omit the genres highlighted by Mikhail Bakhtin in *Problems of Dostoevsky's Poetics*. The presence of masqueraders, the mummer's play, carnival celebration, and a species of 'dialogue of the threshold' oblige us to discuss the *Poèma* in terms of the Menippea.[13]

The possibility that the term 'alien word' might constitute an indirect allusion to Dostoevsky is ultimately confirmed by the explicit mention of him in a passage depicting the arrival of the 'Real—not the calendar—Twentieth Century':

> И царицей Авдотьей заклятый,
> Достоевский и бесноватый,
> Город в свой уходил туман,
> И выглядывал вновь из мрака
> Старый питерщик и гуляка,
> Как пред казнью бил барабан...[14]

> And cursed by Tsaritsa Avdotia,
> Dostoevskian and possessed,
> The city receded into its mist.
> And once again from the darkness
> A *pitershchik* and reveller looked out,
> As before an execution, the drum beat...[15]

Dostoevsky is marked out from other writers in the Petersburg literary tradition alluded to in this section of the poem (Gogol, Blok, Bely, and Mandelshtam, to name but a few), by the adjectival use of his name as an attribute of the city. This coinage serves to blur the division between the historical city in which Dostoevsky lived, and the Petersburg of his novels and stories. The epithets 'Dostoevskian' *(dostoevskii)* and 'possessed' *(besnovatyi)* signal not only a

---

[11] Lev Loseff, 'Who is the hero of the poem without one?', *Essays in Poetics*, 11 (1986), 91-104 (p. 93).
[12] Chukovskaia, II, 211.
[13] Anna Lisa Crone, 'Genre Allusions in *Poèma bez geroia*: Masking Tragedy and Satyric Drama', in *Anna Akhmatova 1889-1989, Papers from the Akhmatova Centennial Conference*, pp. 43-59 (p. 54).
[14] *Poema*, I, 3, 367.
[15] The term *pitershchik*, difficult to translate, is discussed at a later point in this article.

specific relationship with *The Devils (Besy)*—which indeed exists—but in broader terms link the hellish 'Petersburg deviltry' of Akhmatova's text with his fictional world and his biography as an entire system.[16] The use of Dostoevsky's name as adjective constitutes one of the most open-ended allusions of the poem.

Dolgopolov was the first to identify allusion to *The Adolescent* in the line 'The city receded into its mist', although he omits to mention important aspects of Dostoevsky's context which relate to *Poem*.[17] Akhmatova alludes to Arkady's daydream, one of the most striking moments in the novel:

> But in passing, however, I'll remark that I consider St Petersburg mornings, apparently the most prosaic on earth, probably the most fantastic in the world. [...] On such a St Petersburg morning—so raw, damp, and foggy—I have always thought that the wild dreams of someone like Pushkin's Germann in *The Queen of Spades* (a colossal character, an extraordinary and completely Petersburg type—a type of the Petersburg period!) must be strengthened and receive endorsement. A hundred times over amid such a fog I have had the strange but persistent notion: 'What if this fog were to disperse and rise up into the sky, wouldn't the whole rotten, sleazy city go up with it and vanish like smoke, and all that would remain would be the original Finnish marsh with, in the middle of it, for decoration perhaps, a bronze horseman on a snorting, rearing steed?' In short, I cannot express my feelings, because they're all fantasy, just poetry, after all, and therefore nonsense.[18]

Despite a general tendency to neglect *The Adolescent*, critics turn admiringly to this passage as the archetypal expression of 'Dostoevsky's Petersburg'.[19] Dostoevsky directs the reader to pre-existing discourses of myth and literature (especially Pushkin) which have shaped his protagonist's distinctly negative view of the city, but develops them idiosyncratically: instead of being submerged in a flood, the city threatens to rise upwards with the fog. This image of the ephemeral, unreal city is unmistakably Dostoevskian, expressing the essence of his view of Petersburg, with its typical duality of the prosaic and the fantastic. As

---

[16] The passage 'Shutki li mesiatsa molodogo,/Ili vpravdu tam kto-to snova/Mezhdu pechkoi i shkafom stoit?/Bleden lob i glaza otkryty...' (I, 1, 168) recalls Kirillov's suicide: his open eyes and the pallor of his face are specifically mentioned by Dostoevsky. See Naiman, *Rasskazy o Anne Akhmatovoi* (Moscow: Khudozhestvennaia literatura, 1989), p. 130.

[17] Dolgopolov, p. 472.

[18] *An Accidental Family* [I have used an English title closer to the original, *The Adolescent*], trans. by Richard Freeborn (Oxford: Oxford University Press, 1994), pp. 143-44. For the Russian text, see *PSS*, XIII, 113.

[19] Volkov calls it the 'crowning moment' in the novelist's interpretation of the Petersburg myth, p. 53. See also Donald Fanger, *Dostoevsky and Romantic Realism* (Cambridge, MA: Harvard University Press, 1965), p. 132. There is another version of this image in the story 'A Weak Heart', the action of which is set on New Year's Eve, like that of *Poema*. However, *The Adolescent* has more fundamental similarities.

Bakhtin claims, Dostoevsky's Petersburg exists on the threshold between being and non-being, always on the point of dispersing into the fog and vanishing.[20]

In *Poem Without a Hero*, Akhmatova places Dostoevsky in the context of their shared mythological heritage by juxtaposing his name with that of Peter the Great's wife, Tsaritsa Avdotia, who predicted doom for Petersburg. However, Akhmatova also gestures beyond Dostoevsky to the twentieth century, blending his discourse with that of his Symbolist successors, particularly Blok and Bely. Her allusion to *The Adolescent* immediately evokes the latter's *Petersburg* (1913), a subsection of which is entitled 'Petersburg disappeared into the night' ('Peterburg ushel v noch'') and contains a similar image of the city disappearing, clearly inspired by Dostoevsky.

Akhmatova's line 'The city receded into its mist' is not a verbatim repetition of *The Adolescent*. The effect of her tense change from Dostoevsky's 'were to [...] rise up' (in Russian the perfective future form *uidet*) to 'receded' (*ukhodil*, the imperfective past of the same Russian verb) is to transform what Arkady merely envisages into something that her speaker witnesses, albeit in a figurative sense. Moreover, whereas Arkady imagines the city rising with the fog, owing to the change of preposition from 'up' (*kverkhu*) to 'into' (*v*), in Akhmatova's version it sinks back into it as if it were stage-scenery. In Bakhtinian terms, her line is genuinely double-voiced: Arkady imagines the demise of the city and how it might appear, and Akhmatova's speaker describes the event in progress, establishing a dialogue between the two texts. Arkady's query, 'What if' is, in effect, responded to in *Poem*. He comments that this is 'just poetry, after all', and the essence of his dreamer's view of Petersburg is accordingly crystallized into a line of verse by Akhmatova.

Dolgopolov makes the points raised above and draws further pertinent comparisons with Bely's *Petersburg*. He omits to mention, however, that recognition of the Dostoevskian context furnishes the reader with a means to decipher the otherwise puzzling reference to the '*pitershchik* and reveller'. The noun *pitershchik* is an unusual word, originally denoting a peasant who had seasonal work in Petersburg (see Dal). *Guliaka*, on the other hand, means literally 'reveller', 'rake', or 'debaucher'. In *The Adolescent*, Arkady's daydream evokes Peter the Great, in the form of Etienne Falconet's statue (via Pushkin's *Bronze Horseman*). Although there is no overt reference to Peter in Akhmatova's context, the word *pitershchik* is applicable to the tsar for several reasons. He was fond of manual labour and 'perfectly in his element as a common worker', prompting Pushkin to refer to him as 'worker' (*rabotnik*) in his lyric 'Stanzas' ('Stansy').[21] . The word *guliaka* could also readily be interpreted as referring

---

[20] *Problemy poetiki Dostoevskogo* (Moscow: Khudozhestvennaia literatura, 1972), p. 288.

[21] Nicholas Riasanovsky, *The Image of Peter the Great in Russian History and Thought* (Oxford: Oxford University Press, 1985), p. 188.

to Peter, who was notorious for his 'blasphemous, quasi-ritualistic debauchery'.[22] Further evidence of allusion to Peter is the verb 'looked out' (*vygliadyval*), reminiscent of the famous introduction to *The Bronze Horseman*, in which he 'looked into the distance' ('i vdal gliadel'). Akhmatova, in fact, builds upon an established tradition of periphrasis relating to Peter in Russian literature. He not named directly in *The Bronze Horseman* and in a variant of 'Ariost', Mandelshtam refers to him as 'beard-shaver' (*bradobrei*), owing to his prohibition of beards.[23] In *Petersburg*, Bely casts him as the Flying Dutchman, drawing attention to his connections with the West and implying that he was cut off from his native soil.

Akhmatova's use of intertextuality sets her elegiac evocation of turn-of-the-century Petersburg against a dialogizing background which enables her to conflate different temporal planes and relate diverse historical periods to one another. The mention of the execution is a case in point. On the one hand, it provides a further reminder of Peter, who was responsible for the brutal mass execution of the *strel'tsy*, an élite Moscow guards regiment. In 'Stanzas', written after the Decembrist uprising, Pushkin observes:

> Начало славных дней Петра
> Мрачили мятежи и казни.

> Mutinies and executions darkened
> The beginning of the glorious days of Peter.

On the other hand, Akhmatova's mention of execution in close proximity to Dostoevsky's name is a reminder of the commuted death sentence he received, along with other members of the Petrashevsky circle, on 22 December 1849 in Nicholaevan Russia. Akhmatova invokes this event explicitly in her prose, where she remembers 'Semyonovsky Square, where Dostoevsky awaited death', and in 'Prehistory', she alludes to his imprisonment in Omsk:

> Страну знобит, а омский каторжанин
> Все понял и на всем поставил крест.
> Вот он сейчас перемещает все
> И сам над превозданным беспорядком,
> Как некий дух, внесется. Полночь бьет.
> Перо скрипит, и многие страницы
> Семеновский припахивают плацем.[24]

> The country is in a fever, and the convict from Omsk
> Understood everything and gave it all up for lost.
> Now he mixes everything up

---

[22] Riasanovsky, p. 76.
[23] Mandel'shtam, I, 178.
[24] 'Dal'she o gorode', Akhmatova, II, 250; Akhmatova, I, 253.

> And, rises up over primordial chaos.
> Like some kind of spirit. Midnight strikes.
> The pen squeaks, and many pages
> Stink of Semyonovsky Square.

Akhmatova clearly indicates here that Dostoevsky's experience at the hands of the state informed his art. This is equally true of her own: her later poetry also reeks of execution, and the allusions to Peter the Great and Nicholas I in both 'Prehistory' and *Poem* are thinly veiled references to Stalin and the actual executions of writers in the twentieth century. As Amert observes:

> This new myth of origins proclaims a new source of authority for the poet, one suited to the inimical age in which she found herself [...]. In 'Prehistory', Dostoevsky exemplifies the tragic and supreme role of the writer in Russian society: despite being persecuted, threatened with death, and deprived of freedom, he writes, judging his age and transcending it in his art.[25]

Akhmatova suggests in a prose fragment that *Poem Without a Hero* and the 'Northern Elegies' are products of the same creative impulse, and the two are undoubtedly closely related, particularly where allusion to Dostoevsky is concerned.[26] In 'Prehistory' Akhmatova focuses upon the fateful birth of her generation into Dostoevsky's Russia, and in *Poem*, she meditates upon the demise of Petersburg (now war-torn Leningrad) and of her generation, building, through reference to Dostoevsky's near-execution, upon the 'myth of the artist as a tragic hero'.[27] The cornet who commits suicide in Part One embodies the lot of Akhmatova's generation: premature, and probably violent, death. However, Akhmatova highlights in an encoded way the differences between the form of death he chooses and the state-sanctioned murders of other poets, such as Gumilev and Mandelshtam:

> *Сколько гибелей шло к поэту,*
> *Глупый мальчик: он выбрал эту.*
> *Он не знал, на каком пороге*
> *Он стоит и какой дороги*
> *Перед ним откроется вид..*[28]

> *Of all the deaths coming to the poet,*
> *Stupid boy: he chose this one.*

---

[25] '"Predystoriia": Akhmatova's Aetiological Myth', p. 24.
[26] 'Iz pis'ma k ***', Akhmatova, II, 251.
[27] Victor Erlich, *The Double Image: Concepts of the Poet in Slavic Literatures* (Baltimore, MD: John Hopkins Press, 1964), p. 100.
[28] *Poema*, I, 4, 440.

> *He did not know on what threshold*
> *He stood and what road*
> *Opened out before him...*

The threshold is that of the 'Real' Twentieth Century, and the road ahead is the road to Siberia.

Mark Lipovetsky, making a distinction between Russian and Western postmodernism, remarks that the former 'arises from the search for an answer to [...] cultural fragmentation and disintegration, together with the literal (rather than metaphysical) "death of the author"'.[29] This serves to articulate the significance of the deaths-of-poets theme in *Poem*, in connection with which Akhmatova quite naturally aligns herself with Dostoevsky.

Dostoevsky is not only an important point of reference for *Poem* as regards the Petersburg and poet-as-martyr themes, but his influence is also perceptible in formal and structural terms. Once again, a consideration of *Poem* in the light of 'Prehistory', illuminates the issue. A number of scholars have pointed out that there is an important metapoetic level to 'Prehistory'. Timenchik, for example, argues that the description of Dostoevsky's creative work in the elegy also characterizes Akhmatova's own late poetics. She too 'mixes everything up', including fact and fiction, different literary and cultural discourses, and diverse temporal levels.[30] These metapoetic features of the portrait of Dostoevsky in 'Prehistory' establish a further connection with *The Adolescent*, which relates in turn to the conception of *Poem Without a Hero*: namely, the issue of the modern artist's relationship with chaos and disorder.[31]

The creative act—the passage from chaos to cosmos—forms the central focus of 'Prehistory'. In depicting Dostoevsky rising up above primordial chaos, Akhmatova establishes an obvious parallel with the second verse of Genesis: 'Now the earth was formless and empty, darkness was over the surface of the deep, and the Spirit of God was hovering over the waters' ('Zemlia byla bezvidna i pusta, i t'ma nad bezdnoiu; i Dukh Bozhii nosilsia nad vodoiu').[32] Exploring the implications of this, Amert convincingly demonstrates, basing her argument on the work of the French anthropologist Mircea Eliade, that the description of Dostoevsky engaged in creation conforms to the different stages of mythical models of creative acts. The first component of cosmogonic myths

---

[29]'On the Nature of Russian Post-modernism', in *Twentieth-Century Russian Literature: Selected Papers from the Fifth World Congress of Central and East European Studies*, ed. Karen L Ryan and Barry P Scherr (London: Macmillan, 2000), pp. 319-38 (p. 321).

[30]See Roman Timenchik, 'K semioticheskoi interpretatsii "Poemy bez geroia"', *Trudy po znakovym sistemam*, 6 (1973), 438-42; and Amert, 'Akhmatova's Aetiological Myth', p. 23. Kees Verheul also points to the 'recurrent motif of literature and literary creation' in his *The Theme of Time in the Poetry of Anna Axmatova* (The Hague: Mouton, 1971), p. 172.

[31]Kornei Chukovsky mentions the 'close link' between *The Adolescent* and 'Predistoriia', without expanding on it, in 'Chitaia Akhmatovu', *Moskva*, 5 (1964), 200-3 (p. 201).

[32]See Verheul, p. 174.

is the restoration of primordial chaos, through the 'abolition of contours, fusion of all forms, return to the formless'.[33] This return to primordial chaos is enacted in 'Prehistory' with the words 'Now he mixes everything up'. The second stage concerns the point when 'linear time [is] suspended', producing a coexistence of past and present. This is achieved in 'Prehistory' by a sudden shift to the present and the words 'Midnight strikes'.[34] The final stage is the conquering of chaos and the emergence of cosmos, depicted by Akhmatova in Dostoevsky's rising above primordial chaos and in the image of him in the act of writing ('The pen squeaks').[35] Literary production is thus equated with cosmogony, and 'cast as demiurge, Dostoevsky re-enacts the creation of the world in his art'.[36]

But this creative act ultimately produces a peculiarly chaotic cosmos. The opening words of the elegy, 'Dostoevsky's Russia', refer simultaneously to the real world in which the novelist lived, and to his fictional world. The division between these two distinct ontologies is blurred throughout the elegy, as it is in *Poem*, so that Akhmatova seems to be suggesting not only that Dostoevsky lived in a chaotic era, but that his work itself is characterized by chaos. The following lines could apply equally to the real nineteenth century, or to the world of Dostoevsky's novels:

> Все разночинно, наспех, как-нибудь...
> Отцы и деды непонятны. Земли
> Заложены. И в Бадене—рулетка.
>
> Everything out of order, in a hurry, slap-dash...
> Fathers and grandfathers incomprehensible. Lands
> Mortgaged. And in Baden—roulette.

As Amert remarks, 'chaos and disorder are expressed here lexically, thematically, as well as rhythmico-syntactically'.[37] In short, Akhmatova's view of Dostoevsky, as extrapolated from 'Prehistory', is of an author who takes the chaos of reality as his subject matter and conveys its texture in his equally chaotic writings. The image of Dostoevsky's art expressed here is, in this sense, reminiscent of Blok's famous observation that instead of creating *out of* chaos, Dostoevsky created *on* chaos.[38]

The passage from chaos to form characterizes any creative act, but of Akhmatova's literary predecessors it is arguably Dostoevsky who most strove to

---

[33] Mircea Eliade, *Cosmos and History: The Myth of the Eternal Return*, trans. Willard R Trask (New York: Harper & Row, 1959), p. 59.

[34] Eliade, p. 62.

[35] Eliade, p. 54.

[36] Amert, *In A Shattered Mirror*, p. 67.

[37] Amert, *In a Shattered Mirror*, p. 83.

[38] See for instance his letter to E P Ivanov of 1909, in *Pis'ma A Bloka k E P Ivanovu*, ed. Ts Vol'pe (Moscow: Akademiia Nauk, 1936), p. 74. Akhmatova's words 'nekii dukh' also have strong overtones of the Symbolist image of Dostoevsky.

make chaos his subject, resulting in a marked transformation of classical aesthetics that paved the way for Russian Modernism. When writing *The Adolescent*, he was particularly occupied with the issue of form. In his notebooks, he repeatedly exhorts himself to be concise and direct, to 'learn from Pushkin', and to 'imitate Pushkin'. At one point he even exclaims frustratedly, 'Form, form!'[39] However, as Robert Louis Jackson remarks, 'the ideal, sculptured forms and images he admired in Pushkin are hardly typical in the landscape of the Dostoevsky novel.'[40] Nor could they be, given his preoccupation with abnormal psychology, crime, and the grittier aspects of urban life. This is certainly true of *The Adolescent*: Dostoevsky's working title was *Disorder (Besporiadok)*, and he states in his notebooks that 'disintegration is the principal visible idea'.[41] Many critics concur that the novel can best be understood as a sustained, sincere attempt to depict chaos and to seek appropriate forms to represent it. William Leatherbarrow remarks, for instance, 'perhaps the greatest question raised by *A Raw Youth* is that of how the modern writer should respond in his art to the disordered texture of contemporary life'.[42] Similarly, Jacques Catteau calls *The Adolescent* 'the most modern in form' of Dostoevsky's novels and observes that the author was 'affirming the possibility of a new aesthetics which could express modern chaos and complexity'.[43]

This artistic problem is raised explicitly at the close of *The Adolescent*, in a passage with striking relevance for *Poem*. Having written his account of his experiences, Arkady sends it to his fictional mentor, Nikolai Semyonovich, who writes him a letter evaluating it, the conclusion to which forms the final paragraph of the novel:

> But 'Notes' such as yours could, it seems to me, serve as the basic material for a future artistic work, for a future picture of a disorderly but already bygone epoch. Oh, when the burning issue of the day has ceased to be topical and the future has arrived, then a future artist will seek beautiful forms even for depicting past disorder and chaos! That is when 'Notes' like yours will be needed and will provide material; they would be sincere, despite all their chaotic and haphazard character... Certain truthful features would survive, at least, through which it would be possible to guess at the secrets of the soul

---

[39] *The Notebooks for 'A Raw Youth'*, ed. Edward Wasiolek, trans. Victor Terras (Chicago, IL: Chicago University Press, 1969), pp. 80, 240, and 187.

[40] Robert Louis Jackson, *Dostoevsky's Quest for Form: A Study of his Philosophy of Art* (New Haven, CN: Yale University Press, 1966), p. 3.

[41] *Notebooks*, p. 37.

[42] W J Leatherbarrow, *Fedor Dostoevskii* (Boston, MA: Twayne, 1981), p. 137.

[43] *Dostoyevsky and the process of literary creation*, trans. Audrey Littlewood (Cambridge: Cambridge University Press, 1989), pp. 254-325 (pp. 255 and 299).

of an adolescent at that confused time—an insight of no small value, since it is from adolescents that the generations are made ...[44]

This metapoetic comment articulates the problems the text poses for both author and reader, highlighting the difficulty (or even paradox) involved in finding aesthetically successful forms for the depiction of chaotic subject matter. It also provides a paradigm for a hypothetical text by a future artist who might use Arkady's notes as source material for a new creation.

Poem Without a Hero closely fits this description of a hypothetical text: not only does Akhmatova use *The Adolescent* as material for her depiction of Petersburg, but she is concerned with depicting the chaos of a past era, and evaluating that past with the benefit of hindsight. She provides a rejoinder to Dostoevsky by modelling part of her text on his paradigm.[45] The first part of *Poem* is constructed as a discrete text-within-a-text, with a complete paratext of its own. It is preceded by an introduction and has its own title, 'The Year Nineteen Thirteen' ('Deviat'sot trinadtsatyi god'), and subtitle, 'A Petersburg Tale' ('Peterburgskaia povest''). It is comprised of four chapters, is followed by an Afterword and, like *The Adolescent*, by the reaction of a fictional reader. Its temporal structure is as described by Dostoevsky: Akhmatova portrays the year 1913 from the vantage-point of 1940, reflecting on her own youth and that of her generation. She develops Dostoevsky's words 'when the burning issue of the day has ceased to be topical and the future has arrived' to denote a historical watershed. *Poem* is set on New Year's Eve 1940, the eve of war in Russia, and reflects upon 1913, which for Akhmatova marks the end of the nineteenth century proper. Significantly, 'Prehistory' and *Poem Without a Hero* are the only poems by Akhmatova to refer to Dostoevsky by name, and they are also unique in containing the words 'chaos' (*khaos*) or 'disorder' (*besporiadok*).[46] These concepts are alien to her early verse, with its neo-classical aura and traditional forms, but their later appearances suggest that they were, for Akhmatova, not only intimately connected with Dostoevsky's art but had also become central to her own.

The past era described in *Poem* is explicitly presented as chaotic:

> Золотого ль века виденье
> Или черное преступленье
> В грозном хаосе давних дней?[47]

---

[44]*PSS*, XIII, 455.

[45]Dostoevsky himself used Arkady's notes as 'material' for his subsequent novel, *The Brothers Karamazov*, which continues some of *The Adolescent's* themes, such as the disintegration of the family.

[46]See Tatiana Patera's *A Concordance to the Poetry of Anna Akhmatova* (Dana Point, CA: Ardis, 1995), pp. 9 and 236.

[47]'Reshka', 318.

> Is this a vision of the Golden Age
> Or a black crime
> In the menacing chaos of bygone days?

These lines contain a further reference to Dostoevsky. In *The Adolescent*, Versilov tells Arkady of a dream he once had of an innocent, Edenic society, from which he awoke to find himself in France in the wake of the Franco-Prussian war. Arkady responds, 'you have shaken me to my very core with your vision of a golden age' ('vy potriasli moe serdtse vashim videniem zolotogo veka'), words which are closely echoed by Akmatova.[48] The era upon which *Poem* reflects is, however, the morally suspect Silver Age, and the hints at a black crime raise the idea of transgression *(prestuplenie)* and, by implication, punishment *(nakazanie)*. The pervasiveness of Dostoevsky's discourse throughout *Poem* makes it possible to add his name to the list of possible addressees (or, rather, to the composite addressee) of the first dedication ('I write on your rough draft'), the draft in question being the text ('material', 'Notes') provided by *The Adolescent*.[49]

At the same time as she moves closer to Dostoevsky's worldview than ever before, Akhmatova increasingly adopts elements of the Symbolist idiom.[50] The two impulses are related: Dostoevsky provides a crucial link between the nineteenth-century past, into which her generation was born, and the so-called 'Silver Age', dominated by Symbolism, for which he fulfilled the role of a kind of literary father. The Blok scholar Zinaida Mints therefore regards Dostoevsky as a 'sign-symbol' of the late nineteenth and early twentieth-century worldview.[51] After him, it was not necessary for modernists 'to invent completely new images of fragmentation in order to reflect the chaos of the new age'.[52] Or, as Malcolm Jones puts it:

---

[48] *PSS*, XIII, 375. The golden age motif also occurs in *The Devils* and 'The Dream of a Ridiculous Man'.

[49] See L G Kikhnei and O P Temirshina, '"Poema bez geroia" Anny Akhmatovoi i poetika postmodernizma', *Vestnik moskovskogo universiteta. Seriia 9: Filologiia*, 3 (2002), 53-64 (pp. 57-58) for a discussion of other possible addressees.

[50] On this topic, see Anna Akhmatova, *Stikhotvoreniia i poemy*, ed. V Zhirmunskii (Leningrad: Sovetskii pisatel', 1976), pp. 511-23; Anna Lisa Crone, 'Blok as Don Juan in Akhmatova's "Poema bez geroija"', *Russian Language Journal*, 35 (1981), 145-62; David Wells, 'Folk Ritual in Anna Akhmatova's *Poema bez geroya*', *Scottish Slavonic Review*, 7 (1986), 69-88 (p. 80).

[51] Z Mints, 'Blok i Dostoevskii', in *Dostoevskii i ego vremia*, ed. V G Bazanov and G M Fridlender (Leningrad: Nauka, 1971), pp. 217-47 (p. 217).

[52] Robert Russell, 'The Modernist Tradition', in *The Cambridge Companion to the Classic Russian Novel*, ed. Malcolm V Jones and Robin Feuer Miller (Cambridge: Cambridge University Press, 1998), pp. 210-29 (p. 211).

> What was important about his 'fantastic realism' was [...] what can only be defined, if at all, in terms of a modernist (or even a post-modernist) conception of art on the edge of the abyss.[53]

This feeling of art on the edge of the abyss is precisely that captured by Akhmatova in *Poem*, through allusion to Dostoevsky and his Symbolist descendants. To render the chaotic fabric of the present (the Second World War and its aftermath), she draws upon and develops earlier literary expressions of disorder and uncertainty. In particular, the motif of apocalypse is used to characterize the disruptive arrival of the twentieth century and its catastrophic events: two world wars, revolution, civil war, the Terror. This apocalypticism forms part of Akhmatova's stylisation of Symbolism and characterization of the atmosphere, themes, and techniques of the Silver Age, the eschatological sensibility and religious philosophy of which were influenced directly by Dostoevsky.

In formal terms too, *Poem* is characterized by disorder. The very title, *Poem Without a Hero*, implicitly suggests that content is somehow subordinated to form. The text is a sprawling and amorphous generic hybrid, frequently spilling over its own boundaries into different performances as ballet libretto or screenplay. This proliferation of variants, as well as Akhmatova's excursions into prose, make the poem's boundaries impossible to determine. There is not even a canonical text of the poem: Akhmatova authorized, without perusing them, a great many so-called final versions of the text. These different, but equally definitive, versions of the poem convey the impression that it exists in an unfinished or dynamic state. This is clearly a deliberate strategy, an answer to the problem of finding forms suitable for the depiction of chaos: the *process* of creation is privileged over the finished product. In this sense, Akhmatova makes chaos a participant in the work, consciously entering into a dialogue with it by creating a text that is unpredictable, amorphous, and perpetually in flux.

Lipovetsky has recently argued that Russian postmodernist literature is characterized by a striving for the establishment of a compromise between chaos and cosmos, expressed in the breakdown of the artistic system's traditional structures. This need not necessarily, he notes, result in the loss of artistic unity, but rather it can make possible the formation of a new, non-classical, 'chaosmic' system within a work.[54] Akhmatova's unique stanza form, which combines pattern with a high degree of unpredictability, is a good example of this kind of

---

[53]Malcolm Jones, *Dostoyevsky After Bakhtin: Readings in Dostoyevsky's Fantastic Realism* (Cambridge: Cambridge University Press, 1990), p. x.

[54]*Russian Postmodernist Fiction: Dialogue with Chaos*, ed. Eliot Borenstein (Armonk: M. E. Sharpe, 1999), p. 35. More recently, he and Naum Leiderman have argued that the later Akhmatova can be seen as a 'post-realist', claiming that post-realism is related to postmodernism, but distinct from it in view of its interest in making sense of the world and probing the human personality. Although this argument is broadly persuasive, it still seems better to use the term 'postmodernist', if only because it has more established critical currency.

'chaosmos'. The basic aaBccB rhyme scheme which is established in Part Two and the Epilogue is continually departed from in Part One by the interpolation of extra rhyming lines. Akhmatova worked on the poem for over a quarter of a century, not cutting or altering it, but amplifying it almost endlessly.[55] She develops Dostoevsky's text model freely, synthesising classical form and chaos by creating a stanza, based on the *dol'nik*, which resembles a chaotic system, reproducing symmetries, but at the same time admitting various permutations, asymmetries and unpredictability.

Not only is the conception of *Poem* (finding beautiful forms for the depiction of a chaotic era) suggested by *The Adolescent*, but the structural parallels between the two works testify to Akhmatova's awareness of her poem's novelty. The basic structure of both, as mentioned earlier, consists of a text followed by a fictional reading of it. By dramatizing the relationship between authors and readers in this way, Akhmatova and Dostoevsky foreground questions of reception, hint at the existence of correct and incorrect readings, and indicate their texts' novelty.

After *The Adolescent* had been published in instalments in *Notes of the Fatherland*, Dostoevsky added Nikolai Semyonovich's letter to the first separate edition to counter critical responses.[56] Ivan Turgenev was particularly forceful in his condemnation, describing the novel as chaotic, sour-tasting ('kisliatina'), useless muttering ('nikomu ne nuzhnoe bormotan'e').[57] In some respects at least, the fictional Nikolai Semyonovich appears to be a more discerning reader, and he gives an overall impression which Arkady considers to be 'somewhat enlightening' ('nechto raz'iasnitel'noe').[58] He identifies some important aspects of the text; namely its chaotic quality and its contemporary themes, such as the accidental family. He also recognizes the fact that the disorderly and digressive quality of Arkady's notes reflects the nature of the age and the turbulence of adolescence.[59]

However, Nikolai Semyonovich's response is broadly negative, owing to his strong assumptions and preconceptions about what constitutes literature. Discussing historical novels, he observes:

> If I were a Russian novelist and had talent, I would be sure to choose my heroes from the Russian hereditary nobility, because it is only among that type of cultured Russian that an appearance of beautiful order and a beautiful

---

[55] See Vitalii Vilenkin, 'On A Poem Without a Hero', in *Anna Akhmatova 1889-1989: Papers from the Akhmatova Centennial Conference*, pp. 249-65 (p. 250).

[56] See Nicholas Rzhevsky, '*The Adolescent*: Structure and Ideology', *Slavic and East European Journal*, 26 (1982), 27-42 (p. 39).

[57] I S Turgenev, *Polnoe sobranie sochinenii i pisem*, 28 vols (Moscow and Leningrad: Nauka, 1961-68), II, 164.

[58] *PSS*, XIII, 452.

[59] *PSS*, XIII, 455.

impression is possible, so necessary in a novel for an elegant influence on the reader.[60]

His conservative taste is revealed by his view that art is obliged to be beautiful and orderly, hence his use of terms like 'beautiful order' ('krasivyi poriadok'), 'beautiful impression' ('krasivoe vpechatlenie'), 'elegant [i.e., moral] influence' ('iziashchnoe vozdestvie'). He postulates later that the Russian novel's continued existence depends on beautiful characters: 'If they were not beautiful, then a further Russian novel would be impossible' ('esli nekrasivye, to nevozmozhno dal'neishii russkii roman').[61] The irony here is, of course, that *The Adolescent*'s innovation lies precisely in the fact that its narrator is an emergent, unformed social type, whose style is not orderly and refined. As Jackson observes, 'the letter writer is an educator: his concern is frankly moral and didactic; he seeks, above all, form, beauty, tranquillity'.[62] Ultimately, he rationalizes the text according to his own habits and temperament.

In Akhmatova's case, the fictional reading serves to highlight the seditiousness of the 'formalism' of Part One by drawing attention to its blatant contravention of socialist realism. Like Dostoevsky, she probably had specific readers in mind. The figure of the editor appears to be based, at least in part, on Akhmatova's own editor, the socialist realist poet Andrei Surkov, of whom Nadezhda Mandelshtam writes:

> Literary rules were firmly lodged in his mind. 'His urine is normal', Akhmatova would have said; that is, he had an average writer's understanding of poetry [...] which he approached from the point of view of socialist thinking.[63]

While Arkady solicits Nikolai Semyonovich's opinion, the editor's response is forced upon Akhmatova's speaker. He represents the literary establishment and the speaker's relationship with him is professional. His response is irritation and bewilderment:

> Мой редактор был недоволен,
> Клялся мне, что занят и болен,
> Засекретил свой телефон.
> И ворчал: 'Там три темы сразу!
> Дочитав последнюю фразу,
> Не поймешь, кто в кого влюблен.
>
> Кто, когда и зачем встречался,
> Кто погиб, и кто жив остался,
> И кто автор и кто герой—

---

[60] *PSS*, XIII, 453.
[61] *PSS*, XIII, 454.
[62] Jackson, 114.
[63] *Vtoraia kniga* (Paris: YMCA-Press, 1972), p. 664.

> И к чему нам сегодня эти
> Рассуждения о поэте
> И каких-то призраков рой.'[64]

> My editor was displeased.
> Swearing to me that he was busy and ill,
> He got a restricted phone number.
> And he grumbled: 'Three themes at once!
> Having read the last phrase,
> You can't understand who is in love with whom,

> Who met whom, and when and why,
> Who was killed and who survived,
> And who the author is, and who the hero—
> And what use to us nowadays are
> These discussions about a poet
> And a swarm of ghosts?'

The editor, like Nikolai Semyonovich, unintentionally succeeds in identifying important features of the text, such as its multiple themes and fragmented plot. However, unlike him, he displays total incomprehension, as indicated by his series of questions about the identity of the author and heroes and his concern with utility. His reading (if indeed it can be called one), constitutes an attempt to make sense of 'The Year Nineteen Thirteen' in terms of socialist realist requirements. But *Poem* provocatively displays all the decadence and disintegration of bourgeois literature: Andrei Zhdanov once complained that 'everything is degenerating—themes, talents, authors, heroes'.[65] This concern is echoed almost word for word in the editor's remarks, written at the height of Zhdanov's influence on literary matters in the early 1940s.

Both Dostoevsky and Akhmatova use these fictional readings to indicate to the real reader that they are consciously creating something new, which cannot be judged by prevailing standards. A number of claims Akhmatova makes in the prose to the poem emphasize this point. She remarks, for example, that the poem is untraditional ('v poeme net nikakoi traditsion[nosti]') and that no one had previously written such a poem ('takhikh poem nikto ne pisal').[66] As a result, the poem finds its own rules.[67] Critics are increasingly willing to acknowledge that *Poem*'s rampant intertextuality, self-reflexivity and narcissism, and its

---

[64]*Poema*, II, 1, 1.

[65]Quoted in Eugene Lunn, *Marxism and Modernism: an Historical Study of Lukács, Brecht, Benjamin and Adorno* (Berkeley: University of California Press, 1982), p. 71.

[66]'Proza k Poeme', Anna Akhmatova, *Sobranie sochinenii*, ed. S A Kovalenko, 6 vols (Moscow: Ellis Lak, 1998-2000), III, 261.

[67]T Tsiv'ian, '"Poema bez geroia" Anny Akhmatovoi: Nekotorye itogi izucheniia v sviazi s problemoi "tekst-chitatel"', in *Anna Akhmatova 1889-1989: Papers from the Akhmatova Centennial Conference*, pp. 249-65 (p. 240).

conscious, often ironic, return to modernism make it an early example of Russian postmodernism.[68] Akhmatova's dissident attitude towards socialist realism and emphasis on novelty certainly lend credence to this view.[69] Jean-François Lyotard remarks:

> A postmodern artist or writer is in the position of a philosopher: the text he writes, the work he produces are not in principle governed by pre-established rules, and they cannot be judged according to a determining judgement, by applying familiar categories to the text or to the work. Those rules and categories are what the work of art itself is looking for.[70]

Much the same can be said of *The Adolescent*, in fact, but it remains unproblematic in terms of its genre, despite the manifest differences from historical novels of the Tolstoyan type. However, it is not in the same class as Dostoevsky's other major novels, and Nikolai Semenovich's misgivings about form seem to echo some of Dostoevsky's own concerns about his text, as expressed in the notebooks. *Poem*, conversely, is a highly successful literary experiment, an exercise in cultural preservation and revitalisation which produces a complex generic hybrid. Akhmatova, who had the whole of modernist experimentation upon which to draw, ultimately goes much further than Dostoevsky in her quest for forms to depict chaos. Nonetheless, she does so with a backward glance at *The Adolescent*: Dostoevsky's final paragraph anticipates a response from a future artist, and in *Poem Without a Hero*, Akhmatova provides one.

Since the day, some twelve years ago, when I attended the first lecture of his undergraduate course on Russian Thought at the University of Nottingham, through to my current appointment at the University of Durham, Malcolm Jones has been an unfailingly generous source of knowledge, advice and encouragement. I should like to take this opportunity to thank him.

---

[68] See Dubravka Oraiæ, 'Avangard i postmodern', *Russian Literature*, 36 (1994), 95-114; L G Kikhnei and O R Temirshina, 'Poema bez geroia Anny Akhmatovoi', *Russian Language Journal*, 31, 135-145.
[69] See I S Skoropanova, *Russkaia postmodernistskaia literatura* (Moscow: Flinta, 1999), p. 74.
[70] Jean-François Lyotard, *The Postmodern Condition: A Report on Knowledge*, trans. Geoff Bennington and Brian Massumi (Manchester: Manchester University Press, 1986), p. 81.

WHENCE CAME IVAN KARAMAZOV'S NIGHTMARE? (CORRESPONDENCE AND LITERARY CREATION)

Jacques Catteau

DOSTOEVSKY was always engaged with his own century. But the news he pursued in society and contemporary literature was little more than the spring-board from which he dived into the deep sea of the mystery of human nature. His entire *oeuvre* is dialogue, the original nucleus, the ferment and principle of his writing. His lasting passion as a journalistic writer (the journals *Time (Vremia)* and *Epoch (Epokha)* between 1861 and 1865, and later his *Diary of a Writer*), and above all his correspondence, which after his return to Russia from 'European exile' acquired a new, and universal dimension, testify to this. In effect, if one excludes the intimate letters from those close to him, and in particular from his wife Anna Grigorievna, the majority of Dostoevsky's correspondents between 1871 and 1881 were people unknown to him who wrote to him from every part of Russia: high society ladies, even from court; grand dukes; the future Procurator of the Holy Synod, Pobedonostsev; women of humble origins; young girls dreaming of sacrifice; suicidal lycée pupils; rebellious students; injured Jews such as Kovner; farmers; opera singers; inventors and so on.[1]

These new acquaintances came confiding their worries and also questioning the author about a particular idea or mysterious formulation from one of his novels or from *Diary of a Writer*. Dostoevsky was then compelled to explain, elucidate, develop his ideas, he responded to them and wrote new pages which enter his novelistic writing in substance, or even in entire paragraphs. So that in the musical scores orchestrated in such masterly fashion by the genius of the writer of *The Adolescent, The Brothers Karamazov*, and the short stories of the *Diary of a Writer*, we hear the notes, motifs and themes suggested by his correspondents. This grand 'brotherly commerce of souls' which constitutes a dialogue with the Russian reading public imposes a new respiratory pattern. The *Diary* and the novels alternate henceforth like systoles and diastoles. After *The*

---

[1] For more extensive details, see our recent edition, Dostoïevski, *Correspondance* (Paris: Bartillat, 2003), vol. 3, p. 9.

Devils, there was the editorial work on *The Citizen (Grazhdanin)*, with the *Diary of a Writer* column swallowing up the publication in its entirety. After 1873, this rhythm was set, so that the *Diary* and the novels needed nourishment from each other, sustained from underground by his correspondence. From 1874 to 1875 Dostoevsky wrote and published *The Adolescent*; in 1876 and 1877 he returned to *Diary of a Writer*, at last independent and edited by his own hand; from 1878 to 1880 he worked on *The Brothers Karamazov*, the publication of which stretched out over the latter two years; then in 1880 he returned to *Diary of a Writer* for a single issue, 'Pushkin', and, in 1881, he had time to compose the January issue which appeared the day before his funeral. Only death could break the vast swell of his creative activity and dialogue with Russia.

Dostoevsky had promised to devote a special issue of the *Diary* to 'Replies to letters I have received', which remained a dutiful vow, at least in this form. Nevertheless, as soon as a fundamental question, which is directly perpendicular to his creative work, in the case of *The Brothers Karamazov*, is raised, then he catches fire and develops his novel. We will cite a few examples. In a letter of 7 June 1876, he responds to the bewilderment of Vassily Alekseievich Aleksiev, a soloist at the opera, who had stumbled over the expression 'stones turned into bread', dropped into the *Diary of a Writer* for May 1876. This is already in direct style—the Devil using the familiar form as he tempts Jesus—a sketching out of Ivan's poem 'The Grand Inquisitor', with its admiration for the 'three colossal universal ideas' and Christ's response, 'Man cannot live by bread alone'. This dialogized letter entered the chapter of the novel through these phrases, and confirms that Dostoevsky indeed saw the socialism which 'everywhere dismisses Christ and cares in the first place for the bread'. (*PSS*, XXIX: 2, 84-85) In his letter of February 1878, the author replies to Nikolai Lukich Ozmidov, a farmer who doubts the concept of the immortality of the soul, by saying that without this faith, man is refusing to live. (XXX: 1, 10-11) These are the remarks of Zosima, the reverse side of the logic of Ivan Karamazov, who states that without God, 'everything is permitted'. To Nikolai Pavlovich Peterson, the disciple of N F Fedorov, on 24 March 1878, Dostoevsky declared his lively interest in the central idea of the philosophy of 'communal work' ('obshchee delo'), which is the duty to resurrect one's ancestors. (XXX: 1, 14) He referred to Renan and made a mental note of the words he would put into Alyosha Karamazov's mouth, suggesting he would know that life consists equally of 'resuscitating the dead, who would otherwise perhaps never die'...And so on.

However, these sketches for the novel, discovered by interpreters of the genesis of *The Brothers Karamazov*, did not come solely from the correspondence, or, rather, if they did appear there, then it was following another impulse, after another source of fertilization introduced by life. This seems to be the case with the famous Chapters Nine and Ten of Book XI: 'The Devil. Ivan Fyodorovich's Nightmare', and 'It was He who Said That', whose latent progression is astonishing.

Even if the economy of the novel seems more predetermined in *The Brothers Karamazov*, Dostoevsky did not manage without improvising, modifying and disclosing as he went along.[2] As always, the instinct of the genius guided him, and the search for compositional harmony was performed painstakingly. As he explained to N A Liubimov, the co-editor of *The Russian Messenger (Russkii vestnik)*, it was not until 16 November 1879 that the author realized that there would be four parts of three books each, and not three as he had initially foreseen. He wrote, 'I forgot (or neglected) to rectify that which I thought of long ago'. (XXX: 1, 131) The expression speaks volumes about the unconscious, but effective attainment of an exemplary equilibrium.

As far as one can judge from the few surviving pages of the plans for *The Brothers Karamazov*, *there was no question* of the extraordinary scene of Ivan's hallucination, of his dialogue with the devil, in the initial plan for Part Four, titled 'Project'. (p. 134) (XV, 315-316) There is a single allusion to this on page 138: 'Ivan is alone. Satan.' (XV, 319) On the other hand, page 139 witnesses the birth of Ivan's nightmare:

> Ivan is alone. The devil enters and sits down (a hoary old man, a verruca). A conversation. 'You are a vision'; Satan: 'I advise you to take care of yourself' [...] Satan to Ivan: 'You believe, and therefore I am'. Ivan: 'Not for a single moment (I would like you to be).' (XV, 320)

Unfortunately, this page is not dated. However, page 145 has a precise date: 16/17 June [1880] (XV, 325), which allows the suggestion that page 139 goes back, perhaps, to the preceding week. Be that as it may, it was not until 30 June that the nightmare scene, titled 'Satan', took on a larger scale and became apparent in all its dialogic details. (XV, 333-335) When Dostoevsky sent Book XI of *The Brothers Karamazov* to N A Liubimov on 10 August 1880, he made an important confession about Chapter Nine, 'The Devil. Ivan Fyodorovich's Nightmare': 'And if I think myself that this ninth chapter *might not have existed*, I wrote it, I don't know why, with *pleasure*, and I do not disown it in any way.' (XXX: 1, 205) In plain language, this chapter, which he is defending tooth and nail, *was not initially anticipated*. The 'I don't know why' reflects the unconscious role of genius which creates with felicity and grace. The invention of this fantastic chapter has a history which I propose to reconstruct here in broad outline.

The pivotal moment is Dostoevsky's celebrated speech on Pushkin, given on 8 June 1880 in Moscow. We will not recount the history of this event in Russian literature, except to recall that Dostoevsky, interrupting his work on the novel, had been fervently preparing for it since 1 May 1880, the date of his invitation from S A Iuriev, the president of the Society of Lovers of Russian Literature.

---

[2] See my chapter 'Activity by day and improvised writing', in Jacques Catteau, *Dostoyevsky and the Process of Literary Creation*, trans. Audrey Littlewood (Cambridge: Cambridge University Press, 1989), pp. 177-179.

Commissioned by the charitable Slavic society to inaugurate the monument to Pushkin, he dedicated his discourse to works which glorified the Russian Idea, Russian men and women, and the popular, national and universal genius of the poet, but curiously did not tackle the modern and fantastic vein of Pushkin's work, although in his preparatory notes there is a reference to *The Queen of Spades*. (XXVI, 213) The political weight of his speech, the anti-occidentalist fight against Turgenev and his acolytes, did not give him the leisure to develop this aspect of Pushkin's art which, nevertheless, the author of *The Adolescent* had previously evoked so masterfully:

> Mornings in St Petersburg, which seem to be the most prosaic on earth, are for me the most fantastic in the world [...] On this sort of Petersburg morning, putrid, damp and foggy, the wild dream of someone like Pushkin's Germann from *The Queen of Spades* (a colossal character, an extraordinary, perfect Petersburg type—a type from the Petersburg period of Russian history, must, I think, become even more intense. A hundred times in this fog I've been struck by a strange but persistent reverie: 'and what if, when this fog disperses and lifts, this entire putrid and sleazy city were to rise up with it and disappear like smoke, and all that remained would be the old Finnish swamp and in the middle of it, perhaps, for decoration, a bronze horseman on a snorting, driven steed'.

And to end with this admirable plunge in the manner of Calderon:

> You see, here they are, all hurrying and rushing on their way. But how do you know, it may all be nothing but somebody's dream. Maybe there's not a single true, genuine human being, a single real act between them. If the person dreaming it all woke up, it would all suddenly disappear. (XIII, 113)[3]

After his resounding triumph of 8 June 1880, which saw him in turn hailed as a prophet, Dostoevsky, overexcited, prepared to leave Moscow and return to Staraia Russa and his *Brothers Karamazov*. At the hotel Loskutnaia, on the evening of 9 June, his departure having been set for the following morning, he received Maria Alexandrovna Polivanova, wife of the president of the Commission for the Inauguration of the Pushkin monument. She was soon joined by Iuriev, who was trying to obtain the first copy of the speech for publication. Always full of his subject, Dostoevsky finished up as it were with praise for the genius of Pushkin and broached a subject on which he had not spoken in his speech, but which he held close to his heart. We have the evidence of Polivanova's account, noted in rough draft:

> He began to speak again about the Pushkin festival, about Pushkin: Dostoevsky was animated to an inexpressible degree. 'We are all pygmies before Pushkin, there's no such genius amongst us', he exclaimed. 'What

---

[3] Translation based on Fyodor Dostoevsky, *An Accidental Family*, trans. Richard Freeborn (Oxford: Oxford University Press, 1994), pp. 144-145, with some modification (*Translator's note*).

beauty, what strength in his use of the fantastic! I recently re-read *The Queen of Spades*. That's the fantastic. I would like to write a fantastic story myself. My characters are all ready. I just have to finish *The Brothers Karamazov*. It's dragged on too long'. Iuriev jumped at the opportunity: 'Fyodor Mikhailovich, if you write something, would you be so kind as to promise it to me for *Russian Thought (Russkaia mysl')*'. 'Ah, sir, but I will be publishing *Diary of a Writer* myself from the new year, Sergei Andreevich. What will I do? I really don't know [...] Pushkin on his own is an inexhaustible subject. I promise you that if I write something...'[4]

Iuriev, whom the writer did not like, received neither the speech, which was given to Katkov, nor the fantastic story. That went into *The Brothers Karamazov*; it would soon be Chapter Nine. Let us return to the meeting of 9 June; as he was leaving, Iuriev reminded Dostoevsky of his promise for a fantastic story:

> Then Dostoevsky began to tremble. As if he was gripped by a fever, with a glint in his eyes, he began to speak of *The Queen of Spades*. He followed subtly all the movements of Germann's soul, all his torments, all his hopes, and, finally, his awful, sudden defeat, as if he were Germann himself [...] It seemed to me that I was in that company, that Germann was in front of me, I was seized by a nervous shaking and, following Dostoevsky's example, I set out to experience what Germann had felt...[5]

A conversation born out of the excitement of the moment, one might say. No, the idea had already germinated to tie in with the fantastic vein in the spirit of Pushkin. The proof, on this occasion, comes not from the life but from the correspondence. On 15 June 1880, replying to Iulia Fyodorovna Abaza, the wife of the Minister of Finance, a singer and unconditional admirer of the writer, who had submitted to him her own attempt at literature, an implausible story, Dostoevsky gave a lesson in the true fantastic:

> Let us admit that it might be regarded as a fantastic tale, but, in art, the fantastic has its limits and its rules. The fantastic must so closely conform to the real that you should *almost* believe it. Pushkin, who has bequeathed us just about all our art-forms, wrote *The Queen of Spades*, the pinnacle of fantastic art. And you believe that Germann has had a vision which conforms precisely to his conception of the world, so that at the end of the story, that is to say, after reading it, you do not know what to think: does this vision come from within Germann's own nature, or does it really come from those who have drawn near the other world, the world of spirits which are malign and hostile to humanity? (NB. Spiritualism and its teaching). That is art. (XXX: 1, 192)

---

[4] A S Dolinin (ed.), *F M Dostoevskii v vospominaniyakh sovremennikov*, II (Moscow: Khudozhestvennaia literatura, 1964), p. 361.

[5] Dolinin, p. 363.

And the day after writing this letter, on the night of 16 to 17 June, the author of *The Brothers Karamazov* applied these precepts of the fantastic, whose power comes from its fundamental ambivalence, its supreme uncertainty, to himself. Of the eighteen points he made in roman numerals, ten refer to Satan, and of these four are explicit:

XV. Satan. 'I'.
XV. Ivan apropos of conscience. Satan.
XVI. Satan (a verruca and the rest).
XVII. Satan ('I have become superstitious'). (XV, 326)

On 30 July, the writer recorded the essential details which we meet in Ivan's nightmare. Dostoevsky here accentuates the principles of realism, with the grotesque humanization, the vulgarity and the lack of imagination of a devil who dreams of becoming a Russian merchant's wife. Some significant extracts:

S[atan]. It is supposed that I am a fallen angel. I am on the contrary a respectable man (what am I if not a sponger?) (XV, 333)
S[atan]. To rest your beak in the water. Rheumatism. Hof's treatment.
Satan has a slight cough from time to time (realism, a verruca);
The beak in the water or without a beak. (XV, 334)
A 150-degree frost [...] Through stupidity, I didn't want to change my clothes and I risked this flight and I've picked up rheumatism.
S[atan]. About realism and dreams.
Catarrh of the respiratory tracts. And imagine the fear; twice I've been vaccinated.
Satana sum et nihil humanum a me alienum puto.
Iv[an]. Humanum? That's not a bad idea for Satan. Where did you unearth it from? (In dreams reality is stronger than in the waking state, or that wouldn't have been invented). (XV, 335)

One could multiply here the quotations where Dostoevsky, while elaborating the philosophical ideas to which Ivan gives expression with the aid of his devil—because, as he confesses with his repeated response 'It was he who said that', it is half himself—maintains the ambivalence of the Pushkinian fantastic, which leaves the reader uncertain, troubled and destabilized right up to the end. The sudden appearance of the uncanny opens a fissure that the real then mockingly closes: the glass of tea that Ivan throws in the face of the devil, like Luther's bottle of ink long ago, is quietly in its place, the damp towel he had applied to his forehead is quite definitely dry, and so on. The materiality of objects contests the hallucination. And yet it persists: Ivan, in the presence of Alyosha (in Chapter Ten) continues his dialogue with the devil and confirms in this manner the *reality of the unreal*, at least in the eyes of his young brother. One has as proof only the declaration of Ivan, who claims to know that Smerdyakov has hanged himself, whereas in the dream, the devil confined himself to saying, '"Listen, you'd better open the door", cried the visitor, "it's your brother Alyosha who's come to tell you the most unexpected piece of news,

I can assure you"' (XV, 84) The fantastic lack of resolution is maintained right up to the end, just as in Pushkin.

Pushkin's legacy of the fantastic,[6] reactivated by the speech of 8 June, is undeniably the element which triggers off Ivan Karamazov's nightmare: the lively dialogue with Polivanova, later pursued in his correspondence with Abaza, was its medium; emulation and stimulating rivalry with the great Russian poet were played out in equal measure. The routes to literary creation are always complex, and one should not reduce Dostoevsky's achievement in Chapter Nine, Book XI of *The Brothers Karamazov*, to this initial trick. The novelist's casual 'I don't know why' when he sent his text to Liubimov reflects the part played by the unconscious in artistic creation, and a double logic, which has played a decisive role.

The first of these runs through the entire work. Dostoevsky, in The *Diary of a Writer* for November 1877, recalled his 1846 novel, *The Double: The Adventures of Mr Golyadkin*, in the following terms:

> I made a total mess of this novel, but the idea behind it was quite clear and logical, and I have never expressed anything more serious in my writing than this idea. But the form I gave this story was completely wrong [...] If I were to take up the idea now and develop it again, I would choose an entirely different form.' (XXVI, 65)

The idea is that of *doubling*, which is for all that abundantly commented upon in his letters. The error of the young writer, still too much under the influence of Gogol, was to have invented a real, flesh-and-bone double who was also perceived by others, to have made his Golyadkin Junior a public figure in reality, instead of confining himself to depicting schizoid delirium seen from within. With Ivan Karamazov and his nightmare, the hero is perfectly conscious that it is a part of him which is talking through the devil, however he wants the devil to exist in itself, also marking Mitya's famous phrase: 'The devil is fighting with God there, and the field of battle is the human heart'. The novelist has corrected his youthful error, he has chosen 'another form' in order to recover his expression, thanks to Pushkin. The fantastic is handled *not from the exterior but from the interior*, although this interiority institutes belief in its exteriority. The hallucination, the strength of the conviction of which is no less than permanent delirium, maintains the fantastic ambivalence. It remains a real event which reveals the soul. The true fantastic, a fissure opened to another world or a gulf above the hidden self, can only be inscribed in a secure and stable reality.

The second logic is dealt with by the composition of *The Brothers Karamazov*. It is a theme on which I have already commented in the chapter 'The

---

[6]When examined closely, Pushkin's legacy can also be seen in the three visits Ivan makes to Smerdyakov. With his wrinkled left eye, the latter recalls the winking eye of the countess appearing to Germann and repeated by that of the Queen of Spades on the fatal playing card.

spiral and its golden number'.[7] The number three, as in the Russian folktales about the three brothers, governs, in space just as much as in time, the architecture of the novel. Dostoevsky had already, in Book VII, 'Alyosha', revealed the destiny of the youngest brother through the dream of Cana of Galilee; in Book IX, 'The Preliminary Investigation', he had given Mitya the revelation of his destiny, to suffer for others, through the dream of the baby. Whether unconsciously, or by conscious genius, he completed the structural harmony of the novel with Ivan's hallucination in Book XI. Three *visions* thus consecrate the destinies of the three Karamazov brothers: 'the road of crystal with the sun at the end' for Alyosha, redemption through the acceptance of suffering for Mitya, and final judgement for Ivan, brought about by the devil in the darkness.

Of course, there were these 'underground' motivations for the novelistic genius, but it is none the less the case that the festival and his speech at the inauguration of the Pushkin monument constituted the trigger which gave birth to the celebrated chapter of *The Brothers Karamazov*, 'The Devil. Ivan Fyodorovich's Nightmare'.

Translated by Sarah Young[8]

---

[7] Catteau, *Literary Creation*, pp. 360-362.

[8] My thanks to Edward Welch of the University of Durham for his advice on certain aspects of this translation—SY.

PART II

Dialogue

APOLLON MAIKOV AND THE CULT OF THE LEADER

Richard Peace

THE name Apollon Maikov is often encountered by students of Dostoevsky. It is hardly surprising; the two writers kept up a constant correspondence, and Maikov was perhaps Dostoevsky's most trusted confidant. As young men in the 1840s they were both associated with the Petrashevsky circle, but when Dostoevsky tried to recruit his friend to an inner revolutionary circle, his advances were rejected—their role, said Maikov was to be writers, not revolutionaries.[9] Maikov was arrested in the general sweep up of the Petrashevtsy, but was later released.

Apollon was born in 1821 into a very cultured family. His father was a talented artist, who became an academician in the fine arts. His mother was a writer and, of his brothers, the most famous was Valerian, who, although he died young, established a reputation as a literary critic. Vladimir published *The Snowdrop (Podsnezhnik)*—a magazine for children, and Leonid was a Pushkin scholar and literary historian. The boys had the distinction of having Goncharov as a tutor, and he was to remain a friend of the poet in later life. Like Dostoevsky, Maikov moved away from the earlier left-wing sympathies associated with the Petrashevsky circle towards a more Slavophile view of Russian life. His political reliability may be judged from the fact that in 1852 he was appointed a censor (even before his friend Goncharov in 1856) and he served for forty years.

Maikov himself described his life as uneventful. He studied law at St Petersburg University, and but for his poor eyesight might have pursued an artistic career. His poetry, it is said, often reveals a painter's eye. He undertook two journeys abroad. From 1842 to 1844 he visited Italy, France Germany and Czechoslovakia. In 1858 he went on a maritime expedition to Greece and Italy. Italian themes are quite prominent in his work, and he had an interest in the Czechs. His longer poem, *Prigovor* ('The Sentence') (1859) is about the Czech dissident, Jan Hus. Maikov died in 1897.

---

[9] See Letter of A N Maikov to P A Viskovatov (1855), reproduced in N F Bel'chikov, *Dostoevskii v protsesse petrashevtsev* (Moscow, 1971), pp. 264-268 (esp. p. 265).

Although this article has as its title 'Apollon Maikov and the cult of the leader', in order to give a less partial view of his poetic output, it is necessary to touch on other aspects of his work. Maikov's early, so-called, anthological poetry won the praise of Belinsky, and in a review of his poetry in the *The Contemporary (Sovremennik)* in 1855, apparently written jointly by Nekrasov and Chernyshevsky, he is referred to as 'a poet, to whom, at the present time, Russia scarcely has an equal'.[10]

Mirsky lists him among the Eclectic Poets, and his judgements are dismissive: 'Máykov was mildly "poetical" and mildly realistic; mildly tendentious, and never emotional. Images are always the principal thing in his poems'.[11] Nevertheless, given the qualification that he has 'no style, no diction', Mirsky does single out some of Maikov's poems for praise, and there may well have been a degree of political bias which coloured his view.

Many of Maikov's early poems have classical themes, but 'Razdum'e' (1841) begins: 'Blazhen, kto pod krylom svoikh domashnikh lar/Vedet spokoino vek!'.[12] ('Happy the man, who leads a quiet life under the wing of his household gods'). It seems like an imitation of the fourth-century poet, Claudian: 'Felix, qui propriis aevum transegit in arvis' ('Happy the man who has passed his life in his own fields'); or of Pope's 'Ode on Solitude': 'Happy the man whose wish and care/A few paternal acres bound'.[13] But its title is 'Razdum'e', ('Meditation' or 'Change of Mind') and it ends by rejecting a life without emotion *(bez volnen'ia)*. Romanticism has in fact now conquered Classicism, and this theme is carried on in an even shorter poem with the more positive title, not 'Change of Mind' ('Razdum'e'), but 'Thought'—'Duma' (1841).[14] Maikov is, perhaps, seen at his best with nature themes. Even Mirsky describes what he calls his 'short and very well-known poems on spring and rain' as 'happy discoveries'. Such poems are: 'Peizazh' ('Landscape') (1853); 'Vesna! Vystavliaetsia pervaia rama' ('It is Spring! The first window pane is out') (1854); 'Bozhe moi! Vchera—nenast'e' ('Oh Lord! Yesterday was bad weather') (1855).[15]

It is particularly worthwhile looking at one of his most successful poems in this genre—'Senokos' ('Haymaking') (1856):[16]

---

[10] N A Nekrasov, *Polnoe sobranie sochinenii i pisem v piatnadtsati tomakh* (Leningrad (St Petersburg), 1981-2000), XII: 2, 172.

[11] D S Mirsky, *A History of Russian Literature*, (ed. and abridged F J Whitfield) (New York, 1960), p. 220.

[12] A Maikov, *Stikhotvoreniia* (Moscow, 1980), p. 42.

[13] See: *The Penguin Book of Latin Verse* (Intro. and ed. F Brittain) (Harmondsworth: Penguin, 1962), pp. 84-85; *Pope: Poetry and Prose: With Essays by Johnson, Coleridge, Hazlitt &c.* (Introduction and Notes H V D Dyson (Oxford: Clarendon Press, 1933), p. 32.

[14] Maikov, p. 48.

[15] Mirsky, p. 220. See: Maikov, pp. 79, 80, 81.

[16] An English translation of this poem may be found in: Evelyn Bristol, *A History of Russian Poetry* (New York, Oxford, 1991), p. 145.

First stanza: Пахнет сеном над лугами...
                     В песне душу веселя,
                     Бабы с граблями рядами
                     Ходят, сено шевеля

('There is a scent of hay over the meadows. In a song that gladdens the soul the peasant women go in rows raking the hay').

The scene evoked is very visual, yet the very first word of the poem, 'pakhnet' ('there is a scent'), immediately brings the dimension, of smell, of scent, to our attention—a heady element in the process of haymaking. The second line with its opening phrase 'V pesne' ('in a song') introduces an auditory element—the songs of the women.

Second stanza: Там—сухое убирают:
                      Мужички его кругом
                      На воз вилями кидают
                      Воз растет, растет как дом...

('Over there they are gathering the dry [hay]: around it the peasant men are tossing it on to the cart with pitchforks...the cart grows, grows as big as a house...').

In the second verse the hay is referred to merely as the substantivized adjective 'Sukhoe'—'dry'. The onomatopoeic quality of the word conveys the rustle, almost the feel of hay itself. So here we have another sense added to sound—touch.

Third stanza: В ожиданьи конь убогий,
                   Точно вкопанный, стоит...
                   Уши врозь, дугою ноги
                   И как будто стоя спит...

('Waiting, a poor horse stands as though fixed to the earth...its ears sticking out, its legs bent, and as though asleep standing up...').

The first two verses show the bustle of the work on the hayfield. The third verse is one of stasis, conveyed through the description of the waiting horse. This animal, patiently waiting for its load betrays no hint of movement—no flicking of the tail or tossing of the head to ward off flies, as one might expect. Its stillness is somehow emblematic. The final line gives the clue: 'kak budto stoia spit...' ('as though asleep standing up'). It is the epitome of somnolence—an effect which is also associated with the summer heat and the heady smell of hay.

If such somnolence is subtly, and indirectly, suggested through the description of an animal, in the final verse another animal conveys yet another aspect of haymaking. It is an occupation not available to those who have to work, but a dog might enjoy frolicking and tumbling in the hay.

Fourth stanza: Только жучка удалая,
В рыхлом сене, как в волнах,
То взлетая, то ныряя,
Скачет, лая впопыхах.

('Only the bold [dog] Zhuchka jumps in the loose hay, as though they are waves, now flying up now plunging down, and barking in his haste.')

For all its apparent simplicity and directness, I would suggest that this is really a very subtle and evocative poem. It employs very little direct imagery (hay—'as a house'; the dog playing 'as though in waves''—even perhaps the 'dead' image for the horse—'as though fixed to the earth'), yet the whole poem is an image in itself, and this would seem to reinforce Mirsky's view that 'images are always the principal thing in his poems'. Nevertheless, despite its largely visual impact, the poem also manages to convey senses of smell, sound and touch. There is also a noticeable formal characteristic. The division of the poem at its middle into two sets of binary stanzas sets up a contrast between the world of human beings, and the world of animals: the world of work, and the more 'animal'-like connotations evoked by hay in high summer—drowsiness in the third stanza; frolicking—in the fourth. It is this activity which ends the poem, and is aptly conveyed through the internal rhymes of the final couplet: vzletaia, nyriaia, laia: 'To vzletaia, to nyriaia, / Skachet, laia vpopykhakh' ('Now flying up, now plunging down, and barking in his haste').

One of Maikov's most impressive nature poems is the much longer 'Rybnaia lovlia' ('Fishing') (1855), which even the usually dismissive Mirsky calls a 'delightful idyll'.[17] It is in fact an evocation of the Russian countryside at various times of day. Not without humour he records the characters he meets whilst out fishing. and the censure he encounters from his family for engaging in this occupation instead of writing poetry. In many respects the poem reminds one of Wordsworth. A shorter poem of 1841, 'EPM' (the initials of his mother) had already recorded his delight in nature and in fishing which significantly he links to his muse.[18]

Maikov had initially acquired a reputation as a poet with liberal sympathies. Public readings of *Prigovor*, his poem on the trial of Jan Hus, were acclaimed in this sense, and the poem 'Dushno il' opiat' Sirocco' ('It is airless or is it again the Sirocco') (1858), which ends with the Sicilians celebrating the arrival of Garibaldi, was interpreted by some as a call to revolution. An adaptation of the poem's first stanza was actually used in 1901 as an epigraph for the proclamation '!!Ko vsem!!' ('!!To Everyone!!'), calling for a demonstration outside the Kazan Cathedral in St Petersburg.[19]

---

[17] Mirsky, p. 220. See: Maikov, pp. 86-92.

[18] Maikov, p.53.

[19] See: Nekrasov, *PSS*, III, 419; Maikov, p. 141.

It is interesting that this 'liberal' poem of Maikov's ends with the acclaim of Garibaldi, because a notable feature of his poetic output is the political theme of the leader. At the time of the Crimean War he achieved some notoriety for his poem, 'Koliaska' ('The Coach') (1854), in praise of Nicholas I, and for 'Arlekin' ('Harlequin') (1855) which appeared to disparage the French democratic movement. Even though 'Arlekin' was mentioned favourably in the review, written by Nekrasov and Chernyshevsky, already referred to, it did not deter Nekrasov from writing a vicious attack on the poet in 1855:

На Майкова (1855 года)

Давно ли воспевал он прелести свободы?
А вот уж цензором...начальством одобрен,
Стал академиком и сочиняет оды,
А наставительный все не кидает тон.
Неистово браня несчастную Европу,
Дойдет он до того в развитии своем,
Что станет лобызать он Дубельтову <- - ->
И гордо миру сам поведает о том.[20]

('Was it long ago that he sang the charms of freedom?/And now he is approved by the censor and the authorities,/He has become an academician and composes odes, but still does not quit his didactic tone./Frenziedly cursing unfortunate Europe,/He will get to a point in his development/where he will start kissing Dubelt's (arse)/And will proudly inform the world of this.')

'Koliaska' was not published, but it circulated in manuscript form and did much to damage his reputation. His fellow poet N Shcherbina wrote epigrams about him, calling him Apollon Koliaskin. Maikov himself later seemed to regret ever having written it, but it does reveal in Maikov a certain veneration for authority, however dubious its claim to respect.

In Ryleev's 'Dumy' ('Thoughts') we encounter a series of portraits of Russian leaders and historical figures, but these are all seen from the viewpoint of a Decembrist, who is keener on opposition than authority itself. Thus, in Ryleev, we have a poem about the renegade Kurbsky rather than Ivan IV, and in another 'Duma' 'Petr velikii v Ostrogozhske' ('Peter the Great in Ostrogozhsk'), praise of Peter I comes not from the poet himself, but from the traitor Mazepa. Maikov's approach to the question of leadership is quite different.

In 'Kto on?' ('Who is He?') (1841 [1857]) a mysterious horseman helps a poor fisherman mend his boat. It has been maliciously holed during the skirmishing going on between Russian troops and Swedes. The mystery man, it is suggested, is Peter I, and for all that the fisherman grumbles about the boyars, the political situation of the time, and appears to make no distinction between Russians and Swedes, the tsar is presented as his saviour. He is the helper and

---

[20]Nekrasov, *PSS*, I, 458. Dubelt was a secret police chief.

defender of the people—*narod*.[21] In Pushkin's *The Bronze Horseman*, by contrast, Peter is the persecutor of the little man.

The poem 'V Gorodtse v 1263 godu' ('In Gorodets in 1263') (1875) describes the death of Alexander Nevsky on his return from the Golden Horde, where he has successfully pleaded the case of the Russians. He is haunted by visions—the humiliation of having to bow down to the Tatars, but by so doing he knows he has saved the people:

> Боже! ты знаешь—не ради себя—
> Многострадальный народ свой лишь паче
> души возлюбя

('Oh Lord! Thou knowest—not for my sake—/but because, more than my own soul, I love my much suffering people.')

Here again the leader is linked to the theme of the narod. He also remembers the triumphs against the Livonian Knights and the Swedes, and he has a prophetic vision of his own canonized bones being carried to the new city of St Petersburg and a new leader a tsar, Peter I, who will carry on his work.[22]

The most interesting poem of all in this genre is 'U groba Groznogo' ('At the tomb of Ivan the Terrible') (1887). The poet muses on the tomb of Ivan IV in the Cathedral of the Archangel in the Kremlin. He is, Maikov thinks, a misunderstood figure. One senses that fate has not yet pronounced the final judgement on him. The heavy weight of disgrace has not yet been lifted from his grave, though the sum of his guilt and of his crimes has already been drawn up. The verdict has been pronounced, and yet some higher instance is still delaying its confirmation, and the crowd is filled with perplexity. However, Maikov, seems to have his own view:

> что, быть может, никогда
> На свете пламенней души не появлялось...
> Она—с алчбой добра—весь век во зле терзалось.

('That perhaps there has never/appeared a more ardent soul in the world.../Thirsting for what is good, it has been a whole life tormented in evil.')

This last line about a soul thirsting for good and being tormented in evil all its life is almost Dostoevskian.

Maikov imagines Ivan the Terrible rising from his tomb, and justifying himself. He has preserved Russia; he is the founder of a state which has lasted four centuries. Those who were able to see Stalin lying embalmed in the Lenin mausoleum before he was moved, could quite credibly feel that at any moment he would arise, and in similar fashion justify himself. When I saw him in 1957 he looked very much alive beside the doll-like body of Lenin. We know that

---

[21] Maikov, pp. 123-124.

[22] Maikov, pp. 179-183.

Stalin himself was a great admirer of Ivan the Terrible, and perhaps saw similarities in the situations they both found themselves in, and the policies they carried out. Stalin even had his Kurbsky in Trotsky. Common people openly wept when Stalin died, just as Ivan in the poem claims the frightened *narod* wept at the news of his death. Parallels which may be drawn from this poem with the death of Stalin, and the drive amongst certain sections of the Russian public for some sort of rehabilitation of the ogre's reputation, may not be too far fetched:

> Да! Мой день еще придет!
> Услышится, как взвыл испуганный народ,
> Когда возвещена царя была кончина,
> И сей народный вой над гробом властелина—
> Я верую—в веках вотще не пропадет,
> И будет громче он, чем этот шип подземный
> Боярской клеветы и злобы иноземный...

('Yes! My day will still come!/There will be heard how a terrified people howled,/When the death of the tsar was announced,/And this howling of the people over the coffin of the ruler—/I believe—for centuries will not be lost in vain,/And it will be louder, than the subterranean hissing/of the boyars' slander and the malice from abroad...')

There is a real sense of threat in these words.[23]

'Skazanie o 1812 gode' ('A Legend of the Year 1812') (1876) is a poem about a foreign leader. It describes Napoleon's retreat from Moscow, and as such obviously invites comparison with the first part of Victor Hugo's 'Le Châtiment' (1853). Its images, however are not as stark. Maikov's Russian perspective tends to stress the pillaging of church goods rather than the extremes of suffering endured by the French. But there is the presence of another leader in the poem. When Napoleon had threatened the ambassadors of the crowned heads of Europe in the Tuileries Palace, the Russian ambassador had refused to be bullied. Napoleon has miscalculated—the poem asserts—the whole of the Russian people stands behind the emperor. Once again the tsar (in this case Alexander I) is linked to the narod.[24]

In examining Maikov's poems on leadership, we may come to a strange conclusion. Maikov could well have been a poet under Stalin—certainly of that period before, and during the second world war, which encouraged literature characterized as 'heroic nationalism'.[25] This was the period of Aleksei Tolstoy's novel on Peter the Great, who, as we have seen in 'Kto on?' Maikov portrays as a man of the people, and who, in his poem on the death of Alexander Nevsky, he refers to with the title that Stalin himself would acquire, 'helmsman'—

---

[23]Maikov, pp. 194-197.
[24]Maikov, pp. 184-186.
[25]See: 'Editor's Postscript' in Mirsky, p. 513.

kormchii. This was also the period of Eisenstein's films celebrating Alexander Nevsky and more significantly the figure with whom Stalin himself seemed to wish to identify—Ivan the Terrible. Maikov had shown that it was the people behind the leader who had ousted the French in 1812, and a similar message was being conveyed during the second world war by the publication of a mass edition of *War and Peace*. That such comparisons can be made should come as no surprise. The whole drift of Maikov's poems on leadership is to emphasize the continuity from one age to another. As he says of Ivan the Terrible—his labours were to be completed by the heroic efforts of Peter the Great, the intelligence of Catherine the Great and the achievements of the nineteenth century: 'I trud byl dovershen/Uzh podvigom Petra, umom Ekateriny/I vashim vekom...'[26] ('And the labour was completed/by the feats of Peter, the mind of Catherine/and by your century...'). In this context Stalinism itself may be seen as no wild aberration, but a new version of much that had gone on before.

Other longer poems on the theme of 'heroic' figures are *Savonarola* (1851) and *Prigovor* (1859).[27] *Savonarola* is unfinished. It is based on the irony of the burning of Savonarola on the very spot on which he himself had burned the 'bonfire of the vanities'. It may, perhaps, be interpreted as a sly blow against repressive censorship—more openly against bigotry, and the Catholic church. In a somewhat similar vein *Prigovor* deals with the trial of Hus by the princes of the Catholic church. At a critical moment in their deliberations the singing of a nightingale pricks the consciences of the clerical judges—a natural note in a false world. Nature, it seems, could be a force for reconciliation and forgiveness. Unfortunately the revelation is in vain, it is just a passing moment: Hus is condemned to death.

This inquisitorial theme in his portrayal of the western church reveals his affinity to the thought of his friend Dostoevsky, who would later, through the mouth of his character Ivan Karamazov, produce his own *poema*—'The Legend of the Grand Inquisitor'. A poem of 1890, 'My vyrosli v surovoi shkole' ('We have grown up in a harsh school'), has another theme dear to Dostoevsky (particularly prominent in *The Idiot*)—the image of the knight, who, like Don Quixote may be mocked, but is, nevertheless, the champion of good and challenger of evil.[28]

'There is reason to think that Máykov the poet did not come up to the caliber of Máykov the man. At any rate Dostoévsky had more respect for him than for any of his contemporaries and found him the most stimulating and responsive of correspondents'.[29] Mirsky's assessment of the poet seems unduly harsh, for all its occasional flashes of approbation. It is perhaps significant that he passes over

---

[26]Maikov, p. 196.
[27]Maikov, pp. 72-77; 128-133.
[28]Maikov, p. 208.
[29]Mirsky, p. 220.

in silence the more 'political' poems, concerned with the strong leader and his relationship to ordinary people—the *narod*. Yet here is a theme explored at a more philosophical level in the novels of Dostoevsky: the 'Napoleonic' pretensions of Raskolnikov in *Crime and Punishment*; Pyotr Verkhovensky's ambitions for Stavrogin in *The Devils*; the political philosophy of the Grand Inquisitor in *The Brothers Karamazov*. Maikov sees the strong, often ruthless, leader as a recurrent (and not entirely negative) figure in Russian history: a view whose reverberations may well go beyond his own time.

Maikov's poetic range is wide—from short lyrical poems, often of a personal nature, to grand set pieces on civic themes. Yet it is these, with their apparent glorification of tsardom, which did much to damage his reputation among his contemporaries. As a result a poet, who began his career with eulogies comparing him to Pushkin, would later suffer scorn and neglect often from those who had earlier praised him. Maikov is not Pushkin, but at his best he produced some memorable and enchanting poetry, and did so in more than one genre. Perhaps it is time to look at him afresh.

DOSTOEVSKY, 'BOBOK', PIERRE BOBO AND BOBORYKIN

John McNair

THE largely unknown and mostly untold story of Dostoevsky's relations with his younger literary contemporary Pyotr Boborykin, and the complementary story of Boborykin's relations with Dostoevsky, are presented together here in the belief that readers and scholars may discover in them an interest which as separate narratives they could hardly pretend to. For while (as one might say) the monologic exposition of literary minutiae may enhance our understanding of any one writer, it is the dialogic perspective which is more likely to take us beyond the extended footnote to some enriched sense of the personalities, ideologies and aesthetic agenda that constituted the dynamics of the literary life of the time. Moreover, in the case of Dostoevsky, the exercise may afford some specific insight into the myriad ways in which the writer contrived, as Bakhtin put it, to 'think in voices', to express ideas—in his notebooks and journalistic writing as much as in his novels—'through a labyrinth of voices, semi-voices, other people's words, other people's gestures';[1] balancing this, in the case of Boborykin, with even rarer insight into the particular predicament of those who through no desire or agency of their own found themselves appropriated, however marginally, by this dialogic art and inscribed in its rhetoric of topical allusions and competing discourses.

Separated by an age difference of more than fifteen years, as well as by no less significant disparities in their social origins, economic circumstances and life experience, the two writers were linked more fatefully than by their direct literary contacts. More than sixty years later, Boborykin could recall precisely that Dostoevsky's name 'first reached his ears' in the spring of 1849,[2] five months before his thirteenth birthday; for among the Petrashevsky 'conspirators' arrested with Dostoevsky on April 23, sentenced like him to death but in the event transported to Siberia, was Boborykin's own maternal uncle, Nikolai

---

[1] M Bakhtin, *Problemy poetiki Dostoevskogo*; cited from *Problems of Dostoevsky's Poetics*, ed. and trans. Caryl Emerson (Minneapolis: University of Minnesota Press, 1984), pp. 93, 95.

[2] P D Boborykin, 'Bol'shoi dom: iz semeinoi khroniki', *Niva: ezhemesiachnoe literaturnoe i populiarno-nauchnoe prilozhenie* (1913), IV, 554.

Petrovich Grigoriev, cavalry officer and amateur author.[3] The experience which became so traumatic a turning-point in Dostoevsky's life therefore had its repercussions too for the boy growing up in his grandfather's mansion in Nizhny Novgorod, where the occasional visits of Uncle Nikolai had brought rare moments of relief from the routine of a solitary and cheerless childhood. It is unlikely that either his nephew or his fellow-accused were ever aware of Grigoriev's attempt to intercede for his friends in a contrite letter written to Nicholas I from his prison cell:

> My recent acquaintances the Dostoevskys, Durov, Palm, Mombelli and the others always seemed to me to be people with no malice, incapable of any great evil, though fond of talking, chattering and occasionally swearing. I believe that, if given the chance and the means of a comfortable existence, they would turn out to be useful men and loyal to you, Sire.[4]

His plea fell on deaf ears and he received a sentence of fifteen years' hard labour. Following a mental breakdown in 1856, Uncle Nikolai was released into the care of his family the next year and returned to end his days an invalid in his father's house. His fate cast over Boborykin's adolescence and early manhood a shadow with which, it might be surmised, the name of Dostoevsky would ever be associated.

Whether or not he was aware of the connexion with Grigoriev, Dostoevsky must certainly have become familiar with Boborykin's name soon after his own return from exile, towards the end of 1861, when as co-editor and chief polemicist of *Time* (*Vremia*) he would not have missed the début of a new *feuilletoniste* (writing usually as 'Pyotr Neskazhus'') in Pisemsky's 'thick' journal *The Reading Library* (*Biblioteka dlia chteniia*).[5] The fact that much of this first contribution was devoted to the review of a performance of Boborykin's play *The Smallholder (Odnodvorets)* provided a substantial clue as to the identity of the pseudonymous author. A few months later, in March 1862, Pyotr Neskazhus' became the centre of a minor *skandal* following some disparaging remarks about Chernyshevsky's shortcomings as a public speaker and the personal hygiene of some *nigilistki* in his audience at the literary-musical soirée organized in aid of needy students following the closure of St Petersburg University. Dostoevsky, who read some chapters from *The House of the Dead* at the gathering (itself the inspiration for the soirée in aid of indigent governesses

---

[3] See V R Leikina-Svirskaia, ed., *Delo Petrashevtsev* (Moscow/Leningrad: 1951), III, 233-250. The specific charge against Grigoriev centred on his 'seditious' tale, 'Soldatskaia beseda', read aloud to other *petrashevtsy* at a dinner party on April 2.

[4] Leikina-Svirskaia, III, 239.

[5] Piotr Neskazhus', 'Nevinnye razmyshleniia nachinaiushchegosia', *Biblioteka dlia chteniia* (1861), 11 (October). On Boborykin's career as contributor to and later editor of *Biblioteka* see John McNair, '*The Reading Library* and the Reading Public: the Decline and Fall of *Biblioteka dlia chteniia*,' *Slavonic and East European Review*, 70.2 (April 1992), 215-227.

in *The Devils*) and took a keen interest in the satirical sallies of the radical press,[6] must have been aware of this. Within a year, Boborykin, a major contributor to the journal thanks to the monthly instalments of his first novel *On the Road! (V put'-dorogu!)*,[7] had become editor of *The Reading Library* with ambitious plans to revive it as 'a broadly liberal organ'.[8] Though this position was far enough from the blend of Slavophilism and pochvennichestvo that was increasingly to characterize Dostoevsky's line in *Time*—and from 1864 in *The Epoch (Epokha)*—, Boborykin's rejection of routine radical 'tendency' may have made him seem more ally than adversary in the 'journalistic wars' of the early and middle 1860s,[9] and *The Reading Library* was never a target for the kind of polemical attacks Dostoevsky launched most famously against *The Contemporary (Sovremennik)*. Although they were not to meet until 1865, the two editors had some indirect contact through Mikhail Dostoevsky and Strakhov, with whom Boborykin was personally acquainted, as well as through Nikolai Voskoboinikov, a member of Dostoevsky's circle who was eventually to become business manager of the *Library*. According to Dostoevsky, it was through his brother that in May 1863, following the government's interdiction on the further publication of *Time*,[10] Boborykin approached him as a prospective contributor. Negotiations were conducted through Strakhov, but were suspended in July when Boborykin jibbed at the requested fee of 1,500 roubles. In late September, in desperate financial straits following sojourns with Suslova in Wiesbaden, Paris and Baden-Baden, Dostoevsky urged Strakhov to return to Boborykin: 'it's the time subscriptions come in, and he must have the money. And anyway, I'm not asking for 1,500 roubles, but only 300'.[11] What he had in mind was a short story, as yet unwritten, about a gambler—'no ordinary gambler, just as Pushkin's miserly knight is no ordinary miser'.[12] It would be ready by 10 November, in time for publication in the November issue—'on that I give my word of honour'—and occupy 1·5 printer's sheets at 150 roubles per sheet, payable in advance:

> Boborykin should know, as do *The Contemporary* and *Notes of the Fatherland* [*Otechestvennye zapiski*], that (apart from *Poor Folk*) I have never in all my

---

[6] See Piotr Neskazhus', 'Piostrye zametki', *Biblioteka dlia chteniia*, 1862, 2 (February-March), 146-147; and e.g. [V S Kurochkin,] 'Tsepochka I griaznaia sheia: Stseny iz sovremennoi komedii', *Iskra*, 1862, 11 (March 23), 149. On Dostoevsky at this gathering, see Joseph Frank, *Dostoevsky: the Stir of Liberation*, 1860-65 (London: Robson, 1986), pp. 141-4.

[7] Boborykin's first novel was published in (sometimes irregular) monthly instalments between January 1862 and December 1864.

[8] P D Boborykin, *Za polveka*; in his *Vospominaniia v dvukh tomakh*, ed. E Vilenskaia, S Roitberg (Moscow: 'Khudozhestvennaia literatura', 1965), I, 334.

[9] Frank, *Stir of Liberation*, p. 47.

[10] See Dostoevsky's letter to Strakhov from Rome, 18 (30) September 1863: F M Dostoevskii, *PSS*, XXVIII: 2 (1985), 50.

[11] *PSS*, XXVIII: 2, 50.

[12] *PSS*, XXVIII: 2, 51.

life sold any work without taking the money in advance. I am a proletarian writer, and if anyone wants my work, they must pay me in advance. I myself deprecate this way of doing things. But so it has become established, and it seems it will never change.[13]

Within the fortnight, Strakhov was able to report Boborykin's ready acceptance of these terms,[14] and the full 300 roubles were sent at his request to await Dostoevsky in Turin. While progress on the story proved slower than its author had hoped, the October issue of *The Reading Library* advertised a new (as yet untitled) work by Mr Dostoevsky as one of the principal attractions for 1864.

In the interval, Dostoevsky had set his gambling story aside to complete work on *Notes from Underground*, a task made more difficult by new demands on his time associated with the launch of *The Epoch*, his own poor health and the continuing burden of his wife's illness, now in its final stages. It was a few days before her death, in the middle of April 1864, that he learned from his brother of Boborykin's indirect attempts through Strakhov to enquire about the fate of the promised contribution and moot the possibility of the return of the fee which had been paid.[15] Anxious lest Boborykin suspect him of any dishonest dealing, Dostoevsky contrived (in a manner reminiscent of the Underground Man himself) to shift any blame on to the latter:

> ...God knows, had circumstances been different [he wrote to Mikhail], I would have sent them my story straight away. If not, then it would be because I will not have anyone dare to make fun at my expense for 300 roubles. Had I not already taken their 300 roubles, I would have dismissed the jibe and, had circumstances so eventuated, would have sent them my story. But once the editorial board of *The Library* itself had bound me, not just by a promise, but by my word of honour and by money, it ought not to have permitted jibes at my expense to appear on the pages of the journal: as much as to say 'we've bought you, don't you dare wriggle out of it or take offence, and hand over your story regardless.' No sir, I will not sell my person or my freedom of action for 300 roubles.[16]

The offending 'jibe', brought to Dostoevsky's notice by his brother two months before, had appeared in the December issue of the *Library* the previous year in some satirical 'sketches of literary life' belonging to the pen of V P Burenin. Here a somewhat harassed editor is offered, among other contributions, 'a little piece in the heart-warming style, you know, à la Dostoevsky...The diary of a

---

[13]*PSS*, XXVIII: 2, 50.

[14]N S Strakhov, letter to Dostoevsky from St Petersburg, 29 September 1863, in N K Piksanov, O V Tsekhnovitser, eds., *Shestidesiatye gody: materialy po istorii literatury I obshchestvennomu dvizheniiu* (Moscow/Leningrad: AN SSSR, 1940), p. 256.

[15]See Dostoevsky's letter to Mikhail Dostoevsky from Moscow, 13 April 1864: *PSS*, XXVIII: 2, 86.

[16]*PSS*, XXVIII: 2, 86.

prisoner...'[17] Judged by the usual standards of journalistic scurrility—Burenin was certainly capable of much worse, as his subsequent baiting of Boborykin would show,[18] and Dostoevsky himself was hardly above reproach—this may seem mild enough; and in any case it was surely unreasonable to hold the editor personally responsible. Nor could Dostoevsky's righteous indignation obscure the fact that he had pocketed the fee but failed to deliver the story. It was, however, the line he had determined upon and was to follow in replying to the letter Boborykin sent him from St Petersburg on 11 April:[19]

> This explanation consists in my frank admission that, apart from my grievous domestic misfortunes and long illness which have long hampered my work, I was visited about two months ago by a certain unwillingness to place my work in your journal, although at the same time I was most anxious to keep my word. I could furnish you with positive proof that until then, that is until two months ago, I had the firm intention and sincere desire of fulfilling my obligations to *The Reading Library*. In spite of this, however, my ideas changed when I had the dissatisfaction of reading in your journal a jibe directed at my work. There have been numerous jibes made in the press about my work throughout my literary career. Although I have paid heed to very many of them, I have never on that account entered into explanations of any kind, either publicly or privately. But the present case is a special one, and in consequence of my views on certain matters, I could not altogether ignore a jibe, albeit such a modest one, from *The Library*. The statement was made in an article published by you that I write 'in the heart-warming style', and this was said in a sufficiently mocking tone. Of course, this is all innocent enough, but such a tone, in view of my relations with *The Library*, was even—forgive me—impossible. Had I not received from you the money in advance, and importantly, had I not bound myself to you by my word of honour, this jibe, however I might regard it, would have had no influence on my ability to publish in *The Library* or not. But now it concerns me, bound as I am hand and foot. It might be supposed that I do not dare to change my situation and must put up with any tone at all just because I have taken the money. Of course, I do not suggest that such a view of our relations is possible in the offices of *The Library*. But in such a case even the possibility is by itself a delicate matter. I agree that these are 'niceties' on my part. But in my view even an excessive nicety in certain circumstances in life is nevertheless better than any 'coarseness' in relations—forgive me, I can find no better word to

---

[17] V P Burenin, 'Ocherki literaturnogo byta. Priemnyi den' redaktora', *Biblioteka dlia chteniia*, 1863, 12, ii, 8.

[18] See John McNair, 'Persecution by Parody: the Literary Trial[s] of Piotr Boborykin', *New Zealand Slavonic Journal*, 1994 (Festschrift in Honour of Patrick Waddington), 113-126.

[19] Boborykin, letter to Dostoevsky from St Petersburg, 11 April 1864: *F M Dostoevskii, Pis'ma v 4-kh tomakh*, ed. A S Dolgin (Leningrad/Moscow: Academia/GIKhL, 1928-1959), I (1928), 571.

designate the kind of cynicism I have always avoided in my dealings with people.[20]

Noting Boborykin's 'tactfulness' in putting their relations on a 'purely commercial' footing, Dostoevsky ended by agreeing that an immediate reimbursement of the 300 roubles would be 'the best conclusion of these relations'.[21]

There can be little doubt that Dostoevsky derived more satisfaction from this exchange than Boborykin. The restitution of his original investment did nothing to compensate the latter for the lack of a story which, as he explained in his letter of 11 April, he had been particularly anxious to place in the first issues of the new year.[22] His efforts to 'raise' *The Reading Library* after more than two decades of gradual decline had been hampered by his failure to attract contributions from any major literary 'name', and the publication of a new work by Dostoevsky could have made a significant difference. As it was, he had gone to press instead with *Nowhere to Go (Nekuda)* by 'M Stebnitsky', Leskov's intemperate satire on fashionable nihilism, and was very soon to regret it. In June he had to print an 'essential explanation' disclaiming any slanderous intent and refuting the more bellicose attacks from the radical camp. A further conciliatory 'explanation' from the editor accompanied the final instalment of the novel in December, but the damage had been done and subscriptions for the coming year suggested a mass defection by 'progressive' readers. By the beginning of 1865, Boborykin, bound by his terms of purchase to remit sizeable monthly payments to Pechatkin (his predecessor as editor) and by a 'fateful penalty clause' to hand over ten thousand roubles in the event of any default, stared ruin in the face.[23] In fact, his situation resembled that of Dostoevsky, who following the death of Mikhail in July 1864 was left to cope with the hopeless financial affairs of *The Epoch* on his own. It is therefore perhaps unaccountable, and in the light of their recent dealings somewhat unexpected, that they should turn to each other for help. It was probably Dostoevsky who initiated negotiations for an arrangement whereby *The Epoch* could cut its losses and clear a substantial part of its debts to its subscribers in effect by selling to *The Reading Library* the balance of their subscriptions for the remainder of the year; *The Library*, for the relatively low figure of five thousand roubles (payable in instalments), would thus acquire for the remaining months of 1865 several thousands of new subscribers, many of whom might be expected to renew their order for the following year.[24] It was now that the two editors met for the first time in Dostoevsky's 'cramped' flat;[25]

---

[20] Dostoevsky, [draft] letter to Boborykin from Moscow, April 14 1864: *PSS*, XXVIII: 2, 89-90.

[21] *PSS*, XVIII: 2, 90.

[22] F M Dostoevskii, *Pis'ma v 4-kh tomakh*, I, 571.

[23] For a detailed account see McNair, '*The Reading Library* and the Reading Public', 223-225.

[24] Dostoevsky's calculations are to be found in various fragments in his notebooks: e.g. 'Ot izdatelei zhurnala *Epokha*. Konspekty i zabroski', *PSS*, XXVII (1984), 203.

[25] Boborykin, *Za polveka*, p. 391.

listening to Dostoevsky's 'quiet, deep and somehow slightly strained voice',[26] it seemed to Boborykin that *The Epoch* would accept almost any terms in exchange for 'some hope that the deal might be done'.[27] The last issue of Dostoevsky's journal appeared in March, 1865, and on June 9, the newspaper *The Voice (Golos)* carried an announcement explaining the arrangement which its editors, in consequence of 'many unfavourable circumstances' had been obliged to enter into with *The Reading Library*.[28] By the time the identical announcement appeared in the combined issue (No. 7-8) of *The Library* later that month, however, unfavourable circumstances had overtaken that journal too. No further issues appeared, and within a few weeks Boborykin had fled to France, leaving Voskoboinikov to salvage what he could. It was he who later that year declined Dostoevsky's offer of a new work—the future *Crime and Punishment*—in exchange for an advance of three hundred roubles.[29]

Selling or mortgaging his family estates to keep the creditors of *The Reading Library* at bay and finally assuming personal responsibility for the settlement of its remaining debts, Boborykin returned to Russia only in 1871. Dostoevsky, in the meantime, having delivered *Crime and Punishment* to Katkov and *The Gambler* to Stellovsky, set out for Europe with his new wife in April 1867, returning also in 1871. Thereafter, although their personal contacts remained minimal (Boborykin was only to recall two actual encounters following the outcome of the *Epoch* negotiations)[30], they continued to move in the same small world and in the course of things were not infrequently to be found attending the same gatherings and functions. Both were present, for example, at the celebrated trial (early in 1876) of Mlle Kairova, an actress accused, and subsequently acquitted, of stabbing her lover's wife; and, within a matter of days, at a demonstration séance given by the British medium Miss Saint Clair at Alexander Aksakov's house, when, as Boborykin recorded for the readers of *The St Petersburg News (Sankt-Peterburgskie vedomosti)*, the performer interpreted some comments by 'Mr D' as a reflection on her experiments.[31] Over and above their shared interest in the jury system and spiritualism, the two men were again

---

[26] Boborykin, *Za polveka*, p. 391.

[27] Boborykin, unpublished letter to A I Urusov from St Petersburg, 26 April 1865 (IRLI RAN (Pushkinskii dom), R. III, op.1, no. 609, 21 verso.

[28] *Golos*, 1865 (9 June), No. 157.

[29] See the notes to the novel in Dostoevskii, *PSS*, VII (1973), 310. The offer was made simultaneously (in August 1865) to *Otechestvennye zapiski* and *Sovremennik*, who both declined. Katkov's *Russkii vestnik* sent Dostoevsky the advance he required in October.

[30] Boborykin, *Za polveka*, pp. 391-392.

[31] The séance, together with the commission of enquiry set up to investigate its proceedings, was the subject of Boborykin's column in *Sankt-Peterburgskie vedomosti* Nos. 75, 82 and 89 (March 1876); on the incident involving 'Mr D', see No. 75 (March 16); and *PSS*, XXIV (1982), 439. Both Dostoevsky and Boborykin were sceptics, but believed the commission of enquiry biased in its report. On the Kairova case see especially *PSS*, XXIII (1981), 355ff.

colleagues, since Boborykin (now as much a 'proletarian' writer as Dostoevsky had been) was obliged to earn his living as a jobbing journalist, and Dostoevsky was still publishing his *Diary of a Writer* in Meshchersky's *The Citizen (Grazhdanin)*. When (also in 1876) he launched it as a separate periodical, his younger confrère signalled support: 'Mr Dostoevsky's initiative will demonstrate again that among our writers there has begun a much more serious trend in the sense of the economic organization of literary labour'[32]—though notably without any endorsement of the ideological aspect of the venture. In fact, Boborykin took a generally independent if not critical stand on his colleague's opinions and pronouncements, as in a piece on the official celebration of literary jubilees published a month before:

> ...nor do I intend to avoid the issue and remain silent about F M Dostoevsky, a man who has worked tirelessly for more than 25 years, a man who has had to undergo great ordeals and who deserves sympathy for the services he has rendered in the past, no matter how strange the ideas he puts in his novels these days.[33]

While it is natural that Dostoevsky, now as much a public figure as a literary celebrity, should loom large in Boborykin's journalism during the 1870s, it is less easy to explain why Boborykin should come to play so particular a role in Dostoevsky's writing over this same decade. In part, this reflected the fact that, thanks to his regular despatches from Europe as foreign correspondent for a number of newspapers between 1867 and 1871, and again from 1873 to 1875, and to his Sunday feuilletons in *The St Petersburg News* (1875-1876) and other occasional pieces, as much as to the public lectures and critical studies which occupied more and more of his time and the novels, stories and plays which continued to flow from his pen, Boborykin had established a public profile he had not enjoyed before, and might at once be 'placed' with relative ease, whether as a disciple of Comte and Littré, an apologist for Zola, an indefatigable public lecturer, a champion of moderate westernist liberalism or the author of *Victim of the Evening (Zhertva vecherniaia)*, a 'scandalous' novel in which Saltykov-Shchedrin could find nothing but 'nymphomania and priapism'[34]—none of them roles likely to find particular favour with Dostoevsky. For the rest, through the conspicuous efforts of Burenin and his other detractors, Boborykin, notwithstanding the great seriousness with which he took himself, had become something of a comic creation, a favourite target of the satirists and epigrammatists who let pass few opportunities to mock dogged productivity so incommensurate with

---

[32][Boborykin], 'Voskresnyi fel'eton', *Sankt-Peterburgskie vedomosti*, 1876 (11 Jan), No. 11: 59; *PSS*, XXII (1981), 290-291.

[33]Boborykin, 'Novye ptitsy, novye pesni,' *Sankt-Peterburgskie vedomosti*, 1876 (18 May), No. 136; 'Voskresnyi fel'eton,' *Sankt-Peterburgskie vedomosti*, 1876 (29 February), No. 59; and *PSS*, XXIV (1982), 440.

[34][Saltykov], 'Novatory osobogo roda', *Otechestvennye zapiski*, 1868, 11, ii, 35.

native talent.[35] Both circumstances may have suggested the possibility of deploying some version of the Boborykin persona as one of Dostoevsky's most characteristic rhetorical devices or 'voices': the cipher created to embody some false premise or point of view, the man of straw set up to collapse under the weight of counter-argument or ridicule.

Already in *The Devils* (1871), Dostoevsky had permitted himself an oblique slighting remark at the expense of his fellow-novelist. In Part II, Chapter Six ('Pyotr Stepanovich is busy'), the younger Verkhovensky, when questioned by Karmazinov about his reading habits, confesses to having read a single work of Russian fiction: 'I believe I have read something. *Along the Road* or *By the Road* or *At the Crossroads*, or something of the kind. I can't remember. I read it a long time ago, five years or so'.[36] Although no published commentary on the novel seems to have taken it up, this must surely be a reference to Boborykin's first novel *On the Road!* whose protracted publication in monthly instalments in *The Reading Library* over three years attracted more than a little ribald comment at the time.[37] To recognize here only some general parodic play with the titles of certain 'anti-nihilist' classics (*Nekuda, Nakanune*)[38] is to overlook the more pointed irony of Pyotr Verkhovensky in contemplation of a novel which ends by calling on the youth of Russia to the 'new ideal' of a 'healthy, beautiful union' with the spiritual strength of the People.[39] Certainly, the comic possibilities of intertextual reference were not lost on Dostoevsky, who remarked in his notebook early in 1865 that: 'Mr Boborykin, having travelled the length of his *Road*, has reached the conclusion that he now has *Nowhere to go*...'[40]—a sally he presumably thought better of publishing, and certainly one more mordant than anything he himself had suffered at the hands of *The Reading Library*.

It was perhaps another of Boborykin's novels which preoccupied Dostoevsky when, in January 1873, having seen *The Devils* through its first publication in book form, he turned his attention to the next instalment of his writer's diary column for *The Citizen*. *Victim of the Evening*, a *succès de scandale* on its first (serial and book) publication in 1868 thanks to what were assumed to be thinly-disguised portraits of real personalities (as well as to rumours that only the personal intervention of the Sovereign had saved the novel from the censor)[41] had appeared in a second, 'revised and expanded' edition the previous summer.

---

[35] For a selection, see McNair, 'Persecution by Parody'.

[36] *PSS*, X (1974), 286.

[37] See McNair, 'Persecution by Parody', p. 116; book publication followed in 1864.

[38] See e.g. the notes and commentaries to the novel compiled under the editorship of G M Fridlender, *PSS*, XII (1975), 326.

[39] Boborykin, *V Put'-dorogu!* in his *Sochineniia* (St Petersburg: T-vo M.O. Vol'fa, 1884-1886), III, 418.

[40] *PSS*, XX (1980), 184 (and 372).

[41] See Liudmila Saraskina, 'Modnyi pisatel' v salone i doma (Versiia P D Boborykina)', *Znamia* (1988), 4, 205-219; esp. pp. 206-207.

Mikhailovsky's strictures notwithstanding, therefore, this tale of sexual abandon and moral depravity in the *haut monde* ran into none of the obstacles which frustrated Dostoevsky's attempts to publish Stavrogin's 'confession,' and his reflections on the contrast might well have inspired his macabre tale of immorality beyond the grave, 'Bobok'.[42] Whether or not the 'bold assonance'[43] linking the story's title with the name (or pseudonym or nickname) of Dostoevsky's fellow novelist was intentional, it has become part of the mythology of the story,[44] so that in ways hardly flattering for him Boborykin may forever be associated with the strange subterranean murmur of the waking dead, 'a single little word, meaningless of course, about some sort of bean', finally snuffed out by a sneeze and replaced by 'the true silence of the grave.'[45] Apart from that, however, there are other textual features suggestive of some conscious reference to Boborykin's work: for example, the name of the narrator-hero, the hack journalist Klinevich, contrives to suggest both Boborykin's sybaritic man of letters Dombrovich, and one of his companions in debauchery Baldevich (who according to his creator bore more than a passing likeness to the novelist Markevich);[46] while Avdotia Ignatievna, in proclaiming her desire to know no shame ('I desperately, desperately want not to be ashamed of anything'),[47] echoes not only Dombrovich's call to orgiastic abandon, but also the words of the Victim herself as she records her own excesses in her diary: 'I outdid them all! Not a drop of shame was left in me!'I was like a thing possessed'.[48]

If, as has been suggested, 'Bobok' in some sense pursues the account of this 'hellish scene' beyond the point where Boborykin's heroine, overcome by conscience and remorse, can write no more,[49] the point might be to underline the contrast between what, despite its generally unconvincing exposé of low life in high places, remains a conventionally 'progressive' tale touting the prospect of regeneration through education, emancipation and high-minded radicalism, and the infinitely more disturbing vision of a depravity that spares 'not even the final minutes of consciousness.'[50]

Boborykin's continued journalistic engagement with the topicalities of the day no doubt explains his gradual assimilation over the next three years into the rhetorical and ideological design of The *Diary of a Writer*. His name is a parti-

---

[42] Saraskina, pp. 216-217.

[43] Saraskina, p. 218.

[44] *PSS*, XXI (1980), 404-405.

[45] Dostoevskii, 'Bobok', *PSS*, XXI, 43, 51, 53.

[46] A contributor to Boborykin's *Biblioteka dlia chteniia*, Markevich was also known as 'Boboshka': *PSS*, XXI, 405.

[47] *PSS*, XXI, 52.

[48] Boborykin, *Zhertva vecherniaia. Roman v 4-kh knigakh*. 2 ed. (St Petersburg: N.A. Shigin, 1872), p. 169.

[49] Saraskina, p. 218.

[50] 'Bobok', *PSS*, XXI, 54.

cularly recurrent feature in drafts and jottings dating from the early months of 1876:

> ...The letter about our young folk. Right-wing, left-wing. Belinsky. Boborykin. Mikhailovsky and the Tuileries. On the instability of notions'
> ...Letter about young folk [going] to the people. Left, right. Vacillation. Left closer to the Slavophiles. Belinsky and Boborykin. Boborykin on my lyricism. But refuting himself...
> ...On our instability. I've promised to speak of it...
> right and left...right-left, à la Boborykin...[51]

In some way we can now only guess at, these fragments must relate to polemical exchanges inspired by the rise of populism and the impulse of young intellectuals to 'go to the people.' In common with most of the progressive and radical press, one of Boborykin's most successful Sunday feuilletons in the *St Petersburg News*, 'New Birds—New Songs' (May, 1876) had expressed solidarity with Dostoevsky's 'brilliant protest' in his *Diary* on behalf of 'the people' and his denunciation of 'Westernists' who would or could not recognize the moral superiority of the apparently 'backward' masses vis-à-vis 'the trumpery, falseness and worthlessness of the aristocratic cultural world.'[52] It seems to have been Dostoevsky's intention to have identified him with some new phase in the relationship between the intelligentsia and the people: the weakening of old shibboleths ('Belinsky', 'the left', socialism) perhaps, or the promise of some reconciliation between radicalism and slavophilism, or the emergence of some new enlightened 'middle way'; although whether this was a great leap forward or a further example of the 'instability [*shatanie*] of notions' is perhaps less certain. In the event, of course, the suggestion of a new ideological alignment 'à la Boborykin' was never presented to Dostoevsky's public in these terms, and the former eluded the notoriety that was often the lot of the latter's stooges and mouthpieces.[53] Yet Boborykin did not entirely escape the irony of immortalization at Dostoevsky's hands. In 1878, in what seems to be a curiously and gratuitously *ad hominem* jibe, Boborykin—or at least his alter ego—makes a brief appearance in a *Citizen* sketch as a piece of fountain statuary come to life:

> Some people expressed the view that it was some Pierre Bobo or other who had risen out of the water for original effect. Of course, this assumption could not be sustained, since Pierre Bobo would inevitably have emerged in morning dress complete with cravat, albeit a wet one. Whereas this triton was

---

[51] *PSS*, XXIV, 213, 218.

[52] *Sankt-Peterburgskie vedomosti*, 1876, 136 (May 18); see also *PSS*, XXII (1981), 301.

[53] For example, in this instance, the novelist V G Avseenko, Dostoevsky's chosen opponent in the anti-populist camp.

dressed precisely in the manner of classical statues, that is without any clothes at all.[54]

The comic distortion of his name was hardly anything new, and the presumed target of the satire—his dandyism and his penchant for recording the most recondite details of fashionable attire—were familiar enough objects of criticism,[55] but there is perhaps also a suggestion of exasperation or even malice in the intention to belittle a figure who in the final analysis cannot be taken seriously. If Boborykin was ever aware of this squib, he left no record of it.

While Dostoevsky's view of Boborykin finally resolved itself into the somehow unsatisfactory and ultimately ridiculous figure of Pierre Bobo, it was the more disturbing and intractable image of Nikolai Grigoriev which superimposed itself on Boborykin's attempts to inscribe Dostoevsky in his narratives of their interaction. Writing many years later of their first encounter, he found it worth noting that on that occasion his colleague 'did not produce on me the impression of a mystic or neurasthenic';[56] by the time of their third and final encounter, in the foyer of the Maly Theatre in Moscow, Dostoevsky's annoyance at some trifle or other 'revealed too plainly in him a sick man who could never hold himself in check.'[57] For the proponent of objective 'scientific-philosophic' criticism, the student of the 'psychology of creativity' and the advocate of 'sober realism' in art, Dostoevsky would remain irreconcilably a contradiction in terms, a great novelist 'fatally obsessed' in life as in art with the workings of 'unhealthy mental processes',[58] an obscurantist and metaphysician whose 'neoslavophilism of the soil' was so grotesquely at odds with the ideas for which he had suffered so much.[59] Unable to deny his talent, the younger writer could only condemn his 'mystical slavophilism' and express distaste for 'a good half of what is contained in *Crime and Punishment*';[60] confronted with the scenes surrounding the Pushkin speech and Dostoevsky's funeral, he could only concede that 'the author of *The Devils* not only forced everyone to forgive him everything, but at the end of his life became some kind of sage...popular in all circles and classes of Russian society.'[61]

---

[54]'Triton. Iz dachnykh progulok Kuz'my Prutkova i ego druga', *Grazhdanin*, 1878, 23-25 (10 Oct), 495-6; see also *PSS*, XXI (1980), 248-251 and 503-505.

[55]It is difficult to date the début in print of 'Pierrre Bobo', but it was certainly current by the end of the seventies. 'Skorobrykin' and 'Boborysak' appeared in 1875 and 1879 respectively (see McNair, 'Persecution by Parody', p. 114). Examples of satire directed at Boborykin's sartorial eccentricities include Burenin's drama *Rozy progressa* (1875; McNair, 'Persecution by Parody', pp. 117, 124). The term translated above as 'cravat', *fokoli*, is especially recherché.

[56]Boborykin, *Za polveka*, p. 391.

[57]Boborykin, *Za polveka*, p. 392.

[58]B.D.P. [Boborykin], 'Motivy i prremy russkoi belletristiki', *Slovo*, 1878, 6, 52.

[59]Boborykin, *Za polveka*, p. 281.

[60]Boborykin, *Za polveka*, p. 391.

[61]Boborykin, *Za polveka*, pp. 281, 282.

In this context, perhaps, it becomes easier to understand why in the essays in literary history and criticism which became an increasing part of his output in later years, Boborykin should have devoted so much energy to putting the record straight, to correcting posterity's judgement on Dostoevsky by dwelling at every opportunity on the inconsistencies, contradictions and discontinuities that characterized the biography of this 'neurasthenic' and tragically divided soul. His novels are found to be 'subjective'[62] or overloaded 'with a multiplicity of interpretations, tales-within-tales, authorial interventions.'[63] Critics err in propagating the facile view of Dostoevsky as heir to the 'humane realist' tradition of Gogol,[64] or like the Frenchman de Vogüé in making him the centre of a cult of the Russian Soul and glorifying 'this mixture of slavophilism and humanitarian piety' forged together by Dostoevsky from his Siberian experience:

> Here we have to do with a literary personality which would not in any country represent the general average, not even in Russia, where the contrasts in culture between the social classes—the intense religiosity of the masses, their conservative spirit and intellectual benightedness on the one hand, and on the other those profound movements which for half a century have fashioned the educated classes, and especially the young people of successive generations—do not rule out the existence of certain foundations which are much more normal, more healthy, more likely to promote the progressive growth of the nation taken as a whole.[65]

Boborykin's most comprehensive verdict on Dostoevsky (and on his literary contemporaries and compatriots in general) was no doubt intended to be the magisterial history of the Russian novel on which he worked between 1901 and 1914, and which survives only as an incomplete manuscript.[66] Implementing the complex and eclectic critical framework elaborated from the writings of Taine and Brunetière and Hennequin and other exponents of 'scientific criticism' for his earlier volume on the novel in Europe, Boborykin recapitulates arguments that are by now familiar: Dostoevsky's 'bio-psychological type' is distinguished by spiritual disharmony and neurasthenic extremes of feeling and thought, his popularity is attributed to the contradictory appeal of romantic humanitarianism and mystical nationalism, his style combines 'excesses of lyrical moralizing' and

---

[62] Boborykin, 'Motivy i priemy...', p. 48.

[63] B D P [Boborykin], 'Belletristy staroi shkoly', *Slovo*, 1879, 7, ii, 16.

[64] Boborykin, 'Sud'by russkogo romana', *Pochin: Sbornik obshchestva liubitelei rossiiskoi slovesnosti na 1895 g.*, (Moscow: Obshchestvo liubitelei rossiiskoi slovesnosti, 1895), p. 206.

[65] P. Boborykine, 'L'évolution du roman russe', *L'Humanité Nouvelle* 7, 1900, 421.

[66] P.D. Boborykin, *Istoriia evropeiskogo romana v XIX stoletii. Tom II: Sud'by russkogo romana*. Incomplete MS: IRLI RAN (Pushkinskii dom), Rukopisnyi otdel, R 1, op. 2, ed. khr. 274. See John McNair, 'P.D.Boborykin and his *History of the European Novel*,' *Irish Slavonic Studies*, 3 (1982), 14-38.

interminable passages of 'colourless' debate.[67] Circumscribing his idea of Dostoevsky in his narrative of the Russian novel, Boborykin too has learned to 'think in voices', and understood the importance, not of having the last word—how indeed could there be one?—but of ensuring (again in Bakhtin's phrase) the 'endlessness of dialogue'.[68]

---

[67]Boborykin, *Istoriia evropeiskogo romana*, II, [MS], 674 verso; 316; 461 verso.
[68]Bakhtin, p. 252.

PUBLIC EDUCATION IN ENGLAND IN THE PAGES OF *THE CITIZEN* (1873-1874) DURING DOSTOEVSKY'S EDITORSHIP

Irene Zohrab

A NUMBER of discoveries about the impact of British Protestantism in Russia during the nineteenth century, especially on Dostoevsky's *Diary of a Writer*, have been made by Malcolm Jones in a series of articles. These culminated in the chapter on 'Dostoevskii and Radstockism' in the volume *Dostoevskii and Britain* (1995).[1] In this tribute to Malcolm Jones the theme of education in England as represented in the pages of *The Citizen* (*Grazhdanin*) during Dostoevsky's editorship (where he also began his column *Diary of a Writer*) is examined further. It is a topic that is encountered in Dostoevsky's literary-political newspaper-journal more than once. In one of *The Citizen*'s most significant articles the teaching in some leading public schools in England is considered; also that in the charitable institution Christ's Hospital or the 'Blue Coat School' in London. It appeared in the review section of *The Citizen* where reviews of books and monthly 'thick' journals were published. The review was of the journal *Russian Messenger* (*Russkii vestnik*) for January, 1874. It was entitled 'Notes of an idle reader. *Russian Messenger* 1874, No. 1', signed: 'Pavel Pavlov'.[2] Its author was probably Prince V P Meshchersky, the owner-publisher of *The Citizen*, who on this occasion wrote under the pseudonym Pavel Pavlov.[3] The review article discusses the article in *Russian Messenger*, No. 1 on the topic

---

[1] Malcolm Jones, 'Dostoevskii and Radstockism', in *Dostoevskii and Britain*, ed. W J Leatherbarrow (Oxford/Providence, USA: Berg, 1995); See also Malcolm V Jones, 'Dostoevsky. Tolstoy, Leskov and "*Redstokizm*"', *Journal of Russian Studies*, 23 (1972), 3-20; M V Jones, 'A note on Mr J G Blissmer and the Society for the Encouragement of Spiritual and Ethical Reading', *Slavonic and East European Review*, 58 (1975), 92-96. See also passages *passim* in Malcolm V Jones, *Dostoyevsky after Bakhtin: Readings in Dostoyevsky's Fantastic Realism* (Cambridge: Cambridge University Press, 1990).

[2] 'Pavel Pavlov', 'Kritika i bibliografiia. Zametki dosuzhego chitatelia', *Russkii vestnik*, January 1874; *Grazhdanin* No. 9, (1874), 268-275. (Further references to this article are given with the abbreviation *Grazh.* and the cited page numbers in parentheses).

[3] V A Viktorovich, 'Dostoevskii i V P Meshcherskii (K voprosu ob otnosheniiakh pisatelia s okhranitel'nym legerem)', *Russkaia literatura*, No. 1 (1988), 205-216.

'Public education in England', which was signed with the initials KNM.[4] It is possible that they conceal the identity of M N Katkov (1818-1887), the publisher of *Russian Messenger* and editor of *Moscow News* (*Moskovskie vedomosti*),[5] who earned the reputation during the 1860s of being an 'anglophile'.[6]

But even before the appearance of this review, we find public education in Britain being championed as a brilliant example of 'foreign pedagogical activity' in the early issues of *The Citizen* during the first year of Dostoevsky's editorship. In the column 'Moscow Notes' (*Moskovskie zametki*), *The Citizen*, No. 8, 1873, the author advises readers to read the biographical sketch of the English pedagogue Thomas Arnold (1795-1842), 'headmaster of Rugby public school' (*Moskovskie vedomosti*, 1873, No. 17, 19, 20, 23, 27, 28): 'you will see what are, so to speak, strong social arguments in favour of classicism...you will see the whole vital educational significance of religious principles'.[7] It is stressed that under Arnold's system (unlike the St Petersburg example) 'vital, truly democratic convictions were organically unified with piety and adherence to classicism'. Dostoevsky would have seen these articles in Katkov's *Moscow News*, since in one of the same issues, No. 20, there appeared an unusually long advertisement about *The Citizen* (possibly written jointly by Dostoevsky and Prince Meshchersky), that included the contents of its third issue for the year 1873 and the Supplement volume for 1872.

The most vivid picture of public education in England and Arnold's activities is provided by the novel *Tom Brown's Schooldays* (1857) by Thomas Hughes. It was this work which was offered to subscribers of *The Citizen* in advertisements 'From the Editor', which were repeated over several months at the end of 1873 and the beginning of 1874.[8]

Apart from information about model examples of pedagogy in public schools like Harrow (which, *The Citizen* reminds us, Byron, Peel and Palmerston attended (*Grazh.*, 272)), Dostoevsky also published articles relating to popular and higher education in England. *The Citizen* No. 43 published an article 'Herbert Spencer on popular education', which was an excerpt from Spencer's

---

[4]'KNM', 'Obshchestvennoe vospitanie v Anglii. Iz dorozhnoi zapisnoi knigi', *Russkii vestnik*, 109 (January 1874), 244-268. (Further references to this article are given with the abbreviation *RV* and cited page numbers in parentheses).

[5]According to the supposition of V A Viktorovich in a personal communication to the present author.

[6]V P Meshcherskii, *Meshcherskii. Moi vospominaniia* (Moscow, 2001), p. 130. Katkov championed the study of classical languages, mathematics and scripture in education.

[7]'Moskovskie zametki', *Grazhdanin*, No. 8 (1873), 223.

[8]*Grazhdanin* (1873), No. 42, 46, 50, 52; (1874), No. 1. The advertisement declared that by the end of May 1874, *The Citizen* (*Grazhdanin*) would send all 1873 subscribers a copy of *Tom Brown's Schooldays*, translated from English, in two parts, and not just at a reduced price, but FREE OF CHARGE. All new annual subscribers to *The Citizen* for 1874 would also receive the novel free of charge.

latest work *The Study of Sociology*.[9] An exceptional example of 'higher education' in Britain was discussed in the pages of *The Citizen* in two studies devoted to J S Mill's *Autobiography*, which was published in London not long before this.[10] The principle of human development as a whole was discussed in *The Citizen* in a review of the works of Charles Darwin.[11]

There are grounds for supposing that Dostoevsky himself could have recommended to Meshchersky that he prepare a review about the January issue of *Russian Messenger*. It is known that Dostoevsky as an editor showed a special concern for the 'Criticism and bibliography' section and wished to introduce review articles on the latest journal issues as well as books.[12] He wrote about this to M P Pogodin,[13] and made requests about it to the regular critic N N Strakhov.[14] Likewise, the fact that *The Citizen* was preparing to send 1873 and 1874 subscribers a copy of the English novel *Tom Brown's Schooldays* could have been a stimulus to the intention of informing readers about the English system of education.

Many aspects of the article in *Russian Messenger* could have attracted Dostoevsky's attention. Some positive attributes relating to public education in Britain were possibly features which Dostoevsky wished to see in Russia also. For example, the article stresses that with the pupils of English schools a character engendered by a feeling of self-possession and awareness of one's responsibilities comes out in everything. Simultaneously with the development of mental and physical powers, everything in English schools is directed towards the development of independence of character and responsibility. (*RV*, 258) The

---

[9]'Gerbert Spenser o narodnom vospitanii', *Grazhdanin* No. 43 (1873), 22 October, 1150-1152. See also I Zohrab, 'Otnosheniia Dostoevskogo k britanskim Predvoditelem evropeiskoi mysli (Stat'ia vtoraia, "Dostoevskii i Gerbert Spenser")', *Dostoevskii i mirovaia literatura*, 19 (St. Petersburg, 2003), 105-121.

[10]'V', 'Kartina vysshego vospitaniia (Avtobiografiia Dzh. Stiuarta Millia)', *Grazhdanin*, No. 45 (5 November), 1190-1193. N N Strakhov, 'Avtobiografiia Dzh. Stiuarta Millia', *Grazhdanin*, No. 6 (1874), 12 February, 180-182. See also I Zohrab, '"Evropeiskie gipotezy" and "russkie aksiomy": Dostoevskii i Dzhon Stiuart Mill', *Russkaia literatura*, No. 3 (2000), 37-52.

[11]N N Strakhov, '"O proiskhozhdenii vidov" soglasno Charl'za Darvina', trans. S Rachinskii. 3 ed., corrected (Moscow, 1873); 'Zum Streit über den Darwinismus. Von K A Baer (aus der "Augsburger Allgemeine Zeitung")' (Dorpat, 1873); 'KE', 'On the controversy over Darwinism (from the Augsberger Allgemeine Zeitung)', *Grazhdanin*, No. 29 (1873), 809-812. Irene Zohrab, 'Dostoevskii and British Social Philosophers', in *Dostoevskii and Britain*, ed. W J Leatherbarrow (Oxford/ Providence, RI: Berg, 1995), pp. 177-206.

[12]As an editor and columnist Dostoevsky was always concerned about the criticism and bibliography section, taking an interest in the analyses of journals and literary columns. See V N Zakharov, 'Geneal'nyi fel'etonist', F M Dostoevskii, *Polnoe sobranie sochinenii: Kanonicheskie teksty* (Petrozavodsk: Petrozavodsk University Press, 2000), IV, 801-822 (p. 802).

[13]See Dostoevsky's letter to M P Pogodin: *PSS*, XXIX: 1, 262.

[14]'Ia eto delal po nastavleniiu Dostoevskogo'. See Strakhov's letter to Tolstoy of February 22, 1874, in *L N Tolstoi—N N Strakhov: Polnoe sobranie perepiski*, II, compiled L D Gromova and T G Nikiforova, ed. A A Donskov (Ottawa, 2003), p. 153.

basic foundations of English life, such as family and church, are reflected in the observances of schools, such as, for example, in the way pupils every day take part in 'edifying readings and exegesis of the Gospel and the apostolic letters'. (*RV*, 256) Respect for one's parents, for one's forefathers, for tradition is encouraged in the pupils, and this is expressed in the passing down of memories and remembrances. From the viewpoint of the modern reader the article gives quite a stereotypical picture of the spirit of old England, the foundations of society, family traditions and the 'general character of the people', about that England which had 'succeeded in attaining the height of power, glory and prosperity and performing a great service for the whole of humanity'. (*RV*, 245) At this point the author cites from a poem about England by the Slavophile Khomiakov:

> How brightly the crown of learning
> Glitters on thy head!
> How beautiful are the sounds of the songs
> Thou voicest to the world...
>
> How mightily over the waves
> Glides thy broad flag![15]

In *Russian Messenger*, KNM, the author of the article, attaches huge significance to the influence of Thomas Arnold represented in the novel *Tom Brown's Schooldays*, noting that 'England is indebted to him for a great deal in the cause of education'. (*RV*, 252) Mentioning all six 'public schools' in England,[16] he singles out Rugby (where the novel is set) as one of the most remarkable and which 'became renowned through the work of the great Arnold, and did much by its example to improve the system of education in other schools as well'. (*RV*, 246) The headmasters of English public schools were also ordained as pastors, delivered sermons in the school chapel and, as KNM writes, held 'a very visible position and now it has even become customary to select from amongst their ranks future bishops'. (*RV*, 252) Along with encouraging the educational significance of religious principles, they taught their charges independent thinking and judgment and, above all, the development of a moral sense. As was noted *The Citizen*: 'the entire system of English education is simply a matter of personalities and not institutions'. (*Grazh.*, 274) Arnold's

---

[15] A S Khomiakov, 'Ostrov' (1836): Beloved daughter of liberty/How thy nations teem,/How thy fields bloom!/How mightily over the waves/Glides thy broad flag!/How bloodily over land/The sword burns in thy hands!//How brightly the crown of learning/Glitters on thy head!/How exalted are the sounds of the songs/Thou voicest to the world!/All bathed in a glow of gold,/Illuminated by thought,/Thou art fortunate, thou art wealthy,/Thou art splendid, thou art strong./ And distant powers,/Timidly direct their gaze to thee, await/Await what rules thou/Wilt prescribe anew for their destiny?

[16] KNM mentions: Eton, Winchester, Westminster, Charterhouse, Harrow, Rugby: 'These schools provide preparation for university and correspond approximately to our gymnasiums'. (p. 246)

motto: 'It is not measures (*mery*) that are needed, but people' was also encountered in the pages of *The Citizen* (*Grazh.*, 272).

Even the very first paragraph of the review in *The Citizen* declared that such was the principle of this ancient school, which nurtures 'people who ardently love their homeland, people who are moral, developed, honest and endowed with a character which develops independently'. (*Grazh.*, 272) In Dostoevsky's works too one can meet an original transposition of Arnold's slogan (already well known by the end of the 1850s after the publication of the two-volume biography and correspondence of Arnold compiled by one of his pupils, Arthur Stanley).[17]

One of the most popular accounts of this book appeared in the journal *The Reading Library* (*Biblioteka dlia chteniia*) in 1858, when Dostoevsky was able to read this journal (in Semipalatinsk) and seemingly to be a subscriber for a time.[18] This book by Stanley was used by the compilers of the series of articles in *Moscow News*, No. 17, 19, 20, 23, 27, 28 (which are cited in *The Citizen*); they mention[19] that 'the following account was compiled predominantly from this latter book, and the compilers used the sixth edition, which came out in London in 1846 (it contains 746 pages of fine print and a portrait of Arnold)'. The series of articles was taken from the *Calendar of the Tsarevich Nikolai Lyceum (Kalendar' Litseia Tsesarevicha Nikolaia*) for the current year (1873), (while the authors of the Lyceum Calendar in turn also used Stanley's book).[20] The name of Arthur Penrhyn Stanley (1815-1881), the Dean of Westminster appeared rather often on the pages of *The Citizen* during Dostoevsky's editorship (especially after Stanley's arrival in Russia in early January, 1874 to officiate at the English wedding ceremony of Prince Alfred of Great Britain and the Grand Duchess Maria Alexandrovna).[21] *The Citizen* was the only paper to publish in full a series of sermons by Dean Stanley, a review of his book on the Eastern

---

[17] *Life and correspondence of Thomas Arnold, DD, late headmaster of Rugby School, and Regius Professor of Modern History in the University of Oxford*, by Arthur Penrhyn Stanley, MA, Fellow and Tutor of University College, Oxford, 2 vols. (London : B Fellowes, 1844).

[18] 'Pis'ma o vospitanii v Anglii (Doktora Vise)', *Biblioteka dlia chteniia* XI-XIV (1858), CXLIX, otdel II, No. 5, 116-206. (See also the same, pp. 206-217). Semipalatinsk apparently had a good library, because in Tver' Dostoevsky mentions 'there isn't even a decent library', *PSS*, XXVIII: 1, 337. In Semipalatinsk Dostoevsky subscribed to some journals, although by December 12 (24) 1858, he was no longer subscribing on the assumption that he would soon be leaving, *PSS*, XXVIII: 1, 318. Before his departure he gave A I Geibovich most of his library, which has not survived. See 'Neizdannye pis'ma Dostoevskomu', *Dostoevskii: materialy i issledovaniia*, II (Leningrad: Nauka, 1976), pp. 297-322 (p. 299-301).

[19] *Moskovskie vedomosti* (1873), No. 17, p. 4.

[20] Stanley's book had been already reissued 9 times by 1868.

[21] Irene Zohrab, 'Ob odnom intertekste v "Brat'iakh Karamazovykh"', *Evangel'skii tekst v russkoi literature XVIII-XX vekov*, III (Petrozavodsk: Petrozavodsk University Press, 1998), pp. 424-441. I Zohrab, 'Redaktorskaia deiatel'nost' F M Dostoevskogo v zhurnale '*Grazhdanin*' i religiozno-nravstvennyi kontekst "Brat'ev Karamazovykh' (k istorii sozdaniia romana)', *Russkaia literatura*, No. 1 (1996), 55-77.

church, as well as detailed reports of his activities and speeches in general (including the one to the Society of Devotees of Religious Enlightenment in St Petersburg).[22]

Thus *The Citizen* avowed the firm conviction that in every society in the matter of education, as in public order as a whole, what are needed are 'people, not rules *(mery)*'. In a series of articles of an editorial nature under the heading 'Unavoidable reflections', the subheading in the second section proclaimed: 'People, where are the people?'[23] What was discussed here was the relationship of contemporary reforms to people, including those in the field of education, and in conclusion it was acknowledged that 'in essence the matter not in any way lie in the lack of an institution, but in the people. There is a lack of people—that is what all our complaints boil down to...' (p. 1077) It is further noted that: 'The best people went from one reform to another, and compiled a chain of them; while the mass gathered as it could and where it could...These solitary individuals, remote from one another, actually comprise the force which is moving Russia ahead; they are tying the knot of a proper new life, and this life is beginning to produce strong shoots'. (p. 1080)

Dostoevsky himself in *Diary of a Writer*, in the chapter 'Dreams and reveries' wrote: 'People, people—this is the most essential need. People are dearer even than money.[24] In no market, and no matter for what amount of money, can people be purchased, because they are neither saleable nor purchasable, but again, they are evolved by centuries. A man of ideas and of independent learning, a man independently versed in business, is capable of being moulded only by the long independent life of a nation, its century-long labours full of suffering; in short, he is produced by the country's historical life in its totality'. (p. 607)

Dostoevsky persistently thought about the problem of 'the best people' *(luchshie liudi)*, combining hopes with fears, from the very beginning of his work on the *Diary of a Writer* of 1873 (see, for instance 'Environment' *(Sreda)* in *The Citizen*, No. 2) and later the novel *The Adolescent*, and still after that in 1876-1877.[25]

In the review in *The Citizen* great attention is given to a description of a school for the poor, 'Khristov priiut' (Christ's Hospital), which was situated in what was then one of the most dismal areas of London, not far from St Paul's Cathedral, in the centre of the City, 'where the irrepressible hum of London's

---

[22] *Grazhdanin* (1873), No. 27, 32; (1874), No. 2. 3, 5, 7, 8, 9, 12. See: Irene Zohrab, 'Dostoesvky's encounter with Anglicanism', *Australian Slavonic and East European Studies*, 10.2 (1996), 187-208.

[23] 'Neizbezhnye razmyshleniia', II, 'Liudi, gde zhe liudi?' *Grazhdanin*, No. 40 (1873), 1 October, 1077-1080. (Further references to this article are given in the text with the page number in parentheses).

[24] F M Dostoevskii, *Dnevnik pisatelia*, XI, 'Mechty i grëzy', *Grazhdanin*, No. 21 (1873), 21 May, 606-608.

[25] F Ia Galagan, 'Problema "luchshikh liudei" v nasledii F M Dostoevskogo (1873-1876)', *Dostoevskii: materialy i issledovaniia*, XII (St. Petersburg: Nauka, 1996), pp. 99-107.

working and business life does not abate, where the breath of a million panting, bustling busy people is stifled...' (*Grazh.*, 273) This part of London (not far from the 'toxic Thames' and in the neighbourhood of Whitechapel to the East, the Haymarket to the West, and Pentonville to the North) was familiar to Dostoevsky. It was here that he used to stroll by day and night during his stay in London in July 1862.[26]

Christ's Hospital was maintained from funds provided by donations from benefactors, who bore the title of governor and numbered up to 500. They had the right to choose the 'stipendiaries'—up to 700 boys aged between 14 and 19, mainly from poor families. Apart from this, in Hertford, close to London, the school had a primary division. It is mentioned that former pupils of Christ's Hospital included William Camden (1551-1623), Samuel Taylor Coleridge (1772-1834) and Charles Lamb (1775-1834). The day-to-day life of the pupils at Christ's Hospital is described in great detail, particularly their religious and physical education. The reader gains a full picture of the organization of the school, which was divided into sixteen wards, of the school infirmary, kitchen, dining room, swimming pool, bathhouse, etc. After lessons there were 'endless games, marching and gymnastics' for recreation, as well as swimming in a magnificent pool with crystal clear water. The author (KNM) is quoted as finally leaving Christ's Hospital in a very joyous disposition: 'since for me there was no more radiant and refreshing impression than the sight of the rising generation properly nurtured consciously and zealously being prepared to take our place, for the benefit of family, country and humanity...' (*Grazh.*, 274)

Perhaps the editorial decision to quote in full this particular section on Christ's Hospital was influenced by *The Citizen*'s policy of encouraging the maintenance of charitable institutions in Russia, as well as Dostoevsky's own interest in orphanages and institutions for adolescents.

The review in *The Citizen* concludes with a commentary on the author's (Pavel Pavlov's) doubts about the possibility of transferring the inclusion of physical education with its games, exercises and amusements 'to Russian soil': physical education in England is part of a whole: it is not possible to tear off one part and 'transfer it to us: it would be much more possible to transplant the whole system of English education to our soil than one part of it'. But this is also impossible because schools in Russia are run by institutions and bureaucrats: 'The spirit of our schools is the spirit of our bureaucratic institutions: it is not pedagogues who educate but bureaucrats, and what the children turn into are not individual personalities but bureaucratic mummies'. (*Grazh.*, 274)

On the other hand, in England, education is simply a matter of individual personalities. But even in Russia individuals are sometimes encountered: 'In the village of Ivanovo I saw a school run by a priest, where, I can assure you, the sons of workmen were physically and mentally developed to a level incompa-

---

[26]F M Dostoevskii, *Zimnie zametki o letnikh vpechatleniiakh*, PSS, V, 49-50 and 69-70.

rably higher than our gymnasium pupils; whereas the charter and statutes (*ustav*) of this school was minute compared to that of a gymnasium'. (*Grazh.*, 274)

In the opinion of KNM a lot of good things in England with regard to education are 'inaccessible for us. But, in my opinion, we must take some tips from England's centuries-long experience'. However, apart from the mental side it is necessary have a care also for the physical side, and the moral side. Schools in Russia sometimes have to overcome and struggle with the influence of family, because the family has been 'undermined'. On the other hand a lad of extraordinary gifts from the common people, when sent to the capital for tuition, discovers taverns and revelry and returns home 'fundamentally initiated into all the mysteries of the capital's civilization'. (*RV*, 268)

According to Dostoevsky in *The Citizen*, the availability of teachers committed to their calling, especially in the milieu of popular national education, was essential in post-reform Russia, when 'the people began revelling and drinking'. Teachers, especially schoolteachers who were coming into being, together with the temperance society could accomplish a great deal: 'even the poorest schoolteacher of some sort may accomplish a great deal by his initiative, if only he should wish to! Herein is the real point: that in this matter the personality and character are important; the businessman of the moment, one who is really exercising his will'.[27]

Dostoevsky's views on the attributes necessary for a good teacher largely coincided with Arnold's requirements for public education in England. What Arnold wanted to see in a teacher was a true Christian and apart from that a person who was well educated, active, blessed with common sense, who would be able to understand boys. 'In the first place he will be involved with the junior classes, for which reason I was about to say that I do not require special learning from him'.[28] Arnold said that a teacher must strive first and foremost for three goals in the cause of education. The first goal consisted in making the pupil a Christian in the most moral and highest meaning of the word. The second was to make him a gentleman in daily life, and the third was then to enrich his mind with various information. The last goal can be easily attained, if the instructor himself is educated and industrious, but the first two are not within the power of a pedagogue who undertakes the task without a fervent commitment to it.[29] 'In education the most important thing is the system of education, which gives the country people who are rational and courageous, and this should concern society a hundred times more than some idle talk about electoral rights'.

In the coverage of Arnold's life in *The Citizen*, No. 8, the first thing that is conveyed to the reader is the necessity of nurturing independence and morality

---

[27] F M Dostoevskii, *Dnevnik pisatelia*, XI, 'Mechty i grëzy', *Grazhdanin* (1873), 606-608.

[28] (A V Druzhinin) 'Doktor T. Arnol'd (Pribavlenie k pis'mam D. Vize)', *Biblioteka dlia chteniia* (1858), CXLIX, otdel II, No. 5, 206-217.

[29] Druzhinin, p. 212. (Further references to the article in *Biblioteka dlia chteniia* are given in the text with the page number in parentheses). See also *Moskovskie vedomosti*.

in the individual: 'a strict scholarly education always educates the character of the individual as well; it is reflected in the latter in the form of an independent moral cast of mind, a rational self-reliance. It is truth validated by century-old experience. And if, in our society, young people who, to quote the old Russian expression, have marred their human image, have recently been emerging from schools and are probably still doing so, whom is one to blame for this if not the school, whatever category it belongs to? But the listless, colourless character of the school remains such a historic charge against Russian society, which takes a frivolous attitude towards the goals, content and methods of education and instruction. And thus amidst this chaos of vague impressions, which the unsightly general picture of Russian schooling gives us (there are very few bright spots in it as yet), you can't help finding contentment in brilliant examples of foreign pedagogical practice'. (*Grazh.*, 223)

In *Russian Messenger* the importance of developing independence is also stressed: 'In this, however, as in everything, English life finds an invaluable support in the firmness of its own moral, political and social principles and in a profound sense of legality'. (*RV*, 258) Quoting Arnold according to Stanley's book, *The Reading Library* also says that the main thing in education is the development of independence, and self-perfection: 'the private individual and a small private world around him—such is the basis of true, beneficial reforms in the state'. (p. 209)

What emerges is that the independent, moral cast of the personality was always linked (in Arnold and in the pages of *The Citizen*) with a person's obligations or responsibilities. The foundation of all wisdom in young men, Arnold considered, lies in the fear of God, courage, and a clear view of a person's obligations. (p. 212) The basis of teaching talent is the ability to encourage and inspire in the pupil moral development and a sense of obligation or responsibility. In *The Citizen* it is noted that, although

> Arnold's entire life was given over to teaching children, at the same time he said the following: 'In comparison with the most modest step of moral development I set all human learning at naught'. Besides that, he studied all his life, was also a professor of modern history at Oxford and belonged with all his heart to the Whig party. (*Grazh.*, 223)

The author of the article in *Russian Messenger* was apprehensive that in Russia it was immensely difficult to do anything 'serious with regard to the moral aspect of education, because it depended on the religious, moral foundations of society'. (*RV*, 266-267) The author quotes the view of a partner in discussion from abroad on this question: 'No, it behoves us, it seems, to get down to a sober, basic restructuring *(perestroika)* or, where it is still possible, a consolidation of society's foundations, to start from scratch *(priniat'sia...za azy i za zady)*, as your people say. Es ist die höchste Zeit, as the Germans say...'. (*RV*, 268)

The article also says a lot about the environment of one of the 'most famous schools of England', Harrow: 'Who has not heard, if only by name, of this virtual pedagogical shrine of England' It is a nursery of great people in all fields of learning, arts, and civil activity in particular. Here Byron was educated, here were educated many who went on to gain great celebrity'. (*RV*, 246) It is said that in everything the pupils of Harrow manifest a character and a composure engendered by a sense of self-possession: 'It is apparent that each of them knows what he wants, knows where he is going, knows both the end and the means, as well as his rights and obligations'. (*RV*, 247)

On examining the schools the author comes face to face at every step with demonstrations of the fundamental bases of English life, church and family. In the school church the author turns his attention to the bronze and marble plates on the walls passing down from generation to generation the memory of teachers as well as of pupils already deceased. The author emphasizes repeatedly: that the school houses 'memories of former pupils at every step'. (*RV*, 247) 'The memory of former pupils is sacredly preserved by the school which nurtured them over the centuries for the encouragement and edification of new generations'. (*RV*, 247)

Finally, after discussing the influence of memory and remembrances on the world outlook of pupils, the author proceeds to a poetic examination of England as a wondrous emerald isle identified intertextually with the 'finest emerald gem, in a deep crown of sea'. Thus the metaphor of Khomyakov's gem is picked up by KNM and transferred to the grave stone on the terrace of Harrow cemetery, where Byron loved to sit and dream. Since those times his fellow countrymen in an endless procession have been visiting this national shrine and breaking off even just a small piece from the 'happy grave as a souvenir'. (*RV*, 249) The fact that England remembers and honours its great people is noted more than once by the author, and he cites it as an example to Russian young people.

All these Victorian motifs (linked with the representation of memory, religion, moral responsibility, grave stones and so on, that are also so abundant in *Tom Brown's Schooldays*) could have attracted the attention of Dostoevsky because several years later he constructs similar motifs with regard to moral responsibility, memory, Ilyusha's gravestone, and so on in *The Brothers Karamazov*.[30] (Unfortunately, it is not possible to discuss these constructs and correspondences here. It is worth noting however, that in the study *Slovar' iazyka Dostoevskogo (Dictionary of Dostoevsky's Language)* this terminology is not mentioned, apart from the word *pamiat'*. Purely mechanically, it is possible to check the presence and predominance of these words in the concordance).[31]

---

[30] Irene Zohrab, 'Dostoevsky and Protestantism: *Tom Brown's Schooldays* and *The Brothers Karamazov*', paper presented at the Eighth International Dostoevsky Symposium, Oslo, 1992.

[31] *Slovar' iazyka Dostoevskogo: Leksicheckii stroi idiolekta*, ed. Iu N Karaulov (Moscow, 2001), pp. 262-272; 'Konkordans proizvedenii Dostoevskogo':
<http://www.karelia.ru/~Dostoevsky/dostconc/alpha_e.htm>.

In *The Reading Library* the author of the article (A V Druzhinin), apparently via his own translation into Russian from a German adaptation, quotes from *Tom Brown's Schooldays* a scene in which the pupils reminisce about their former mentor Dr Arnold. (This scene appears in a completely different translation/adaptation in *The Citizen*'s version of *Tom Brown's Schooldays* published by A Transhel in 1874.) The pupils relate (in Druzhinin's early translation) how every year on the anniversary of Arnold's death, the school buildings are filled with visitors from all corners of England—old pupils of the great mentor come to pray and recall their school days at his grave:

> I still see before me that tall, energetic figure, I still hear that voice, now quite and tender, now sonorous and rousing, like the horns of our army's chasseur regiments. I remember how and what this voice spoke to us, when he talked to us every Sunday about God, love and truth, and the divine spirit and strength with which he, our mentor, was filled.
>
> The attentive rows of fresh children's faces stretched for several tiers in the chapel. There we all were, from children who had just parted with their homes and mothers the previous day to young men who faced in a week's time the prospect of plunging into all the cares of the big world...What compelled us to sit and listen so attentively, us restless kids, still incapable of understanding the grandeur of the words we were hearing?
>
> We barely understood half the Doctor's words, nor did we yet know the secrets of the human soul, or of our own souls. But we listened avidly, as children always listen to someone who is dear to them. We were vaguely aware that this man, with all his heart and all his strength, was opposed to what was unworthy, incorrect and unmanly in our little school world. It was not from some cold, inaccessible heights that the voice of our mentor rang out.
>
> His was the vital and fervent voice of a warrior battling for us and alongside us, bidding us to stand stoutly beside him and be prepared for everything. And gradually, slowly, but not tardily, life's true significance was revealed to each child for the first time, and he began to understand that our life was no heaven for sluggards and imbeciles, but a battlefield given to man by his creator, a field on which there were no spectators, but where young and old endure a struggle whose pledge is either life or death.
>
> And the one who told us this instructed us through all his words and his whole life on how we ought to struggle with life, and stood before us as our comrade-in-arms and leader. And there was no better leader in the whole world for an army of children because our leader never wavered, never gave a mute or ambiguous command, taught us never to give in to harsh untruth and come to terms with it. In this first childhood of ours, while still not understanding our spiritual obligations, we had faith in Doctor Arnold, and he, relying on this faith, taught us to believe in our Lord and Creator. (pp. 215-216)

In *The Citizen* it is said in conclusion that the Tsarevich Nikolai Lyceum (established by M N Katkov and P M Leontiev in Moscow in 1867-1868) is the sole purely English institution in Russia in which the headmaster does *everything he wants*. It is based on love for young people.[32] And, like English schools, the Tsarevich Nikolai Lyceum will bloom with a good director and deteriorate with a poor one: 'Just provide more opportunities to open such Lyceums and in fifty years we can reshape our up and coming generations'. (*Grazh.*, 274)

---

[32] For some background on Tsarevich Nikolai and his friendship with Prince Meshchersky, see Irene Zohrab, 'The correspondence between Prince V P Meshchersky and the Grand Duke Nikolai Alexandrovich. A friendship, its aftermath, and the creation of scandals', in *Slavic Journeys Across Two Hemispheres. New Zealand Slavonic Journal*, 37 (2003), 237-280.

DIALOGUES WITH DOSTOEVSKY IN TOLSTOY'S RESURRECTION

Sarah Hudspith

IT is well known that Lev Tolstoy made very few written comments about his contemporary Fyodor Dostoevsky. It is a reticence that has intrigued and puzzled many critics, given that the two giants of nineteenth-century Russian literature together invite studies of comparison and contrast in terms of their views, subject matter and artistry. Dostoevsky, conversely, had more to say about his rival, most notably concerning the latter's novel *Anna Karenina*, which he discussed at length in his *Diary of a Writer*. In this series of reviews, he praised the author for the mastery of the scene of reconciliation at Anna's bedside and called the novel 'a fact of special importance' for its 'Russian' response to the theme of guilt and transgression.[1] It was because of the 'special importance' he attributed to this scene that his disappointment at Tolstoy's handling of the 'Eastern Question' in Part Eight of the novel was so acute: he could not reconcile the novel's overall message of compassion with Levin's refusal to understand those who volunteered for active service in sympathy for the suffering of fellow Slavs. Tolstoy made no published direct response to Dostoevsky's criticisms. However, it may be said that despite the lack of specific comments, Dostoevsky and his works frequently occupied a crucial position in Tolstoy's thought and writings. Robert Louis Jackson writes of 'Tolstoy's deep interest in, and involvement with, Dostoevsky's work', and notes: 'That interest, finally, is fully disclosed not so much in Tolstoy's casual remarks about Dostoevsky but in his fictional works. Here we find convincing evidence of his creative dialogue with Dostoevsky.'[2] I would like to examine such dialogues in Tolstoy's last novel, *Resurrection*.

Of all Dostoevsky's works, *Notes from the House of the Dead* was the one that Tolstoy admired most. It is natural, given its subject matter, that he should re-read it in preparation for writing his own story of convicts, retribution and repentance. This of course was territory that Dostoevsky had very much made his own, not only with *The House of the Dead* but also with *Crime and Punishment*. The latter novel also has its role to play in the development of *Resurrection*. Tolstoy had read the work at least once; he admired it, particularly the first part; he discussed it with G A Rusanov when the latter visited Yasnaya Polyana in

---

[1] *PSS*, XXV, 198-202. All translations of extracts from *Diary of a Writer* are taken from Fyodor Dostoyevsky, *A Writer's Diary*, 2 vols., trans. K Lantz (London: Quartet, 1994-1995).

[2] R L Jackson, *Dialogues with Dostoevsky: The Overwhelming Questions* (Stanford, CA: Stanford University Press, 1993), p. 112.

1883,[3] and an 1884 edition of the novel is among one of the most annotated of the volumes of Dostoevsky's work in Tolstoy's personal library.[4] Moreover, in his 1890 essay on the moral damage caused by tobacco, alcohol and other narcotics, 'Why do Men Stupefy Themselves?', which was written concurrently with *Resurrection*, Tolstoy used Dostoevsky's Raskolnikov as an example of how the simplest decisions may affect the course of events, thus necessitating a constant sharpness of mental and moral faculties. An engagement with *Crime and Punishment* is therefore not unlikely in *Resurrection*, and evidence of this can be found.

During their initial acquaintance, Nekhliudov gives Maslova classics of literature to read, among which are novels by Dostoevsky and Turgenev. In the early drafts of *Resurrection*, Tolstoy specifies that the Dostoevsky work is *Crime and Punishment*. Subsequent drafts transfer the gesture to after Maslova's conviction, when Nekhliudov gives her an unspecified work by Dostoevsky (here *The House of the Dead* might be more appropriate). The finished version reverts back to the giving of a Dostoevsky novel (this time not named) before Maslova's seduction. It is possible to attach some significance to the fact that Tolstoy originally placed *Crime and Punishment* as that work, when one remembers that 'Why do Men Stupefy Themselves?' was written alongside *Resurrection*. It presents an interesting subtext in Tolstoy's novel, and suggests that its relationship to *Crime and Punishment* functions as more than the epilogue suggested by George Steiner.[5]

In 'Why do Men Stupefy Themselves?' Tolstoy, likening the conscience to a compass or a Swiss watch, explains how this precision instrument inside each of us points in one true direction, and how easy it is to deviate from the course it shows. He takes the example of Raskolnikov, and demonstrates that long before he committed his murder, Raskolnikov was already drifting off course in the tiny decisions governing his day-to-day life.

> He lived his true life when he was lying on the sofa in his room, deliberating [...] whether he ought to live in Petersburg or not, whether he ought to accept money from his mother or not, and on other questions not at all relating to the old woman. And then—in that region quite independent of animal activities—the question whether he would or would not kill the old woman was decided.[6]

---

[3]G A Rusanov, 'Poezdka v Iasnuiu polianu', *Tolstovskii ezhegodnik* (1912), 51-87 (p. 60).

[4]*Biblioteka L'va Nikolaevicha Tolstogo v Iasnoi poliane: Bibliograficheskoe opisanie*, ed. V F Bulgakov, I (Moscow: Kniga, 1972), pp. 268-70.

[5]G Steiner, *Tolstoy or Dostoevsky: An Essay in Contrast* (London: Faber and Faber, 1980), p. 93.

[6]L N Tolstoi, *Polnoe sobranie sochinenii*, 91 vols, ed. V G Chertkov et al. (Moscow: Gosudarstvennoe izdatel'stvo khudozhestvennoi literatury, 1928-1958), XXVII, 280. All translations of extracts from 'Why Do Men Stupefy Themselves?' are taken from Leo Tolstoy, *Recollections and Essays*, trans. A Maude (London: Oxford University Press, 1937).

Raskolnikov could not be expected to know, of course, that the outcome of these decisions could lead him to murder, but Tolstoy implies in 'Why Do Men Stupefy Themselves?' that if one does not smother one's conscience with drugs, pride or selfishness, then one will make the correct choice in those vital day-to-day decisions without even really being aware of it. Care should be taken to note that Tolstoy does not intend that once Raskolnikov had made those critical, seemingly trivial decisions, from then on there was no going back. In fact he is suggesting how long ago Raskolnikov began to deviate from the course indicated by his conscience compass; his decisions at the points indicated by Tolstoy makes it easier to follow the direction away from the compass at the next moment of decision, but it is still possible to turn back to the correct path.

Here, Tolstoy's interest is in responsibility for one's actions. This is an area of his world view that demands cautious and meticulous attention. We know from his analysis of history in *War and Peace* that Tolstoy does not view the question of human actions in polarized terms of either freedom or necessity, but in terms of the relationship between necessity and the reality of a consciousness of free will. He writes: 'Reason gives expression to the laws of necessity. Consciousness gives expression to the reality of free will. [...] Only by uniting them do we get a clear conception of the life of man.'[7] This is why he states in 'Why Do Men Stupefy Themselves?' that discussion on the question of free will or determinism is 'superfluous for my purpose' and 'a question in my opinion not correctly stated.' Instead, he argues: 'We must, as far as it depends on us, try to put ourselves and others in conditions which will not disturb the clearness and delicacy of thought necessary for the correct working of conscience';[8] in other words, Raskolnikov was, at least to some extent, responsible for his decisions and their outcomes.

In *Resurrection*, the theme of responsibility is strongly associated with both Nekhliudov and Maslova: they each have opportunities to make alternative decisions that would lead to a more positive course of events for them. If we envisage that the Dostoevsky novel given by Nekhliudov to Maslova was *Crime and Punishment*, then it is plausible that it functions as a symbolic indicator of the importance of making the right decisions. Maslova, for instance, initially had the option of a frugal, yet respectable life as a peasant's wife. After her seduction, although her options became more limited, she could have chosen the physically demanding, yet honest work in her aunt's laundry. The subtext becomes more evident in comparing and contrasting the decision-making processes leading up to Raskolnikov's crime and Nekhliudov's immoral act. In the case of Raskolnikov, it is easy to see why the imagery of the compass occurred to Tolstoy, since Dostoevsky's hero wanders in confusion through the streets of Petersburg, as he tries to decide, both literally and morally, which path to take. Should he 'find a way out in the person of Razumikhin', or 'is *that* really

---

[7]Tolstoi, *PSS*, XXII, 336.

[8]Tolstoi, *PSS*, XXVII, 281. For a fuller discussion of this question, see I Berlin, 'The Hedgehog and the Fox', in *Russian Thinkers* (Harmondsworth: Penguin, 1979), pp. 22-82; and G S Morson, *Hidden in Plain View: Narrative and Creative Potentials in War and Peace* (Stanford, CA: Stanford University Press, 1987), p. 92.

going to happen?'[9] Crucially, the choice between fulfilling or abandoning his murderous plan is before him right until the last moment, but Raskolnikov is so out of touch with his conscience-compass that he interprets this not as a decision for which he is responsible, but as fate. He constantly asks himself, 'Is it really going to happen?' After his dream of the beaten mare, in which his stifled conscience shows him the full horror of his intention, he experiences a sense of release: 'Freedom, freedom! Now he was free from that sorcery, that witchcraft, that fascination, that infatuation!'[10] By seeing his idea as an external force that held him in its power, he fails to realize that the choice cannot go away until he has actively made a decision, so when he learns that Lizaveta will not be at home (thanks to his seemingly unconnected decision to return to his apartment via the Haymarket), he feels powerless: 'His mind was completely empty, and he was quite incapable of filling it with anything; but with his whole being he suddenly felt that he no longer possessed any freedom of thought or of will, and that everything had suddenly been decided once and for all.'[11]

The disordered ramblings and dialogues that pass through Raskolnikov's mind represent a highly complex struggle with conscience. When not viewing his plan as something separate from his will, he sees it as a statement about his capabilities, hence his other frequent question, 'Am I really capable of this?' Here, pride is the dominant note, for an answer in the negative all too frequently reflects not the triumph of conscience but his own hatred of himself and his frustration at his inability to come up with a more glorious idea: 'Oh God! How loathsome all this is! [...] It shows what filth my heart is capable of, though.'[12] Alcohol quickly restores what he believes to be clarity of purpose: 'One glass of beer, a *sukhar'*—and in a single moment the mind gains strength, one's thoughts grow lucid and one's intentions firm!'[13] On the other hand, when his conscience does make itself felt it is not in conscious dialogue but in dreams and instinctive gestures, such as leaving money for the Marmeladovs and helping the abused girl in the street. This demonstrates how apparently unrelated incidents are in fact closely connected to the vacillations in his moral trajectory. So Dostoevsky, that well-known advocate of man's fundamental freedom of will, chooses to emphasize Raskolnikov's blindness to his conscience and his perception of what appears to him to be necessity. It is through conversations with Sonya and Svidrigaylov that the issue of free will in Raskolnikov's act is elucidated.

By contrast, Tolstoy's technique is considerably more explicit. When describing Nekhliudov's preparation to seduce Maslova, he makes the dialogue with conscience more prominent so as to emphasize the element of responsibility. After a formative three years of army service, during which he has acquired a taste for alcohol,

---

[9] *PSS*, VI, 44-45. All translations of extracts from *Crime and Punishment* are taken from Fyodor Dostoyevsky, *Crime and Punishment*, trans. D McDuff (Harmondsworth: Penguin, 1991).
[10] *PSS*, VI, 50.
[11] *PSS*, VI, 52.
[12] *PSS*, VI, 10.
[13] *PSS*, VI, 11.

Nekhliudov makes the decision to call on his aunts and renew his acquaintance with Maslova. Tolstoy indicates that already Nekhliudov is moving closer to his immoral act: 'Perhaps in his inmost heart he had already formed those evil designs against Katyusha which the brute beast in him suggested, but he was not conscious of this intention.'[14] On the eve of the seduction, Nekhliudov's conscience pricks him in the form of a dim feeling that for some reason he ought to leave his aunts, but instead he chooses to attend the midnight Easter service. This, it might be assumed, would be a step in the right direction. But beneath the surface of this ostensibly virtuous act, his animal self continues to steer him away from the right course. He thinks of something trivial to say to Maslova, so that he might come close to her in church. Even this apparently insignificant decision edges him nearer to the point of his crime. The voice of conscience continues to plead with him, but his determination grows. As with Raskolnikov, his pride is one of the key elements in bolstering his resolve: 'he did not realize that this uneasiness and shame were the finest qualities of his soul begging for recognition, whereas, on the contrary, he thought it was only his stupidity, and that he ought to behave as everybody else did'.[15] Nekhliudov also suffers a degree of physical discomfort; although his symptoms are not as developed as Raskolnikov's feverishness, he experiences restlessness, a pounding heart and laboured breathing. After the act, his choice of words indicate that like Raskolnikov he evades the thought of his personal responsibility and prefers to think instead in terms of fate: 'Has a great happiness or a great misfortune befallen me?'[16]

Tolstoy's protagonist differs most from Raskolnikov in one significant way. A key factor in Raskolnikov's deviation from the morally right course is his isolation. The more he indulges his tendency to aloofness and scorns company of any kind, the more he succumbs to the 'outrageous but seductive daring'[17] of his idea. Hence the importance of his hesitation over whether to visit Razumikhin before the murder. The isolation in which Dostoevsky places Raskolnikov helps to underscore his freedom of will in murdering Alyona and Lizaveta. Conversely, Nekhliudov finds himself becoming more morally corrupt the more he allows himself to follow the example of his peers. It is the gradual persuasion of his army colleagues to give in to drink, gambling and womanizing that leads to the moral erosion resulting in his seduction of Maslova. Here Tolstoy is pointing to the interrelationship of freedom and necessity. This contrast between the effect of isolation and the influence of others forms the crux of a divergence between Tolstoy and Dostoevsky, and underlies a further dialogue with Dostoevsky in *Resurrection*, this time with *Diary of a Writer*. It centres on the question of the environment as a factor in giving rise to crime.

Following Dostoevsky's criticism of *Anna Karenina* in *Diary of a Writer*, it might be expected that Tolstoy would react in his diaries or letters. There is no such direct reaction, but we should not take this to mean that Tolstoy was not familiar with *Diary of a Writer* or the articles on his novel. In 1883 he wrote a long letter to M A

---

[14] Tolstoi, *PSS*, XXXII, 50-51.
[15] Tolstoi, *PSS*, XXXII, 58-59.
[16] Tolstoi, *PSS*, XXXII, 63.
[17] *PSS*, VI, 7.

Engelhardt on the question of non-violent resistance to evil, and here, obviously referring to the *Anna Karenina* criticism, he mentioned that he found what Dostoevsky wrote on the subject repugnant.[18] Later, his diary from 1910 records the receipt from N N Gusev of a letter the latter had written to A K Chertkova, discussing not only Dostoevsky's *Anna Karenina* criticism but also his *Diary* article on the environment theory. Tolstoy's reaction is thus: 'Gusev sent me his letter about Dostoevsky; as it happens it says just what I feel.'[19] Tolstoy was not keen on *Diary of a Writer*, and whereas he was happy to re-read many of Dostoevsky's fictional works, when he was brought the *Diary* to read in 1909, he refused it, saying that he found it a difficult read.[20] Nevertheless, the themes and ideas concerning crime, the environment and justice in the *Diary* would undoubtedly have been of great interest to Tolstoy, and there is evidence for reading *Resurrection* as a polemical engagement with *Diary of a Writer*.

In the 1873 *Diary* article 'Environment', Dostoevsky discusses jury trials and the moral considerations involved in judging one's fellow man. Using one of his favourite techniques, he imagines a conversation with several speakers, and offers replies to their points of view. One of the imaginary voices argues thus:

> We have been frightened by this dreadful power over human fate, over the fates of our brethren [...]. We sit as jurors and think, perhaps: 'Are we any better than the accused' We have money and are free from want, but were we to be in his position we might do even worse than he did—so we show mercy'.[21]

Nekhliudov has a very similar thought as he reflects on the prison population and the reasons for their imprisonment:

> The second category was made up of persons sentenced for crimes committed in peculiar circumstances: while drunk, for example, or in a fit of passion or jealousy, and so on—crimes which those who sat in judgement and meted out punishment would almost certainly have committed themselves in like circumstances.[22]

Nekhliudov's implication is as expressed by Dostoevsky's imaginary interlocutor: that if we might do the same ourselves, we have no right to judge. However, Dostoevsky's answer to such a view is that those who feel they do not have the right to judge are simply shying away from a painful and difficult moral duty. He argues that the pain of the heart caused by recognition of one's own capacity for crime, one's unworthiness to judge, and by sympathy for the criminal being

---

[18] Tolstoi, *PSS*, LXIII, 114. The editors note that Tolstoy was making reference to a letter written by Engelhardt to Ivan Aksakov, in which the *Diary* articles were mentioned explicitly.

[19] Tolstoi, *PSS*, LVIII, 122. (My translation.) Gusev's letter to Chertkova is reproduced in Tolstoi, *PSS*, LVIII, 554-555.

[20] Tolstoi, *PSS*, LVII, 388.

[21] *PSS*, XXI, 15.

[22] Tolstoi, *PSS*, XXXII, 311.

punished, is the rightful punishment and necessary burden for those who sit in judgement: 'If this pain is genuine and severe, then it will purge us and make us better. And when we have made ourselves better, we will also improve the environment and make it better'.[23] Igor Efimov remarks that in *Diary of a Writer* Dostoevsky is interested in the question of how to reconcile the Christian demand for unlimited mercy with the necessity of protecting the weak from evil. As this is a choice between two noble things, he offers no easy answers.[24] Instead, by comparing and contrasting a variety of contemporary domestic and child abuse cases, he demands, in Boris Sorokin's words, 'compassionate involvement' in the judging process.[25]

Nekhliudov also identifies other types of criminal in his analysis. He notes that there are some who commit acts which they do not consider to be crimes, such as gathering firewood on private land, but who are therefore deemed criminals by the men whose arbitrary decisions made the laws. There are others who are considered criminals only because they oppose the authorities, such as strikers, sectarians and oppressed minorities, but who in Nekhliudov's opinion are morally 'head and shoulders above the common run of society'. Finally there are the criminals who he categorizes as 'more sinned against than sinning', because 'the conditions under which they lived seemed to lead on systematically to those actions which are termed crimes'.[26] Here Nekhliudov is making a statement about the role of the environment in driving these people to crime. Dostoevsky discerns a similar point of view in his imagined debate. He argues that to acquit a man so as to avoid a burdened conscience can encourage the view that the criminal is not to blame, and thus the theory that the environment is to blame takes hold: 'We inevitably reach the point where we consider crime even a duty, a noble protest against the environment. "Since society is organized in such a vile fashion, one can't get along in it without protest and without crimes"'.[27] For Dostoevsky, to say that a criminal was driven to his crime by his social environment is tantamount to denying his essential moral freedom and thereby his humanity.

However, we must remember that Tolstoy approaches human actions not in terms of either freedom or environment theory, but in terms of 'both/and'. *Resurrection* can be viewed as an attempt to answer Dostoevsky's objections to man's avoidance of judging his fellow man on the grounds of denying his free will. Nekhliudov realizes that all those in positions of power over others, including those involved in the judicial process, are corrupted by their power, not

---

[23] *PSS*, XXI, 15.

[24] I Efimov, 'Nesovmestimye miry: Dostoevskii i Tolstoi', *Zvezda*, 11 (2002), 187-192 (p. 189).

[25] B Sorokin, 'Dostoevsky on Tolstoy: The Immoral Message of *Anna Karenina*', *Connecticut Review*, 6: 2 (1973), 25-33 (p. 29).

[26] Tolstoi, *PSS*, XXXII, 311-312.

[27] *PSS*, XXI, 16.

purified as Dostoevsky would have it. For Tolstoy, man's judgement of another will always be flawed because, just as it is impossible for historians to know the infinite number of events in the causal chain and the impact of seemingly insignificant events on the course of history, so it is impossible to unravel the interconnecting circumstances and decisions that result in a crime. For example, nobody really knows what caused the teenage Fedosia to attempt to poison her husband, shortly after their marriage. Whereas Dostoevsky deplores the verdict of a village court who advised a woman and her abusive husband to 'learn to live together',[28] Tolstoy demonstrates that whilst awaiting trial, Fedosia and her husband did indeed learn to live together and fell in love, and yet in spite of their improvement in relations, Fedosia is punished for her crime. In breaking Christ's commandment not to judge one another, we try to do what only God is capable of, and this is what damages our humanity. Therefore, *Resurrection* is populated by portraits of morally disfigured judges, prison superintendents and politicians, all of whom believe that they have the right to dispose of people's lives, and that their victims deserve such treatment.

Another aspect of crime upon which Tolstoy engages with Dostoevsky is the traditional Russian practice of referring to crime as a 'misfortune' and the criminal as an 'unfortunate'. Dostoevsky identifies this as an instinctive idea of the Russian *narod* that recognizes both the guilt and the humanity of the criminal, through the notion that each is responsible for all. But he warns in 'Environment' that this noble instinct may be misrepresented by proponents of the environment theory, who would argue that the criminal is 'unfortunate' because not he but the environment is to blame. He asserts that if this interpretation of the misfortune of crime leads to acquittals, then the consequences will be serious: 'You only plant cynicism in their hearts; you leave them with a seductive question and with contempt for you yourselves'.[29] He tackles the point made by Nekhliudov that some may not regard as crimes certain acts which are committed in opposition to or as a result of social conditions:

> What if the criminal, consciously preparing to commit a crime, says to himself: 'There is no crime!' Will the People still call him an 'unfortunate'? Perhaps they would; in fact they certainly would. The People are compassionate, and there is no one more unfortunate than one who has even ceased to consider himself a criminal: he is an animal, a beast. And what of it if he does not even understand that he is an animal and has crippled his own conscience? He is only doubly unfortunate. Doubly unfortunate, but also doubly a criminal.[30]

For Dostoevsky, an awareness of mutual responsibility should not undermine recognition of the individual's personal responsibility for his own acts.

---

[28] *PSS*, XXI, 20.
[29] *PSS*, XXI, 19.
[30] *PSS*, XXI, 18.

Tolstoy makes his most overt engagement with Dostoevsky in *Resurrection* on this issue. It comes in the form of an incident involving a minor character by the name of Makar Devkin. Some research has already been done in this area. M I Varets notes not only the similarity of name to that of the hero of Dostoevsky's *Poor Folk*, but also that Tolstoy's Devkin is imprisoned for attempted murder with an axe, that he experiences a 'double' in the inner voice urging him to commit his crime, and that in prison he is involved with an instance of 'name-swapping', a practice Dostoevsky recorded in *The House of the Dead* whereby one convict persuades another to change places with him in order to receive a lighter punishment.[31] Whilst these points are evidence of a dialogue with Dostoevsky, I would place more emphasis on one question mentioned by Varets only in passing, namely the association of Devkin with the notion of crime as a misfortune.

Devkin figures as an example of the phenomenon Dostoevsky speaks of in *The House of the Dead* where a man who has lived quietly and morally for many years may suddenly act in a manner totally out-of-character and commit a crime. For Dostoevsky, such sudden outbursts are desperate but vain attempts to express the perpetrator's frustrated and humiliated individuality. In Devkin's case there is no such psychological insight. We learn only that he is a man of previous good character, who abruptly succumbs to the temptation, voiced, as he believes, by the Devil, to murder a wealthy peasant he is accompanying to a nearby town. His attempt is foiled and he meekly submits to his punishment. In prison he demonstrates his moral qualities by risking his life to save a convict fooled into swapping his name with another due to receive a harsher sentence. The incident in the final version of *Resurrection* occupies no more than one very short chapter, but Varets points out that in earlier drafts Tolstoy devoted more space to the episode. Originally, he included more detail about Devkin's motives, that he needed the money to establish his own household and become independent from his father with whom he quarrelled, and that Devkin's attention was firmly fixed on theft. Varets also notes that one draft included the following comment: 'He was one of those convicts who more visibly than others confirmed for Nekhliudov the truth that crime is not essentially a result of corruption or an evil will, as it is said, but an occurrence of misfortune'.[32] Alongside the original detail about Devkin's financial and domestic troubles, it could be argued that this statement might allow the interpretation that Devkin's crime was a misfortune because he was driven to it by his social circumstances. It is plausible that Tolstoy stripped away those details and sharpened his focus on the uncharacteristic nature of Devkin's crime in order to head off any criticisms of the kind voiced by Dostoevsky in *Diary of a Writer*.

---

[31] M I Varets, '"Zapiski iz mertvogo doma" i epizod v romane "Voskresenie" (po materialam neopublikovannykh rukopisei)', *Filologicheskie nauki*, 4: 124 (1981), 62-65.

[32] Varets, p. 64. (My translation.)

Yet Tolstoy's understanding of the misfortune of crime is different from Dostoevsky's. Devkin is an 'unfortunate' because he has been sentenced to four years' hard labour, in spite of his hitherto upright life. Nekhliudov sees that his generosity of spirit in trying to save the 'swapped' convict is evidence of a lofty moral character, which should have the opportunity of developing and making a difference in the world. But because he has been judged, Devkin's potential is severely hampered. Nekhliudov reflects:

> In the light of what was done to them, people who had been in prison came to see and realize with every fibre of their being that all the moral laws of respect and compassion for man preached by religious and moral teachers were set aside in real life, and that therefore there was no need for them to adhere to them either. Nekhliudov noticed evidence of this in all the convicts he knew: in Fedorov, Makar [Devkin], even in Tarass [...].[33]

Once again, Tolstoy takes issue with Dostoevsky's belief that judgement of criminals is a necessary response to crime, because in his view, those who in spite of their crimes might otherwise be capable of worthy contributions to society, are labelled as evil by the criminal justice system and put in conditions where their moral qualities are eroded.

Therefore in *Resurrection* Tolstoy takes up the debate about crime upon which Dostoevsky had dwelt in so much detail and subtlety in his works. He acknowledges the issue of personal responsibility elucidated in *Crime and Punishment*, but he challenges Dostoevsky's arguments against the theory of environment by demonstrating how human judgement is flawed and how it disfigures not only the condemned but also those who condemn. This is in line with his similar critique of history in *War and Peace*. Had Dostoevsky lived to see the publication of *Resurrection*, he would no doubt have responded. He may have remarked that *Resurrection* lacks the truly evil convicts like Gazin and Aristov who commit crimes for pleasure and spite, and that analysis of such characters plays a vital part in the debate about judgement. I feel certain that he would have taken issue with Nekhliudov's five categories of convict, because of the words he gave to Dmitry Karamazov: 'Man is broad, too broad.'[34] Whereas Tolstoy spoke on behalf of the potential for good in everyone, Dostoevsky warned of the corresponding presence of evil in each of us, and of the need to act in defence when that evil was expressed. Tolstoy once described 'the whole of' Dostoevsky as 'struggle'.[35] Dostoevsky almost certainly would have agreed, and then added that so are we all.

---

[33]Tolstoi, *PSS*, XXXII, 412.

[34]*PSS*, XIV, 99 (my translation).

[35]Tolstoi, *PSS*, LXIII, 142. The remark was made in Tolstoy's reply to Strakhov's attack on Dostoevsky's moral character. For more information, see Jackson, pp. 104-120.

DOSTOEVSKY IN THE LECTURES AND CONVERSATIONS OF MERAB MAMARDASHVILI

Vladimir Tunimanov

MERAB Mamardashvili is, as is generally accepted today, a significant figure: an outstanding lecturer and educator, and a refined aesthete. He is recalled with gratitude by those who had the pleasure of hearing the philosopher who, rather than familiarizing the auditorium with the history of the development of science in its 'progressive' movement from the old European materialists and idealists to the radiant 'heights' of Marxism, instead in the most direct sense taught his students to think, taught the art of being a free citizen. He became free himself, crossing the difficult path to true knowledge, together with his listeners, who were encumbered with numerous internal obstacles, which resulted in stagnant habits and routine, stereotypical thinking. A master of oral genres, he found inspiration in conversation, needing retorts, objections, questions; he would declare openly in the middle of lectures, 'I am simply discussing this out loud with you now, and am in no way imparting anything absolute in the sense of knowledge; I have none; I am attempting to approach it together with you'.[1] He considered it essential to share with his listeners his own experience of the 'road to Damascus':

> Most frequently of all history, is a graveyard of still-births, of unfulfilled hopes and strivings for freedom, love, thought, honour, virtue. I lived through an experience like 'non-birth' myself, and lived through it profoundly, it is my personal experience. But thanks to it... I truly understood that man's passion lies in fulfilment.[2]

As a Soviet philosopher, Mamardashvili belonged to a privileged caste of guardians of 'truth', ideological priests. Naturally, he followed the party line (to present oneself as a non-party philosopher or historian in the land of 'real' socialism was impossible; such people by their very trade automatically became party members). But as with the 'seminarists' of pre-Revolutionary Russia, whose ranks were successfully reinforced with radicals, nihilists and atheists, Soviet philosophers and historians quite frequently became dissidents, opportunists and ideological trouble-makers. Called to battle against the idealistic and positivistic trends of Western philosophy (an absurd situation—the philosopher on whom is

---

[1] M Mamardashvili, *Kartezianskie razmyshleniia* (January 1981) (Moscow, 1993), p. 276.
[2] M Mamardashvili, *Kak ia ponimaiu filosofiiu* (Moscow, 1993), pp. 313-314.

imposed the obligation to fight against philosophy), they instead successfully propagated it (as, for example, in the fascinating form in which P Gaidenko acquainted his compatriots with existentialism) and, at the first opportunity, translated it (Mamardashvili spoke with gratification of the translation at the end of the 1950s of Ludwig Wittgenstein's *Tractatus Logico-Philosophicus*).

Mamardashvili belonged to the generation of the sixties, whose worldview was formed in the mid-fifties and later underwent an intensive evolution. Under pressure of external circumstances, this generation first abandoned politics for professional research and educational work, then made a brilliant reappearance in the social arena in the second half of the 1980s and beginning of the 1990s (the period of 'perestroika'). Today, the sixties generation is in the shadows and is not honoured. In fact, only a handful of them remain alive, and their voices, if they still ring out at all, are barely heard. They belong to other times, other orientations, another atmosphere. At the beginning of the new century in Russia, concepts of toleration, free democratic elections, the wider European family, the free press, and so on, are regarded with a large share of scepticism, as is the unfailingly enclosed in quotation marks 'friendship between nations'. The men of the sixties are looked upon in the best case as groundless idealists and romantics, and in the worst case as people who promoted the disintegration of the Empire, from which, in truth, only the music of the national anthem has been successfully defended. But romanticism can under no circumstances be ascribed to Mamardashvili; he foresaw the undesirable development of events in the 'independent' states, populated by people who were internally enslaved, raised in the spirit of slaves.

He called himself a metaphysician, having found himself right from his youth in internal emigration, and having assimilated the salutary device of a 'spy', an indispensable condition of whose existence is to resemble those around one. He quoted Flaubert fondly, saying that in one's private life it was preferable to be a petty bourgeois, as this gives absolute freedom for literary work. However, he also laughed at his own dangerous position:

> ...I am quite a ridiculous character, the sort that theatrical plays are full of. You know, the sort that appears for a second on the stage and then immediately runs off. And then appears again a little later for no apparent reason, and vanishes again. This usually provokes wild laughter amongst the audience.[3]

Mamardashvili's credo for life was: 'A philosopher needs solitude and silence. If I throw myself into political battles, I will lose the sense of silence and solitude necessary for my work'.[4] And in changing conditions he remained true to this credo, rejecting direct participation in political battles, not wishing to read instructions or exhortations, or to thrust himself on the younger generation, but

---

[3] *Kak ia ponimaiu*, p. 352.

[4] *Kak ia ponimaiu*, p. 352.

instead observing nervously as 'passions, emotions and ambitions flooded' this purified space (interview given by the philosopher in Tbilisi, August 1990)—a natural reaction of a 'citizen of the world' to the nationalistic mood of his Georgian homeland. He knew only too well that emotional conversations about freedom and democracy were one thing, but real freedom and democracy were quite another: 'Quite recently forbidden words like "democracy" and "private property" were liberated, as in the biblical parable of the Gadarene swine. Now they may be pronounced, but are they embodied in concrete reality? No, they are devoid of roots in the depths of the soul'.[5]

There is in these confessions by Mamardashvili an element of over-statement. He was never apolitical, and in his own sphere, as a lecturer, he did more than a little for the development of free thought in the USSR. He was a contributor to journals with a strong oppositional bias, such as *Problems of the World and Socialism (Problemy mira i sotsializma)* and *Philosophical Questions (Voprosy filosofii)*—which were at one point the most authoritative ideological 'organs', but it is indeed no accident that it is said that 'the fish rotted from the head down'. The philosopher was well acquainted with the main actors in the Prague Spring (prominent film directors and the editor of the newspaper *Literarny Listy*, Antonin Lim).[6] His friends—philosophers, historians, economists, political scientists and writers—not only thirsted for political change, but even prepared it. Some of these are named in a certain conversation of Mamardashvili's (Boris Grushin, Vadim Zagladin, Boris Pyzhov, the distinguished philosopher Evald Ilenkov). Mamardashvili singled out in particular Aleksei Matveevich Rumiantsev ('In terms of human qualities he is undoubtedly a brilliant man. He has integrity, decency and stability in friendship and enmity'),[7] at that time editor of the main newspaper *Pravda*, and later vice-president of the Academy of Sciences.

He also credited Rumiantsev with putting forward on the Academy's list for elections to the Supreme Soviet the historian, literary critic and political activist with radical-democratic tendencies, Iurii Fyodorovich Kariakin, with whom Mamardashvili sympathized, having been infected by him with interest in the works of Dostoevsky.

Of course, it would be naïve to suggest that Mamardashvili was not familiar with Dostoevsky's works before his conversations with Kariakin, or his reading of the latter's clear and sharp articles and books. Indifferent to pre-Revolutionary criticism of the writer, publicistic and ideologized, shuddering at the cliché-ridden language of Soviet literary critics, and unswerving in his opposition to engaged, politicized literature, Mamardashvili, reflecting on the strange fate of the writer in Russia, where Dostoevsky was first rejected, then raised higher than

---

[5] *Kak ia ponimaiu*, p. 354.

[6] It was Mamardashvili's idea, incidentally, to create the 'Prague Encounters' club.

[7] *Kak ia ponimaiu*, p. 358.

the heavens, with pleasure recollected his true idol Marcel Proust, who had dedicated a few pages of his novel *The Captive* to the writer:

> I have always been troubled...by the fate of Dostoevsky as a writer in the eyes of our literary criticism and our perception as readers. It always has in mind some sort of special teaching or message of Dostoevsky's in his novels, whether about Russia or the human soul. And these messages are periodically rejected, then accepted, one minute they appear reactionary, the next progressive. In all cases, it suggests that the writer has some sort of system, which we can explain, having read the book, and that he himself exists as its bearer and guardian.

This sort of tendentious attitude to Dostoevsky's works was alien to Mamardashvili as, in contradicting the democratic principles of thought, and ignoring the freedom of the artistic work, it is in essence utilitarian. He is much closer to Proust's position:

> In Proust there is an unexpected phrase (startlingly close and intelligible to me): for some reason, talking and writing too solemnly about Dostoevsky is accepted. And really, clearly (and I perceive it thus), in our eyes Dostoevsky is dealing with himself, he is writing himself as if in a 'mirror', he is seeking the means, the existence, and correcting them through his experimental realization in verbal actuality, and not expounding any kind of teaching. And if we perceive this as something 'teacherly', then it is only because we are able to make close to us the path of a man who, in the existing conditions of culture, casting off its prejudices and permanent problems, and suspending within himself the spiritual displacements and conditions it creates spontaneously, wonders at the actual meaning of his existence, and at the fact that it stands as witness to his own, so to speak, 'person' which surrounds it.[8]

Obviously, the philosopher's position differs fundamentally, conventionally speaking, from that of the slavophile (Iu Seleznev), the Marxist (V Kirpotin, G Fridlender), the liberal-positivist (A Dolinin) and other interpretations of the writer's works coloured in one ideological tone or another. In part, he was probably close to Dostoevsky's phenomenology of style, as developed in M Bakhtin's classic study. But only in part. Mamardashvili's ideas about Dostoevsky blend in perfectly with the metaphysical aesthetic of his thought, developed in his lectures on Descartes, Kant and Proust, and in his interview-conversations. It is not surprising that he proves to be so close to Proust's phrase,[9] which was not in the least 'unexpected' (it was, evidently, unexpected in the sense that its provocative tones rang out at a time when the solemn rhetoric of 'sublime idiots' held sway). Other judgements by Proust of Dostoevsky are also probably close

---

[8] *Kak ia ponimaiu*, pp. 157-158.

[9] 'What I find so boring is the solemn manner in which people talk and write about Dostoievsky', Marcel Proust, *The Captive; Remembrance of Things Past*: 3, trans. C K Scott Moncrieff, Terence Kilmartin and Andreas Mayor (London: Penguin, 1983), p. 387.

to the philosopher; here is one which chimes clearly with Mamardashvili's own ideas:

> For one thing, the world which he describes does really appear to have been created by him. All those buffoons who keep on reappearing, like Lebedev, Karamazov, Ivolgin, [...] that incredible procession, are human types even more fantastic than those that people Rembrandt's *Night Watch*. And yet perhaps they're only fantastic in the same way, by the effect of lighting and costume, and are quite normal really. In any case the whole thing is full of profound and unique truths, which belong only to Dostoevsky.[10]

It is necessary to add here that Mamardashvili sympathized with Proust's attitude to literary criticism of his own time: 'We, as a rule, treat books with great reverence. I would sooner stick to a disrespectful attitude to literature, so to speak, and would even advocate, after Proust, a special genre of literary criticism, which would be called the genre of disrespectful literary criticism'.[11] Iurii Kariakin was, it appears, ascribed by the philosopher to the amiable ranks of disrespectful literary critics. Evidently, the conversation of these two friends referred to the 'Zhdanov fluid' about which Rogozhin, the murderer of Nastasya Filippovna, worries: 'I've wrapped her in oilcloth, good quality, American oilcloth, and put a sheet on top of that, and I've put four open bottles of Zhdanov fluid by her, they're standing there now'.[12] In his article '"Zhdanovskaia zhidkost"', ili Protiv ochernitel'stva',[13] Kariakin re-examined this piece of everyday realia in the context of political events of Soviet times, turning to the activities of the butcher of Russian culture, Andrei Zhdanov: 'Well, quite naturally, the "fluid" which Zhdanov "sprinkled" on culture could not but be named after him. Only this time, unlike in Dostoevsky, the fluid itself was deadly, putrid, stinking, but was passed off as ideological nectar'.[14]

Mamardashvili also used this sinister detail from Dostoevsky's novel in an analogical context, when he discussed an astonishing Soviet phenomenon—the corruption, distortion and poisoning of consciousness:

> ...this corrosive Zhdanov fluid—from within, from inside the skull, it penetrates to the very sources of the will and the formation of ideas. Previously we understood that it is possible, of course, to forbid the utterance of ideas and feelings, but it is impossible to prevent people feeling for themselves. The whole of classical culture is based on this. But the experience of the twentieth century has shown that it is possible to encroach on the very sources of

---

[10] Proust, p. 386.

[11] *Kak ia ponimaiu*, pp. 159-160.

[12] *PSS*, X, 504.

[13] First published in *Ogonek* in 1988, and later appearing, with major additions, in Iu Kariakin, *Dostoevskii i kanun XXI veka* (Moscow, 1989).

[14] Kariakin, *Dostoevskii i kanun XXI veka*, p. 595.

> thoughts and feelings themselves, to cut off the very possibility of thought, the very possibility of feeling for oneself...[15]

Mamardashvili employs Kariakin's metaphor, but by moving away from this or that concrete external event or political figure, he deepens and strengthens it, revealing its mechanism, plunging into the ins and outs, into the destructive results of the totalitarian experiment, transferred from the laboratory of Nechaev—Bakunin—Lenin to the daily life of the people, the results of which were prophetically foreseen by Dostoevsky, who gave the phenomenon an apt name in *The Devils: Shigalevshchina*. This phenomenon became an object of intense study for many of the generation of the nineteen sixties; it is particularly necessary to single out Kariakin (and his friend the historian E Plimak)—their contribution to the destruction of the totalitarian system was significant, although, it seems, external facts pushed the internal side of things somewhat into the background: the consciousness of the generation brought up behind the iron curtain in many ways remained the same as previously, which was exactly what worried Mamardashvili most of all; he suggested that the most important and fearfully difficult task was tireless and patient instruction, enabling people to learn the lessons of the twenties and thirties, in order to achieve a final and irrevocable break with the past. His particular interest in *The Devils* is also understandable, as it inevitably falls at the very centre of the philosopher's reflections about the meaning not only of the past, but also through the prism of its on-going results, and in the artistic experience of Dostoevsky, which was simultaneously also the writer's personal confessional experience.

Mamardashvili frequently returns to the same theme—that of the anthropological catastrophe which had, in his opinion, already begun. 'I have a feeling', he said at a conference in the mid-1980s,

> that amidst all the many catastrophes with which the twentieth century has weakened and threatened us, one of the major ones, which is often hidden from view, is the anthropological catastrophe [...] I have in mind events occurring to man himself, and linked to civilization in the sense that something vitally important could irreversibly be broken within him, owing to the destruction or simply to the absence of civilized bases for the process of life.[16]

He makes recourse to vivid metaphorical comparisons (taken from literature, folklore and eschatology) to explain what it is precisely that causes alarm, and why. The space into which humanity is steadily sliding is likened to Lewis Carroll's looking glass, where:

> left and right change places, all meanings are overturned, and the destruction of human consciousness begins. The anomalous signified space drags into it

---

[15] *Kak ia ponimaiu*, p. 206.
[16] *Kak ia ponimaiu*, p. 107.

everything with which it comes into contact. Human consciousness is annihilated and, falling into a state of uncertainty, where everything hints at having not simply two meanings, but multiple meanings, man himself is also annihilated: neither courage, nor honour, nor virtue, nor cowardice, nor dishonour survives.[17]

Humanity disappears into the 'black hole' foreseen by fantasy writers:

> ...I believe instinctively that such a black hole already exists, and that it is moreover quite a common, well-known idea for us. And that we quite often dive into it, and that everything passing its horizon falls into it, immediately disappearing, becoming inaccessible, as is presumed to be the case with black holes. Evidently, there exists some kind of fundamental structure of consciousness, by virtue of which the heterogeneous microscopic, macroscopic and cosmic phenomena under observation, which are outwardly in no way linked to each other, appear to be analogous at their very depths.[18]

A fantastic atmosphere arises, involuntarily recalling absurdist and surrealist art—the works of Kafka and Kharms, the theatre of Artaud and Beckett, Platonov's *The Foundation Pit*, Robert Musil's unfinished épopée *The Man without Qualities*, the anti-utopias of Zamyatin and Orwell. A kind of 'zombification' is created, 'entirely resembling man, but [which] is in actuality other for man, only imitating what is in fact dead. The product of this, as distinct from *Homo sapiens*, that is, from a person who *knows* good and evil, is an "alien man", an "indescribable man"'.[19]

The philosopher also touches on the anthropological catastrophe in one of his conversations, recalling Dostoevsky's metaphor and attempting to explain more graphically what happens if 'man's capacity *to be*, and his possession of living differences, which are unceasingly, again and again renewed and broadened', are perpetually crushed. Mamardashvili's conclusion is categorical, but justified:

> Otherwise one can fall from any height. This is obvious in today's *anthropological* catastrophe, in the appearance among us of the other, the zombie, with whom 'historical man' has nothing in common and in whom he cannot recognize himself, but can only—when the opportunity arises—'return the ticket'. [...] First man dies, then nature dies. That is, I want to say that first man 'made of paper' appears...and then already this displaced otherness, which is not subject to development, that is to say, which is only imitating life, wields power over nature—and this final part of the noetic sphere, the sole natural part of our nature, dies.[20]

---

[17] *Kak ia ponimaiu*, p. 119.

[18] *Kak ia ponimaiu*, p. 108.

[19] *Kak ia ponimaiu*, p. 111.

[20] *Kak ia ponimaiu*, p. 189.

'Returning the ticket' is of course Ivan Karamazov's eternally hackneyed formula of universal rebellion. The man 'made of paper' is Shatov's ironic response from *The Devils*, in his tireless denunciation of liberals: 'People made of paper: it all comes from a lackey's way of thinking...'[21] Mamardashvili invests this accusatory formula with an additional meaning: people made of paper are phantom beings, the issue of imperial bureaucratic offices.

Most of all, the process of the elimination-expulsion of 'devils' in Dostoevsky, the fearless submergence into the depths of consciousness, the overcoming of stereotypical notions of the age (the distinctive cult of the insulted and injured), attracted the philosopher. He interprets Dostoevsky's spiritual feat from the philosophical point of view thus:

> He appears to us as the first example of contemporary intellectual work... and this work reveals certain ideas, conceptions, moral structures which were simply not formed according to the usual laws of ideas or moral structures. He eliminates from himself everything that unbeknown to his will has entered into him in the shape of the instincts of the Russian mass of that time. For example, the strange, fantastic deference for the 'insulted and injured...' He drew attention to the fact that poverty is also in fact a possession, which also contains its own kind of pride and its own ability to oppress others. And, 'possessing poverty', it is possible to be exactly the same sort of scoundrel as one who is shaped by the possession of riches. [...] Such people are at first drawn by Dostoevsky into some sort of mill, a maelstrom, from which they emerge with a completely unforeseen appearance. No real thought or characteristic of a protagonist in his works is 'pre-given', but rather they appear only in the white heat of the process of writing—they are born only in the movement of mind and soul. This is why, for example, the problem of 'devils' is for him more a problem of certain structures of the soul than of social opposition...But such 'spiritual experience' in its historical moment remained as a fatal image, if you like, almost unassimilated, 'omitted' by the Russian intelligentsia.[22]

The philosopher was struck not only by the exceptionally important role of ideas in Dostoevsky's artistic world, but also by the heightened attention given to the personal attributes of the ideologues, as he strives to show, if I may be permitted to express it thus, the 'moral potential' of ideologues:

> For Dostoevsky the rich attractiveness of the idea was not in itself sufficient criteria. It was also necessary to discover what kind of person it was who pronounced it, and what internal rights and foundations he had for it. And to understand whether it was possible in general to teach others on the basis only of certain elevated ideas, without staking everything on a single card. In the

---

[21]*PSS*, X, 110. In the preparatory materials for the novel Shatov's anti-liberal reflections are given a special sub-heading: 'PEOPLE MADE OF PAPER'.

[22]*Kak ia ponimaiu*, p. 129.

final analysis, this relates to the question of whether it is possible to build the life of society or the cosmos on—to use Dostoevsky's terminology—the Euclidean platform of the tiny human mind.[23]

Dostoevsky's artistic discoveries, his fantastic 'realism in a higher sense', are consonant with the philosopher's conceptions of the qualities and attributes of the idea ('the matter of ideas and the events of ideas themselves are plural, distributed simultaneously along many points')—this is the audacious method of a courageous pioneer, who destroys stereotypes and the countervailing aggression of malevolent entropy:

> For us the experience of Dostoevsky, describing real devils, is important, insofar as he was conforming, in his own words, not to a realistic description, but to the realism of his own soul; he was explicating the true meaning and true appearance of reality, which existed above all in the shape of the motives within him himself. That is, he did this with the consciousness that the devils were also him, and he was restraining in himself the demonic possibilities of his soul, which without the accomplishment of such efforts are poured out into other people, and run out of control in them, if they have not been restrained within oneself. Indeed at some points, the acts of birth of devils must be cut short. The best point of access for this cutting off lies within oneself.[24]

That which Mamardashvili calls 'Dostoevsky's experience' includes various weights of the artistic self-consciousness (and self-knowledge) of confessionality, inseparable from the theme of 'repentance', which presupposed a transfer of the theme of responsibility from the environment, of 'the other' within oneself which, of course, is not only characteristic of Dostoevsky, although in his works (as in the works of Lev Tolstoy, although there it is presented in a somewhat different manner) confession has a particularly naked and complex character. From the wider perspective Dostoevsky is continuing the tradition of the hero's reflexive thoughts from Shakespeare's tragedies:

> ...in the foregoing generation even good-humoured people always said one classic phrase, which can summarize their mental world: 'All that is them, but not I. I am other', instead of saying 'All this is I'. Only then can comprehension, interpretation and mutual realization begin. Shakespeare's Hamlet is capable of finding spiritual meaning only because he is capable of universal responsibility, saying, 'How all occasions do inform against me'. And Dostoevsky, in my opinion, tried to do the same, describing devils not from the outside, not saying that they are 'them' (although literally he has none of them), but instead saying that the devils are himself. That is, the possibilities of my soul, which I am obliged in some way to restrain, have run out of

---

[23] *Kak ia ponimaiu*, p. 129.

[24] M Mamardashvili, *Estetika myshleniia* (Moscow, 2001), p. 196.

control in external space, in other people. The vigilant man is a being who is capable of restraining the vicious circle within himself, having ceased to engender that which is spontaneously engendered by this vicious circle'.[25]

Dostoevsky's novels help the philosopher to explain intelligibly the essence of his reasoning about the anthropological catastrophe. Dostoevsky proves to be at the centre of his reflections on 'sublime idiots', 'hysteria at the possibility of the ideal', the torments of the devil, nihilism, fascism, the era of the Great Terror. The idea is reborn into the alchemy of the idea, noble utopias turn out to be the paved road to hell—the mechanism of this metamorphosis, the rules of this diabolical dialectic, Dostoevsky comprehended, according to the philosopher, with the greatest clarity:

> Hysteria at the possibility of the ideal is a truly diabolical torment, because it is directed by sublime feelings, not by self-interest. It issues from the demand that the world should be exactly as it is supposed to be according to the ideal. And this is the reason why it could happen that Dostoevsky could describe the realm of the soul and morality in arithmetical terms: when in order to save the best thousand people we are prepared to sacrifice millions, insofar as at the starting point we acted as though with noble and immediately moral feelings [...] Nihilism as a European phenomenon in the broad sense of that word is the product of precisely such hysteria, which gripped, for example, revolutionaries. A revolutionary, indeed, cannot be human without dreaming of making the whole world humane. And then the alchemy of the idea arises. That is, it presupposes a certain merging of 'pure' elements in a single body, whether that is called a commune, the prototype of all socialist thought, or the state, in the sense of the fascist consciousness, which is expressed in the establishment of *bundles* of people—from the Italian word *fascio*, 'bundle', 'sheaf'.[26]

Freely interpreting the artistic design of Chekhov, Mamardashvili attributes Epikhodov from *The Cherry Orchard* ('twenty-two misfortunes') to the ranks of 'sublime idiots'—'quite a peculiar kind of man', 'a mildly cultured wally, stumbling over his own hands and feet, and highly aggressive...' He considers that 'we are to this day dealing with precisely these Epikhodovs, with this type of consciousness. In different variations: from the revolutionary to the thief'.[27] But Epikhodov is derived from Dostoevsky's Kartuzov-Lebyadkin, to whom the philosopher turns as the godfather of 'sublime idiots':

> From within his 'good-natured' ideas about the Russian Don Quixote, it is as if there arises a grimace of opposition (it is still striking how the level of reflection and the level of real creation are distinguished in his writing!)

---

[25] *Estetika*, p. 215.
[26] *Estetika*, pp. 386-387.
[27] *Kak ia ponimaiu*, p. 133.

which anticipates future Epikhodovs. He has a rough sketch of an exceptionally expressive character called Kartuzov, who then becomes Lebyadkin in *The Devils*... And of this character Dostoevsky writes in his notebooks the remarkable phrase which looks far into the future: 'A fanatic with a pure conscience'. And he adds that he would have become a revolutionary if he had received *any education*... In their dark consciousnesses, overgrown with hair, these Kartuzov-Epikhodovs moved sublime blocks of words (about love, for example, and what is more they demanded their 'rightful amusements'). Out of this obscurity other types were then crystallized, who had received 'some education', that is, who had mastered some fashionable phraseology or other, and who had decided that the whole world belonged to them by right. How did Kartuzov speak of his Amazon? 'For the sake of such beauty I'm ready to die thirty times'. No less. This is indeed just the same as we have heard in *The Government Inspector*: 'I won't spare myself in the cause of learning!' In our century we would hear something closely related to this in...the texts of Kharms and the verses of the early Zabolotsky, in Zoshchenko, Bulgakov and Platonov'[28]

The twenties and thirties were celebrated by the invasion of the inarticulate, illegitimate children of Kartuzov-Epikhodov, who began to speak in Soviet Volapuk. The pages of Orwell's novel *Nineteen Eighty-Four* about 'Newspeak' undoubtedly inspired Mamardashvili in his reflections on the close link between language and politics, and between language and the consciousness of the 'New Man'. He traces the fundamental alterations, the changes in society and culture, imprinted in monstrous forms of language, 'as though' establishing life, when the pyramid of culture is turned completely upside down:

> The language of the lower classes, of the almost unconscious mass, proved to be the standard, 'normal' language of all culture. The language of 'housing committees', which Bulgakov and Zoshchenko portrayed. But over time it became not a subject of writers' artistic representation, but the language of literature itself. The same immobile blocks of words, which not a single healthy mind was, it seems, in a position to move. But in fact for some amongst them it was quite easy! Then indeed for them, in life itself, language became allegorical, so to speak, a system of winking between themselves, with only they knowing what was for whom. That is, for this new breed of people, they knew how to obtain sustenance without any action. A class of Soviet Chichikovs, who by a misunderstanding we called bureaucrats...[29]

The substitution and distortion of understanding are not simply automatically fixed in language; they become the ideal expression of the illusoriness of all state and social pronouncements, the mighty tools of 'fantastic ideocratic power':

---

[28]*Kak ia ponimaiu*, pp. 133-134.

[29]*Kak ia ponimaiu*, p. 135.

Many moral or political manifestations are in essence the manifestations of their linguistic origins. We recall the impatience which in the twenties and thirties caused a careless rush to the future, which was looming magnetically on the horizon. This impatience was in many ways urged on just by language, in which meanings were hastily 'overlooked' and 'consumed', borrowed from without, but plainly not assimilated from within. They did not have support in the internal development of the subjects handling them. The subjects in fact omitted certain moments of their intellectual and spiritual development, but in *language* they proved to be ahead of everyone...[30]

Dostoevsky's 'latent idea',[31] and his unique terminology, entered into the creative consciousness of Mamardashvili. Explaining to his listeners what 'free thought' is, he proposes the representation of a man who finds himself 'in the condition of a particular kind of duration which is not broken down into anything', which begins from a vivid impression, using a 'mysterious and magical image':

...the desire will appear somehow to understand, to decipher this impression. This type of impression is privileged in the sense that we strive to answer the question: what is this? What is this communicating? Where does it come from? This is roughly the same condition as that of Dostoevsky's heroes, who also try to resolve the idea. Not to verify any theory. No. But to resolve some kind of mental anxiety. The rays of the impression arising in space. Here, some space is torn out by the rays of the impression and we, like moths to the flame, keep on flying to this illuminated spot. And this becomes for us, in the literal sense of the words, a question of life and death.[32]

Mamardashvili feels keenly the philosophical acuteness and 'loftiness', the anthropological full-bloodedness of Dostoevsky's creative work. In his lectures, the theme of 'Kant and Dostoevsky' arose logically (Kant was an indisputable authority for Mamardashvili). The philosopher thus freely develops Kant's idea of the negative consequences of a single 'innocent' assumption (human nature is changed and a new man is created):

And then actually in full conformity with logic, then logically to build a society on the knowledge of the movement of history proven to man, and quite logically to develop a world, which has no logical gaps, of spiritual

---

[30] *Kak ia ponimaiu*, pp. 135-136.

[31] The philosopher considers that '...great works are differentiated by the fact that they contain a voice, a latent text in distinction from the overt content. And criticism is an integral part of this, its means of coming into existence; it locates within the infinity of the text (without giving a definitive explanation), in the "mystery of time", the dedication which at one time Chaadaev warmly offered to Pushkin, and brings to us (successfully, of course) fragments of this "unknown motherland" (Proust), which is the only motherland of the artist', *Kak ia ponimaiu*, p. 161.

[32] *Kak ia ponimaiu*, pp. 368-369.

automata, in whom everything is correct, who gesticulate all the time, but in whom there is no life.[33]

From delight at Kant's ability to reason flawlessly and precisely, Mamardashvili shifts to Dostoevsky:

> ...I must tell you that this act of thinking represents the crowning moment of the finest, deepest and richest intellectual world, which arose within European culture on a wave of religious wars, reformation, counter-reformation, heresy, mysticism, scholasticism, religious debates and so on. Here—in these Kantian words—is represented just the very 'wheel', which to all intents and purposes Russia reinvented for itself in the nineteenth century. In particular, the whole of Dostoevsky, with his 'Grand Inquisitor' and his description of that world which tormented him; his novels of ideas, as the critics express it, where the ideas are the heroes, who collide in fantastic battles, take the knife to each other, scream, finding themselves in a perpetual condition of spiritual hysteria. Dostoevsky's contribution, it would seem, consisted in all of this... in the fact that he discovered this wheel for Russian culture, although to reduce to some sort of system the ideas of Dostoevsky himself, who followed his own path—and in this lies his virtue—would be completely absurd.[34]

Mamardashvili overstates the case somewhat: Dostoevsky did not simply reinvent the wheel on which Kant had never had time to travel around Königsberg. It is more that he interprets Kant through the filter of Dostoevsky's 'experience'. In a course of lectures on Descartes' philosophy, he carefully and with reservations states an idea which, unfortunately, he never developed: '...we may consider Dostoevsky to be a man who added to Kant's antinomies his own antinomies, which are truly interesting and, possibly, for our real, conscious life, just as profound as Kant's for the picture of the world and cognition'.[35] We have at our disposal only fragments of that which could have formed a series of lectures or a book by the philosopher on Dostoevsky. He was obviously working towards this, but never completed it.

*

Merab Mamardashvili died in November 1990 in Moscow, the city with which he was linked in so many ways, and where he gave his artistic lectures with such success. Mamardashvili's educational work was cut short at a time when society had set off down the difficult path of democratic changes, when timid hopes alternated with bitter disappointments, and it was becoming all the more obvious that the consciousness of society was not ready for fundamental spiritual transformation. Mamardashvili foresaw such a turn of events, and did not put his

---

[33] *Estetika*, p. 285.

[34] *Estetika*, pp. 284-285.

[35] *Kartezianskie razmyshleniia*, p. 264.

trust in rapid progress, but instead continued tirelessly to caution and educate. Mamardashvili's books (his lecture courses, prepared for publication by his devoted students) appeared after his death, and became a prominent phenomenon in the cultural life of 'post-imperial' society, which is hardly surprising: they are full of talent, brilliantly written, the ideas are outlined with pedagogical clarity, and fascinatingly, have not dated at all, but read as if they have been written on the current issues which occupy us today.

He never dabbled in prophecies, and did not see himself as being called to fulfil a higher mission, suggesting that such 'games' were dangerous and harmful. Both Russian and Georgian nationalism were alien to him. His two motherlands were, of course, dear to Mamardashvili, but above all he preferred to remain a European, a 'citizen of the world'. He was always faithful to the democratic traditions of Descartes, Kant, Proust, Pushkin, Dostoevsky, Tolstoy, Mandelshtam, Pasternak. He tirelessly repeated a truth which is far too often forgotten:

> ...the artist may see himself as a prophet, and act like one, and consequently treat his work, the Word, as a missionary would. However, it must be understood that such an attitude is in essence socio-utopian. And this we see in the fate of the moral orientation of Russian literature, which is supported by such a purpose. On the contrary, there can be another, far more modest attitude to the word: the personal-individual attitude, which in the first place foregrounds the problem of the word as such. This is the position of service, which in its modesty is close to so-called 'art for art's sake'.[36]

The philosopher himself gave preference to modest (but not meek) service, persuaded that it is necessary for the educator, in order to achieve the desired results, to efface himself, rather than adopt the pose of the all-knowing teacher:

> ...we anticipate and read the lesson—that is certainly the reverse side of the missionary purpose of the artist. The teacher serves not 'the word' but 'the people', that is he instructs them, he communicates a certain truth, about himself, which it is as if he cannot realize himself, because of his insignificance—he appears in the role of an orphaned child. But the artist (or thinker) then stands in the position of the father, the adult guardian... This is the ancient, classical arrangement, if you like. And in my understanding it is particularly undemocratic. Service of the very word as such is far more modest, it presupposes personal responsibility and equality with those who heed you, which seems to me to be one of the triumphs of the democratic tendency in the sphere of art and culture in general.[37]

This is a characteristic example of Mamardashvili's educational activity: he did not teach democracy, but tactically introduced it to the stupefied, distorted

---

[36] *Kak ia ponimaiu*, p. 127.

[37] *Kak ia ponimaiu*, p. 127.

consciousness of the 'serfs' of 'real socialism' who had become estranged from it, relying on the experience of his favourites, Descartes and Kant. And also Dostoevsky, fittingly making use of the terribly difficult work of the thinker, who is magnificently aware of the necessity of 'resolving the idea' in every present moment, because in these moments are found what we cannot have: 'In the given instant, in the present interpretation of people, light, sound—*to fall* into the truth. So as at the next moment to re-gain it'. According to the philosopher, Dostoevsky

> came into being as an author and thinker by such discrete momentary births in the course of his writing [...] The artist must constantly win back his own insight; each time anew. And on the wave of such effort and strain is created a kind of special time of life, not the present chronologically, but the time in which you reside. The intensive zone of consciousness is created.[38]

Mamardashvili often spoke of his own country as a country of constant and negative repetitions, of eternal gestation:

> ...we are still being born without the solution to problems which ought to have been resolved long ago, and from which some meaning ought to have been elicited. For that reason we are striving towards a terrible infinity, although we in fact live in the finite world, and we are at the mercy of a certain reality, although we are in no way able to see it. And this means that we do not have the historical power to become, to be realized, to fulfil something to the end [...] Events, so to speak, occur in a surprising manner, but they are not concluded and, moreover, not completed.[39]

From generation to generation, from decade to decade, the same endless conversations have continued, accompanied by 'pseudo-acts of the idea, its simulacra', which fill literature, theatre, the ether. The country continues to live 'in the fumes of slavery', there hangs over everything a certain

> absolute repetition of fate—the absolute past, consisting of the dead, and of unrealized things [...] and at the same time the absolute future, which we are powerless to influence. And when this terrible dilemma repeats itself, it will be possible to predict that in twenty years there will be an argument in Russia about whether it is ethical to steal from the state or not.[40]

This dreadful repetition is organically linked with infantilism, a sense of 'never growing up': 'In a certain, sense slaves never grow up. They remain permanently as children. And that leaves an absolutely terrifying reserve of evil'.[41] The evil and corrupted children of a degenerate people are doomed, like Mandelshtam's

---

[38] *Kak ia ponimaiu*, pp. 138-139.

[39] *Estetika*, p. 48.

[40] *Estetika*, pp. 255-256.

[41] *Estetika*, p. 377.

swallow, to return to the 'hall of shadows'. This is a fantastic dream, but in truth it is nightmarish, a dream of Kafkaesque metamorphosis:

> If we slept for seventy years, then it would be by no means the sleep of the just, from which we would awaken in all our glory and purity. In sleep we are both regenerated and degenerated. And we might indeed awake as insects, like one of Kafka's characters [...] People might awaken from hibernation and already have turned into insects. So many unseen changes occurred in the past within Soviet man. Soviet man is the product of such changes, degradations and progressive deformations. And it is difficult to break the chain of these changes. The are perhaps already irreversible.[42]

These words about irreversible changes might seem pessimistic and so, to tell the truth, they are. But they are realistic; events and certain tendencies of development of post-imperial society in the years following the philosopher's death have, unfortunately, repeatedly confirmed their correctness. In the first place, there continues 'the burden of negative repetitions and dreadful, never-ending torments, when one cannot die and must chew one and the same crumb over and over again', and instinctively the metaphor of hell from Evgeny Trubetskoi's book *The Meaning of Life* springs to mind: eternal non-death: 'As if bogged down in a terrible dream, here the same story is being played out, where there is no death which would throw the light of conclusive meaning on events'.[43]

Reflecting on the fates of those who were called the 'sixties generation', Mamardashvili recalled more than once the words of the Gospels, endowing them simultaneously with a metaphorical and a concrete, contemporary, and very clear meaning: 'In the Gospels it is said: there is a generation which shall not pass [...] These words referred to the generation which committed the acts as a result of which Christianity arose, and they changed history in an irreversible way'.[44] Without the least leniency to the people of his own generation, he had the courage to warn that:

> ...we live and are formed according to biological laws and, in accordance with their order, at the stage of the child's development there is already a definite sequence: something of our capacities must develop precisely in the period, say, from three to six years. And if that does not happen at that time, then even using powerful means of education, it will be impossible. This is the danger that faces us: we also have our sign of the times, and if we fulfil it, then we will be the generation which shall not pass, that is, the generation after whom something different, another world, will begin.[45]

---

[42] *Kak ia ponimaiu*, p. 345.
[43] *Kak ia ponimaiu*, pp. 398-399.
[44] *Estetika*, p. 193.
[45] *Estetika*, p. 211.

He emphasized that 'the generation *which shall not pass* is capable of crossing over, of leaping into the other world, from the world in which dilemmas and oppositions have been fixed'.[46]

The generation of the sixties has done much to halt the long and idly-turning cycle of negative repetitions. Nevertheless, it is difficult to assert optimistically that they have 'not passed' in a higher sense; the all too frequent relapses in history, which would seem to have slipped past, the unexpected returns, even in the distant time of the cavemen, and the sluggish ideas of the 'slave' consciousness, which has entered into the brains and blood of some generations, are all still alive, and cannot be abolished by decree from above, but will demand a huge effort and a great deal of time. We can only hope and suggest that the experience of this glorious generation, having absorbed the experience of Pushkin, Dostoevsky, Tolstoy, Chekhov, Mandelshtam, Pasternak, Platonov (all these, and many other writers and thinkers were discovered and 'returned' anew, in the eyes of free people reading them, in the second half of the twentieth century), cannot pass without leaving a trace. Nor, in 'post-modern' Russia, I would add, has readers' interest passed in the books, articles and philosophical conversations of Merab Mamardashvili.

Translated by Sarah Young

---

[46]*Estetika*, p. 212.

'A MORE IMPORTANT CONNECTION THAN PEOPLE THINK': DOSTOEVSKY AND RUSSIAN MUSIC

Arnold McMillin

IT is a great pleasure to write an article on music in honour of Malcolm Jones, one of the most harmonious of all Slavists. The bold quotation in the title comes from a typically generous endorsement by Shostakovich (1906-1975) of Abram Gozenpud's 1971 *Dostoevskii i muzyka (Dostoevsky and Music)*,[1] a pioneering but not particularly enterprising study, superseded a decade later by the same scholar's *Dostoevskii i muzykal'no-teatral'noe iskusstvo: Issledovanie (Dostoevsky and Musical-Theatrical Art: Research)*, where the endorsement is printed.[2] This comment, however, is radically tempered by Gerald Abraham's wry assessment: 'Dostoevsky's writings certainly do not cry out for musical treatment; nevertheless, they have been given it.'[3] Whatever the merits of the first half of Abraham's proposition, the second half is reasonably true; indeed, his article omits one of the most important such works, namely Shostakovich's song cycle, *Four Verses of Captain Lebyadkin*. In addition to the latter masterpiece, there are at least eight Russian operas, dating from 1903 to 1985, on themes from Dostoevsky's works, most of them rarities nowadays. Numerous films and dramatizations have, of course, been and continue to be made of the work of this most dramatic of writers, but two of them stand out for their brilliant musical scores, namely that by Nikolai Karetnikov (1930-1994) for Alexander Alov and Vladimir Naumov's 1966 film version of 'A Nasty Story' and that by Alfred Schnittke (1934-1998) for Iurii Lyubimov's 1985 English production of *The Possessed*.[4]

Since there is no obvious chronological way of arranging the material in this survey, it is proposed to consider the film scores and theatrical accompaniment first, followed by the song cycle, and ending with a survey of the attempts to

---

[1] Abram Gozenpud, *Dostoevskii i muzyka* (Leningrad: Muzyka, 1971).

[2] Abram Gozenpud, *Dostoevskii i muzykal'no-teatral'noe iskusstvo: Issledovanie* (Leningrad: Sovetskii kompozitor, 1981), p. 3.

[3] Gerald Abraham, 'Dostoevsky in Music', in *Russian and Soviet Music: Essays for Boris Schwarz*, ed. M H Brown (Ann Arbor: UMI Research, 1984), pp. 193-199 (p. 193). This view is shared by Mark Manuilov, 'New Operas by Alexander Kholminov', *Music in the USSR*, July-September (1986), 91-93 (hereafter Manuilov), p. 92.

[4] We are using *The Possessed* here to refer specifically to the English title of this production; for references to the novel itself, and to other Russian productions of it, we use, as in the other essays, the title *The Devils*. (*Editor's note*.)

make operas from Dostoevsky's prose. Not surprisingly, many of the varied films in this genre have background music that fulfils the accepted criterion that such music should support the action of the film without drawing attention to itself.[5] In fact most of the composers of music to Russian 'literary' films are not known as 'serious' composers outside the cinema studios.[6] Before turning to the major exceptions,[7] it is worth mentioning that several films have been based on more than one of Dostoevsky's works and some have used them without acknowledgment: of the former, Grigory Roshal's *Petersburg Night* (1934), for instance, mixed 'White Nights' with *Netochka Nezvanova* to a score by Dmitry Kabalevsky (1904-1987). More interesting, perhaps, is the unacknowledged use of *The Devils* in Fridrikh Ermler's *The Great Citizen*, Part II, about the murder of Kirov, where Dostoevsky's revolutionaries, naturally, become counter-revolutionaries. Direct quotations from *The Devils*, such as the plotter Borovsky's use of Pyotr Verkhovensky's words, make the background text unmistakable.[8] Of the exiguous music for the film by Shostakovich, only a single concert piece survived, the restrained Funeral March, which he later incorporated in his Eleventh Symphony (1957).[9]

As in the West, some Russian films are not shy of taking well-known classical pieces as background music, and it may be argued that this practice, with regard to films based on Dostoevsky's prose, has as little relevance to the musical interpretation of the works as, for instance, the insistent use of the first movement of Brahms's First Piano Concerto in the British romantic weepie, *The L-Shaped Room* (1962). Amongst such Russian films may be mentioned Ivan Pyrev's 'White Nights' of 1959,[10] that is accompanied by the music of a

---

[5] Such Western films as, to take two prominent examples, *Doctor Zhivago* (1963) and *Lawrence of Arabia* (1965), with Oscar-winning scores by Maurice Jarre (b. 1924) are, for many people, memorable on account of their insistent theme music. Russian film scores tends to be more varied.

[6] The main filmography referred to here is that in N M Lary, *Dostoevsky and Soviet Film: Visions of Demonic Realism* (Ithaca and London: Cornell University Press, 1986) (hereafter Lary), pp. 268-271. For the later period (the last film in Lary's filmography dates from 1980) there is a useful website of films based on Russian literature: <httw//www.surrey.ac.uk/LIS/LVMG/>. The present writer would like to acknowledge here the help he received from Gillian Long in using SSEES/UCL's excellent video collection. There are at least two valuable bibliographies of settings of writers to music: Ernst Stöckel, *Puškin und die Musik* (Leipzig: VEB Deutscher Verlag für Musik, 1974), and Boris Rozenfel'd, *Anna Akhmatova, Marina Tsvetaeva, Osip Mandel'shtam i Boris Pasternak v muzyke: Notografiia* (Stanford: Stanford University, 2003).

[7] A minor exception is Lyutsiyan Pirozhkov (b. 1926), an adaptable composer who has written choral, symphonic and chamber music as well as scores for the theatre and cinema. His varied but unobtrusive music for Alexander Borisov's 1960 film of 'A Gentle Creature' highlights the story's pathos admirably.

[8] For a more detailed analysis see Lary, pp. 69-77.

[9] Shostakovich wrote music for films from early in his career with *New Babylon*, op. 18 (1928-1929) to one of his last works, the music for *King Lear*, op. 137 (1970).

[10] This was one of the three Dostoevsky films made by Pyrev after the death of Stalin, the others being *The Idiot* (1958) and *The Brothers Karamazov* (1967-1968).

disparate triumvirate: Glazunov, Skriabin and Rachmaninov. More remote still is the 1992 film of Igor and Dmitry Talankin, *The Devils* (*Nikolai Stavrogin*) in which the background music is taken from Glinka and Tchaikovsky. Finally may be mentioned a version of *The Idiot* by Roman Kachanov, *Down House* (2001) whose music is credited to the suspiciously pseudonymous sounding DJ Gruv.[11]

Two dramatizations, one for the screen, one for the theatre, stand out musically. Nikolai Karetnikov's score for the film version of 'A Nasty Story' is as innovative and striking as Naumov's daring dramatic and cinematic experiments. These include rapid switches in mood, and highly mobile, often wobbly, camera combined with grotesquely caricatured, somewhat Gogolian characters, and particularly, a graphic depiction of an authority figure brought low. These may well have been amongst the elements that led to this masterpiece's being banned immediately after its first showing in 1966. Karetnikov's music responds admirably to the swiftly changing accents of the film, making extensive use of silence, and underlining the absurdity of the action, pointing up in particular the contrasts between servility and malice, pomposity and maudlin idiocy. The film opens with a sea of grimacing faces, and the music reinforces the tone by an insistent, barely changing rhythm over which a squeaky, rather bitter off-key tune rises in varying intervals to the highest registers. This thematic material recurs with variations at a number of particularly drunken scenes when Bakhtinian carnival is taken to extremes. This is in maximal contrast to the demure quadrille that Pralinsky imagines before gate-crashing his subordinate, Pseldonimov's party. The folksy music played 'live' at the real party bears a generic resemblance to the opening music, though the insistent background rhythm has, naturally, gone. It too, however, is extremely repetitive. A sad broken waltz accompanies the film's more pathetic moments, including the times when Pseldonimov tries to be intimate with his bride on a rickety bed (the bridal bed being occupied by the drunken Pralinsky) before it collapses. This may not be a great film,[12] but the music is exceptional.[13]

Also exceptional, but mainly in the context of Liubimov's brilliant production (the latter available only in a poor video recording) is Schnittke's music for the Almeida Theatre's production of *The Possessed*. As a short three-movement suite ('Winter Road', 'Budding Song' and 'March'), it is entitled *Music to an*

---

[11]This recalls the translator of Vasily Belov's generally unpleasant and, in particular, anti-Semitic novel, *Vse vperedi: The Best Is Yet to Come* (Moscow: Raduga, 1989): P O Gromm.

[12]Lary, pp. 171-174, for instance, regards it as being too Gogolian and a misrepresentation of Dostoevsky's ideas and tone.

[13]The distinguished scholar Mikhail Tarakanov in an article intended to restore the reputation of a neglected composer believes that this is by far Karetnikov's finest film score, and goes so far as to compare its accomplishment in the sphere of applied sound creativity with that of Prokofiev in Eisenstein's film scores: Mikhail Tarakanov, 'A Drama of Non-recognition: A Profile of Nikolai Karetnikov's Life and Works', in *'Ex oriente...-II'. Nine Composers from the Former USSR* (Berlin: Verlag Ernst Kuhn, 2003), pp. 109-131 (pp. 123-124).

Imagined Play, and was first performed by the redoubtable Gennady Rozhdestvensky in Moscow in 1985, the same year as Liubimov's London performances. The suite is written for an ensemble comprising a flute and piccolo, trumpet and timpani, piano, violin, guitar, mouth organ and two vocalists (singing with combs). Schnittke, clearly Shostakovich's principal successor in Russian music,[14] was also very interested in literature and wrote settings and accompaniments to the work of many Russian and other writers. It was, however, Dostoevsky with whom he felt the greatest affinity. He believed that his music, like the writer's prose, demands an active response from the listener/reader,[15] particularly liking the impossibility of finding a final single meaning in Dostoevsky's novels and responding to his lofty ideals and inexhaustible vision, expressed through what he saw as contradictions and irrationalism.[16] The London production of *The Possessed* itself begins with a chorus in the sardonic manner of Carl Orff's *Carmina Burana*, as the characters, initially presented as expressionist puppets, introduce themselves with slapstick gestures and movements. The main furniture in the minimalist set is a honky-tonk piano, extensively used for glissando slides, an instrument such as might have been drummed on by Lyamshin at the Verginskys' to keep the conspiracy from prying ears, when the row drowns out the discussion and, as an unnamed participant remarks, 'We don't understand ourselves'.[17]

Dmitry Shostakovich felt a distinct affinity with Dostoevsky and, indeed, with some of his characters. Volkov recalls that 'he kept trying to convince people that Shostakovich was the Dostoyevsky of music'.[18] The composer's last song cycle, *Four Verses of Captain Lebyadkin*, op. 146 (1975) which immediately followed his very different *Suite on Verses of Michelangelo Buonarotti*, op. 145a

---

[14]This appellation requires qualification in so far as that Schnittke, with not a drop of Russian blood in his veins, felt a foreigner everywhere; although he lived most of his life in Russia, Vienna was perhaps his cultural motherland: see Alexander Ivashkin, *Alfred Schnittke* (London: Phaidon, 1996) (hereafter Ivashkin, *Schnittke*), p. 10.

[15]Ivashkin, *Schnittke*, p. 169.

[16]See Aleksandr Ivashkin, *Besedy s Al'fredom Shnitke* (Moscow: Klassika-XXI, 2003), p. 35, and Ivashkin, *Schnittke*, p. 154.

[17]*PSS*, X, 309. Further references to the volume and page number of this edition are in parentheses in the text.

[18]Allan B Ho and Dmitry Feofanov, *Shostakovich Reconsidered*, with an Overture by Vladimir Ashkenazy (Exeter: Toccata Press, 1998) (hereafter Ho and Feofanov), p. 345. Rather more convincingly, Gozenpud compares the writer's and the composer's concern for the world's wretched and unfortunate, as well as their ability to show 'how evil is born, and how what appears to be harmless in origin can turn into something dangerous and destructive': see Elizabeth Wilson, *Shostakovich: A Life Remembered* (London and Boston: Faber and Faber, 1994) (hereafter Wilson), pp. 458-462 (p. 459). Gozenpud compares Lyamshin's increasingly sinister improvisation in *The Devils* to the development of the obsessive marching song in the first movement of Shostakovich's Seventh Symphony.

(1974),[19] is a fascinating work, revealing his close and lasting knowledge of Dostoevsky's novels and of *The Devils* in particular, although the latter, denounced by Lenin, had not been republished when the composer first made reference to it.[20] *The Devils* was not only Shostakovich's favourite Dostoevsky novel, but the songs of the sinister buffoon Captain Lebyadkin had been referred to by him early in his life as a term of abuse, as his teacher Maximilian Shteinberg recalls, when the twenty-two-year-old complained about the Second Symphony of Vladimir Shcherbachev (one of his seniors who was later to be very loyal to Shostakovich over his difficulties with *Lady Macbeth of Mtsensk* and at other times) saying that Alexander Blok in this symphony was 'not Blok at all, but the poetry of Captain Lebyadkin from *The Devils*'.[21] For all this youthful show of disrespectful high spirits, some thirty-six years later the composer approached his second-to-last published work with great seriousness, as is underlined by his letter to Boris Tishchenko dated 24 August 1974, where he identifies precisely the places in the novel from which the songs are drawn, insisting that they be performed in the right order.[22]

They have been described as 'in some ways, as the oddest and most opaque of Shostakovich's late works',[23] and thus it is not surprising that this highly original late flowering of Shostakovich's satirical and parodic gifts has been subjected to considerable analytical enquiry, most notably from his principal Russian biographer, Sofya Khentova, as well as from Western commentators such as Malcolm MacDonald, Dorothea Redepenning and Esti Sheinberg, as well as, most recently, with perceptive thoroughness, from Caryl Emerson.[24]

---

[19] Dorothea Redepenning analyses the relationship between these two cycles in '"And Art Made Tongue-Tied by Authority": Shostakovich's Song-Cycles', in *Shostakovich Studies*, ed. David Fanning (Cambridge: Cambridge University Press, 1995) (hereafter Fanning), pp. 205-228 (p. 226). See also Bernd Feuchtner, *'Und Kunst geknebelt von der grossen Macht': Schostakowitsch, künstlerische Identität und staatliche Repression* (Frankfurt: Sendler, 1986), pp. 255-257.

[20] Shostakovich's letter to Tanya Glivenko of 24 January 1924 shows that he had admired *The Devils* from as early as his middle teens: Ho and Feofanov, p. 539.

[21] See 'Shostakovich v dnevnikakh M I Shteinberga', in *Shostakovich mezhdu mgnoveniem i vechnost'iu*, ed. L Kovnatskaia (St. Petersburg: Kompozitor, 2000), pp. 83-148, entry for 19 March 1928 (p. 104).

[22] *Pis'ma Dmitriia Dmitrievicha Shostakovicha Borisu Tishchenko* (St Petersburg: Kompozitor, 1997) (hereafter Tishchenko), p. 46. This care over the songs reflects the importance given to Lebyadkin (at first called Kartuzov) by Dostoevsky himself in the creation of *The Devils*, as may be seen from the Notebooks: *The Notebooks for 'The Possessed'*, ed. Edward Wasiolek, trans. Victor Terras (Chicago: Chicago University Press, 1968), pp. 36-42.

[23] Malcolm MacDonald, 'Words and Music in Late Shostakovich', in *Shostakovich: The Man and His Music*, ed. Christopher Norris (London: Lawrence and Wishart, 1982), pp. 125-147 (hereafter MacDonald), p. 42.

[24] Sof'ia Khentova, *Shostakovich: Zhizn' i tvorchestvo* (Leningrad: Sovetskii kompozitor, 1985-86), pp. 125-147; Esti Sheinberg, *Irony, Satire, Parody and the Grotesque in the Music of Shostakovich: A Theory of Musical Incongruities* (Aldershot etc.: Ashgate, 2000), pp. 285-289; and Caryl Emerson, 'Shostakovich and the Russian Literary Tradition', in *Shostakovich and His World*, ed. Laurel E Fay

The cycle comprises four songs drawn from various parts of the novel, three of them to words by Lebyadkin himself. The first, 'Captain Lebyadkin's Love', consists of snatches of the Captain's drunken amatory verses to Liza Tushina from Part One, III, chapter 3; from Part One, IV, chapter 2; and from Part Two, II, chapter 2. The linking prose includes Lebyadkin's explanation that although the (first) verse describes his being hit by a cannonball at Sebastopol, he was neither there nor lost an arm, but only included these details for the rhyme ('But what a rhythm!') (*PSS*, X, 95); this note of Lebyadkin's characteristic ambiguity is brilliantly caught by Shostakovich throughout the four songs of the cycle. In the first of them the simplistic, harsh music in a crude triple rhythm admirably conveys the Captain's violent, lascivious nature, highlighting his semi-literacy (for instance, by the vivid musical reproduction of his several attempts to enunciate a complicated word like *aristokraticheskii* ('ari-sto-krati-cheskii', bars 66-73).[25] Emerson draws attention, amongst other things, to the vulgarity of the Captain's language, when he uses, for example, the word *chlen* for Liza's erotically charged broken leg,[26] but the overwhelming impression of this song and, indeed, the cycle as a whole, is distant parody or imitation, as the bibulous Lebyadkin introduces into his songs snatches of well known operas and popular songs, though the crowded bars, simplistic musical timing and what MacDonald with vivid accuracy describes as 'textures [...] spare to the point of desiccation, the harmony almost entirely limited to bare octaves, with the occasional buzzing dissonance or triadic gesture, the voice-part "unvocal" in its register, narrow compass, and doggedly syllabic setting'.[27] Like so much seeming simplicity (MacDonald calls it 'stark artlessness')[28] in late Shostakovich, the Lebyadkin songs offer a mine of half-hidden allusions, and great scope for seeking roots and references, not least to his own works.[29] 'Captain Lebyadkin's Love' ends with the remark that 'the song was composed by an untutored man during an

---

(Princeton: Princeton University Press, 2004), forthcoming. The author is most grateful to Professor Emerson for generously allowing him the chance to see before publication what is undoubtedly the best study of this song cycle. Malcolm MacDonald, amazingly, suggests that Dostoevsky's 'genius no more embraced satire than Gogol's embraced tragedy' (MacDonald, p. 83). This seems a reversal of Aaron Copland's dictum that 'If a literary man puts together two words about music, one of them will be wrong': *The Guinness Book of Poisonous Quotes*, ed. Colin Jarman (Enfield: Guinness Publishing, 1991), p. 149. For once, the hoot seems to be on the other flute.

[25] See Sheinberg, p. 288. In the next poem the word 'bla-go-rodneishii', drawn out in Dostoevsky's text, is spread over several notes, but more conventionally than 'ari-sto-krati-cheskii'.

[26] Emerson, typescript, pp. 38, 42.

[27] MacDonald, p. 142. Esti Sheinberg refers to 'Shostakovich emphatically [using] the dilettante device of accommodating the text into the music by crowding many syllables into one bar, resulting in its filling with short rhythmic-value notes': Sheinberg, p. 287.

[28] MacDonald, p. 142.

[29] Malcolm MacDonald relates Lebyadkin to Lear's Fool (Shostakovich had set Lear's songs for a 1941 production of the play in Leningrad), but, more convincingly, sees a link between the songs and the Thirteenth 'Babi Yar' Symphony, notably the 'Humour' and 'Career' movements: MacDonald, pp. 143-145.

argument', these words being set with very low minor seconds in the accompaniment before a sequence of violently triumphant chords reminds us of Lebyadkin's crude braggadocio, and, indeed, the threat that lies behind this and the other songs.[30]

The second song 'The Cockroach' recalls the well-known children's ditty, 'Chizhik-Pyzhik', but sung in a sinisterly burlesque manner. The song includes Varvara Petrovna's outraged intervention and a reprise louder and in a higher register. Shostakovich's song ends on a note of real bathos, referring to the most noble man Nikifor after Lebyadkin's song in the novel is over: 'As for Nikifor, he represents nature'. (*PSS*, X, 141) It is difficult, however, to fully accept Tamara Levaia's suggestion the song is 'a grotesque symbol of the disintegration of personality [or that] the idea shimmers through the Holy Fool character'.[31]

The third song, 'A Ball in Aid of Governesses' is read by another buffoon, Liputin, at the celebration, although those present immediately recognize Lebyadkin's authorship of the scurrilous and disrespectful lines. The music of this crude lampoon is aggressively simple to match the words, and the banging piano accompaniment with which it begins sets the tone of cruel burlesque. All the words are set but, in this case, without the prose interventions of Dostoevsky's text, such as 'Hurrah! Hurrah!' and 'Quite right, quite right, that's realism for you, you can't do anything without the "doings"'. (*PSS*, X, 362-363)

The last song of the cycle, 'A Shining Personality', which occurs before the other items in Dostoevsky text (*PSS*, X, 273) differs from them in that the words are not by Lebyadkin himself, although von Lembke's copy, read aloud by Pyotr Stepanovich in the novel, had been obtained from the bullying and stupid Lebyadkin. In the song the simple revolutionary message is underlined ironically by Shostakovich, using a rather pathetic elementary tune and crude cries of 'Ekh!' at the end of each of the three verses. There can be little doubt that this setting illustrates Shostakovich's view of the lack of seriousness that characterizes revolutionary ideology both in Dostoevsky's time and in his own.

Apart from scores to accompany Dostoevsky-related films and shows, and Shostakovich's amazing Lebyadkin song cycle, there are at least eight Russian operas based on the novelist's works: one on *Poor Folk*, two on 'White Nights', one on *The Gambler*, one on 'The Little Boy at Christ's Christmas Tree', two on *The Idiot* and one on *The Brothers Karamazov*. Taking them in order of composition, the earliest is *The Christmas Tree* (1902-1903) by Vladimir Rebikov

---

[30] Caryl Emerson, more fully than the other commentators, demonstrates the place of these songs in their literary context (typescript, pp. 37-46). She also highlights Khodasevich's views not only on the importance of Lebyadkin's songs but also on their role as caricature: V F Khodasevich, 'Poeziia Kapitana Lebiadkina' (1931), in his *Sobranie sochinenii* (Ann Arbor: Ardis, 1983), II, 194-201.

[31] Tamara Levaia, 'Taina velikogo iskusstva: O pozdnikh kamerno-vokal'nykh tsiklakh D D Shostakovicha', *Muzyka Rossii*, 2 (1978) (hereafter Levaia), p. 326. In the same vein, she relates the fourth song's prelude to the Kromy scene at the end of Mussorgsky's *Boris Godunov* (Levaia, p. 325).

(1866-1920). Written over a period of six years (1894-1900), with a rather weak libretto by I Plaksin,[32] it is described as musico-psychological drama, and is one of his best-known works. Rebikov was widely travelled and interested in the new schools of art, literature and music. In literature he was closest to the Symbolist movement, and he enjoyed a long friendship with Valery Briusov who, for his part, like his fellow-Symbolist Konstantin Balmont, interested himself in contemporary music.[33] Rebikov, known to many schoolchildren in Russia for his music for beginners, also set several scenes from Briusov's work in vocal scenes, but soon after completing *The Christmas Tree* he joined the avant-garde, making many technical innovations of his own, and pioneering whole-tone music. *The Christmas Tree*, like many of Rimsky-Korsakov's operas, became best known as an orchestral suite consisting of a charming, wistful waltz, a march of the gnomes (closer to Tchaikovsky than to Grieg), a boisterous dance of the clowns, and a dance of the Chinese dolls, making much use of the piccolo, followed by the angel's ladder (an orchestrally imaginative piece switching skilfully between the wind instruments against a background of tremolo strings); the suite ends with a short depiction, mostly pianissimo, of a dark night. Musically rather simple, like Tchaikovsky's far better-known *Nutcracker Suite*, it lacks the latter's easy charm, but is far from facile. Rebikov's early attempt to create a Dostoevskian opera is in one act and four scenes, the second incorporating the gnomes, clowns and Chinese dolls, the third and fourth scenes being purely orchestral. This work, described by Karatygin as 'monotonous and pathetic',[34] enjoyed considerable popularity in the composer's lifetime, being performed not only in Russia but also in Prague and Berlin.

Next chronologically is *The Gambler* (1917, 1929) by Prokofiev (1891-1953). The second of the composer's eight operas, it is a far cry from the first, *Magdalen* (1911-1913), a technically unadventurous but over-rich marshmallow of a romantic melodrama. In *The Gambler*, despite avowing that he wished, above all, to be simple, Prokofiev wrote a large-scale opera in four acts and six scenes, calling on a huge orchestra and cast of twenty-nine singers, but with none of the set pieces of traditional opera, such as arias and choruses. Instead he turned back to the ideas of Dargomyzhsky's *The Stone Guest* (1860s) and Mussorgsky, particularly in his opera *The Marriage* (1868),[35] attempting to

---

[32]The libretto incorporates Andersen's *The Little Match Girl* (1845) and Hauptmann's *Hannele* (1894).

[33]For a perceptive and thorough review of Balmont's relations with Prokofiev see Pamela Davidson, 'Music, Magic and Poetry: Prokof'ev's Creative Relationship with Bal'mont and the Genesis of *Semero ikh*', *New Zealand Slavonic Journal*, 36 (2002), 67-79.

[34]V G Karatygin, *Izbrannye stat'i* (Moscow and Leningrad, Muzyka: 1965), p. 259. Such strictures seem harsh, to judge by the suite.

[35]Prokofiev had been greatly impressed by the performances of Mussorgsky's opera in 1906 and 1909. Daniel Jaffé notes that the comments made by Prokofiev to the press about *The Gambler* are strikingly similar to those of Mussorgsky in letters round about the time he wrote *The Marriage*:

relate the music as naturally as possible to the words, in what he called 'an opera in the declamatory style', written in 'an ultra-left idiom',[36] including outlandish intervals and enharmonic tones. Prokofiev declared himself to have been attracted by this particular work on account of the fact that it 'apart from its thrilling subject, consists almost entirely of dialogues, which gave me the opportunity of preserving Dostoyevsky's style in the libretto';[37] indeed, he almost obsessively tried to preserve the novelist's actual words, taking care that the subtly deployed orchestra should not drown the singers. For all that, the most spectacular part of the opera is the penultimate scene in the last act, depicting the frenzy of the casino, which offers less scope for dialogue, authentic or otherwise, than the rest of the novel. Spurning a chorus, Prokofiev portrays the frenetic atmosphere created by Aleksei's run of wins and eventual breaking of the bank, using the voices of various individual gamblers in a near-cacophony of fragmentary comments, as the tension rises to a powerful climax,[38] in which Aleksei's voice, always a source of nervous tension in the opera, becomes just one amongst many. The running music, so brilliantly employed in *The Love of Three Oranges* (1919), is used to maintain the tension in this most imaginative scene. The other main characters, Polina and Babulenka, are also well depicted. Babulenka's mainly wistful music changed little between the first and second versions of the opera, and also forms the best part of the suite derived from it (see *infra*); Polina comes between two other hysterical women in Prokofiev's operas: the eponymous Magdalen and Renata in *The Fiery Angel* (1927), based on Briusov's novel. The whirring of the roulette wheel is vividly conveyed by woodwind and a xylophone, to mention just one example of Prokofiev's imaginative orchestration.[39] The composer, perhaps wisely, chooses to end the opera before the conclusion of the novel, with the parting of Aleksei and Polina. Whilst Dostoevsky's main concern in this tale was the fatal attraction of gambling, the opera focuses on the tragic destiny of human characters and the breakdown of personal relationships, failure and disappointment.

Daniel Jaffé, *Sergei Prokofiev* (London: Phaidon, 1998), pp. 47-8.

[36] Sergei Prokofiev, *Soviet Diary 1927 and Other Writings*, ed. and trans. Oleg Prokofiev (London and Boston: Faber and Faber, 1991) (hereafter *Soviet Diary*), p. 254.

[37] Sergei Prokofiev, *Materials. Articles. Interviews* (Moscow: Progress Publishers, 1978), p. 28.

[38] Comparable devices are to be heard, in perhaps even more adventurous ways, in early Shostakovich, notably his opera *The Nose* (1927-28), but there the crowd scenes, be they a hocket or the hunt for the Nose, often contain a powerful note of chaos and potential violence, whereas in *The Gambler* Prokofiev's aim is to create a feeling of fevered passion. For a view of the setting of Gogol's stories in context see Arnold McMillin, 'Gogol''s St Petersburg Stories in the Hands of Russian Composers', *New Zealand Slavonic Journal*, 37 (2003), 171-182 (hereafter McMillin).

[39] For more detail, see David Nice, *Prokofiev: From Russia to the West 1891-1935: A Biography* (New Haven and London: Yale University Press, 2003) (hereafter Nice), pp. 120-125; and Harlow Robinson, 'Dostoevsky and Opera: Prokofiev's *The Gambler*', *The Musical Quarterly*, 70 (1984), 96-106.

Prokofiev's *The Gambler* might never have been written and was, in any case, for many years suppressed or neglected. Diaghilev, with whom the composer was collaborating at that time, had made serious attempts to persuade him that the future lay with ballet rather than with opera, but, together with Nikolai Myaskovsky (1881-1950), Prokofiev had been strongly attracted by the idea of writing operas based on Dostoevsky, whom they thought neglected by musicians.[40] Myaskovsky's plans to create an opera based on *The Idiot* (as late as 1916) came to nothing, but Prokofiev's opera was written in five and a half months between 1915 and 1916, with the orchestral score completed in the following year. The coming of the February Revolution less than a month after the first orchestral rehearsal was doubtless one of the reasons why for over eleven years the opera had to remain unperformed. When, in 1929, Prokofiev completely revised it, the work received a premiere in Brussels. It finally reached the Bolshoi Theatre only in 1974; in the year 2000 Gennady Rozhdestvensky conducted a performance of the original version. Unusually, the suite made from the opera, *Four Portraits and a Denouement*, is less attractive than its source, as the portraits lose life without their context.[41] Like Shostakovich's Lebyadkin songs, Prokofiev's first full-length opera responds in modern idiom to Dostoevsky's texts, albeit, in each case, very different and perhaps untypical ones.[42]

There are two operatic versions of 'White Nights', of which the least known and earliest (1933) is by Mikhail Tsvetaev (1907-1982), a pupil of Myaskovsky, who spent most of his life working in Dushanbe. Attracted to large forms, he produced, in addition to *White Nights*, a ballet, seven symphonies and a number of piano sonatas. He also wrote a number of successful romances, some to classical poetry,[43] as well as several works with Tajik themes and melodies. It is not known, however, when his opera *White Nights* was last performed, and no recordings are available.[44]

The other opera based on Dostoevsky's story is by a somewhat better-known composer, Iurii Butsko (b. 1938) who, amongst other things, produced an impressive opera based on Gogol's *Notes of a Madman* (1963-1964).[45] Naturally, less frenzied than his Gogol opera, Butsko's *White Nights* (1968) is a fine

---

[40] It may be noted, however, that Prokofiev was not drawn to Dostoevsky as a writer in the way that, for example, Shostakovich and Schnittke were: he was 'a writer for whom I don't always feel the greatest love': Harlow Robinson, *Sergei Prokofiev, A Biography* (New York: Viking, 1987), p. 67.

[41] For more detail see Nice, pp. 292-293.

[42] Prokofiev himself considered *The Gambler* the least Dostoevskian of all Dostoevsky's works: *Soviet Diary*, p. 287.

[43] There are particularly fine versions of Blok's 'Slowly Streaming' ('Medlitel'noi cheredoi') and 'Some day' ('Kogda-to').

[44] Tsvetaev does not even warrant an entry in the most recent Grove dictionaries.

[45] See McMillin, p. 173. Other literary works by this composer include vocal cycles on the words of Blok (*The Twelve*, 1957-1962) and Khodasevich (*Solitude*, 1966).

chamber opera for two singers, less than an hour in length and deliberately static, but full of the feeling of frustrated romance and dreaming. It is in four scenes, the first comprising the meeting of the Dreamer and Nastenka, the second including the latter's tale of her beloved Lodger, the third combining Dostoevsky's third and fourth nights—the declaration of love—and the conclusion, whilst the fourth is a brief and tranquil picture of morning. Dostoevsky's text is followed faithfully and treated with imagination, as for example when the Lodger appears in Nastenka's narration, sung by the Dreamer. Butsko justifies this device by referring to the frequent use of doubles in the novelist's work, and there is, in any case, some echoing of lines between the Dreamer and the Lodger. Unlike many twentieth-century chamber operas, *White Nights* does not depend on recitative but, for the most part, has a cantilena texture with the voices (tenor and soprano) not greatly differentiated, and moving between the various instruments of the orchestra. It is only at the climax that the music becomes more disjointed and agitated, accentuated by the brass and timpani, and there is a particularly successful use of these instruments at the quiet end, after lofty words of prayer-like resignation, when a persistent six-note motif recurs with increasing remoteness, as the Dreamer's disappointment recedes in his mind. There are no leitmotifs as such, but each part of Butsko's rather symphonic score has its own shape and melodic fragments which help to give a feeling of wholeness.

Of the two attempts to create operas from *The Idiot*, the first is a rare piece by Valerian Bogdanov-Berezovsky (1903-1971), who was better known as a critic. In his youth he was a friend of Shostakovich and collaborated with the leading music critic of the time, Boris Asafiev, a.k.a. Igor Glebov (1884-1949), who also combined criticism with composing. *Nastasya Filippovna* (1964) received a concert performance in 1968, but the present writer has no other first-hand information, apart from the fact that this Dostoevskian work was written in a more modernistic style than his earlier operas on non-literary themes.[46]

Nearly two decades later, another opera based on *The Idiot* was written by Maisei Vainberg (Mieczysław Weinberg, 1919-1996), a Russian composer of Polish origin, whose friendship with Shostakovich, to whom he dedicated many of his works, including, posthumously, *The Idiot* (1980), greatly influenced his ideas on composition.[47] *The Idiot* was the last of his seven operas, written

---

[46] For more information on this composer and critic's (earlier) life see: I Gusin, *Valerian Bogdanov-Berezovskii* (Moscow and Leningrad: Muzyka, 1966). Specifically on *Nastasya Filippovna* see L Dan'ko, 'Novaia opera na siuzhet Dostoevskogo' in *Muzyka i muzykanty Leningrada*, ed. L N Raaben, E A Ruch'evskaia and A N Sokhor (Leningrad and Moscow: Muzyka, 1972), pp. 231-241.

[47] Vainberg played duets with Shostakovich both privately and publicly, and the latter always defended his music, but Vainberg was sometimes mocked as an epigone of the older composer. Worse still, Ivashkin mentions Vainberg as being part cause of 'a sort of weariness with this [Shostakovich's symphonic] style [...]' covering 'it over with a scab of numerous and bad copies':

towards the end of a very difficult life, during which he had never ceased to write prolifically, maintaining high ideals of philosophical harmony and musical clarity. Like Shostakovich, Vainberg was particularly fond of Gogol and Dostoevsky.[48] *Idiot* is a four-act opera, scored for a huge orchestra including Russian bells, glockenspiel, marimba, xylophone, celesta and offstage piano. The work is also available in a version for small orchestra.[49] There are eight scenes, with no part for Ippolit, but considerable roles for Ganya and Lebedev, the latter at times seeming something like a typically Dostoevskian unreliable narrator, but in scene four singing to a cheap tune, and in scene eight accompanied by a banal triple rhythm, like a parody of a waltz. The declaration of his grand plans is against frenetic 12/8 arpeggio-like figures. The musical characterization of the singers is, in general, well done, although Myshkin seems even more passive than in the novel. When he first tells his story to the Epanchins, however, the orchestral accompaniment varies imaginatively to accentuate the different moods. Throughout the opera the orchestra often mimics or introduces the music of the singers, which follows the words carefully. Nastasya Filippovna sings at first in a rather hysterical, capricious, almost crooning voice, whilst Aglaya's first musical entry (offstage) is highly lyrical. Finally, the build up to the stabbing is against a sinister offstage knife-grinder advertising his services to a monotonous, quietly percussive, almost oriental theme. This dramatic rather than philosophical opera ends with Rogozhin and Myshkin sitting together by the corpse.

The chamber opera based on *Poor Folk* (1974) by Gleb Sedelnikov (b. 1944), already known for his children's music, was submitted as a diploma piece at Moscow Conservatory and later won first prize for a composition by a blind or partially sighted composer in 1978. It is in one act and composed for soprano, baritone and string quartet, with a libretto by Sedelnikov himself. A gramophone record of the opera was issued in 1980 and a disc in 1997. Despite this attention, Sedelnikov, like Tsvetaev, has no mention in either of the Grove dictionaries. This quintessentially chamber opera consists of thirteen of the letters: Makar's (hereafter M) of 8 April; Varvara (hereafter V) of 8 April; M 8 April; V 9 April;

'Shostakovich and Schnittke: The Erosion of Symphonic Syntax', in Fanning, pp. 254-270 (p. 255). It cannot, however, be said that Vainberg is totally neglected, since Olympia in 2004 brought out sixteen discs of his music, and he has several websites devoted to him, for the most part concerned with his life and his symphonic and chamber music, but not the operas, and certainly not *The Idiot*. See, for example, Robert R Reilly's article, 'Light in the Dark. The Music of Mieczyslaw Vainberg' [sic]: <http/ww.freewebs.com/black-arrow/biography 1.html>. A quarter of a century earlier, in 1956, Flora Litvinova asked Shostakovich about his other pupils and friends: 'Is Weinberg composing, and Levitin?' to which the composer apparently answered disapprovingly, 'Only theatre and film music': Wilson, p. 270.

[48] See Mecheslav Vainberg, 'Chestnost', pravdivost', polnaia otdacha', an interview with I Zhmodiak, *Sovetskaia muzyka*, 9 (1988), 23-26 (hereafter Vainberg) (p. 23).

[49] The piano score, on which the present writer has had to rely, in addition to an ancient recording, omits the breathy quiet flute motif with which the opera opens, perhaps representing, albeit briefly, the quiet of Switzerland. It is soon interrupted by a discordant crashing chord (where the piano score begins), representing the 'civilization' of the train and its passengers.

M 12 April; V 25 April; M 12 June; V 27 June; M 1 July; V 3 September; M 5 September; 23 September; final passage. There is little or no direct indication of the characters' impoverished background, and no mention of the novel's other characters (except for Mr Bykov when he comes to claim his bride). Sedelnikov eschews the opportunity for duets, instead rendering the dialogue mainly in a fairly melodious, tonic recitative, to which at moments of high emotion, he introduces elements of a dramatic or lyric line. Sedelnikov has used some of Dostoevsky's words, not necessarily precisely (after all, it can only be a selection). The atmosphere of the novel is, however, well achieved at one level, but there is no humour and Varvara's somewhat terse, even brusque, manner compared with Devushkin's loquaciousness is eroded. Both characters are, in fact, made pathetic: at first Makar has an almost jaunty accompaniment, but gradually his music becomes sadder or agitated, as when he compares himself to a rag (in the letter of 12 June) or at the end as he realizes that he is losing Varvara. The latter is something of a tragic heroine; her mood changes from dramatic victim, rescued damsel and doomed victim, well caught by Sedelnikov. Makar goes from lively and insistent to deeply despondent, whilst Varvara's music ranges from that of a heroine in grand opera to a fading flower (V April 9) or a long reminiscence of the country (V 3 September) where the music is intensely lyrical. The string quartet provides a vividly imaginative accompaniment to the bathos and pathos of the couple's feelings and thoughts. This chamber opera is one of the most successful transformations of a Dostoevsky text into music.

Finally, may be mentioned one of the most ambitious projects of all, that by Alexander Kholminov (b. 1925) to set *The Brothers Karamazov* to music.[50] Subtitled 'A Few Pages from the Novel by Fyodor Dostoevsky', it is in two acts and ten scenes, a full-length opera, written with great invention and skill rather than genius. The influence of Shostakovich, as on many twentieth-century Russian composers, is clearly evident (for instance, the quasi-simplistic, rhythmically repetitive accompaniment to Fyodor is comparable to the music for Boris Timofeevich in *Lady Macbeth of Mtsensk*). Nonetheless, there is much to admire. The opening vividly set the scene with the bereaved woman's lamentations, whilst in Ivan's gruesome catalogue of cruelty to children, the moans of the child tortured to death are very effectively heard offstage. Many readers of the novel are obsessed with Dmitry and his problems, and he is also at the centre of Kholminov's opera. His two women are more distinctly differentiated in the music than by their physical appearance in the Moscow Chamber Opera's production: Grushenka's music is considerably more down to earth, even folksy, than the more sophisticated Katerina Ivanovna's. But it is the character of Smerdyakov that seems to provoke particularly strong responses in Kholminov, as he does in other composers. In Shostakovich's *The Nose* (1927-28), for example, Smerdya-

---

[50] For many, Kholminov is best known for his Leniniana: 'Songs about Lenin' (1955), the cantata 'Lenin is with us' (1967) and music to three documentary films: *The Living Lenin, Memories of Lenin* and *The Lenin Museum* (all 1958).

kov's song, 'An invincible power' (Part II, 5, chapter 2), given to the lackey Ivan, was the only part of that opera with words not by Gogol. In Kholminov's work Smerdyakov's famous words, 'It's interesting to have a chat [*pogovorit'*] with a clever man' (in Act 1, scene 3 of the opera) begin off stage with a series of repeated Cs leaping to, at first B on the last syllable of *pogovorit'*. As the scene progresses his leaps vary, often accompanied by a shrill clarinet, but the vocal line's instability very successfully creates a sense of cunning, combined with neurotic weakness. Later the leaps stabilize to some extent into a sixth from G to E in a sinisterly simple motif that perhaps might recall for some Western listeners Universal Studios' Woody Woodpecker's call sign.[51] Later, in Act 2, scene 9, after the murder, Smerdyakov has a long laughing passage of terrifying intensity, beginning with 'Everything is permitted' ('Vse dozvoleno'), which recalls the earlier unbalanced leaps, but achieves its memorable effect mainly by quickly repeated notes against a grotesquely cacophonous background. In the background, a faint bell ostinato seems to symbolize the inevitability of universal justice.[52] Whether or not Fyodor's death is the central point of the novel, it is certainly one of the highpoints of Kholminov's ambitious opera.

In conclusion, it may be wondered, what is the purpose of setting novels like *The Idiot* and *The Brothers Karamazov* to music? Undoubtedly, some works of literature, like Mérimée's 'Carmen' or Leskov's 'Lady Macbeth of Mtsensk', have gained a tremendous new lease of life from their operatic reincarnations. In the case of Dostoevsky, however, it would seem that, whilst many interesting compositions have been written under his inspiration, it is the less well known works such as 'A Nasty Story' with Karetnikov's film score or, especially, the songs of Captain Lebyadkin which can benefit most from transposition into music. Nonetheless, the writer who, with the help of Bakhtin, brought the concept of polyphony to many who do not know their arias from their Elgar, has undoubtedly attracted a quantity of interesting music—the connection is, indeed, more 'than people think'.[53]

---

[51]This is not nearly so obvious a coincidence as is 'Three Blind Mice' in the slow movement of Rachmaninov's Fourth Piano Concerto.

[52]Manuilov, p. 92.

[53]Professor Jones has written about the musical qualities of Dostoevsky's prose, with reference to *Notes from Underground*: M V Jones, *Dostoyevsky: The Novel of Discord* (London: Paul Elek, 1976), pp. 63-65. Although 'from another opera', it may be mentioned that Dostoevsky himself had a general rather than specific fondness for music, most enjoying Beethoven, also Rossini, Glinka and Serov. According to Anna Snitkina, his appreciation was emotional and could extend to a barrel organ: for more detail see J Catteau, *Dostoyevsky and the Process of Literary Creation*, trans. A Littlewood (Cambridge University Press, 1989), pp. 27-32. There may well also be scope for analysing Dostoevsky's novels through comparison with musical works. For an interesting attempt to relate *The Brothers Karamazov* to Wagner's operas, in particular, *Parsifal* see: R Bartlett, 'Dostoevsky's *The Brothers Karamazov*: The Novel as Fugue or Music Drama?', in Phrase and Subject: *Studies in Music and Literature*, ed. D Da Sousa Correa and R Samuels (Oxford: Legenda, forthcoming).

PART III

Text and Reader

THE *SIUZHET* OF PART I OF *CRIME AND PUNISHMENT*

Robert L Belknap

THE *siuzhet* of *Crime and Punishment* falls into two unequal parts. For certain kinds of study it is useful to pretend that the first seven chapters, ending in the murder, are a novella named *Crime,* that can be separated from the remaining thirty-four chapters, a novel named *Punishment*. These two works share their hero, but not the rest of the cast; among all the characters, Raskolnikov actually meets only two major figures in both parts, the Marmeladov parents. The two parts also share a fractal quality. The first chapter embodies Part I in some of the same ways Part I embodies the whole, and the first page does several of the same things on a tiny scale.

On this first page, the first paragraph introduces two characters. One, Raskolnikov, goes unnamed for several pages, and the other, the narrator, never receives a name, though we all know that Dostoevsky had toyed with the idea of also naming him Raskolnikov. In the printed text, this narrator is so far from being Raskolnikov that he has to deduce Raskolnikov's state of mind from the slowness of his actions, *'medlenno, kak by v nereshimosti'* ('slowly as if in indecision'). In the second paragraph, the narrator introduces another character, the landlady, and moves closer to Raskolnikov. *'On blagopoluchno izbegnul'* ('he successfully avoided') implies that the narrator knows Raskolnikov had tried or at least wanted to avoid meeting the landlady, and later in the paragraph, the narrator knows that Raskolnikov *'chuvstvoval kakoe-to boleznennoe i truslivoe oshchushchenie'* ('experienced a certain sort of morbid and cowardly sensation'). At the end of the next paragraph, he slips into *erlebte Rede,* using words like *vzdor* ('nonsense') and *drebeden'* ('trash') that plainly reflect Raskolnikov's mind, although the voice is technically the narrator's. Only in the fifth paragraph does the narrator's voice disappear behind Raskolnikov's reflections on his own morbid and cowardly feelings, which are presented in quotation marks.

Symmetrically, in this paragraph, as the narrator's presence recedes, another important character comes into play, the reader. Here, for the first time, the narrator is visibly manipulating the reader, when Raskolnikov says to himself, *'Na kakoe delo khochu pokusitsia'* ('I want to make an attempt like that'). The narrator is doing two things: loading the *delo* with the importance for Raskolnikov and the reader that comes, as Meerson has shown, from being spookily unmentionable, tabooed; and at the same time introducing the standard narrative device of *curiosité,* that counterpart of suspense which arouses doubt in the reader not about the future, but about what is going on at the moment.

On the first page, Dostoevsky has introduced his hero and the murder without naming either, and also his interest in complexities of narrative technique. At the end of this paragraph, the hero asks, '*Nu zachem ia teper' idu? Razve ia sposoben na eto?*' ('So why am I on my way now? Can it be that I'm capable of *that*?'). These two sentences introduce the central activity of Chapter One, of the novella *Crime*, and of the entire novel: the rehearsal of an intimidating action. Most important, this page has led the reader from experiencing the happenings as an outsider to internal participation in Raskolnikov's thinking. The whole 'novella' repeats this pattern on a larger scale.

The first three chapters of the novella *Crime* introduce the reader to most of the characters Raskolnikov does not actually meet within the novella, using a variety of narrative techniques, as does the first page. Causally, these three chapters are curiously isolated from one another. The first presents Raskolnikov's situation and his first rehearsal of the crime. The second allows Marmeladov to recount the woes of his family (pp. 14-21)[54], and the third embeds the letter from Raskolnikov's mother about the Svidrigaylovs, Luzhin, and Dunya (pp. 27-34). Raskolnikov is a bystander in the affairs of the Marmeladov family, and has little influence on the events in his mother's letter beyond his absence and his need for money, about which his mother's account is silent. The two heroines, Sonya and Dunya, come into their own only in the sequel, but they share one property with Lizaveta and her sister, Alyona: all four are victims.

The causal separation between the Raskolnikov plot, the Sonya plot, and the Dunya plot forces the reader to notice another kind of connection among these plots. Dunya's plan to sacrifice her happiness to support her brother's career is one of the strongest motives for the murder, and Dostoevsky takes great pains to remind the reader of the parallel between the situations of these two heroines. In the fourth chapter, Raskolnikov responds to the monologic statements of his mother and Marmeladov with an interior monologue of his own that is almost as long as theirs (pp. 35-39), and is basically a literary criticism of his mother's letter, partly of its diction, use of the word 'apparently', etc., but also of its plot, particularly the motivation of Luzhin, Dunya, and his mother. This third monologue includes a comparison of the earlier two: 'Oh, dear and unjust hearts!... Sonechka, Sonechka Marmeladova, the eternal Sonechka, as long as the World lasts!...Do you know Dunechka, that Sonechka's destiny is in no way more vile than a destiny with Mr. Luzhin?' (p. 38). Dostoevsky is using Raskolnikov to instruct his readers on how to understand the relationship between the Sonya plot and the Dunya plot, since this relationship is not causal. Characters in Dickens, Hugo, Sand, and other favourites of Dostoevsky's have compared calculated marriages to prostitution, but the nagging attention to the parallel in Raskolnikov's interior monologue is then enacted in the second part of Chapter Four.

---

[54]*PSS*, VI. Page references to this volume are given in the text in parentheses.

When Raskolnikov meets a dishevelled teenager staggering down the Boulevard, he reflects that her destiny is also prostitution and death before she is twenty, and he calls the hovering lecher 'Svidrigaylov', creating a cluster of three helpless women sacrificed to the lust of moneyed selfishness. By calling our attention to this 'situation rhyme', Dostoevsky shifts his reader's attention from the parallels among the three women to the consistency in Raskolnikov's responses to their situations. With Sonya's family, his first impulse is generous; he leaves money on the windowsill as he leaves, then in a fit of literal *esprit d'escalier* repents his generosity, saying to himself, 'they have Sonya...' (p. 25). With the drunken teenager, he gives a policeman money to help her home, then calls to the puzzled policeman to forget the whole idea, telling himself cynically that statistics prove that a certain percentage of women have to be ruined every year (p. 43). With Dunya, his reaction to the Luzhin engagement is more spirited. His generosity takes the form of preventing the marriage, but suddenly he asks himself what right he has to forbid it, which leads him to thoughts about murdering the pawnbroker (pp. 38-39). By the end of the fourth chapter, therefore, Dostoevsky has trained his readers to expect parallel events producing parallel responses, and specifically to expect Raskolnikov to alternate between impulsive generosity and cynical afterthought.

These four chapters position the reader to experience the second, far more horrible rehearsal of the murder, the dream of the beaten horse. In this scene, Dostoevsky uses the child Raskolnikov to guide the reader's moral response, but such guidance is hardly necessary; the brutality speaks for itself, and Raskolnikov's alternations of mood have been established, so that the reader expects some contrary response also. But Chapter Five is divided into three unequal parts, and the dream sequence, followed by the waking Raskolnikov's first response to it (pp. 46-50) are much longer than the reversal passage (pp. 50-52). His waking response begins with the same incredulous revulsion against the idea of murder that the first rehearsal produced: 'God!...can it be, can it really be that I will actually take an axe and undertake to slam her head, to brain her skull... and slither on sticky, warm blood...' The revulsion leads to a resolution:

> No, I won't endure it! Even though there should be no slightest doubt in all these calculations, though everything I've been deciding all this month should be clear as day, as just as arithmetic. Lord! I still would not decide to do it. I just won't endure it, won't endure it...
>
> He suddenly began to breathe more easily. He felt that he had already cast off this fearsome burden that had been crushing him so long, and in his heart it suddenly grew easy and peaceful. 'Lord!' he prayed, 'Show me my way, and I renounce this damned—daydream of mine!'
>
> ...Freedom, freedom! He was free now from all these enchantments, from charms delusions, and deceptions (p. 50).

This second part of Chapter Five systematizes a set of opposed abstractions that Dostoevsky has been constructing for five chapters:

Dream (*son*)	vs Daydream (*mechta*)
Unconsciousness	vs Consciousness
Impulse	vs Afterthought
Generosity	vs Economics
Religion	vs Mathematics
Nature	vs Science
Humanity	vs Statistics
Intuition	vs Reason
Freedom	vs Determinism
Air	vs Crushing burdens
Revulsion	vs Murder

After the murder, more elements enter the picture, notably the opposition between confession and suicide, and between resurrection and death, but once Dostoevsky has established this system, the plan for the book is in place, and it is daringly simple. The alternations he has established in Raskolnikov's mind take place between the two sides of this list, very often signalled by the word so many Dostoevskians have loved, *vdrug*.

The expected shift in Raskolnikov's position takes place in the last part of Chapter Five. Upon learning that Alyona will be alone at seven the next night, he goes home like a man 'condemned to death', with neither 'freedom of judgment, nor will', and everything 'suddenly definitively decided'.

Having trained us to read this pattern, Dostoevsky starts to work to implicate us in Raskolnikov's crime as powerfully as the dream of the horse has implicated us in the revulsion against it. At the very end of Chapter Seven, Raskolnikov, whose actions, passions, and experiences we have shared without interruption, waking, sleeping, reading, listening, and committing murder, has unlocked the door and listened at the stairhead, waiting patiently to escape. He hears voices in the distance, then silence, then the noisy painters quitting work, and then someone's footsteps approaching, heavily, evenly, unhurriedly. He freezes, as in a nightmare when one dreams pursuers are catching up, close, want to kill, and it is as if one has taken root there and cannot move one's hands. He finally slips back to the pawnbroker's room, rehooks the door, and hides, not breathing (p. 67). While Raskolnikov stands in the room with two bleeding corpses, holding his breath as he listens at the door, inches from his potential discoverers, who may leave or may bring the police, we readers hold our breath, exert our will upon him not to give up and confess, and then suddenly realize that we are accessories after the fact, trying to help this merciless, calculating hatchet-murderer to escape.

This complicity in the crime alternates with the reader's horror and revulsion at it, just as Raskolnikov alternates between a drive to murder and escape and a drive toward freedom, generosity, humanity, and all the elements contributing to his revulsion. At the end of the novella, *Crime*, Dostoevsky's rhetoric has established a *raskol* in his reader, who participates actively on both sides of Raskolnikov's split drives.

OF SHAME AND HUMAN BONDAGE: DOSTOEVSKY'S *NOTES FROM UNDERGROUND*

Deborah A Martinsen

Human infirmity in moderating and checking the emotions I name bondage: for, when a man is prey to his emotions, he is not his own master, but lies at the mercy of fortune: so much so, that he is often compelled, while seeing that which is better for him, to follow that which is worse.

Spinoza, *Ethics*, Part 4, 'Of Human Bondage, or the Strength of Emotions'

DOSTOEVSKY'S underground man is not only a paradoxicalist, he *embodies* shame's paradox, i.e., its capacity to isolate yet relate. Though he has isolated himself, he reaches out to readers. Though he champions free will, he acts unfreely. By creating these disjunctures between the underground man's words and deeds, his theory and practice, Dostoevsky reveals that which his underground man would conceal. He fashions a first-person narrator whose narrative strategies serve as shame defences that both reveal his shame and limit his freedom. In doing so, Dostoevsky explores the psychological and metaphysical relationship between shame and unfreedom.[1]

---

[1] Other helpful studies of the underground man are: Roger B Anderson, *Dostoevsky: Myths of Duality* (Gainesville, FL: University of Florida Press, 1986), pp. 27-47; Robert L Belknap, 'The Unrepentant Confession', in Belknap, ed., *Russianness* (Ann Arbor MI: Ardis, 1990), pp. 113-123; Michael André Bernstein, *Bitter Carnival: Ressentiment and The Abject Hero* (Princeton, NJ: Princeton University Press, 1992), pp. 87-120; Carol Flath, 'Fear of Faith: The Hidden Religious Message of *Notes from Underground*', *Slavic and East European Journal*, 37, 4 (1993), pp. 510-529; Joseph Frank, *Dostoevsky: The Stir of Liberation*, 1860-1865 (Princeton, NJ: Princeton University Press, 1981), pp. 310-347; Robert L Jackson, *The Art of Dostoevsky: Deliriums and Nocturnes* (Princeton, NJ: Princeton University Press, 1981), pp. 171-188; Malcolm V Jones, *Dostoyevsky: The Novel of Discord* (New York: Harper & Row, 1976), pp. 55-66 and *Dostoyevsky after Bakhtin: Readings in Dostoevsky's Fantastic Realism* (Cambridge: Cambridge University Press, 1990), pp. 59-73; Liza Knapp, *The Annihilation of Inertia: Dostoevsky and Metaphysics* (Evanston, IL: Northwestern University Press, 1996), pp. 15-43; Olga Meerson, 'Old Testament Lamentation in the Underground Man's Monologue: A Refutation of the Existentialist Reading of *Notes from Underground*', *Slavic and East European Journal*, 36, 3 (1992), pp. 317-322; Robin Feuer Miller, 'Dostoevsky and Rousseau: The Morality of Confession Reconsidered', in Robert L Jackson, ed., *Dostoevsky: New Perspectives* (Englewood Cliffs, NJ: Prentice Hall, 1984), pp. 82-98; Irina Reyfman, *Ritualized*

The underground man's shame makes him universal. According to the biblical myth informing Dostoevsky's understanding, shame originates in the Fall. After transgressing in the Garden, Eve and Adam become self-conscious. Realizing their nakedness, they hide themselves. Expelled from the Garden, they lose their unselfconscious relationship to one another, their environment, and God. Dostoevsky explicitly locates his underground man in this fallen world. Like our mythical forebears, Dostoevsky's antihero has lost his sense of wholeness and belonging and thus experiences shame and self-consciousness. Just as Eve and Adam fabricate clothes that conceal their physical nakedness but reveal their transgression, so the underground man fabricates an egoistic philosophy that conceals the narcissistic, shame-based psychology that his biography reveals.

Dostoevsky discloses his ethical agenda in *Notes from Underground* by linking the underground man's metaphysics and his ethics, attending closely to his shame and guilt issues. Shame is broadly linked to human identity; guilt more narrowly to human action. Shame arises from feelings of exclusion, objectification, or negative self-assessment; guilt from transgression of personal, moral, social, or legal norms. Shame and guilt can be related, but need not be. The underground man's unattractive appearance makes him feel shame, for instance, not guilt. When he passes his shame on to Liza, however, he acts in a way that harms her and haunts him. He also compounds his original shame with the shame of knowing that he is the kind of person who has deliberately harmed another. In creating a character who hides his guilt behind a confession of shame which he aggressively generalizes to include his readers, Dostoevsky complicates his narrative. Guilt often follows the sequence—transgression, repentance, expiation, and, in Christian scenarios, redemption. Shame has no fixed script. Nor can a single action heal feelings of shame. The underground man responds to shame by excluding, objectifying and negatively assessing others, by struggling to be perceived as a worthy self-presenting agent, or by actively sharing his shame, contradictory responses that also characterize his writing project. He exposes himself partly to relieve his guilt and isolation, but he fails: to expiate his evil action, he must acknowledge its evil. To do so, he must accept universal moral norms, which, Dostoevsky shows, the underground man will not do. His egoism taints his ethics. The underground man repeatedly chooses aggressive self-protection over the vulnerability of relation.[2] Instead of appealing to our

---

Violence Russian Style: The Duel in Russian Culture and Literature (Stanford, CA: Stanford University Press, 1999), pp. 192-261; Richard H Weisberg, *The Failure of the Word: The Protagonist as Lawyer in Modern Fiction* (New Haven, CN: Yale University Press, 1984), pp. 24-41. James P Scanlan, *Dostoevsky the Thinker* (Ithaca, NY: Cornell University Press, 2002), pp. 57-76 deserves special mention for its analysis of the underground man's theorizing.

[2]Some of the most useful psychological shame studies are: Francis Broucek, *Shame and the Self* (1991); Gershen Kaufman, *The Psychology of Shame: Theory and Treatment of Shame-Based Syndromes* (1993); Michael Lewis, *Shame: The Exposed Self* (1992); Susan Miller, *The Shame Experience* (1993); Andrew Morrison, *Shame: The Underside of Narcissism* (1989); Donald L. Nathanson, *Shame and Pride: Affect, Sex and the Birth of the Self* (1992) and ed., *The Many Faces*

common experience of shame as grounds for bonding, he claims shame superiority, thus reinforcing his isolation by justifying it.

By having the underground man claim self-consciousness as his defining condition, Dostoevsky prepares the ground for existentialist thinkers to claim his antihero as their forebear. By having his character elaborate a philosophy that justifies inaction while arguing for free will, Dostoevsky reveals the flaws in his arguments. By employing 'surplus vision',[3] Dostoevsky demonstrates that his narrator is emotionally stuck in an underground of his own making. Hell is not other people, but his own construct—as readers learn in Part II, when the underground man tells his story.

Aggression

Throughout *Notes from Underground*, Dostoevsky uses the underground man's shame defences to expose his antihero's shame. From his narrative's first chapter, the underground man employs the two standard, socially acceptable defences of denial and flight, manifest largely as grandiosity and repression (denial), or as intellectualizing, fantasizing, and self-enclosure (flight). The underground man fortifies these standard defences with the third, non-standard, unacceptable defence of aggression, as he does in his famous first three sentences: 'I am a sick man...I am a spiteful man. I am an unattractive man'. In Russian, these are all three-word sentences. The first two start with the first-person pronoun 'I', the third with the adjective. The adjectives occupy three different positions: third, second, first. In English they would awkwardly read: 'I—man sick. I—spiteful man. Unattractive—I man'. In Russian, the adjective in second position— 'spiteful'—is unmarked syntactically, while 'sick' and 'unattractive' compel notice.

Dostoevsky double-voices these provocative sentences, thus demonstrating his authorial control while exposing his anti-hero's psyche.[4] When the underground man announces that he is 'sick' and then that his liver hurts, he encourages readers to regard his illness as physical, an explanation he subsequently repudiates. As Olga Meerson demonstrates, however, Dostoevsky uses this diagnosis to suggest metaphysical illness: the underground man alludes to Galen's theory of humours, but Dostoevsky alludes to the Old Testament book of Lamentations. While the underground man remains resolutely earthbound,

---

of Shame (1987), and ed., *Knowing Feeling: Affect, Script and Psychotherapy* (1996); Carl Schneider, *Shame Exposure and Privacy* (1977; 1992); and Leon Wurmser, *The Mask of Shame* (1981). The most useful philosophical analysis of shame for my work on Dostoevsky is J David Velleman, 'The Genesis of Shame', *Philosophy and Public Affairs* 30, no 1 (Winter 2001), 27-52.

[3]M M Bakhtin discusses this strategy in 'Author and Hero in Aesthetic Activity', in *Art and Answerability: Early Philosophical Essays by M M Bakhtin*, ed. Michael Holquist & Vadim Liapunov, trans. Vadim Liapunov (Austin, TX: University of Texas Press, 1990), pp. 4-256.

[4]M M Bakhtin, *The Dialogic Imagination*, ed. Michael Holquist, trans. Caryl Emerson and Michael Holquist (Minneapolis: University of Minnesota, 1984), p. 324.

Dostoevsky suggests that he suffers from metaphysical desolation due to separation from God.[5]

The underground man's second adjective, 'spiteful,' reinforces the story's metaphysical dimension, for he uses the Russian word *zloi*, which also means 'evil.' By constantly emphasizing his spitefulness, the underground man encourages the psychological reading. Dostoevsky, however, evokes the concepts of 'good' and 'evil', thereby underscoring the story's ethical dimension and suggesting a relationship between spite and evil. The sentence's central placement rather than its syntax thus reveals Dostoevsky's authorial emphasis.

The third adjective, 'unattractive', reads as awkwardly in Russian as in English. The first two adjectives 'sick' and 'spiteful' are not only short and common, they rhyme—*bol'noi/zloi*. The underground man's third, multisyllabic, non-rhyming adjective—*neprivlekatel'nyi*—thus strikes a dissonant chord. Literally translated 'unattractive', the adjective can refer to physical appearance or moral qualities. Not surprisingly, the underground man focuses on his appearance, a major source of his shame-sensitivity, while Dostoevsky focuses on his moral condition. The underground man's first words dramatize his obsession with how others perceive him. His last adjective reveals that he frets more about his identity than his ethics. The adjectival progression—sick, spiteful, unattractive—also reflects the story's structure: the underground man aggressively exposes himself, yet, here as elsewhere, he places the most painful revelation last.

The aggressiveness of these opening sentences prepares readers, as much as anything can, for the hostility that follows. Most strikingly, the underground man aggressively assaults his readers with a narrative strategy that reflects his behaviour in the story: just as he aggressively passes his shame on to Liza, so he aggressively passes it on to his narrative audience.[6] By self-consciously admitting to his own shame, the underground man establishes himself as a fellow sufferer in our fallen world. By assaulting his narrative audience, he protects himself as he alienates us.

In Part II, Chapter Nine, Dostoevsky has the underground man explain the dynamics of passed-on shame to Liza:

---

[5]Meerson, p. 319.

[6]I take the terms 'narrative' and 'authorial' audiences from Peter Rabinowitz, *Before Reading: Narrative Conventions and the Politics of Interpretation* (Ithaca, NY: Cornell University Press, 1987), pp. 93-104. As members of the narrative audience, we participate as observers of the text's mimetic illusion, i.e., we treat the fictional action as real; as members of the authorial audience, we are equally aware of the text as synthetic construct. Dostoevsky exploits our divided roles as members of both audiences. In the narrative audience, we respond viscerally to characters' shame; in the authorial audience, we witness and experience that shame yet retain the cognitive engagement, surplus vision and aesthetic pleasures provided by the text. I elaborate this strategy in my book, *Surprised by Shame: Dostoevsky's Liars and Narrative Exposure* (Columbus, OH: The Ohio State University Press, 2003).

You've come because I spoke *pitiful words (zhalkie slova)* to you then. So you went soft and wanted 'pitiful words' again. So know, know that I was laughing at you then. And now I'm laughing. Why are you trembling? Yes, I was laughing! I had been insulted earlier at dinner by the fellows who came ahead of me. I came there to thrash one of them, an officer. But I didn't succeed, I didn't find him. It was necessary to avenge my offence on someone, to take my own back, you turned up, and I poured out my spite on you and laughed. I had been humiliated, so I wanted to humiliate; I had been ground into a rag, so I too wanted to show power'. (V, 173)[7]

With these words, Dostoevsky reveals how shame can lead to guilt. Humiliated by others before their initial encounter, the underground man assaults Liza sexually. Humiliated by her rebuff of his kindness, he humiliates her verbally. Their second encounter likewise begins with his humiliation. Liza arrives just as he is impotently raging at Apollon. This time he assaults her verbally—because she witnesses his humiliation in front of his servant, then sexually—because she witnesses him break down and cry. When Liza leaves, the underground man fabricates and then attacks his narrative audience.

The underground man's assaults on Liza and his readers explain his failure. Imprisoned by egoism and shackled by shame, he cannot envision true freedom. He defines free will negatively and thus fails to recognize its positive manifestation in Liza. The underground man adopts the form of confession for his *Notes*, but he cannot escape his bad conscience because, as Robert Belknap has noted, he does not repent.[8] Confession can provide relief for both shame and guilt only if the one confessing gives his audience the authority either to accept him as he is (shame) or to forgive his transgression (guilt).[9] The underground man refuses to relinquish authority because he fears loss of control. By repeatedly choosing egoism and isolation over relation and community, he fortifies his prison.

The underground man's repetition compulsion further limits his freedom. He not only assaults Liza twice following humiliation by others and twice following emotional exposures before her, he also forces himself on those who do not seek his company—first the officer on the sidewalk, then his classmates, then his servant, and finally Liza. Dostoevsky uses this progression both to stress his antihero's ethical inertia[10] and to highlight gender politics. The underground man cannot dominate his male interlocutors, neither his social equals nor his servant, so he channels his rage onto his female interlocutor, the more vulnerable Liza.

---

[7] Citations are from *PSS*. All translations are my own.

[8] Belknap, p. 120-121.

[9] Michael Lewis identifies four methods of dealing with shame: 'owning it', which allows shame to dissipate with time; denial/forgetting; laughter, which allows individuals to distance themselves from feelings of shame; and confession (Lewis 1992, pp. 127-128).

[10] See Knapp, pp. 15-43.

His writing also repeats a pattern: the underground man feels so marginal, he creates dialogic situations to prove he exists. Thus, when he chooses to write his 'notes', he constructs a narrative audience with whom he acts out his patterns of behaviour. His sense of shame leads him to expose himself; exposure inevitably leads to more shame, which leads to flight—isolation, intellectualizing, fantasizing, or a combination. Fortified by his defences, he sallies forth aggressively, only to be defeated yet again. And so the cycle goes on.

These repetitions prepare us for his project's ultimate failure, for in his 'notes', the underground man turns on us, his imaginary interlocutors. He periodically exchanges his habitual first-person singular pronoun 'I' for the collective 'we', projecting his beliefs or habits onto his narrative audience, as he does in his final paragraph:

> Permit me, ladies and gentlemen, I am not justifying myself with that 'all of us'. As for what touches me personally, I have only in my life carried to an extreme that which you have not dared to carry even halfway . . . We are even oppressed at being humans, humans with *our own* real bodies and blood; we are ashamed of it, we consider it a disgrace, and we keep trying to be some sort of fairy-tale universal beings. (V, 178-179)

The argument of the paragraph (including the omitted parts) runs as follows: I am part of all of us (we). I do what you do, only I go further (boast—I). We are all fallen creatures; we are all ashamed of ourselves; we are all seeking to be other than what we are (we). Inside his universalizing claim, the underground man grandiosely declares superiority. He thus reveals the flaw in his strategy—though he hopes to alleviate his shame by sharing it,[11] he aggressively places himself first, isolating and alienating himself from the community he longs to join.

His writing project as explained in Part II thus resembles the toothache he discusses in Part I. The hypothetical toothache is an image of pain. Unlike the golden pins, which represent pain inflicted by someone more powerful, or the slap in the face,[12] which represents pain inflicted by a social equal, the toothache is a form of bodily pain. It thus resembles mortality, a source of shame that Dostoevsky's Ippolit will rail against in *The Idiot*. Faced with this hypothetical evidence of his human condition, the underground man posits two responses: seeking help or suffering in silence. The first strategy he rejects in Part I, Chapter One when he declares that he refuses to accept medical help 'out of spite'. Though he later explains this decision in terms of free will, another dynamic actually obtains. To accept medical help requires acknowledgment of the doctor's superior knowledge or skill, and, as Belknap shows, the underground

---

[11] Camus borrows this strategy of having a first-person narrator share his shame when writing *La Chute*. Since he writes allegorically about the occupation of France as well as the human condition, however, Camus emphasizes his narrator's attempt to share guilt.

[12] See Reyfman for a discussion of the sociopolitical dimensions of slaps in the face.

man refuses to acknowledge others' authority.[13] He also rejects silent suffering. If he must suffer, he wants others to acknowledge his pain and suffer with him. His moans provide sensual pleasure because they indicate his control over his pain's expression. He knows 'that he might moan differently, more simply, without trills and affectations, and that he is only indulging himself like that from malice, from venom. Well, in all these recognitions and disgraces there lies voluptuousness'. (V, 107) By analogy, Dostoevsky reveals that the underground man's pleasure in writing derives from embellishing his pain and thus sharpening others' awareness of him. Faced with isolation and exclusion, he chooses self-exposure. Like his interlocutor Rousseau,[14] the underground man forces others to acknowledge his presence, revels in his revelations of shame, and acts out a script in which he is the primary actor. His discourse on toothaches reveals his egoism, his anguish, and their correlation. His self-imposed isolation is agonizing, but to accept help from an other would mean forfeiting his self-declared superiority.

The underground man's defences thus expose the causes of his failure: while he addresses an audience, he wants to feel in control. Because he is socially inept, he feels most in control when alone. But when he is alone, there is no one to admire him—or even to acknowledge his existence. He writes in order to be. His writing becomes an existential project which takes the form of self-aggrandizement. He draws attention to himself to undo the pain of his insignificance. Exposing himself may be painful, but it proves he is alive. As he says in Part I, Chapter Nine: 'Well, even though the same result obtains with consciousness, that is, one will also do nothing, at least one can sometimes whip oneself, which livens it up somewhat. While it's retrograde, it's nonetheless better than nothing'. (V, 119)

Throughout his *Notes*, the underground man claims moral superiority by declaring the superiority of his self-consciousness. But such a claim rings hollow in the face of Liza's magnanimity. He argues for self-awareness; she demonstrates awareness of an other. When she offers him love, he aggressively punishes her. He sees her generosity as a threat to his autonomy. His egoism blinds him, but not Dostoevsky's readers. We see that Liza embodies the elusive ideal the underground man cries out for at the end of Part I: 'Well, change, seduce me with something else, give me another ideal. (V, 120) Liza shows him something better—love and compassion, a way out of his prisonhouse of shame. He intuits but represses that knowledge.

---

[13]Belknap, p. 122.

[14]On Dostoevsky and Rousseau, see Belknap; Miller; J M Coetzee, 'Confession and Double Thoughts: Tolstoy, Rousseau, Dostoevsky', *Comparative Literature*, 37, 3 (Summer 1985), pp. 192-232; and Barbara F Howard, 'The Rhetoric of Confession: Dostoevskij's *Notes from Underground* and Rousseau's *Confessions*', in R F Miller, ed., *Critical Essays on Dostoevsky* (Boston MA: G K Hall, 1986), pp. 64-72.

Denial

Repression is one of the underground man's major denial defences; grandiosity the other. Though one operates covertly and the other overtly, both defences protect his narcissistically vulnerable ego. The underground man's grandiosity expresses itself flamboyantly as a rhetorical strategy. He boasts his intellectual superiority as a cover for his social ineptitude, but he also flaunts his narcissistic vulnerability as a sign of his superior self-consciousness. He grandiosely denies that rejection by his classmates represents a loss, for example. In the Liza story, his greatest denial merges with fantasizing, one of his favourite flight defences. He runs after Liza but returns to his apartment where he stifles 'the living heartfelt pain with fantasies'. (V, 177) He fantasizes that the pain he has inflicted will prepare her for the degradation ahead: 'offence will elevate and purify her...by hatred...hmm...perhaps, also by forgiveness'. (V, 178) The anti-utilitarian underground man thus justifies his action by positing its utility. Although he projects his own strategy—'by hatred'—onto her, his hesitating 'by forgiveness' indicates awareness of Liza's autonomy. This hesitation reveals the authorial message: the underground man's awareness of an alternative accounts for his anguish. Likewise, his choice reveals his tragedy: forgiveness entails reciprocity; isolation and hatred are safer.

The underground man's other denial defence, repression, fittingly conceals itself. Grandiosity and repression unite in the second paragraph, where the underground man boasts that he can repress his positive emotions—an acknowledgment that clues Dostoevsky's authorial audience to look for repression in the text's unusual structure. While the underground man declares that he is going to talk about himself, he carefully controls his public image, repressing some facts as he reveals others. He confesses to secret debaucheries without openly stating that he visits brothels (Part II, ch. 2)—a strategy of partial disclosure whereby he mentions his vice without naming it and thus implicates his narrative audience by assuming shared knowledge or experience. Most strikingly, the man from underground delays the pain of self-exposure for as long as possible. Only at the end of Part I, for example, does he reveal that he began his writing project to gain relief from an oppressive memory. In Part II he writes first about his co-workers, his sidewalk duel, and his former schoolmates, saving the haunting story of Liza for last. These delaying tactics reveal the underground man's defences: He conceals his emotional vulnerability by constructing an abrasive exterior. His denial merges with aggression.

Flight

The underground man flees his shame by intellectualizing, fantasizing, and isolating himself. In Part I, he grandiosely shows off his intellect and thus his qualifications as a social agent. After reading Part II, we realize that this initial theorizing derives from the underground man's painful experiences of twenty years earlier. In Part I, for instance, he calls himself 'unattractive'. In Part II, he reveals the narcissistic pain behind his intellectualizing strategy: 'I hated my face, for example, found it odious, and even suspected that there was some mean expression in it...The most terrible thing was that I found it positively stupid. And I would have been quite satisfied with intelligence. Let's even say I would have agreed to a mean expression, provided only that at the same time my face be found terribly intelligent'. (V, 124) He thus compensates for his negative self-image with a rhetorical display of intellect.

The underground man generalizes his personal experiences into metaphysical pronouncements. In Part I, he compares the laws of nature and the theory of determinism to a stone wall. He argues that men of action accept the existence of stone walls and work around them, while men of consciousness bang themselves against stone walls, deliberately causing themselves pain in order to protest the laws of nature. In Part II, readers discover the main source for the underground man's metaphor in his servant Apollon, a rigid man who withstands his master's attempts to bend him to his own will. When we realize that the underground man's metaphysics derives from a particular psychological dynamic, we are prepared to see how Dostoevsky extends the metaphor to the underground man, who hides his emotional pain behind a stone wall of theory. Furthermore, we see that while the underground man cannot break down Apollon's rigid defences, he weakens and demolishes Liza's more flimsy ones. She, in turn, crumbles his by offering him the metaphorical cup of tea with sugar that he writes about in his second paragraph: 'I might be foaming at the mouth, but bring me some kind of doll, give me a cup of tea with sugar, and I, if you please, will calm down. I will even go soft in the soul, although, undoubtedly, I will then grind my teeth at myself and for several months suffer insomnia from shame'. (V, 100) As he admits, the underground man cannot bear emotional vulnerability.

The shame theory of the philosopher David Velleman interestingly illuminates the underground man's theorizing. Velleman views shame as anxiety about exclusion from the social realm where individuals act as self-presenting agents,[15] a view that resonates with the underground man's extreme anxiety about self-presentation. By Part I, Chapter Ten he even attributes to his imaginary interlocutors—a self-constructed audience—the power to ignore him: 'And if you do not want to give me your attention, I am not going to bow and scrape before you'. (V, 120) He declares his autonomy, but the shame of his dependence on others, even imaginary others, then rouses his anxiety and provokes defiance: 'I have the underground'. (V, 120)

Shame and Unfreedom

The underground man argues against the most popular theories of his day—positivism, determinism, and materialism—by pointing to the disjuncture between

---

[15] Velleman, p. 50.

theory and practice. Buckle's theory that human beings become less bloodthirsty as civilization advances sounds good, he argues, but history provides ample evidence to the contrary. Dostoevsky employs a similar strategy with his unsocial protagonist—the theory he proposes in Part I represents the logical outcome of the choices he makes in Part II. Dostoevsky thus uses the underground man's biography to expose the sources and weaknesses of his theory. Most strikingly, Dostoevsky reveals that his theorist of free will acts unfreely.

In Part I, the underground man argues that his opponents' theories do not account for free will, even though it is man's 'most advantageous advantage'. Free will proves man is an independent agent with choice—choice to act against his own perceived or material advantage. Exerting free will in defiance of the laws of nature may be irrational, but it also proves his individuality, thereby elevating him above those who act unthinkingly. He may harm himself by refusing medical help, but he also asserts his autonomy by exercising choice. Throughout Part II, the underground man provides concrete examples of how he has harmed himself through exercising free will. He chooses to give up the prestigious civil service job he was offered in order to cut ties with his past. He lives with Apollon, who torments him. He engages in a one-sided duel. He invites himself to the celebratory dinner for Zverkov and behaves badly.

In these cases, the underground man chiefly harms himself. But in both encounters with Liza, he inflicts deep suffering on another—a socially humiliated and defenceless woman. When the underground man argues theoretically against the view that individuals always act in accordance with their perceived best interests and argues instead that humans do not always act rationally, he commands reader agreement. When he advocates ethical egoism, i.e., a theory which holds individuals free to act upon their desires,[16] he gives us pause. When he acts on his desire to harm Liza rather than on his desire to help her, we are forced to re-evaluate his theory. By structuring the narrative this way, Dostoevsky reveals that the underground man's theory of free will is negative and reactive. He protests against his opponents, but he does not propose an alternative. As Velleman argues, free will involves resisting desires as much as acting upon them. On his account, an agent's capacity to resist desires (i.e., to exercise his free will) enables him to choose which desires his behaviours will express.[17] In Part II, Dostoevsky demonstrates that his antihero reacts more than he acts. He may advocate free will, but he does not act freely; his emotional defences rather than his intellect guide his actions. His irrational choices are largely shame-driven and unfree. Instead of protesting the laws of nature, the underground man is protecting his fragile ego.

Dostoevsky continually underscores the disjuncture between the underground man's theory and his practice. While the underground man proclaims that free

---

[16] Scanlan, pp. 70-73.

[17] Velleman, p. 35.

will manifests personality and individuality, he repeatedly exhibits lack of moral imagination. He longs for an identity but has no idea what he would choose to be. (Part I, ch. 2) He fantasizes but steals his plots from books. (Part II, ch. 2) He pines for the sacred but cannot comprehend it. (Part I, ch. 10-11) In mythic terms, he senses something missing, but he cannot conceptualize it because it is outside him. His self-enclosure verges on solipsism. He cannot understand Liza, because she acts autonomously. She thus haunts him.

In Part II, the underground man confesses that he fantasizes to escape and thus to live safely and vicariously. He spends long hours engaged in solitary, reactive fantasies that derive from his reading. For the most part, he indulges in grandiose hero-fantasies:

> For example, I triumph over everyone; everyone, of course, is lying in the dust and is forced to voluntarily acknowledge all my perfections, and I forgive them all. I fall in love, being a famous poet and court chamberlain; I receive countless millions and donate them immediately to mankind, and then and there confess before all the world my disgraces, which, of course, are not mere disgraces, but contain an exceeding amount of 'the beautiful and the lofty,' of something manfredian. Everyone weeps and kisses me (what blockheads they'd be otherwise), and I go barefoot and hungry to preach new ideas and crush the retrograde under Austerlitz. (V, 133)

While others populate his fantasies, they have only one actor: the underground man. Again Dostoevsky provides his authorial audience with a metaliterary clue to his underground man's text. His fantasies replicate his text's structure: while it seems open to readers, it is actually closed. The underground man's contemporaries as well as his narrative audience are cast as the conquered or the adulatory or both.

Both Dostoevsky and his underground man emphasize the latter's self-enclosure. He simply cannot envision a relationship based on mutuality. As he confesses: 'with me to love meant to tyrannize and to excel morally. For my whole life I have been unable even to imagine any other kind of love...Even in my underground dreams I did not imagine love as anything but a struggle'. (V, 176) His view of love as a power struggle locks him into a dynamic that permits only two outcomes: mastery or submission. He articulates the crux of his tragedy: 'I began it always with hatred and ended it with moral subjugation, and afterwards I never could imagine what to do with the subjugated object'. (V, 176) This stunning statement exposes the underground man's greatest limitation. By choosing to see others as objects rather than equals, he denies himself the possibility of meaningful relationships. He also deprives himself of the possibility for self-knowledge. In creating the world in his own image, he perpetuates his self-enclosure.

In Velleman's view, when an agent shows something private, he fails to manage his self-image, which becomes an occasion for shame.[18] The underground man's fear that he is not a qualified self-presenting agent pervades the discourse of Part I and drives the action of Part II. In the autobiographical part of his story, each incident he relates follows a similar pattern—shame-exposure-exclusion-more shame, etc. By witnessing this repetition, Dostoevsky's authorial audience sees that to escape the underground means stepping out of this vicious cycle.

Liza represents a way out. She is also isolated, humiliated, and poor. She also erects stone wall defences. Yet when she sees the underground man's pain, she opens to him as a fellow sufferer and freely offers to share his pain. Dostoevsky employs Liza not only as an alternative to the underground man, but as a model reader. At first she only hears him assault her, but gradually she sees through his defences and empathizes with the suffering behind them: 'Liza, offended and crushed by me, understood much more than I had imagined. From all of it, she understood what a woman, if she loves sincerely, always understands above all, and that is: that I myself am unhappy'. (V, 174) Instead of responding to his words, she responds to the misery behind them. Like Liza, we are meant to see the misery—and the choices that led to it. Liza escapes his script, because she acts out of compassion—an emotion that he represses. She challenges his solipsism by acting as an equal self-presenting agent. The underground man, however, sees her autonomy as a threat. In social interactions, he attempts to dominate others. Because of his bureaucratic power, he succeeds with the sabre-rattler. He declares success with the sidewalk duel. He pretends success, boasting of his evening out with friends when borrowing money from his supervisor. But he cannot repress the memory of Liza's compassion. Her generosity shames him. His shame-based cruelty haunts him. He does not harm the sabre-rattler, the officer, or his classmates. He harms Liza. AND he cannot save face—either before himself or his readers. So, just as he turns on Liza for witnessing his shame, he turns on us. He says to her:

> Have you really not even now guessed that I will never forgive you for having found me in this bathrobe when I was throwing myself like a spiteful cur at Apollon... The saviour, the former hero throwing himself like a mangy mongrel at his lackey, who laughed at him. And for my tears just now, which I, like a shamed woman, could not hold back in front of you, I will never forgive you. And for that which I've just now confessed to you, I will also never forgive you. (V, 173)

The same applies to his narrative audience: He can never forgive us for witnessing his shame.

The underground man speaks loudly to readers because he embodies shame's paradox. Perceiving the openness of relation as a threat to his autonomy, he

---

[18] Velleman, p. 42.

embraces isolation. Isolated, he longs for relation. He reaches out to readers yet pushes us away. His desire for audience approval conflicts with his fear of negative response. Self-consciousness paralyses him. Dostoevsky masterfully portrays this dialectic of shame. In the person of the underground man, Dostoevsky dramatizes shame's self-conscious essence—its acute awareness of self and other. He creates a narrator who constructs his text the way he protects his ego: his shame defences serve as narrative strategies that allow Dostoevsky to reveal to his readers that which the underground man would conceal from his. The underground man writes aggressively. Every sentence is a struggle: he intellectualizes yet emotes; he embraces yet rejects isolation; he reveals yet represses his positive emotions; he confesses self-loathing yet grandiosely declares his superiority; he retreats into bookish fantasies which he tries to impose on others. But the structure of his text—which is both his creation and Dostoevsky's—exposes him. Brilliantly reversing the structure of St. Augustine's *Confessions*, which begins in autobiography and ends in theology, Dostoevsky uses his underground man's autobiography in Part II to discredit his philosophy in Part I. By creating a character who boasts of his consciousness and self-consciousness yet makes many unconscious, unself-aware choices, who champions choice yet repeatedly chooses to limit his own options, Dostoevsky demonstrates how his underground man's shame defences make him unfree.

NARRATIVE TECHNIQUE AS 'MAIEUTICS': DOSTOEVSKY'S *CRIME AND PUNISHMENT*

Horst-Jürgen Gerigk

I

'MAIEUTICS' is the art of midwifery. In Plato's dialogues, Socrates is presented to us as the master midwife of the philosophical dialogue. Socrates guides this dialogue in such a way that his conversation partner finds the truth by himself. The truth is not handed to him on a plate in a summary of the argument, it is rather revealed to him in such a roundabout way that he suddenly stumbles across it himself. It is born before the eyes of Socrates' interlocutor, as it were: through their dialogue, the truth comes into the world like a newborn child. Socrates supervises and directs this process of finding the truth as a midwife guides a delivery. He himself never intervenes explicitly, yet he also never allows his conversation partners to whittle the truth down to a single point. The main aim of Socrates' philosophical endeavour is to make his interlocutors conscious of their latent thoughts, and not in the least their erroneous thoughts.

The New Shorter Oxford English Dictionary defines the adjective *maieutic* as follows: 'Of a mode of inquiry: Socratic, serving to bring out a person's latent ideas into clear consciousness'. And *maieutics* is 'the maieutic method'.[1]

Yet what does this have to do with Dostoevsky's narrative technique? In order to answer this question, we will turn our attention to *Crime and Punishment*. The central character in this novel is the twenty-three-year-old former law student Rodion Raskolnikov. Even though the novel has a third-person narrator, the reader sees events through Raskolnikov's eyes. In fact, Dostoevsky manages to draw us, the readers, so deeply into the inner world of his central character that we can not only 'understand' him, but that we also become his accomplices. We share Raskolnikov's anxiety about the execution of his plan to kill the moneylender Alyona Ivanovna, and we share his regret at the sudden appearance of her stepsister Lizaveta at the scene of the crime, which forces him to kill her too, in order not to leave any witness. Similarly, we share Raskolnikov's hope to have committed the perfect crime and not to succumb to the psychological hounding of the examining magistrate Porfiry Petrovich.

In other words, Dostoevsky's brilliant narrative technique forces the readers to experience an aspect of themselves. They see that they themselves would be

---

[1] *The New Shorter Oxford English Dictionary on Historical Principles*, ed. Lesley Brown, 2 vols. (Oxford: Clarendon Press, 1993), vol. I, 1666.

capable of doing what Raskolnikov is planning and executing—at least in thought.

II

In his groundbreaking article 'Silence in *The Brothers Karamazov*' (1997),[2] Malcolm Jones indicated that Dostoevsky's narrative technique aims to withhold the 'last word' from the reader. It is no coincidence that Dostoevsky was very fond of quoting Fyodor Tiutchev's famous line 'A thought uttered is a lie' (Mysl' izrechennaia est' lozh'). Dostoevsky only allows the reader to reach the truth about what is said via a number of detours. When Christ remains silent instead of answering the pointed statements of the Grand Inquisitor, as they contain their own contradiction, we could read this as striking evidence that the truth does not have to be articulated in order nevertheless to be present. This is very much in the spirit of Platonic dialectics. In his dialogue *The Sophist*, Plato reminds us with some sense of urgency that the one who gains the upper hand in a discussion is not necessarily on the side of the truth. A sophist is able to make an untruth appear to be a truth.

In *Crime and Punishment*, Dostoevsky uses one particular narrative strategy with an intensity that is absent from all of his other novels. The readers are corrupted, both rationally and emotionally, to the extent that they feel a certain solidarity with the murderer Raskolnikov as they are reading his story. This is the result of a clever manipulation on Dostoevsky's part of the reader's understanding of the text. In this way, the readers come to realise how easy it is for them to be tempted into both evil thought and evil deeds.

Essentially, this temptation is played out in three different spheres. A rational sphere, in which logical arguments speak in favour of Raskolnikov's planned robbery and murder, an emotional sphere, which is fed by the hatred of the morally repugnant and physically ugly moneylender Alyona Ivanovna, and finally an irrational sphere, in which Edgar Allan Poe's *Imp of the Perverse* holds sway, or which, in the words of Dostoevsky himself, is the domain of the devil (*chert*). In this irrational sphere, evil is desired and done for its own sake.

On a rational level, the reader is led to see the financial impotence of Dunya and Sonya as an unwarranted humiliation, from which they have to be saved by the murder committed by Raskolnikov. At the same time, the moneylender Alyona Ivanovna is portrayed as a morally inferior being. From an economic perspective, Raskolnikov triumphs over the scourge of extortionate interest rates with the murder of the pawnbroker. Much later, Ezra Pound would also curse moneylending with a similar intensity to Dostoevsky: 'The Evil is Usury, *neschek*

---

[2]Malcolm Jones, 'Silence in *The Brothers Karamazov*', in *Die Brüder Karamasow. Dostojewskijs letzter Roman in heutiger Sicht*, ed. H-J Gerigk (Dresden: University Press, 1997), pp. 29-46.

the serpent [...] the crawling evil, slime, the corrupter of all things'.[3] In both cases, the antisemitic barb is hard to miss. At the same time, however, Dostoevsky's pawnbroker is morally inferior: hard-hearted in the extreme towards her customers and tyrannical towards her stepsister Lizaveta. But that alone is not enough: she is also the embodiment of physical repulsiveness. Thus we are presented with three reasons for killing her: economic, moral and aesthetic. In the wake of these rational and irrational justifications both of his intention and of his action, yet another 'reason' occurs to Raskolnikov when he is at the scene of the crime-to-be, a reason of a very different nature altogether: the desire to commit evil for its own sake. In a cold and self-destructive trance, he kills not only Alyona Ivanovna, but also her entirely innocent sister Lizaveta, who turns up accidentally at the crime scene.

Dostoevsky succeeds in dragging his affirming readership along this twin current of arguments and trance and sets them on a road to hell—in solidarity with the murderer on moral grounds. Lest we forget, Raskolnikov is portrayed to us as a young man of twenty-three. The murderer with his axe has eyes full of expression, undeniably noble features and he is tall and slender. Of all the murderers depicted by Dostoevsky (Rogozhin, Pyotr Verkhovensky, Smerdyakov), Raskolnikov is undoubtedly the most handsome. He is indeed a moral person. Even his megalomaniac belief in himself as an extraordinary person with exceptional rights seems to flow seamlessly and automatically from his fundamental helplessness in the face of the very tangible injustice in the world around him. He wants to destroy 'the present time in the name of a better one'. All the 'Lycurguses, the Solons, the Muhammads, the Napoleons and so on' are all 'criminals' to a man, Raskolnikov argues in a conversation with Porfiry Petrovich, the examining magistrate.[4] Paradoxically, the only thing left for Raskolnikov to do, if he is to maintain his self-respect as a moral person, is to commit this robbery and murder. All the other ways of reacting to the state of the world as it is, Marmeladov's alcoholism, Razumikhin's stolid self-discipline or Luzhin's cynical meddling, are out of the question to Raskolnikov.

Dostoevsky has structured the character of his double murderer in such a way that we cannot refuse to understand his thoughts, feelings and actions at any point in the novel. Even the murder of Lizaveta, as a consequence of an unfortunate coincidence, becomes part of the state of despair that turns a moral person into a criminal. So could it be said that, on the most fundamental level, the novel has quite literally doomed all morality to burn in hell?

Far from it: Dostoevsky enlightens the readers about themselves. In order to do this, he aligns Raskolnikov's view of the world with that of the reader. Throughout his novel, the author casts a spell over his readers, so they see everything Raskolnikov experiences through his eyes. This method is not merely

---

[3]Ezra Pound, *The Cantos* (London: Faber & Faber, 1975), p. 798.
[4]*Crime and Punishment*, Part III, chapter 5. *PSS*, VI: 189-190.

an instrument to increase the tension, it is the point at which narrative technique becomes 'maieutics'. A false conclusion is suggested to the reader in the form of the sullen Raskolnikov in Siberia, eighteen months into his eight-year sentence, evidently incapable of remorse. Raskolnikov is pictured as having a 'shaven head' (Boris Christa),[5] pondering the possibility that his actions may still have been right, in view of the state of the world. To the last, he remains 'the divided one', as his name suggests.

III

We now come to the point of our argument, answering the question whether Dostoevsky provides an alternative to Raskolnikov's social actions, which inevitably lead the latter to be imprisoned. Has Dostoevsky made his peace with reality by renouncing the revolutionary act of violence? That, at least, is what Maxim Gorky thought.

Nevertheless there is a scene in *Crime and Punishment* which may serve as a programmatic statement of Dostoevsky's alternative. The scene in question comprises the second and third chapters of Part V, which depict the wake in honour of Semyon Marmeladov. First impressions may suggest that Dostoevsky uses this scene to further develop the profile of the murderer Raskolnikov and Sonya, the prostitute, as moral beings, as it is in the next chapter (Part V, ch. 4) that the former confesses his crime to Sonya. Yet this is not the primary function of the funeral meal.

The literal meaning of the wake scene is the public refutation of a false accusation. The lawyer Luzhin accuses Sonya of having stolen a hundred-rouble note from him. This accusation is proven to be unfounded by the public servant Lebezyatnikov, who testifies that he witnessed Luzhin slipping Sonya the hundred-rouble note without her noticing. For his part, Raskolnikov uncovers the motive of Luzhin's disgraceful accusation. This configuration is not dissimilar to a trial, with a prosecutor, two defence counsels and the audience as judge: the accused is acquitted and the slanderer is forced to withdraw.

Next to this literal meaning, Dostoevsky also insinuates an allegorical meaning of the scene. The court proceedings come to represent a society of the future, in which justice is administered only according to a universally acknowledged moral law. Dostoevsky's eschatological hope is that 'the state should become a church'. For one instant during the funeral meal for Marmeladov, this hope becomes reality. It is not without significance that the motley crew of guests, at the suggestion of those who reveal the truth (Lebezyatnikov and Raskolnikov), can sense the living breath of this moral law, whereas the obduracy of the slanderer Luzhin is exposed. The deciding factor for the presence

---

[5]Boris Christa, 'Raskolnikov's Wardrobe: Dostoevsky's Use of Vestimentary Markers for Literary Communication in *Crime and Punishment*', in the present volume.

of this truth is the fact that even those characters whom Dostoevsky does not regard without ambiguity, like Lebezyatnikov, the follower of Chernyshevsky, and the three Roman-Catholic Poles, are suddenly gripped by the holy truth and openly speak out in its favour. It is equally meaningful that the slanderer Luzhin instrumentalizes the role of money to execute his underhand plan. Elsewhere in the novel, he is characterised as a 'Jew and a trickster' (*zhid i figliar*),[6] even though he is not even Jewish. The uncontrolled flow of money sows the seeds of discord. Alyona Ivanovna is described as 'as rich as a Jew' (*bogata kak zhid*).[7] In the society of the future, according to the 'court proceedings' during the funeral meal, the role of money has to be stripped of its destructive character, and not by revolution but by changing people's understanding. The allegorical meaning of chapters two and three of Part V extol the virtue of publicly standing up for the truth whenever it matters. In this context, it is obvious that Sonya, the orphan, becomes an allegory of Russia, with Raskolnikov as the advocate of the insulted and injured, as he has a critical insight into society. The fact that this scene is followed immediately in the next chapter by Raskolnikov's confession to Sonya may serve as further evidence of the importance Dostoevsky attributes to the wake scene.

What is an incidental constellation in the literal context of the novel, the collision of Luzhin and Sonya with Lebezyatnikov and Raskolnikov as advocates of a threatened truth, becomes, on an allegorical level, the emblem of a future society which will judge without violence.

In any case, Dostoevsky has hidden this message by making it inconspicuous. It is up to us to retrace his 'maieutics' in order to see this message, a message which, at the end of the novel, Raskolnikov himself has yet to reach.

Translated by Bram Mertens

---

[6]*PSS*, VI, 156.
[7]*PSS*, VI, 53.

CRIME AND PUNISHMENT IN THE CLASSROOM: THE ELEPHANT IN THE GARDEN

Robin Feuer Miller

ALTHOUGH many of us contributing to this volume are teachers of literature and venture often into the confounding terrain of the classroom, we tend to resist writing about the business of actually teaching a work of literature. I make my own first foray into this realm in honour of Malcolm V Jones, who has encouraged his students and his colleagues to try new things, and to seek always to be ethically sensitive while being intellectually honest. In addition to his important contributions as a scholar of literature and a gifted teacher, Malcolm Jones cares passionately about the life of the university as a whole; he has served his own university and the profession at large in major administrative capacities. This combination of interests on his part emboldens me to offer to this volume an essay devoted to the teaching of Dostoevsky's *Crime and Punishment* within the larger contexts of the teaching of literature in universities and reading generally. In addition to his public life as an administrator, teacher, and mentor, Malcolm Jones has made singular and lasting contributions to our understanding of all of Dostoevsky's *oeuvre*. His compelling essays on *Crime and Punishment*—'*Crime and Punishment*: Transgression and Transcendence' and '*Crime and Punishment*: Driving other people crazy' (to be found in *Dostoyevsky: The Novel of Discord* and *Dostoyevsky after Bakhtin: Readings in Dostoyevsky's Fantastic Realism*) are classic essays and required reading for anyone who seeks both an informed and original reading of this novel.

I. Is reading at risk?

In the United States, I would argue, it is. In June 2004, the National Endowment for the Arts issued a report entitled *Reading at Risk*. Although this agency was, at the time this report was prepared, staffed with political appointments from the Bush administration, its report—an exhaustive one—was based on a large sampling over time and was conducted by the U.S. Bureau of the Census. Seventeen thousand adults from most demographic groups were polled; the results are sobering, to say the least. The report reads in part, 'for the first time in modern history, less than half of the adult population now reads literature, and these trends reflect a larger decline in other sorts of reading'. The report finds that the 'rate of decline has accelerated, especially among the young'. It gloomily concludes, 'More than reading is at stake'.[1]

Reading at Risk cites the ways in which print culture 'affords irreplaceable forms of focused attention and contemplation that make complex communications and insights possible. To lose such intellectual capability—and the many sorts of human continuity it allows—would constitute a vast cultural impoverishment'.[2] This is not to say that literary reading is not still an important component of our leisure activity: the report finds that the proportion of people reading literature is higher than participation in most other cultural, sports, and leisure activities except for watching television, movie-going, and exercising.[3]

The data unambiguously show that people who read also play a more active role in their communities. This may contradict our notion of the reader as someone solitary who escapes society through the intensely private, intimate, often historically subversive act of reading. A decline in reading, in fact, actually

> parallels a larger retreat from participation in civic and cultural life. The long-term implications of this study not only affect literature but all the arts—as well as social activities such as volunteerism, philanthropy, and even political engagement [...] As more Americans lose this capability, our nation becomes less informed, active, and independent minded. These are not qualities that a free, innovative, or productive society can afford to lose.

Finally, as if this were not bad enough, 'At the current rate of loss, literary reading as a leisure activity will virtually disappear in half a century'.[4]

The writers of this document do make a brief comparison with the reading habits of Canadians and Europeans. Canada conducted a similar survey in 1998 and found that 67% (as opposed to our 47%) of its adult population read a book during the survey year. A European study (of October 2002) cited the average reading rate in fifteen European countries as 45%, with Sweden, Finland, and the United Kingdom the highest (72%, 66%, 63% respectively) and Portugal and

---

[1] *Reading at Risk: A Survey of Literary Reading in America: Research Division Report #46.* (To be abbreviated here as *RAR*.) These quotations are drawn from the 'Preface', by Dana Gioia—a poet and the Chairman of the NEA at the time of the preparation of this report. The report defines a reader as anyone who during the past twelve months had read, during leisure time, any novel, short story, play or poem. 'No distinctions were drawn on the quality of literary works' (p. 2). There are problems with this definition of reader: it excludes the reading of non-imaginative literature; it excludes imaginative literature assigned as reading to students, and, conversely, it sets the bar for being designated a reader very low: the reading of a single short poem during the course of a year is enough to make you a reader—and if quality is not taken into account, that could be almost anything—even an ad jingle. But any definition for a report such as this is the obvious product of compromise and utility. The report—despite its shorthand and its shortcomings—has yielded important results.

[2] *RAR*, p. vii.

[3] *RAR*, p. 5.

[4] *RAR*, pp. vii, xiii.

Belgium the lowest (23%, 15%).[5] All western nations, to varying degrees, share the same predicament. We, then, are not just scholars of Dostoevsky; we are labourers in the effort to keep the reading of literature alive.

It is against this backdrop of a decline in reading that professors in the United States assign large, unwieldy, difficult novels like *Crime and Punishment*. In this first context of reading, then, *Crime and Punishment* is merely a stand-in for any other complex literary text, be it poem, short story or novel. Reading is at risk; our first, most basic job, whether we like it or not, the one we tend not to talk about—the elephant in our garden—is to persuade our students to love literary reading and to continue to be readers throughout their lives. They may take only one or two literature courses while at the university. This is our chance.

II. Finding an analogy: the novel as tragedy

Crime and Punishment is the most tautly structured of Dostoevsky's novels. In that way it is somewhat atypical, so that when students go on to read his other novels, they frequently find that the fictional world they have entered—with the possible exception of *The Brothers Karamazov*—does not exhibit the same luminescence of architectural design. Malcolm Jones puts it this way: 'Although the novel takes the hero through successive scenes of disorder, from which he only occasionally finds release, the plot itself is, by Dostoevskian standards, a relatively orderly one'.[6]

One way to engage students quickly with unfamiliar and potentially daunting material is to make an analogy with a text they think they already know. Thus I have found that Konstantin Mochulsky's delightfully old-fashioned but scholarly *Dostoevsky: His Life and Work* (1967) is very helpful in an introductory class of English-speaking students who have read some Shakespeare and one or two classical Greek tragedies. Mochulsky, you remember, argues that *Crime and Punishment* is a 'tragedy in five acts with a prologue and an epilogue'.[7] Others have also made this link to tragedy—Vyacheslav Ivanov first (and famously) called Dostoevsky's novels 'novel-tragedies' and, more recently, Joseph Frank

---

[5]*RAR*, p. 7.

[6]Malcolm Jones, *Dostoyevsky: The Novel of Discord* (New York: Harper & Row, 1976), p. 75. See also '*Crime and Punishment*: Driving other people crazy', in which Jones finds a different, highly original organizing principle. 'Almost any scene in the novel could be analysed in terms of the strategies of driving other people crazy' (*Dostoyevsky after Bakhtin: Readings in Dostoyevsky's Fantastic Realism* (Cambridge: Cambridge University Press, 1990), p. 91). Jones demonstrates how '[t]he techniques of emotional confusion have paradoxically led to the possibility of gradual clarification' (p. 94).

[7]All the following quotations from Mochulsky are taken from Konstantin Mochulsky, *Dostoevsky: His Life and Work*, trans. Michael A Minihan (Princeton, NJ: Princeton University Press, 1967), pp. 300-313. Since all the quotations come from the same thirteen pages of the book, and since there are so many of them, I have decided not to cite them individually but rather as a group.

has maintained that this novel elevates the Russian Nihilist to 'artistic heights equalling the greatest creations of Greek and Elizabethan tragedy'.[8]

A testing of Mochulsky's hypothesis about whether the novel is 'a tragedy in five acts' offers an occasion for fruitful discussion, even before students have actually finished reading the novel. One can throw it out as a hypothesis and return to it in subsequent class meetings for revaluation. Along the way, students will find themselves looking at the action of each part of the novel.

In a nutshell, Mochulsky suggests that Part I is the prologue which 'depicts the preparation and perpetration of the crime'. Part II then is Act I; it portrays the immediate effects of the crime upon Raskolnikov. In Part III (Mochulsky's Act II), Raskolnikov realizes that Porfiry suspects him, and he also has the dream in which he tries to kill the old woman again but finds that despite the blows of his axe, she remains alive and laughs at him. Mochulsky locates the climax of the 'novel-tragedy' in Part IV (Act III), in the counterpoint between Raskolnikov's interactions with Svidrigaylov ('the bath-house with its spiders') and Sonya (the resurrection of Lazarus). Mochulsky identifies an 'unexpected peripeteia' in the painter Nikolai's confession at the moment when Porfiry Petrovich had intended to expose Raskolnikov as the murderer. Part V (Mochulsky's Act IV) contains the scandalous scene of Marmeladov's funeral dinner, Raskolnikov's realization—'Was it really the old woman that I killed? I killed myself'—and his confession to Sonya. These scenes, important though they are, also serve to create a crucial 'slowing of the action before the final catastrophe'. That catastrophe occurs in his Fifth Act (Part VI of the novel). It is here that Dostoevsky depicts what Mochulsky labels as the 'parallel ruin of the two "strong individuals"'—Raskolnikov and Svidrigaylov'.

Mochulsky does not grant that Raskolnikov is undergoing any kind of spiritual change even at this late point in the novel. On the contrary, he asserts that Raskolnikov 'does not have enough strength of will to commit suicide, and so he surrenders himself to the authorities. This is not a sign of penitence but of pusillanimity'. Finally, in his scheme, the tragedy ends with an epilogue, an epilogue that Mochulsky passionately maintains betrays the thrust of the novel as a whole. He concludes, 'The novel ends with a vague anticipation of the hero's "renewal". It is promised, but it is not shown. We know Raskolnikov too well to believe this pious lie'.

I have offered up a summary of an argument some readers of this volume probably know well, because Mochulsky's take on *Crime and Punishment* can offer a valuable approach for beginning a classroom discussion of the novel. Why? First, it casts a kind of order, a semi-familiar structure—that of a tragedy—on to a large mass of turbulent, difficult, often self-contradictory events and utterances with which the students are struggling as they read the novel.

---

[8]Vyacheslav Ivanov, *Freedom and the Tragic Life*, trans. Norman Cameron, ed. S Konovalov (New York: Noonday Press, 1952), *passim*; Joseph Frank, *Dostoevsky: The Miraculous Years, 1865-1871* (Princeton, NJ: Princeton University Press, 1995), p. 100.

Indeed, although *Crime and Punishment* is Dostoevsky's most single-mindedly constructed novel and though it may be the most carefully stitched fiction he ever produced, the construction is more like a hem stitch than a woven tapestry. Tug on one thread, and you may begin to unravel, or at least reconfigure, the whole fabric. For example, Raskolnikov drops a pair of earrings after the crime. The young man who picks them up finds himself swirled into the central vortex of events. If a reader begins to focus on this particular event with microscopic intensity, the shape of the whole alters irrevocably. Choose almost any action, coincidence, or item at random from the novel and it will offer a link to something else; the pattern on the kaleidoscope will change as will the perspective of the whole. Thus Mochulsky's accessible comparison of the structure of this novel with the structure of a tragedy offers a simple way to begin to talk about the organization of the novel.

Nevertheless students find themselves simultaneously drawn to the tangle of events and ideas, to disorder, even as they are seeking pattern and order. Likewise Mochulsky embeds an idiosyncratic, subversive, even cynical interpretation in his orderly description of the novel. He finds Raskolnikov's conversion to be largely bogus, a 'pious lie' on the part of an author opportunistically eager to get his novel accepted by his readers and by his editor Katkov's thick journal. Is he suggesting, then, that the novel's omniscient narrator is, at worst, a liar and at best, unreliable? He hypothesizes that Raskolnikov's primary emotion is not repentance or even regret but shame. Raskolnikov is, above all, ashamed because he had come to his ruin 'blindly...and stupidly...through some decree of blind fate'. Mochulsky's highlighting of Raskolnikov's persistent sense of shame is crucial to his argument and functions, in his view, as a kind of roadblock to any authentic repentance on Raskolnikov's part.[9]

Even as Mochulsky underlines Raskolnikov's sense of shame, he finds no contradiction in continuing to envision him as a grandly tragic hero. Mochulsky concludes, in italics,

> **Raskolnikov has been brought to destruction like a tragic hero in battle with blind Destiny.** *But how could the author present this bold truth about the new man to readers of Katkov's well-meaning journal in the 1860s? He had to cover it by throwing an innocent veil over it. He did this, however, hurriedly, carelessly...*

---

[9] The most interesting, original, and recent analysis of the quality and the ramifications of Raskolnikov's shame can be found in the work of Deborah Martinsen. See her article, 'Shame and Punishment', in *Dostoevsky Studies: New Series*, 5 (2001), pp. 51-70. See also her incisive full-length monograph which explores the question of shame (and its links to the contemporary field of shame studies) throughout Dostoevsky's work, *Surprised by Shame: Dostoevsky's Liars and Narrative Exposure* (Columbus, Ohio: Ohio State University Press, 2003), pp. 20-21 and *passim*.

This careless cover-up, which Mochulsky even implies is a kind of shameful cover-up, is, in his view, the epilogue.

Surely some might argue that Mochulsky is simply wrong (to use an unfashionable word), wrong about the structure (a tragedy in five acts, with prologue and epilogue), wrong about the nature of Raskolnikov's experience, and wrong about the author's reasons for writing his epilogue. Dostoevsky's letters actually chronicle his own growing surprise that the ending to his novel evolved into a short epilogue. Usually his works turned out to be longer than he had planned, but in this case the last part grew shorter.[10] But it is always useful for students to see their professors in dialogue with the critics; it helps them forge their own reading of a text separate from that of professor or critic, yet hopefully informed by them as well. It is the process of making such distinctions and decisions that will fix the novel in their minds.

III. The portability of readerly insight

Although we want our students, in some concrete, intellectually informed way, to understand this difficult writer Dostoevsky and his difficult novels, we also want them to begin, through the act of reading, to learn how to use literary texts to formulate meaningful questions and to empathize with others different from themselves. The most cherished teachers, like the most enduring novels, show how to find and ask questions; they do not claim to offer definitive answers.

The formulation of such questions begins to occur most naturally during class discussions. The American poet Jay Parini wrote recently about his task as a professor in a seminar (and many of our smaller classes, even at the undergraduate level, in fact become seminars):

> It seems useful to recall that one 'conducts' a seminar. The analogy with a musical conductor is appropriate and instructive. The subject of the seminar (and the texts or problems being considered) forms a kind of score; the students will already have, with greater or lesser degrees of success mastered that score before coming to class. The expectation is, in fact, that they will have prepared for class by reading the material, by thinking up something to say. The work of the conductor is to draw out this intellectual music, to arrange it, set the tempo of play.[11]

---

[10] *PSS*, XXVIII: 2, 171, 173, and Fyodor Dostoevsky: *Complete Letters, II, 1860-1867*, ed. and trans. David A Lowe (Ann Arbor MI: Ardis, 1989), letters to Nikolai Liubimov, 9 December 1866, p. 214, and 13 December 1866, p. 216. In the second letter he writes, 'That's the way it's turning out; that way it will be better and more effective in a literary sense'.

[11] Jay Parini, 'The Well-Tempered Seminar', in *The Chronicle of Higher Education*, L, No. 46 (23 July 2004), 16. This is not unlike Northrop Frye's statement that the text is like a picnic to which the author brings the words and the reader the meaning; see *Fearful Symmetry* (Princeton, NJ: Princeton University Press, 1957), p. 427).

Thus the teacher, while remaining as faithful as possible to her understanding of the text, needs also to find a way, within the classroom, to bring it into play. Only then will students begin to possess it. Surely Dostoevsky, the master of polyphony, the seeker after 'a new word', the author of *The Diary of a Writer*, the avid correspondent, the writer whose every utterance is dialogic, the poet of 'ideas in the air' would encourage a free flowing classroom discussion of his work, would consider it an organic part of his work—its existence in the air, in the atmosphere beyond the printed page.

Possession of a novel by a reader is essentially a private, individual act. But the reading of literature in the classroom also serves a more public, even civic function. It is worthwhile, even urgent, for us as teachers to be mindful that literature and discussions about it are important for our lives in the public sphere, in culture. Our responses as readers are partly formative of the entire eco-system of culture, both high and low. Recently the American philosopher Martha Nussbaum has explored the ways in which literature and our readings of it form an essential component of our public discourse, and, by extension, our democratic society. Nussbaum argues that 'thinking about narrative literature' has 'the potential to make a contribution to the law in particular' and 'to public reasoning generally'.[12]

Nussbaum's search for a vehicle which allows one to empathize, to understand 'the other' is no sentimental endeavour; the capacity which literature engenders in us to understand those different from ourselves (or even ourselves) can contribute, she argues, to the rational formulation of just law and policy:

> The literary imagination is a part of public rationality, and not the whole. I believe that it would be extremely dangerous to suggest substituting empathetic imagining for rule-governed moral reasoning, and I am not making that suggestion. In fact, I defend the literary imagination precisely because it seems to me an essential ingredient of an ethical stance that asks us to concern ourselves with the good of other people whose lives are distant from our own. Such an ethical stance will have a large place for rules and formal decision procedures, including procedures inspired by economics [...] On the other hand, an ethics of impartial respect for human dignity will fail to engage real human beings unless they are made capable of entering imaginatively into the lives of distant others and to have emotions related to that participation.[13]

The student of literature, the reader of *Crime and Punishment*, enters emotionally into the lives of precisely such 'distant others', but realizes and necessarily contemplates also the importance, whatever his sympathies might be, of society's 'rules and decision procedures'. Indeed, to read *Crime and Punishment* is to make a perpetual series of journeys back and forth between the

---

[12] Martha C Nussbaum, *Poetic Justice: The Literary Imagination and Public Life* (Boston, MA: Beacon Press, 1995), p. v.

[13] Nussbaum, p. xvi.

intensely private sphere of Raskolnikov's individual consciousness and the communal realm of laws, ideas, religion, and the teeming life of the city that always surrounds and permeates him. More particularly, Nussbaum goes on to argue that the genre of the novel, 'on account of some general features of its structure, generally constructs empathy and compassion in ways highly relevant to citizenship'.[14] Certainly one could read many scenes in *Crime and Punishment* with such civic questions in mind, nearly every scene in fact. Even in the moments of his most private reverie, his dreams, or the narrator's representations of the flowing, fragmented particles of his hero's consciousness, Raskolnikov is always rubbing up against the values and practices of the world in which he lives.

To my mind, Nussbaum argues here as a modern day Portia with much to tell us about the foundational qualities of mercy and compassion, qualities formed and tested in large part by our activity as readers of literature. But most exciting, in her paradigm, the qualities of the best reader in the private world of fiction and the best judge in the real world of events are nearly interchangeable. Near the end of her book she writes:

> Intimate and impartial, loving without bias, thinking of and for the whole rather than as a partisan of some particular group or faction, comprehending in 'fancy' the richness and complexity of each citizen's inner world, the literary judge [...] sees in the blades of grass the equal dignity of all citizens— and more mysterious images, too, of erotic longing and personal liberty [...] But in order to be fully rational, judges must also be capable of fancy and sympathy. They must educate not only their technical capacities but also their capacity for humanity. In the absence of that capacity, their impartiality will be obtuse and their justice blind.[15]

Crime and Punishment offers its readers innumerable fictional opportunities to contemplate the overlap and the friction between individual and social justice and to make weighty judgments both about individuals and the society in which they live. Our capacities of fancy and sympathy are taxed throughout; each of us arrives at her own notion of poetic justice in this novel. If we adhere to Nussbaum's point of view, we can argue that this readerly knowledge is portable and can render us more capable of making rational, ethical judgments in the real world.

---

[14]Nussbaum, p. 10.

[15]Nussbaum, pp. 120-121. The 'blades of grass' reference here is to Walt Whitman (*Song of Myself*), whose work is central to Nussbaum's overall analysis, as is that of Dickens (*Hard Times*), E M Forster (*Maurice*), and Richard Wright (*Native Son*), as well as several others.

IV. Reading and rereading the novel

Crime and Punishment, like *Pride and Prejudice* or *Huckleberry Finn*, is a novel that some of our students have already read in high school. One sometimes hears, with disappointment, 'Oh, I've already read that'. Yet many students quickly decide that it is worthwhile to reread. Teaching any novel that some students have already read can offer an opportunity to engage in a more intensely dialogic exercise, for one can coax students to juxtapose the memory of the first reading, and concurrently of a childhood or adolescent self, with subsequent ones. They can thus engage in an authentic conversation with themselves, while at the same time creating a dialogue with their fellow students, the teacher, the critics, and, most important, the novel.

Whether we first read this novel as an adolescent or as an adult, we are gripped by it. V S Pritchett wrote incisively of Dostoevsky that he 'is still the master [because] he moves forward with us as the sense of our own danger changes'. Octavio Paz, in a different context, has concurred, 'Dostoevsky is our great contemporary'.[16] These statements could serve as epigraphs for *Crime and Punishment*. Our present sense of danger is particularly alert these days to the ways in which ideas—half-baked or otherwise—spread in the same ways that fearsome viruses travel through the world. In this novel, Dostoevsky with his typical novelistic economy, has prophetically conjoined the two. Ideas are viruses; viruses are ideas; they are equally contagious.

In the epilogue that Mochulsky dismisses so angrily and with such contempt is the narrator's description of Raskolnikov's famous final dream, a dream which Raskolnikov has near Easter:

> He had dreamt in his illness that the whole world was condemned to fall victim to a terrible, unknown pestilence which was moving on Europe out of the depths of Asia. All were destined to perish, except a chosen few, a very few. There had appeared a new strain of trichinae, microscopic creatures with intelligence and will. People who were infected immediately became like men possessed and out of their minds. But never, never had any men thought themselves so wise and so unshakable in the truth as those who were attacked...[17]

---

[16] V S Pritchett, *The Myth Makers: European and Latin American Writers* (New York: Random House, 1979), p. 72. Octavio Paz, *On Poets and Others*, translated by Michael Schmidt (Manchester: Carcanet Press, 1987), p. 94. I am grateful to Donald Fanger for turning my attention to both these works. Recently Richard Freeborn described Dostoevsky's still awesome power 'to ambush a part of life and transform it forever'. See his *Dostoevsky* (London: Haus Publishing, 2003), p. 137. Criticism abounds with powerful testaments to Dostoevsky's acute timeliness.

[17] *PSS*, VI, 419, and Feodor Dostoevsky, *Crime and Punishment*, trans. Jessie Coulson, ed. George Gibian (New York: Norton, 1975), p. 461. Subsequent references to both Russian and English versions of the novel will appear in the main body of the text in parentheses, with the Russian page reference first.

What is our current age but one in which each of us, whatever our nationality, our race, our profession, has been, to some degree, infected with precisely such a virus? Moreover, the very language of Raskolnikov's dream, with its references to the chosen few, suggests that he has already been infected. Is the dream itself, like Ivan's encounter with his devil, a marker of the beginning of a homeopathic spiritual and physical recovery?[18] The spectres of the very real AIDS virus and the virus of ideology merge here for a contemporary reader in a way that Dostoevsky would have undoubtedly relished.

The virus Raskolnikov imagines is a disease of certainty (conviction) laced with uncertainty (anxiety). Ideas, motivations, psychology, and by the time of *The Brothers Karamazov*, even the devil himself—most terms in Dostoevsky's world—have a positive and a negative charge. Hence, to return to Raskolnikov's dream in the epilogue, even though each individual stricken with the virus thought himself wise and unshakably possessed of the truth, nevertheless

> [a]ll were full of anxiety, and none could understand any other; each thought he was the sole repository of truth and was tormented when he looked at the others, beat his breast, wrung his hands and wept...they could not agree what was evil and what good. They did not know whom to condemn or whom to acquit. (420, 461)[19]

Is this a representation of the most absolute ideology being wrapped in a paralysing mantle of relativity and undirected, unproductive sympathy? Or is this a visionary dream of a world simply barren of conviction, of empathy, without justice—poetic or otherwise? Both alternatives are dreadful. Passages like these speak to our own contemporary and confusing sense of danger—physical and ethical—in a powerful way.

---

[18] For an extended discussion of Dostoevsky and the practice of metaphysical homeopathy, see my essay, 'Adventures in Time and Space: Dostoevsky, William James, and the Perilous Journey to Conversion', in *William James in Russian Culture*, ed. Joan Delaney Grossman and Ruth Rischin (Lanham, Maryland: Rowman and Littlefield Publishing, 2003), pp. 33-59.

[19] Curiously, in his notebooks of the mid-1860s, before he began work on *Crime and Punishment* as well as various articles, Dostoevsky twice made reference to the contrast between socialism and Christianity by linking, on the one hand, loose twigs (*luchinochki*) with socialism, and on the other, brotherhood—or the collective idea of humanity—with Christianity. See *Neizdannyi Dostoevskii*, 83 (Moscow: Nauka, *Literaturnoe nasledstvo*, 1971) pp. 244-246, and *The Unpublished Dostoevsky: Diaries and Notebooks 1860-1861*, I, introduction by Robert L Belknap, ed. Carl R Proffer (Ann Arbor: Ardis, 1973). See the entries for 19 August and 14 September 1864, pp. 94-95. Proffer (albeit a bit confusingly) glosses these references to twigs in a way that resonates with why the infected individuals in Raskolnikov's dream are doomed to failure: 'When talking about Christianity versus socialism, Dostoevsky apparently uses this word as a shorthand reference to the biblical parable of the strength of many twigs together, while separate and disunited they break easily, seeing socialism as essentially composed of separate individuals—unlike a Christian community bound together by the indestructible idea of God' (p. 142). The Russian editors also write, 'Dostoevsky often speaks about "luchinochki"' (cf. pp. 246, 250) and indicate that he is referring to a parable. But neither source indicates what parable this is, and I have, unfortunately, been unable to locate it by the time of this writing but cite the reference anyway because of its intriguing nature.

Moreover, although this novel has its epilogue, Dostoevsky still manages, as he virtually always does in all his work, to frustrate our expectations of an ending. We hear nothing of the reassuring hammering and banging that accompanies the endings of most nineteenth-century big blockbuster novels. (I am thinking here of E M Forster's remark in *Aspects of the Novel* (1927): 'the writer, poor fellow, must be allowed to finish up somehow, he has his living to get like anyone else, so no wonder nothing is heard but hammering and screwing'.)[20] Our novel may indeed have offered up to us a prologue, five acts of a tragedy, and an epilogue, but despite that formal exterior pattern, there is no inner closure, no answer to any single important question. Questions like 'Why did Raskolnikov commit the murder?' or 'At what moment did he begin to repent his crime?' or 'What constitutes an authentic confession?' or 'Does Raskolnikov undergo a religious conversion?' are fully ripe for discussion, but never for a full solution. Is 'the ripeness all?' The closer one looks at any possible event or motivation, the more important its precursors become. Yet such are precisely the paradoxes we expect from our most deeply engaging literature. Just as Maynard Mack said of *King Lear* that the 'bent of the play is mythic: it abandons verisimilitude to find out truth',[21] so could we perhaps say of *Crime and Punishment* that it abandons answers to find understanding.

***

In conclusion, nearly everything is missing. I have brought up no discussion of crime, of punishment, of fantastic realism, of the polyphonic novel, of the dialogic imagination, of sideward or squinting glances, of thresholds, of coffin-like rooms, and drenching rains. Nothing much about Marmeladov, Sonya, Dunya, Svidrigaylov, Razumikhin, and the magnificent Porfiry Petrovich. Nothing about Dostoevsky's technique of doubling, very little about dreams, about Napoleon, about articles Concerning Crime, about the possibility of authentic confession or solid repentance. Not to mention nothing about five-year old girls hiding behind cupboards, folded one hundred rouble notes tucked in pockets, or watchmen named Achilles. Nothing at all about Dostoevsky's passionate and ongoing polemic with Rousseau. There is nothing to do but return to the text, to its final words, 'All that might be the subject of a new tale, but our present one is ended'. Or, perhaps that tale has already been told by Malcolm Jones and others who have written so forcefully about this monumental novel.

In closing, the most important insight that I have about entering a classroom to teach *Crime and Punishment*, or indeed any hefty novel or the shortest of

---

[20] E M Forster, *Aspects of the Novel* (New York: Harcourt Brace, 1927), pp. 95-96.
[21] Maynard Mack, *King Lear in Our Time* (Berkeley: University of California Press, 1965), p. 97, quoted by R A Foakes (ed.), in *The Arden Shakespeare: King Lear*, 'Introduction' (London: Arden Shakespeare, 2003), p. 1.

poems, is to have yourself recently reread as much of it as possible, or at least some part of it, before going into class. This is more important than reviewing notes or reading secondary material. When some portion of the literary work is alive in my brain, my intellect, my imagination—a virus all its own—infecting me, perhaps confounding me, I tend to be better off than when I have distilled a particular reading of the text and bottled it for a measured dose to distribute to the students.

PART IV

Religion

DOSTOEVSKY ON CHILDREN IN THE NEW TESTAMENT

Boris Nikolaevich Tikhomirov

> I would even have been astonished if Christ's encounter
> with children had been omitted from the Gospels (XXII, 156)

It has been noted more than once that one of the most striking features of Dostoevsky's journalistic writings is the writer's analysis of 'present-day reality' *sub specie aeternitatis*, his connection of criminal chronicles from newspapers with ultimate questions about the fate of man and humankind on earth. In particular, the structure of *Diary of a Writer*, as a unique 'generic ensemble' (the term is D S Likhachev's), proves to be governed by the presence—side by side with direct appeals by the author to topical reality—of distinctive 'breaches' in the metaphysical plan of being, accomplished in 'artistic educations' within the journalistic text, as represented, for example, by the fantastic stories 'Bobok' (a descent into the Inferno of Petersburg) or 'The Dream of a Ridiculous Man' (a flight to another planet, and a picture of a *heavenly* idyll). However, in *Diary of a Writer* such 'breaches' in the metaphysical plan are not only localized and shaped in separate, independent works (which are quite rare), but also literally 'interlay' the whole narrative, and are realized, in particular, in its many biblical allusions and references. One such example provides the first stimulus to the formulation of an entire complex of interconnected problems, the consideration of which is the subject of the present article.

Acquainting his readers in *Diary of a Writer* for 1877 (July-August, Chapter 1) with the case of the Dzhunkovsky parents, accused of torturing their own children and brought before the circuit court in Kaluga on 10 July 1877, and giving a profound and subtle interpretation of the psychology of both the child and adult members of this 'accidental Russian family', Dostoevsky unexpectedly concludes his article with a call to a certain promise by Christ from the Gospels:

> If we cease loving children, whom will we be able to love thereafter, and what will become of us then? Remember as well that it was only for children and their little golden heads that our Saviour promised to 'shorten times and seasons' for us. For their sakes the torments of the regeneration of human society into a more perfect one shall be shortened. And may this perfection

come to pass, and may the sufferings and perplexities of our civilization be brought to an end! (XXV, 193)[1]

Without exaggeration, in spite of its small size and the fact, it would seem, that the rejoinder is 'apropos', before us stands one of Dostoevsky's key pronouncements which reveals his religious worldview.[2] But until now, as far as I am aware, it has not attracted particular attention from scholars. Perhaps it has not become prominent because the quoted lines have not been afforded the necessary textological commentary. To which 'promise' of the Saviour is Dostoevsky referring here? The notes to the *Complete Works* (XXV, 431) give an obscure reference to The Acts of the Apostles, where we read: 'When they [the Apostles—BT] therefore were come together, they asked of him, saying, Lord, wilt thou at this time restore again the kingdom of Israel? And he said unto them, It is not for you to know **the times or the seasons**, which the Father hath put in his own power'. (Acts 1: 6-7)[3] The commentator here (A I Batyuko) obviously went down the easiest, most formal route; he pointed out an instance of the use in the New Testament of the sought-for combination 'times and seasons', and stopped there. But does the suggested reference to Acts clarify the idea behind the biblical allusion in question? On the contrary, it makes it all the more obscure. Moreover, because of the Apostles' lack of understanding of the true meaning of Christ's words in this episode from Acts, it is not entirely clear that 'times and seasons' refers to the fulfilment of the prophecy of the Second Coming and Judgement Day, or that these words in *Diary of a Writer* are the beginning of the expression of an *eschatological theme*. In this connection, reference to another part of the New Testament, Paul's Epistle to the Thessalonians, would possibly be more fruitful: 'But of the **times and seasons**, brethren, ye have no need that I write unto you. For yourselves know perfectly that the **day of the Lord** so cometh as a thief in the night'. (1 Thess. 5: 1-2) But with this commentary as well, the meaning of Dostoevsky's words about the *shortening* of 'times and seasons' still remains incomprehensible; and in neither suggested quotation is there a single word about *children*. Evidently we have to seek other sources.

There is no doubt that in speaking of the Saviour's 'promise', the author of *Diary of a Writer* is very definitely referring the reader to the following prophecy of Christ on the Mount of Olives, in the episode which theologians have named

---

[1] In quotations from *PSS* words in bold type in quotations indicate emphasis by the author of the present article; words in italics indicate emphasis in the original text. The translation of this quotation is based on: Fyodor Dostoyevsky, *A Writer's Diary: Vol. 2, 1877-1881*, trans. Kenneth Lantz (London: Quartet, 1995), pp. 1059-1060, with minor alterations. *(Translator's note.)*

[2] In this pronouncement in the pages of *Diary of a Writer*, the discussion of children and their parents is included in the eschatological context (of which more details below), and, 'in eschatology', according to the subtle comment of Fedotov, 'lies the key to any religion', G P Fedotov, *Stikhi dukhovnye (Russkaia narodnaia vera po dukhovnym stikham)* (Moscow, 1992), p. 105.

[3] Biblical quotations follow the Authorized Version *(Translator's note)*.

the 'little Apocalypse'.[4] In Matthew's Gospel we read: 'For then shall be great tribulation, such as was not since the beginning of the world to this time, no, nor shall ever be. And **except those days should be shortened** there should no flesh be saved: but for the elect's sake **those days shall be shortened**'. (Matt. 24: 21-22) We read the same in Mark's Gospel: 'And **except that the Lord had shortened those days**, no flesh should be saved: but for the elect's sake, whom he hath chosen, he hath **shortened the days**'. (Mark 13: 20) There is no common opinion amongst theologians: is Christ with these words foretelling the future destruction of Jerusalem by the Romans, or prophesying the end of history and the Apocalypse?[5] Apparently, it was precisely to eliminate this double meaning, and to emphasize quite definitely that he is referring precisely to the end of 'our civilization' that Dostoevsky substitutes the indefinite 'those days' with the apocalyptically marked 'times and seasons'—with the biblical cliché expressing the idea of the in principle 'unknowable time of the end of history'.[6] But having settled the first textological problem, we are now faced with a new, much more complex one.

The given sections from the Gospels (both Matthew and Mark) say: '**for the elect's sake** those days shall be shortened'. And in Dostoevsky we have: '**only for children and their little golden heads**...'. In this way, the contamination of the New Testament texts, created in the passage under analysis by the author of *Diary of a Writer*, proves to be not two-sided, but to have multiple components.

---

[4]Referring to chapters 24 and 25 of Matthew's Gospel, and parallel locations in the other synoptic Gospels. However, Derevensky comments: 'Although this speech [by Christ] is often called the "little Apocalypse", it is difficult to relate it to that genre. It lacks the defining signs of apocalyptic works of that time: allegory and metaphor. The founder of Christianity is prophesying the future end of the world in direct language, only rarely accompanying his story with allegories (parables), which are characteristic of the synoptic Gospels. In its form, the speech on the Mount of Olives corresponds more to the prophecies of the "end of days" or the "day of the Lord" of Isaiah, Ezekiel and other Old Testament prophets', B G Derevenskii, *Uchenie ob antikhriste v drevnosti i srednevekov'e* (St Petersburg, 2000), p. 158. However, such a subtle specialist on the question as the archpriest Bulgakov is disinclined to over-emphasize this stylistic difference: according to his assessment, Christ's speech on the Mount of Olives 'is expounded **in the apocalyptic language of the epoch,** making use of Old Testament eschatological images', S N Bulgakov, *Agnets Bozhii* (Moscow, 2000), p. 438. Following Bulgakov, I will henceforth use the definition 'little Apocalypse'.

[5]'...This speech [of Christ's] is one of the most difficult to explain, and not all interpreters, even in ancient times, agree on several points in it, leading sometimes to the most varied explanations, and leaving it to the reader's personal feelings to accept one or another interpretation. The internal foundation of such unification in the speech of subjects both close and distant lies in the very character of this speech, as prophetic: in prophetic contemplation, events close and distant are sometimes presented as if in a single picture in perspective, and it is as if they merge together, especially if one event, the closest one, acts as a prototype of the other, most distant one [...] So it is here as well, in relation to the events of the destruction of Jerusalem and the end of the world, as the former acts as an image of the latter...', *Evangelie ot Matfeia s predisloviem i podrobnymi ob'iasnitel'nymi primechaniiami episkopa Mikhaila* (Minsk, 2000), p. 468 (referred to below as *Tolkovoe Evangelie*).

[6]S N Bulgakov, *Pravoslavie. Ocherki ucheniia pravoslavnoi tserkvi* (Moscow, 1991), p. 375.

In Dostoevsky's artistic work, analogical instances of the synthesis in a single context of different biblical texts as the crucial creative principle of the poetics of the 'great five' novels have been detailed by the research of E G Novikova. This scholar's conclusion that this reception to all intents and purposes 'represents an act of exegesis on the part of Dostoevsky' which 'realizes its interpretation of the sacred text [...] by leaning against another, just as authoritative [biblical] text',[7] seems profoundly true and methodologically fruitful. In our case as well we must speak of an act of exegesis—of Dostoevsky's own interpretation of the biblical prophecy of apocalyptic times, the end of world history and a post-historical eschatological perspective.[8] Moreover—and this must be emphasized immediately—Dostoevsky's exegesis extends here not only to the 'little apocalypse' of the Gospels, but to New Testament eschatology as a whole, as the passage under analysis from *Diary of a Writer*, alongside the words about the shortening of 'times and seasons', also speaks of 'the torments of the regeneration of human society into a more perfect one', of the accomplishment of 'perfection' at the end of time. And this is the problem (and one that is to the highest degree debatable!): chiefly, the last book of the New Testament, the Revelation of St John the Divine, particularly its final chapters (19-22), have no correspondence with Matthew, who *concludes* his 'little Apocalypse' with the Second Coming of Christ and His judgement of peoples. (Matt. 25: 31-46)

The 'lack of coincidence' between the eschatological 'scenarios' of the 'little Apocalypse' in Matthew and Mark and in Revelation sometimes troubles biblical exegetes. But this very distinction in the account of the events of the end of history between the synoptic Gospels and the 'version' given in the final book of the Bible, suggests, as such an authoritative expert on the question as S N Bulgakov commented, that,

> If *Revelation* concerns 'Things which must shortly come to pass' (Rev. 1: 1), that is, to the future, from the perspective of final **substance**, then the aim of the 'little Apocalypse' is **exhortationary**—a forewarning of the sorrows and ordeals which await the faithful instead of the Messianic kingdom [on earth] they expect [...] Accordingly their main problem is the calling of Christians to fortitude, vigilance and patience in these ordeals, as it is chiefly here that the **whole tragedy of history** will be shown. [...] The Lord reveals to his four

---

[7] E G Novikova, *Sofiinost' russkoi prozy vtoroi poloviny XIX veka* (Tomsk, 1999), p. 99.

[8] One is reminded in connection with this of the image of Lebedev, the interpreter of the Apocalypse in *The Idiot* (1868) who, in his own words, is 'good at interpreting [Revelation], I've been interpreting it for fifteen years'. (VIII, 167) Even before this Marmeladov in *Crime and Punishment* (1866) becomes a distinctive interpreter of eschatological prophecy, drawing in his confession an original image of Judgement Day (on this see Novikova, pp. 101-103). In his journalistic works, Dostoevsky first addresses apocalyptic issues in *Winter Notes on Summer Impressions*, written in 1863 (V, 70, 71).

closest pupils that what awaits them is not the kingdom and the glory, not peace and inactivity, but the most sorrowful and difficult trials.[9]

Consequently in the 'little Apocalypse' and in Revelation we do not have different eschatological 'scenarios' but simply differently accentuated accounts —depending on their particular arrangement—of one and the same future event ('the same in essence, although in different images and from different points of view', in Bulgakov's expression).[10] In the representations of Matthew and Mark the centre of gravity is displaced to the period of 'great sorrows', while in John the Divine everything is directed towards the final *transfiguration* of the 'earthly kingdom' into the 'Kingdom of God' (Rev. 11: 15) and the promised *recompense* of the just on a 'new earth' under a 'new heaven'. (Rev. 21: 1) But in both cases the one presupposes the other; they are conceived in unity.

In connection with this it is instructive to turn our attention to Raskolnikov's labour-camp dreams in the epilogue of *Crime and Punishment*, the account of which Novikova qualifies as the first instance in Dostoevsky's artistic work of the author's own interpretation of apocalyptic events.[11] But as distinct from the angle through which she steers her analysis, for me now it is more significant to focus on the 'final accord' of the hero's dreams, when *after* the image of world-wide catastrophe ('Everyone and everything perished') we unexpectedly read: '**Only a few people in the whole world were saved**, they were **the pure and the elect**, predestined to begin a new species of people and a new life, to renew and purify the earth...' (VI, 419) Amongst commentators it has already become almost a commonplace to indicate that Raskolnikov's labour-camp dreams are also genetically linked to the apocalyptic prophecy of 'great sorrow' from Chapter 24 of Matthew's Gospel.[12] This is fair enough, but demands serious clarification. Although in Matthew the motif of *election* is present in this chapter—and moreover not only in verse 22 cited above ('for the elect's sake those days shall be shortened'), but also in the final picture:

> Immediately after the tribulation of those days shall the sun be darkened, and the moon shall not give her light, and the stars shall fall from heaven, and the powers of the heavens shall be shaken: [...] And he [Christ] shall send his angels with a great sound of a trumpet, and they shall *gather together his*

---

[9] Bulgakov, *Agnets Bozhii*, pp. 437-438.

[10] Bulgakov, *Agnets Bozhii*, p. 437.

[11] See Novikova, p. 133.

[12] See, for example, V Ia Kirpotin, *Izbrannie raboty v trekh tomakh* (Moscow, 1978), III, 427-428 (here verses 6-8 and 10-12 from Matthew 24 are placed in parallel with Raskolnikov's dreams); see S V Belov, *Roman F M Dostoevskogo 'Prestuplenie i nakazanie': Komentarii: Kniga dlia uchitelia* (Moscow, 1985), pp. 227-228.

elect from the four winds, from one end of heaven to the other'. (Matt. 24: 29; 31; see also Mark 13: 24-27)[13]

—the motifs of *transfiguration* and *renewal* of the earth, which in Raskolnikov's dreams must be achieved by the elect ('...the pure and the elect, predestined to begin a new species of people and a new life, to renew and purify the earth') are, however, as already noted, not present in the 'little Apocalypse'. And here again, this time from the final images of Raskolnikov's labour-camp dream, so thematically close to the eschatological passage from *Diary of a Writer* of 1877, the threads extend to the final chapter of Revelation.[14] This observation once more emphasizes that the witnesses to the 'little Apocalypse' in the accounts of the Synopsists, and to the Apocalypse itself according to St John the Divine, Dostoevsky *conceives as interconnected*, and he creatively 'smelts' and brings them together into the unified picture of the apocalyptic labour-camp dreams of his hero.

But at this point it is time to pose a question: does not this appeal to specialisms and discussion of theological problems into the bargain (even if it is, perhaps, topical in its interpretation of other works by the writer) lead us away from the theme of contemporary children and their parents, to which the analysis of 'present-day reality' in the pages of *Diary of a Writer*, founded on concrete facts, is devoted?[15] On closer examination it becomes apparent that not only does it not lead us away, but on the contrary reveals, discloses the specifics and the genuine depth of the formulation of this 'topical' theme by Dostoevsky. Speaking briefly and as a preliminary, the specifics of this consist in the facts of a criminal chronicle being examined by the writer through an eschatological perspective and, interpreted in this way, they themselves provide the impulse for setting questions no less important than about the future fate of the world.

---

[13] The elect, those for whose sake the Lord shortened the days of 'great sorrow', apparently, participate with Christ in the judgement of peoples depicted later (see Matt. 25: 31-46; I touch on further details of this aspect below).

[14] Belov, alongside the 'little Apocalypse' of Matthew as a source of Raskolnikov's dreams, also points to chapters 8-17 of Revelation. It is instructive, however, that this commentator 'cuts out' the final chapters from the last book of the Bible, which describe the future *transfiguration* of the world, 'a new heaven and a new earth' (Rev. 18-22): Belov patently fails to take into account the 'final accord' of Raskolnikov's dreams (see Belov, p. 228). As distinct from her predecessors, Novikova focuses her analysis *exclusively* on the proximity of Raskolnikov's labour-camp dreams to Revelation (not taking into account the clear allusions to the 'little Apocalypse' in Matthew and Mark at all), but paradoxically also excludes the final chapters from her comparison (see Novikova, pp. 131-132).

[15] This unwittingly recalls the words of Dostoevsky himself from *Diary of a Writer* for 1876: '...Trace another fact from real life, even if it seems at first glance in no way as clear, and if you have the strength and the eyes, you will find in it depths that don't exist in Shakespeare. But in this lies the whole question: who has the eyes and who has the strength?' (XXIII, 144) These words are, unarguably, characteristic of the writer himself, and the incident under examination is the clearest example of this.

First of all I will note that the question Dostoevsky asks, 'If we cease loving children, whom will we be able to love thereafter...?' allies the 'children' theme in the *Diary* to the writer's (and his characters') reflections over many years of the possibility of man fulfilling Christ's 'greatest' commandment, loving one's neighbour. The very earliest of these notes is the writer's widely known religious-philosophical revelation on the death of his first wife, written on 16 April 1864: 'To love man *as one loves oneself,* according to Christ's commandment, is impossible. The law of personality binds. The *I* is the obstacle.' (XX, 172)[16] It is evident that after a decade of working around these reflections, the phenomenon of *love for children* (whom it is 'impossible not to love')[17] introduces an essential corrective to his initial position. In the extract from 1877, Dostoevsky values the fact of love for children as, perhaps, the sole living witness to the accessibility for earthly human nature of 'Christ's love for people' and, consequently, as the original 'pledge' of the possibility of realizing in principle the 'greatest' commandment of the Gospels. But, on the other hand— and in this controversy lies the whole of Dostoevsky!—the immediate subject of the author's reflections in the text in question from *Diary of a Writer* turns out to be, on the contrary, the threat that in contemporary humanity love for children is *drying up* (and moreover in its most crystal-clear form, parental love); and this is perceived by Dostoevsky as the danger of a final falling away from Christ and as an ominous symptom of the future collapse of 'our entire civilization': 'If we cease loving children, **whom will we be able to love thereafter, and what will become of us then?...**'

But it is right here, in the face of this most terrible danger, as if invoking, in the manner of an ancient prophecy, mankind's approaching of this fatal trait, that Dostoevsky turns to the Gospel promise of Christ on the Mount of Olives: 'Remember as well that it was only for children and their little golden heads that our Saviour promised to "shorten times and seasons" for us.' Precisely here, in this phrase, the 'children' theme, as has already been shown, enters the context of biblical eschatological prophecies. Here the writer's thoughts turns to the apocalyptic time of 'great sorrows'. Moreover, this 'apocalyptic context' is exactly what allows Dostoevsky to convey his highly original view of the *absolute value* of children in Christianity.

But the foretelling by Christ of the epoch of 'great sorrow' is also interpreted by the writer in a particular manner which is some distance from Church

---

[16] See also Versilov's words in *The Adolescent*: 'Man is created so as to make it physically impossible to love those close to one' (XIII, 175), or the words of Ivan Karamazov: 'I can never understand how you can love those close to you. It's precisely those close to you who, in my opinion, it's impossible to love, you can only love at a distance. [...] In my opinion Christ's love for people is a type of miracle that's impossible on earth. True, he was God, but we aren't gods'. (XIV, 215-216)

[17] Just before the extract we are analysing from the *Diary* for 1877, we read: 'and indeed, among all our obligations nature helps us most in our obligations to children, having made it so that we cannot help but love children. How can we not love them?' (XXV, 193)

orthodoxy. It turns out to be not a sign of 'final times', not the threshold of the 'end of history', but—even if it is agonizing and dreadful—a modus of the passage of mankind into a qualitatively new condition of earthly existence: 'For their sakes **the torments of the regeneration of human society into a more perfect one** shall be shortened. And **may this perfection come to pass**, and may the sufferings and perplexities of our civilization be brought to an end'. Interpreting such an interpretation, so to speak, is possible only in the light of the teaching of a thousand years of Christ's kingdom on earth—of the so-called Millennium, which Dostoevsky in the 1870s, apparently fully shared. This is evinced, in particular, by a little-known polemical rejoinder, to be found in the notebooks for the August issue of *Diary of a Writer* for 1880, directed at the publicist G Gradovsky who, ironically as regards Dostoevsky's declaration in his Pushkin speech that Russia, perhaps, will utter the 'word of "ultimate harmony" in mankind', sarcastically recalling the Holy Epistles, wrote: 'In a word it will come to pass that he is not predicting the Apocalypse at all! On the contrary, he is heralding not "ultimate accord", but ultimate "discord" with the coming of the Antichrist. Why refer to the Antichrist, if we will utter the word of "final harmony"?' 'That's terribly clever,' replies Dostoevsky,

> only you have distorted everything. You, evidently, haven't read the whole Apocalypse, Mr Gradovsky. There it says precisely that **at the time of greatest discord it is not the Antichrist, but Christ who will come and build his kingdom on earth (listen, on earth) for a thousand years.** To this can be added that blessed is he who participates in the resurrection first, that is in this kingdom... (XXVI, 322)[18]

The problem of the Millennium is one of the most complex facing Christian theology. Many tomes have been written, and many lances broken, on account of the first verses of Chapter 20 of Revelation, from which both advocates and opponents of the idea of the Millennium have derived their arguments. (see Rev. 20: 1-7) This is not the place to enter into examination of this centuries-old polemic.[19] The highly interesting and complex question of 'The Millennium in Dostoevsky's religious worldview', which has not thus far been resolved by scholarship, goes outside the framework of the current article, and is a problem which demands separate research. Therefore I will limit myself to establishing that in the eschatological 'scenario' as, judging by a whole range of pronouncements, it appeared to Dostoevsky in the 1870s, in the crowning stage of world

---

[18] For more details of this statement by Dostoevsky, see B N Tikhomirov, '"Nasha vera v nashu russkuiu samobytnost'" (K voprosu o "russkoi idee" v publitsistike Dostoevskogo)', *Dostoevskii: materialy i issledovaniia* (St Petersburg: Nauka, 1996), XII, 120-124.

[19] I will point to two very recent publications dedicated to the problem of the Millennium, the authors of which stand in diametrically opposed positions: B Kir'ianov, *Polnoe izlozhenie istiny o Tysiacheletnem tsarstve Gospoda na Zemle* (St Petersburg: Aleteiia, 2001) (from the series 'Antichnoe khristianstvo: Issledovaniia'), and N Kim, *Tysiacheletnee Tsarstvo: Ekzegeza i istoriia tolkovaniia XX glavy Apokalipsisa* (St Petersburg: Aleteiia, 2003) (from the series 'Vizantiiskaia biblioteka. Issledovaniia').

history, after the times of 'great sorrow' foretold in the Gospels (in the quotation above from the polemic with Gradovsky, 'at the time of greatest discord') the Second Coming of Christ and the establishment by Him of the millennial kingdom *on earth* occurs. I would suggest (without introducing here concrete arguments to support my thesis) that Dostoevsky, like, for example, St Irenaeus, 'viewed the millennial kingdom of the Messiah as a **transitional stage** for the devout in the journey to the kingdom of heaven'.[20] Examination of the genesis of such opinions by the writer seems to me to be extraordinarily interesting and important. But, I repeat, this is a specialist question which demands extended study.

For the present research, it is essential to note that in his thus conceived eschatological 'scenario' Dostoevsky endows *children* with exceptional significance. The most agonizing, but salvational 'regeneration of human society into a more perfect one', the very character of the transition from the time of 'great sorrows' to the millennial kingdom of Christ is, in the view of the writer, conditional upon *attitudes to children*. Whose attitude? That, it seems, both of adult humanity and the God of Providence. It is precisely in *the child*, according to Dostoevsky, that there arises (and perhaps, on the contrary, comes undone?) an important kind of 'knot', tying together the interrelations between God and mankind: 'we' have been promised by the Saviour that 'only for children and their little golden heads' (a variant: 'for their sake') 'shall those days be shortened'.

But again, here, and with every acuteness (and not only as a narrowly textological problem), a question arises in which all the other questions raised by the present article come together: what kind of *biblical basis* is there for such a view of the child? From which New Testament text (or texts) has the author proceeded, in order to synonymize concretely the anonymous declaration of the Apostles 'for the elect's sake those days shall be shortened' with the categorical declaration 'only for children and their little golden heads'? What is it that allows Dostoevsky to all intents and purposes to *identify* 'the elect' of the 'little Apocalypse' with children?

I will say immediately that giving a straightforward and unambiguous reply to such a question is, apparently, impossible. This is a problem that must be resolved not so much on the textological as on the conceptual level. Its resolution requires not only analysis of the peculiarities of the text of the New Testament, but also observation of the materials of Dostoevsky's creative work which contain biblical allusions and citations. In particular, analysis of the working materials for *Diary of a Writer* allows one to a certain degree to approach an answer to this far from simple question. The fact is that this original 'manoeuvre'—the introduction of the biblical context into the formulation in a journalistic article of the question of contemporary children and parents—arose

---

[20]*Khristianstvo: Entsiklopediia* (Moscow, 1995), III, 158.

in the plans of Dostoevsky the publicist some time before his consideration of the trial of the Dzhunkovsky parents. In 1876-1877 the author more than once turned in the pages of *Diary of a Writer* to similar trials, the first of which was the case of S L Kronenberg (in Dostoevsky, Kroneberg), a father brought to trial for torturing his seven-year-old daughter. The famous lawyer V D Spasovich acted as barrister in this trial. Indignant at the tricks used by his defence, Dostoevsky recorded in his working notebooks: 'Who defines,' asks Spasovich, 'how many blows a father may inflict before he is judged to be extreme, excessive [...] How can someone define that? In fact the very heart of the father must define that. Christ, embracing children, defined how we must look at them...' (XXIV, 137) In another place, directly working on the text of chapter two of the February 1876 issue of *Diary of a Writer* concerning the Kronenberg case, Dostoevsky points even more precisely to the Gospel episode he has in mind here: 'I would even have been astonished if Christ's encounter with children **and his blessing of children** had been omitted from the Gospels...' (XXII, 156) The commentary to the *Complete Works* glosses these words with the following text from Matthew's Gospel:

> Then were there brought unto him little children, that he should put his hands on them, and pray: and the disciples rebuked them. But Jesus said, Suffer little children, and forbid them not, to come unto me: for of such is the kingdom of heaven. And he laid his hands on them, and departed thence. (Matt. 19: 13-15)

But the detail accentuated by the author in the first note ('embracing children'),[21] compels us to prefer as a gloss the story of the same Gospel event in Mark's version:

> And they brought young children to him, that he should touch them: and his disciples rebuked those that brought them. But when Jesus saw it, he was much displeased, and said unto them, Suffer the little children to come unto me, and forbid them not: for of such is the kingdom of God. Verily I say unto you Whoever shall not receive the kingdom of God as a little child, he shall not enter therein. And he took them up in his arms, put his hands upon them, and blessed them. (Mark 10: 13-16)

'I would even have been astonished if Christ's encounter with children had been omitted from the Gospels...'—this rough note in his workbook reveals that Dostoevsky endowed this episode from the Gospels with particular significance, that he considered it the *key* to uncovering the truth of the Gospels' Revelation. Evidently, this was conditional above all upon the cited words of the Saviour, '**...for of such is the kingdom of God**'. (Mark, 10: 14) Children here, according to Christ's direct assertion, are the *first in line* to inherit the kingdom of God.

---

[21] How touchingly attentive is Dostoevsky to the least appearance of the strictly human hypostasis of Christ disclosed in the Gospel texts!

That is apparently what lies at the basis of Dostoevsky's quite exceptional perception of the 'theme of children' in the New Testament.

And this motif which is actually present in the Gospels is not only sharply perceived and assimilated by Dostoevsky: he also achieves in his work a further and highly original development. Above this finds expression in the words of Arkady in *The Adolescent*: '...a laughing and merry [child] is *a ray from heaven*, a revelation from the future, when man will become pure and simple in his soul, like a child'. (XXIII, 286) In this pronouncement, children are not only the first—at the end of time—to inherit the kingdom of heaven, but it as if they also in today's earthly life carry within them the nature of the future, transfigured mankind. This evaluation can be connected to the words of Zosima in *The Brothers Karamazov*: 'Love children especially, for they are [...] without sin, like angels, and they live to arouse tenderness in us, to purify our hearts and act as a kind of example to us'. (XXIV, 289) This and similar judgements[22] allow us to reinforce our initial notion of Dostoevsky's view on the *absolute value* of children in Christianity.

Turning again to *Crime and Punishment* permits us, possibly, to advance further in our attempt to look at the 'children episodes' from the Gospels through Dostoevsky's eyes. In Part IV of that novel, immediately following the scene of the reading from the New Testament, the author records a conversation between the two main characters, in which Raskolnikov convinces Sonya Marmeladova that Petersburg is the town of the *Antichrist*. At the centre of the hero's monologue is an almost exact quotation from the same Gospel story about Christ and the children cited above (in Mark's version):

> Surely you've seen children here, on street corners, who have been sent out by their mothers to beg for alms? I found out where these mothers live and in what condition. Children there can't remain children. There are seven-year-old perverts and thieves there. But children are the image of Christ: **'Theirs is the kingdom of God'**. He said to honour and love them, for they are future humanity... (VI, 252)

---

[22] I will note that such a view of the child stands in a certain defiance of the Orthodox representation of human nature in its condition after Original Sin. Thus, that subtle and profound interpreter of Dostoevsky's legacy from the Orthodox position, the archpriest V V Zenkovsky, perceived in similar 'teachings on children' the structure of so-called 'Christian naturalism'. Critically assessing the theological content of the well-known note from the preparatory materials for *The Devils*—'Did Christ then come so that humanity would discover that [in] his earthly nature, the human spirit can appear truly in such heavenly splendour, in actual fact in the flesh itself, and not just in a single dream and ideal? *and that this is both natural and possible.*' (Zenkovsky's emphasis)—he in particular writes: 'The whole flavour of naturalism is manifest precisely in the fact that this completeness, this perfection which is conceived in Christ as man is as if related to ordinary man as his hidden, primordial sacred space. **Children for Dostoevsky are radiant with *this* beauty**', V V Zenkovskii, 'Problema krasoty v mirosozertsanii Dostoevskogo', in *Russkie emigranty o Dostoevskom*, ed. S V Belov (St Petersburg: Andreev i synov'ia, 1994), pp. 228, 232.

In this reasoning of Raskolnikov everything is significant: both the alteration in the quotation from the Gospels from 'of such' to 'theirs', and viewing children as 'future humanity'.[23] But above all, what merits attention is the highly unusual view of the child as...an *icon* of Christ: 'But children are the image of Christ'. There is nothing close to this in the cited Gospel story of 'Christ's encounter with the children'. Is it possible to ascertain a New Testament basis for such as view as well?

Apparently here Dostoevsky (and his hero) are giving an original interpretation of yet another episode from the Gospels, which answers the disciples' question: 'Who is the greatest in the kingdom of heaven?':

> And Jesus called a little child unto him, and set him in the midst of them, and said, Verily I say unto you, Except ye be converted, and become as little children, ye shall not enter into the kingdom of heaven. Whosoever therefore shall humble himself as this little child, the same is greatest in the kingdom of heaven. And whoso shall receive one such little child in my name receiveth me[24] [...] Take heed that ye despise not one of these little ones; for I say unto you, That in heaven their angels do always behold the face of my Father which is in heaven. (Matt. 18: 1-5, 10)

In Mark again the story of this incident includes a detail about which we have already spoken above: 'And he took a child, and set him in the midst of them: and when he had taken him in his arms, he said unto them, Whosoever shall receive one of such children in my name, receiveth me: and whosoever shall receive me, receiveth not me, but him that sent me'. (Mark 9: 36-37)[25]

These two episodes involving children in the Gospels (the blessing of children and the appeal to the Apostles to be 'as children') are exceptionally close, both ideologically and textually, even including word-for-word repetition. But it is even more important to point out the new 'ideologeme' of exceptional importance, which appears only in the second incident (and moreover in both Matthew and Mark): the idea of the child as an earthly 'substitute' for Christ (or, to put it into the more usual language of the guild of Dostoevsky scholars, the child as

---

[23] In the present context, this definition can be interpreted in the sense that 'from children the generations grow', but in relation to the general view of the author on children, and in particular alongside the unexpected characteristic 'Children are the image of Christ', the words about 'future humanity' converge with the statement from *The Adolescent* introduced above: children are '**a revelation from the future**, when man will become pure and simple in his soul, like a child'.

[24] The text, so sharply experienced by Stavrogin in *The Devils* (in the chapter 'At Tikhon's'), continues: 'But whoso shall offend one of these little ones which believe in me, it were better for him that a millstone were hanged around his neck, and that he were drowned in the depth of the sea'. (Matt. 18: 6) For a textological analysis of this verse, see below.

[25] This point in Mark's Gospel is probably even more favourable as a commentary for Dostoevsky's note: 'Christ, embracing children, defined how we must look at them?' (XXIV, 137), because it is precisely here that how and why we must behave towards children is grounded and explained by Christ.

a 'double' of Christ): 'And whoso shall receive one such little child in my name receiveth me' (Matt. 18: 5); 'Whosoever shall receive one of such children in my name, receiveth me'. (Mark 9: 37) Moreover, in the second instance the interrelation of Christ and the child is confirmed by analogy with the interrelation of Christ and God the Father: 'and whosoever shall receive me, receiveth not me, but him that sent me'. This suggests that it is precisely this paradoxical Gospel 'ideologeme', formulated as the principle of the interrelation of Christ and the child, which found its expression in the hero's aphorism in *Crime and Punishment*: 'But children are **the image of Christ**'. (VI, 252)

However, in relation to the 'textological' problem which occupies us this observation is not in itself of value. The idea 'the child is an icon', for all its importance, does not yet in itself provide an answer to the question of the basis for identification in the extract under examination from *Diary of a Writer* for 1877 of children with the elect, the virtual reduction by Dostoevsky of the latter to the former. It does not provide an answer but it does, possibly, provide a key...

In the 'little Apocalypse' in Matthew's Gospel, and precisely in the final scene of the judgement of peoples, we encounter in the words of Christ a curious variant of virtually the same 'ideologeme' we have just examined, but *without reference to children*.

> And before him shall be gathered all nations: and he shall separate them one from another, as a shepherd divideth his sheep from the goats: and he shall set the sheep on his right hand, but the goats on the left. Then shall the King say unto them on his right hand, Come, ye blessed of my Father, inherit the kingdom prepared for you from the foundation of the world: for I was hungred, and ye gave me meat: I was thirsty, and ye gave me drink: I was a stranger, and ye took men in: naked, and ye clothed me: I was sick, and ye visited me: I was in prison, and ye came unto me. Then shall the righteous answer him, saying, Lord, when saw we thee an hungred, and fed thee' or thirsty, and gave thee drink? [...][26] And the King shall answer and say unto them, Verily I say unto you, Inasmuch as ye have done it unto one of the least of these my brethren, ye have done it unto me'. (Matt. 25: 32-37, 40)

The same idea, only 'in reverse', is repeated by Christ in relation to 'them on the left hand', who are dispatched, 'cursed, into everlasting fire, prepared for the devil and his angels [...] Verily I say unto you, **Inasmuch as ye did it not to one of the least of these, ye did it not to me**'. (Matt. 25: 41, 45)

Of course, the two variations of this 'ideologeme' also contain serious differences: in particular, the naming by Christ of 'the least of these my **brethren**' is difficult to define as an 'image of Christ' (Raskolnikov's words about the children). But for the aims of our research it is important to emphasize something else. About which of '**these** [my] brethren' is Christ talking here? We find no direct answer in the text of this Gospel. Theological literature points out

---

[26] The reply of the righteous repeats in full all the elements of Christ's utterance (Matt. 25: 38-39).

that those 'named? as Christ's 'brethren' constitute in effect a *third category* of those summoned to judgement by the Saviour: they relate to neither the 'sheep' nor the 'goats', to neither the 'righteous' nor the 'sinners' who, respectively, are warranted 'life eternal' or condemned to 'everlasting punishment' (Matt. 25: 46), *depending on* how in life they treated 'the least of these': 'Here the criterion, the 'touchstone', is the attitude of peoples to those who Christ calls 'My brethren'— as one commentator on the biblical text points out.[27] But it is even more important to answer the question: *Who are they?* Because of the peculiarity of the biblical discussion, all answers given to this question in theological literature inevitably prove to be optional, based on making absolute one or another argument, none of which is sufficient in itself. The close parallelism of the formulae examined above, which express the principle of the interrelation of Christ and the child, on the one hand, and of Christ and 'the least of these my brethren', on the other hand ('And whoso shall receive one such little child in my name receiveth me' (Matt. 18: 5); 'Inasmuch as ye have done it unto one of the least of these my brethren, ye have done it unto me' (Matt. 25: 40)), additionally supported by the parallelism of the definition (Christ on the child: 'But whoso shall offend **one of these little ones...**' (Matt. 18: 6; see also 18: 10, 14); Christ on the 'brethren': Inasmuch as ye did it not to **one of the least of these..**' (Matt. 25: 45)), theoretically allows the possibility of extrapolating that those who make up the 'third category' discussed as being called to the judgement of peoples are in fact *children*.

Whilst in no way insisting on the authenticity of the proposed interpretation as applied to the biblical text as such (insofar as I am a literary critic, not a theologian), at the same time I would suggest it is quite probable that Dostoevsky could have resolved the problem of the exegesis of this 'dark spot' in Matthew's Gospel in just this way. A similar view on the attitude to children as the most important criterion to be taken into consideration on the Day of Judgement was, it seems, quite close to him. In relation to this an early sketch on Versilov's suicide from the preparatory material for *The Adolescent* is exceptionally instructive. Here we read: 'HE speaks the day before his suicide: if you offend one of these little ones, **you will not be forgiven in this world, or in the world to come**'. (XVI, 65) The commentary in the *Complete Works* points to the following biblical source: 'But whoso shall offend one of these little ones which believe in me, it were better for him that a millstone were hanged around his neck, and that he were drowned in the depth of the sea'. (Matt. 18: 6; for variant readings, see Mark 9: 42, and Luke 17: 2).[28] But this gloss again proves patently

---

[27] See, for example, *Bibliia: Knigi Sviashchennogo Pisaniia Vetkhogo i Novogo Zaveta, kanonicheskie, v russkom perevode s ob'iasnitel'nym vstupleniem k kazhdoi knigi Biblii i primechaniiami Ch I Skofilda s angliiskogo izdaniia 1909* (Moscow, 1989), p. 1139 (note).

[28] In the final text of *The Adolescent*, this biblical verse is cited verbatim and in full (in Church Slavonic) in the story of the merchant Skotoboinikov. Here 'to offend' (*soblaznit'*), corresponding precisely with the explanations of biblical commentaries, signifies 'to lead into sin or to place

inadequate: in the sketch for *The Adolescent* we again have an instance of a most interesting *contamination* (see Matt. 12: 32: 'And whosoever speaketh a word against the Son of man, it shall be forgiven him: but whosoever speaketh against the Holy Ghost, **it shall not be forgiven him, neither in this world, neither in the world to come**'). This is yet another example of an 'act of exegesis' by Dostoevsky: here the significance lies both in the fact that as a result of the contamination created by the author offending a child is *equated* with the unforgivable 'sin of sins'—abuse of the Holy Ghost (even abuse of Christ can be redeemed by repentance)—and in the fact that with the introduction of the formula 'neither in this world, **nor in the world to come**', the appraisal of Versilov's sin is not simply strengthened against its biblical origin ('a millstone [...] hanged around his neck'), but also the 'offence' caused to the child becomes an unconditional predeterminant of the fate of the hero on Judgement Day.[29]

However, for all the importance of the above observations, their significance for me is now incidental and subsidiary. We have already shown that the main emphasis made by Dostoevsky in his interpretation of the 'children theme' in the New Testament is not at all related to the idea that the attitude to children will be the main criterion in the appraisal of man on Judgement Day (this is only my critical 'reconstruction' of the writer's position), but rather relates to the idea that children, in the direct words of the Saviour, *are the first to inherit the kingdom of God*. But, based on such declarations, Dostoevsky, naturally, could not but be perplexed at the *absolute absence* of any reference whatsoever to children in Revelation, which depicts phases of the offensive and the final triumph at the end of time of the promised kingdom of God. Nor is there a single word about children in the 'little Apocalypse' of Matthew and Mark. Such a 'silence' must have struck Dostoevsky, having spent ten years reading the verses of the Apocalypse, quite sharply and painfully. Here he evidently also could not but have been

---

obstacles in the way of virtue' (*Tolkovoe Evangelie*, p. 352). We can suggest that Dostoevsky rejected the variant we have already found in the preparatory materials for the novel (see the following note), because the merchant Skotoboinikov's sin does not correspond in gravity to the 'sin of Stavrogin' (or the sin of Versilov in earlier variants).

[29] It is interesting that while working on *The Devils* ('Stavrogin's Confession') Dostoevsky had not yet found this *maximal* solution: '"**Will Christ indeed not forgive**", asked Stavrogin, and in the tone of the question a light hint of irony was audible, "as it says in the book, 'If you offend one of these little ones'—remember? **According to the Gospels, there is no greater crime**, and cannot [be]"' (XI, 28); '"There will be no forgiveness for me", said Stavrogin gloomily, "in your book it says that **no crime is higher** than offending 'one of these little ones', and cannot [be]. That's in this book." He pointed to the Bible'. (XII, 119) Here (in both variants) the assertion that 'according to the Gospels there is no greater crime' is given for the present *without any proofs*. The sketch we have introduced from *The Adolescent*, resorting to contamination, is already attempting to lean this thesis against a Gospel text reproduced word for word.

'astonished'; he must have been 'astonished'.[30] The presence of this inconsistency obviously demanded from the author considerable exertion in his attempts to give it his own explanation and interpretation, to find a solution to the problem, to propose his own interpretation of the biblical text which would remove the inconsistency. The passage from *Diary of a Writer* about the words of Christ, who 'promised to "shorten times and seasons" for us', 'only for children and their little golden heads', inserting, and with such strong emphasis, children into the eschatological 'scenario', is unarguably a *manifest trace* of such 'exegetic' efforts by Dostoevsky.

However it is also important to emphasize something else. Dostoevsky is not simply finding an opportunity to include the figure of the child in the picture of apocalyptic events, as if in order to fill in a 'lacuna' in the canonical biblical text which is painful to him. For the author, apparently, the idea of children taking precisely the place of 'the elect' was a matter of principle. This replacement seems to me to be conceptual.

This is because the question of 'the elect' is also in itself one of the most 'painful' of Dostoevsky's eschatological conceptions.[31] Remember in particular that the *problem* of 'the elect' is formulated with the utmost sharpness by the Grand Inquisitor, the hero of Ivan Karamazov's poem, who in the rebellion of his struggle against Christ also uses among other things arguments 'from eschatology'. Polemically stressing the very principle of *election*, he bases his criticism of Christ precisely on this.[32] 'Your great prophet tells in a vision and in an allegory that he saw all those who took part in the first resurrection, and that they were twelve thousand from each tribe', says the Inquisitor:

> But even if there were so many, they too, were not men, as it were, but gods. They endured your cross, they endured dozens of years of hungry and naked

---

[30] To some extent, such declarations by Dostoevsky might also rely on apocryphal stories, gleaned in part from popular religious legends. Thus, for example, in the legend 'The Godfather' from Afanas'ev's collection, with which the writer must have been familiar, the hero is the godson of Christ himself: in coming upon the 'ninth heaven', he passes on the way to the Lord three palaces, clearly imagined as the 'construction' of the heavenly kingdom. In the first palace the hero sees, 'for the palace was adorned, angels and archangels conversing, singing songs to the glory of the most holy Trinity'; the second palace is 'adorned with greater mouldings than the first, and in it are sitting prophets and **infants**, rendering praise to the Lord'; in the third is found 'the greatest throne of all', of Christ himself (*Narodniye russkie legendy A N Afanas'eva* (Novosibirsk, 1990), pp. 156-157). This text demonstrates expressively the place, according to popular notions, that children ('infants') occupy in the 'heavenly hierarchy'.

[31] See, for example, the discussion about who—the author or the hero—'owns' the idea of 'the elect', and who is 'predestined to begin a new species of people and a new life, to renew and purify the earth' at the end of *Crime and Punishment*, in B N Tikhomirov, 'K osmysleniiu glubinnoi perspektivy romana F M Dostoevskogo Prestuplenie i nakazanie', in *Dostoevskii v kontse XX veka*, ed. K A Stepanian (Moscow: Klassika plius, 1996), pp. 267-268.

[32] For more details on this, see B N Tikhomirov, 'Khristos i istina v poeme Ivana Karamazova "Velikii inkvisitor"', *Dostoevskii i mirovaia kul'tura*, 13 (1999), 162-168.

wilderness, eating locusts and roots, and of course you can point with pride to these children of freedom, of free love, of free and splendid sacrifice in your name. But remember that there were only a few thousand of them, and that they were gods. But what of the rest? Is it the fault of the rest of feeble humanity that they could not endure what the mighty endured? Is it the fault of the weak soul that it is unable to contain such terrible gifts? **Can it be that you indeed came only to the elect and for the elect?** If so, then there is a mystery here and we cannot understand it'. (XIV, 234)[33]

The basis of this tirade by the hero Ivan Karamazov, the charge against Christ that the kingdom of God is accessible only to the *proud and mighty* 'elect', who are able to 'endure the cross' and accomplish a 'great sacrifice', acquires exceptional significance, because in the text under examination from *Diary of a Writer* for 1877, *children* will become the 'elect' at the centre of eschatological events. From such a viewpoint, Dostoevsky's pronouncement that 'it was only for children and their little golden heads that our Saviour promised to "shorten times and seasons" for us' can be perceived as a rejoinder in the distant argument of the author of the future *Brothers Karamazov* with his as yet unwritten hero, who was already, evidently, troubling his imagination—the Grand Inquisitor. And it is precisely in the context of this distant argument, as a counter-argument by the author to the reproach aimed by Ivan's hero at Christ, that he 'came only to the elect and for the elect' that we can perceive the true significance of Dostoevsky's declaration: 'I would even have been astonished if Christ's encounter with children had been omitted from the Gospels' (in the sense that I have attempted to reveal in this article). And this crucial promotion by Dostoevsky of *children* to the forefront of the eschatological 'scenario' becomes in the 'great dialogue' (Bakhtin's term) of the author's artistic work a unique conceptual 'counterbalance' to the Grand Inquisitor's argumentation against Christ. Furthermore, the definite 'making absolute' of the significance of children by Dostoevsky in the prophetic exclamation about the shortening 'of times and seasons' ('**only** for children...') in such a correlation gains explanation as a polemical sharpening, advanced in opposition to the seductive argumentation based on making absolute 'the proud and the mighty'. This suggests that in the ideological structure of *The Brothers Karamazov* itself, the image of the 'wedding feast' in the chapter 'Cana of Galilee', where those called to the 'feast of the Lamb' are not the mighty and the powerful, but the 'many', who 'gave only an onion, only one little onion' (XIV, 327), apparently corresponds *typologically* to this train of thought. In this way, examination of the eschatological passage about children in *Diary of a Writer* for 1877, in the context of the problematics of the author's final novel, reveals that its appearance

---

[33]The translation of this quotation from *The Brothers Karamazov* is based on Fyodor Dostoevsky, *The Brothers Karamazov*, trans. Richard Pevear and Larissa Volokhonsky (London: Vintage, 1992), pp. 256-257, with some alterations. (*Translator's note*).

under Dostoevsky's pen was a matter of principle and *non-accidental*, that it belongs to some latent and agonizing thought-process occurring in the very depths of his soul and concerning the chief questions of being.

The author intends to undertake further work on this problem, in a special study devoted to analysis of Dostoevsky's eschatological ideas.

Translated by Sarah Young

DOSTOEVSKY AND MUSIC

Diane Oenning Thompson

DOSTOEVSKY'S works have long been compared to musical compositions.[1] Some have likened them to symphonies with their build-ups to catastrophic climaxes, some have discerned musical structures in his treatment of time, others remark on his verbal orchestration of leitmotifs, repetitions, and themes and variations. Most famously, Mikhail Bakhtin saw Dostoevsky as the creator of the 'polyphonic novel', whose 'chief characteristic' is: 'A plurality of independent and unmerged voices and consciousnesses, a genuine polyphony of fully valid voices'.[2] These analogies concern the large compositional and generic features of Dostoevsky's works. He also incorporated into his fiction specific musical motifs and episodes, sacred and secular, such as songs, musical fantasies and performances. Here we consider several musical motifs from Dostoevsky's last three novels in order to discover how they reflect his major themes, his aesthetic practice and his Christian worldview. This, in turn, gives us a particular perspective on Bakhtin's concept of polyphony and what bearing it has on Dostoevsky's representation of the divine Logos.

The Devils (1872): The Franco-Prussian War

The Devils is a novel about the roots of Russian nihilism and political terrorism. It is set in a provincial town where a circle of the 'higher liberal[s]' would meet in their club and engage in 'jolly liberal chatter'. (X, 30), (1, 1, IX)[3] There,

---

[1] For a comprehensive treatment of Dostoevsky's relation to music, see A Gozenpud, *Dostoevskii i myzykal'no-teatral'noe iskusstvo* (Leningrad: 'Sovetskii kompozitor', 1981). See also Jacques Catteau's discussions in *Dostoyevsky and the process of literary creation*, trans. Audrey Littlewood (Cambridge: Cambridge University Press, 1989), pp. 27-34, 296-97 and 444-47. Apropos his work on *Notes from Underground*, Dostoevsky himself invoked a musical term: 'You understand what a *transition* is in music. It's exactly like that here. In the first chapter it's evidently idle talk, but suddenly this idle talk in the last 2 chapters resolves into an unexpected catastrophe'. (XXVIII: 2, 85) See Note 3 for reference.

[2] Mikhail Bakhtin, *Problems of Dostoevsky's Poetics*, ed. and trans. Caryl Emerson (Minneapolis: University of Minnesota Press, 1984), p. 6.

[3] Quotations are from *PSS*. English versions generally follow Richard Pevear and Larissa Volokhonsky's translations of *Demons* (London: Vintage, 1992); *The Adolescent* (London: Alfred A Knopf, 2003) and *The Brothers Karamazov* (London: Vintage, 1994), though I have made some minor alterations. Parts, Chapters, and Sections, and Book and Chapters respectively, are given in brackets following the Russian references.

Lyamshin, a servile rascal and buffoon, would entertain the club members by playing the piano, and 'in the intervals, would mimic a pig, a thunderstorm, a mother giving birth with the first cry of the baby'. Once, 'to Lyamshin's accompaniment', they 'even...sang the *Marseillaise*'. (X, 30-31) Into this complacent milieu, Pyotr Verkhovensky, the arch nihilist and deceiver, arrives to form a revolutionary cell, ostensibly to promote the 'common cause'. His real aim is to sow total political, social destruction and enlist the enigmatic Stavrogin as the figurehead of his movement. Lyamshin, along with several other club members, is soon drawn into Verkhovensky's cell of gullible conspirators. Julia von Lembke, the wife of the provincial governor, impressed with Verkhovensky and eager to ingratiate herself with the progressive youth, turns their house into a salon where they discuss the new ideas. There Lyamshin performs his 'new special little piece for piano'. Says the narrator:

> The little piece really turned out to be amusing, with the comical title of 'The Franco-Prussian War'. It began with the menacing strains of the *Marseillaise*:
>
> Qu'un sang impur abreuve nos sillons!
>
> The bombastic challenge was heard, the intoxication with future victories. But suddenly, together with the masterfully varied measures of the anthem, somewhere from the side, down below, in a little corner, but very close by, were heard the vile little strains of *Mein lieber Augustin*. The *Marseillaise* does not notice them, the *Marseillaise* is at the peak of intoxication with her own grandeur; but *'Augustin'* is gaining strength, *Augustin* is becoming more and more insolent, and now the measures of *Augustin* somehow unexpectedly begin to fall in with the measures of the *Marseillaise*. She begins, as it were, to get angry; she finally notices *Augustin*, she wants to shake him off, to drive him away like a nagging worthless fly, but *Mein lieber Augustin* fastens on firmly, he is gay and confident, joyful and insolent; and the *Marseillaise* somehow suddenly becomes terribly stupid; she no longer conceals that she is annoyed and offended; there are cries of indignation, tears and oaths, with arms outstretched to Providence:
>
> Pas un pouce de notre terrain, pas une pierre de nos forteresses![4]
>
> But now she is forced to sing in time with *Mein lieber Augustin*. Her strains somehow most stupidly turn into *Augustin*, she is yielding, dying out. Only an occasional outburst 'qu'un sang impur...' is heard again, but it immediately jumps over in a most vexing way to the vile little waltz. The *Marseillaise* submits entirely: it's Jules Favre, sobbing on Bismarck's bosom and surrendering everything, everything...But now *Augustin* turns ferocious; one hears hoarse sounds, senses measureless quantities of beer being drunk, a frenzy of self-boasting, demands for billions, for fine cigars, champagne and

---

[4]Jules Favre's exact words were 'ni un pouce de la territoire de France, ni une pierre de ses forteresses'. See Émile Bourgeois, *Manuel historique de politique étrangère, 4 vols. (Berlin, Paris, 1897-1926)*, III, *De Metternich à Bismarck (1830-1870)*, dixième édition (Paris: Librairie classique Eugène Belin, 1940), p. 732. I thank the historian Jacques Beauroy for locating this quotation for me.

hostages; *Augustin* turns into a furious roar...The Franco-Prussian war ends. (X, 251-252), (2, 5, I)

Here Dostoevsky presents the Franco-Prussian war (1870-71) as a musical battle between two national popular songs, quite different in style and genre. The *Marseillaise*, is a marching song and the French national anthem. Composed in 1792, it is a musical expression of the spirit of the French Revolution. It sounds a stirring call to revolutionary action, with lofty appeals to world history, to glorious futures. *Mein lieber Augustin* is a sentimental beer-hall waltz, composed for boisterous dancing and singing. The two songs are represented as male and female personifications of their respective nations. In the struggle for supremacy, each song undergoes a radical metamorphosis.

Beginning on a 'bombastic' note, the *Marseillaise*, 'intoxicated with her own grandeur', at first holds her own. But *Augustin*'s voice infiltrates the anthem, and growing stronger, subversively 'falls in' with its rhythms. The *Marseillaise* angrily tries to shake off her 'vile little' assailant, but *Augustin* transmogrifies from an innocuous dance song into a violent male who 'fastens on firmly', insolently enjoying himself. Under attack by *Augustin*, the *Marseillaise* loses her invocatory and militant character, her heroic accents and revolutionary élan. She weeps, curses, pleads with outstretched arms. As *Augustin* overpowers the *Marseillaise* and takes possession of her voice, the French anthem becomes vulgar, stupid, it acquires a character alien to it. Then, in a complete reversal, *Augustin* forces the *Marseillaise* to sing to its tune, to 'jump' to its rhythms until the *Marseillaise*, vainly struggling to sing her words, becomes a whimper, yields, fades away and finally, utterly humiliated in what has become a musical rape, she 'submits entirely'. French revolutionary heroism, as expressed in Jules Favre's heroically defiant call to the defence of France—'pas un pouce...'— collapses in the bathetic image of Jules Favre 'sobbing on Bismarck's bosom'. Prussia is victorious. France 'surrenders everything'. Thus, at one stroke Lyamshin ridicules French revolutionary heroism, German philistinism and arrogant Prussian militarism. But Dostoevsky's parody is not only about the Franco-Prussian war. His concerns go farther, to the baleful impact of European ideas on the future fate of Russia and humankind.

Towards the end of Lyamshin's piece, the *Marseillaise* and *Augustin* merge, and are subsumed by a new composition of aggressive rhythms and crashing chords, which, to 'hoarse sounds' and truculent demands for 'hostages', finally turns into a ferocious roar (*neistovyi rev*), into a beast. Thus, in the juxtaposition and merging of the two songs, a concealed potential is realized, new meanings in their respective texts emerge—in the *Marseillaise*, which is in fact a cruel song, bloodthirsty strata come to the surface. Indeed, of the two songs, the only words quoted are from the *Marseillaise*: 'That impure blood should flood our furrows'. Likewise, the jolly, waltzing Germans, whose song ends on a 'roar', are exposed as capable of ferocious savagery. Dostoevsky uses Lyamshin's parody of the *Marseillaise* to de-heroicize revolutionary ideals by bringing in *Augustin* who is contemptuous of French pretensions to revolutionary heroism.

The radicals looked upon the *Marseillaise* as a sublime expression of their highest ideals. Indeed, the Russian revolutionary movement was to take its inspiration from the French Revolution. In *The Devils* Dostoevsky aimed to expose the fatal consequences of the radical atheistic ideas emanating from Western Europe and being enthusiastically taken up by the Russian intelligentsia, which he passionately believed would lead to Russia's ruin.[5] In these ideas, when taken to their nihilist extremes, he located the roots of Russian nihilism. The Franco-Prussian War was for Dostoevsky a sign of European civilization, corrupted by atheism, tearing itself apart. His musical battle, as the whole novel, thus carries a cautionary and prophetic message. Here, Dostoevsky turns to another text as the ultimate interpretive guide to the novel's tragic events.

Lyamshin's witty musical entertainment has no direct bearing on the plot, but it later turns out to have a powerful symbolic resonance with the Word. Verkhovensky aims to bind the loyalty of his cell by forcing its members to witness his murder of Shatov, a former associate who now wants to break away. He concocts the lie, which he half believes, that Shatov intends to betray them, and lures him to a rendezvous at night in a deserted park. There, in the presence of the other conspirators, Verkhovensky coolly shoots Shatov in the forehead, and sets about tying stones to the corpse so it will sink in a nearby pond. And 'suddenly', says the narrator, 'a strange thing happened'. (X, 461), (3, 6, I) At the sight of the body, two of the conspirators became panic stricken. Virginsky suddenly began to tremble all over, crying out: 'It's not right, it's not right'. (X, 461) Lyamshin, who has been peering out from behind Virginsky's shoulder, suddenly squeezed Virginsky, and, demented with terror, let out an uncanny scream. He 'screamed not with a human voice, but with a voice of some sort of wild beast', 'his eyes goggling...his mouth extremely wide open...rapidly stamping his feet on the ground, as though he were beating out a tattoo on a drum'. (X, 461) Virginsky became so terrified that 'he started screaming like a madman himself', scratching and punching Lyamshin. (X, 461) Lyamshin, seeing Verkhovensky, screamed, tripped over Shatov's body as he lunged at Verkhovensky, who yelled, cursed and pounded him on the head with his fists. Verkhovensky then aimed his revolver right in Lyamshin's screaming mouth, but Lyamshin, in blind animal panic, 'kept on screaming' until Erkel 'deftly stuffed [his foulard] into his mouth'. (X, 461-462) At about the same time, general

---

[5] According to Gozenpud, by 'bombastic', Dostoevsky had in mind 'the degeneration of the great ideals, which the [*Marseillaise*] expressed in the years of revolution 1789-1794, into reactionary ones in the reign of Napoleon III, and 'he thought that '*Mein lieber Augustin* won so easily because the *Marseillaise* stopped being the *Marseillaise*', pp. 141-142. Although Dostoevsky sympathized with France and thought some regenerative idea might emerge from her defeat, for him, regeneration could never come from atheistic, revolutionary socialism. Moreover, considering later developments in the novel, and Dostoevsky's known views, the idea that he regretted the collapse of French revolutionary ideals can hardly be sustained. For his attitudes to the Paris Commune, which 'filled him with horror and rage', see Joseph Frank's excellent discussion in *Dostoevsky: The Miraculous Years, 1865-1871* (Princeton: Princeton University Press, 1995), pp. 418, 471.

mayhem has descended on the town, fires set by arsonists break out, von Lembke goes mad, Marya Lebyadkina, her brother and their servant are found with their throats slit, Liza is lynched, Verkhovensky murders Fedka the convict, Shatov's wife and her baby die of exposure, Kirillov, pressed by Verkhovensky, blows his brains out and, at the very end, Stavrogin hangs himself.

Lyamshin's mimicries of pigs and his entertaining musical improvisation have now to be seen in quite a different light. From his confident chords in a drawing room to his long drawn out screams in the night, from his bravura pounding of the piano keys to his feet frantically tapping out a drumroll—there could hardly be a sharper, more chilling contrast. The human beings have fallen to the level of beasts. The relation of this tableau of violence to the Word is signalled by one of the two epigraphs to the novel, the Gospel passage on the Gadarene swine. It is the squeals of the possessed swine that we hear in the screams of the two terrified conspirators, it is the scuffling of the stampeding herd that sounds in the tapping feet of Lyamshin and the pounding fists of their cursing ringleader. The potential contained within the bloodstained text of the *Marseillaise*, and *Augustin*'s beast within is realized here; and in the 'splashes of blood and brains' of Kirillov, who ends his suicide note with the French Revolutionary slogan—'Liberté, egalité, fraternitié ou la mort'. (X, 476, 473), (3, 6, II) This is the endpoint of Nihilism. You cannot play at nihilism, revolutionary nihilism is not a musical entertainment but a lethal game that leads to real bloodshed, to subhuman chaos.

The Adolescent (1875): Trishatov's opera

Arkady Dolgoruky, the hero of *The Adolescent*, drops into a restaurant where he meets Trishatov, a 'dreamer' with a love of literature and music, who relates to him his idea for an opera that takes its subject from *Faust*. He imagines it thus:

> A Gothic cathedral, inside, choirs, hymns, Gretchen enters, and you know—the choirs are medieval, so that you can even hear the fifteenth century. Gretchen is in anguish, first there's a recitative, soft but terrible, tormenting, and the choirs thunder forth gloomily, sternly, indifferently:
> *Dies irae, dies illa!*
> And suddenly—the devil's voice, the devil's song. He's invisible, just his song, and alongside the hymns, together with the hymns, it almost coincides with them, but yet it's something quite different...The song is long, relentless, it's a tenor, it must be a tenor. He begins softly, tenderly: 'Remember, Gretchen, how you, when still innocent, still a child, used to come to this cathedral with your mama and babbled the prayers from an old book?' But the song grows stronger, more passionate, more impetuous; the notes get higher: in them are tears, anguish, unremitting, hopeless, and, finally, despair: 'There is no forgiveness, Gretchen, there is no forgiveness for you here!' Gretchen wants to pray, but only cries burst from her breast—you know, when your breast convulses with tears—but Satan's song doesn't stop, ever more deeply it pierces into her soul, like a spike, ever higher—and suddenly

it breaks off with almost a shout: 'It's all over, you are damned!' Gretchen falls on her knees, clasps her hands before her—and just here comes her prayer, something very short, half recitative, but naïve, without any ornament, something in the highest degree medieval, four lines, only four lines in all—Stradella has a few notes like them—and on the last note she faints! Commotion. She's lifted, borne up and—and just here suddenly a thundering choir. It's like a great peal of voices, an inspired choir, triumphant, overwhelming, something like our 'Up-borne-by-the-an-ge-lic-hosts',—so that everything's shaken to its foundations—and everything changes into a rapturous, exultant, universal exclamation of—'Hosanna'—as if it were the cry of the whole universe, and she's borne up, borne up, and here the curtain falls! (XIII, 352-353) (3, 5, III)

In this striking composition of contrasting voices and styles of sacred music the similarities to Goethe's *Faust* are readily discernible.[6] Both authors conceive Gretchen's story as a drama of Fall and Redemption, played out as a struggle in her soul between God and the devil. In both works, an invisible devil in a cathedral taunts Gretchen with her fallen innocence by invoking her childhood memories of attending services and babbling her prayers. Brought to utter despair by the devil's pronouncement of damnation, Gretchen prays to God, whereupon she is saved and ascends heavenwards to choral accompaniment.

More illuminating, though, are the differences in the way Dostoevsky re-imagined *Faust*. Goethe sets the first phase of Gretchen's spiritual ordeal in a cathedral where, now pregnant, she appears, suffering from fear and remorse. Behind her an evil spirit mercilessly taunts her with her 'sin and shame', terrifying her with graphic reminders of the Last Judgment and 'the fiery torment'.[7] Interweaving through the scene, a choir, to the sombre accompaniment of an organ, intones the *Dies irae* of the Catholic requiem which warns of divine wrath and vengeance at the Last Judgment. Dostoevsky takes up Gretchen's drama at the crisis point, when she is agonizingly suspended between damnation and salvation, in the 'Gothic cathedral', alone with the devil's voice whose song, as *Augustin* in Lyamshin's piece, surreptitiously emerges from the hymns, becomes stronger and then predominates. Dostoevsky quotes only the first line of the *Dies irae*, whereas Goethe includes nine, thus creating a strong emphasis on terror, judgement and vengeance. Goethe sets the second phase of Gretchen's ordeal in a dungeon prison, a place of punishment and dark enclosure where Faust appears to rescue her. There he presents Gretchen as a criminal, the murderess of her infant, and the cause of her brother's and mother's deaths, maddened by terror before her imminent execution and the torments of her conscience. Significantly,

---

[6]Dostoevsky also knew and appreciated Gounod's *Faust*, but his 'opera' only partially conforms to Gounod's. See Gozenpud, p. 143.

[7]Quotations are from Goethe, *Faust: eine Tragödie*, herausgegeben und erläutert von Erich Trunz, siebente Auflage (Hamburg: Christian Wegner Verlag, 1962). The translations are mine. The passages discussed are from Part One, scenes 23 and 28, and Part Two, scene 23.

Dostoevsky eliminates Faust, thereby dispensing with the love story, and omits the dungeon scene. It is highly pertinent that, whilst in Goethe's work Gretchen's 'sin', 'shame' and crime are powerfully and vividly elaborated, in Dostoevsky's opera they are not even mentioned, nor does the devil conjure up threatening images of hell and the Last Judgement. In Goethe, Gretchen's salvation hinges on her rejection of the temptation of Faust's plea to escape with him, and on her penitent prayer in which she gives herself up to 'God's judgement'. But this does not save her from her execution by beheading. Whilst Goethe means us to know, just after Mephistopheles' climactic curse: 'she is judged and condemned', by a 'voice from above' that 'she is saved', this will only be after her execution. In Goethe, the earthly law is enforced, whereas in Dostoevsky, Gretchen's execution is bypassed, and her naïve penitent prayer, after which she faints, leads straight to her salvation. Goethe's treatment of this theme reflects the juridical theology of salvation of the Catholic Church, according to which the sinner must pay for his sin. For Dostoevsky, it is not the sin or punishment for crime that matters so much as compassion, forgiveness and redemptive Grace, qualities he believed expressed the true spirit of Christianity and were uniquely preserved in Orthodoxy.[8] He shows this by introducing a subtle musical shift in creeds just after Gretchen prays and faints.

Both Dostoevsky and Goethe depict the finale of Gretchen's drama with heavenly choirs, but they markedly diverge in their religious contexts. Goethe's drama is contextualized with elements taken from Catholic and pagan sources, and from German humanist classicism. Dostoevsky's 'opera' divides into two creedal contexts; the Gothic cathedral, Gretchen's initial, tormented recitative, the 'gloomy', 'indifferent' choir, deaf to her plight, singing the requiem in Latin, the devil's taunt 'there's no forgiveness for you here', his final curse, 'you're damned', and Gretchen's nadir of despair are left to the Catholic half of his drama. Then follows 'Commotion', a pause preparing for the transition to an Orthodox finale. Gretchen is 'lifted, borne up', whereupon the music shifts to a major key as there sounds, in answer to her prayer, a new 'thundering', 'inspired choir, triumphant...singing something like our "Up-borne-by-the-angelic-hosts"', where 'our' refers to the mystical *Cherubim Hymn*, a prayer from the Orthodox liturgy of St John Chrysostom.[9] Which is to say that an earthly Orthodox hymn

---

[8]Gozenpud makes a similar point: 'The main thing for Dostoevsky, as always, is not the punishment for crime but the redemption of sin', p. 145.

[9]Dostoevsky originally introduced the 'inspired' choir with 'suddenly an organ frighteningly booms out' (*vdrug strashno gudit organ*). (XVII, 122) Most likely he deleted it because Orthodox services do not employ musical instruments and, more importantly, because he wished to underscore the Orthodox faith as one of mercy, hope and light, as opposed to Catholic gloom, fear and punishment. Gozenpud also notes the presence of the two creeds, but maintains that [...] 'the Catholic requiem and the Orthodox "Cherubim" are transformed. This is not cult [i.e., religious] or theatrical music, but...one which embraces with its rejoicing sounds heaven and earth', pp. 145-146. However, unlike Lyamshin's Franco-Prussian War, there is no transforming merger here of the two liturgical songs. Dostoevsky clearly demarcates them; the *Cherubim* follows and supersedes the Requiem.

is 'something like' heavenly music. In the Russian text, Dostoevsky quotes, in liturgical Church Slavonic, syllables separated as in singing, the hymn's final words: *Dori-no-si-ma chin-mi*. The text, familiar to Orthodox Russians, reads in full:

> Let us who mystically represent the Cherubim,
> and who sing the thrice-holy hymn
> to the life-creating Trinity,
> now lay aside all cares of this life,
> that we may receive the King of All,
> who comes invisibly upborne by the angelic hosts.
> Alleluia, alleluia, alleluia.[10]

This is sung by the choir during the Eucharist, a sacrament held to impart grace and salvation, when the priest brings the bread and wine in which Christ is believed to be present. This allusion to the hymn is followed by: 'everything's shaken to its foundations' (*vse potriaslos' na osnovaniiakh*), a phrase that is a reminiscence of the Crucifixion when 'the earth shook' (*zemlya potriaslas'*) and the Resurrection. (Matt. 27: 51, 28: 2) These evocations of Christ's redemptive death and resurrection liken Gretchen's ascension, 'carried upborne by the angelic hosts', to the 'King of All', a traditional Orthodox epithet for the image of Christ Pantocrator. She thus attains *theosis* (divinization), a central Orthodox concept according to which human beings, by grace, may gradually assimilate to God?s likeness, and thus may share in His divinity, the supreme goal of a Christian life.[11] At the end of Goethe's drama, Gretchen, soaring upwards, is reunited with her lover Faust, whereupon the Mater Gloriosa appears, urging her on to 'higher spheres'. Goethe's concluding 'Mystical Chorus', which celebrates the 'Eternally Feminine', is not canonical or even markedly Christian. Dostoevsky's choir culminates in a universal, communal 'exclamation' (*vozglas*) of 'Hosanna', where *vozglas* denotes the final words of an Orthodox prayer or service, exclaimed in a loud voice. In Goethe, Gretchen is associated to the Virgin Mary and her apotheosis is a non-canonical poetic image of the Catholic Marian cosmos, in which neither God nor Christ appears.[12] In Dostoevsky, Gretchen is

---

[10] In fact, Dostoevsky quotes only the last two words of the final line: *Angel'skimi nevidimo dorinosima chinmi*. For the sake of clarity, I have followed Pevear and Volokhonsky's insertion of 'angelic'. I thank Father Sergei Hackel and Peter Scorer for checking the accuracy of this anonymous translation from Church Slavonic. I also thank Jostein Børtnes for discussing an earlier version of this paper with me.

[11] For a clear and concise explanation of this concept, see Timothy Ware, *The Orthodox Church*, (Harmondsworth: Penguin, 1986), especially pp. 224, 236-242.

[12] As Trunz remarks in his commentary to *Faust*, 'Goethe gives no final scene in which Christ or the Lord God as Judge appears, or which alludes to [Christ's] sacrificial death?, p. 631. David Luke also notes the 'absence of God, and especially of Christ'. Johann Wolfgang von Goethe, *Faust, Part Two*, trans. David Luke (Oxford: Oxford University Press, 1998), p. lxxvii.

associated to Christ, and her *theosis* is celebrated with the 'exultant cry of the whole universe', thus turning it into an event of the liturgical Orthodox cosmos.

The Brothers Karamazov (1880)

Dostoevsky sometimes subjected his most cherished beliefs and aspirations to parody by putting them in the voices of those who mock or oppose them. During Ivan Karamazov's conversation with his nightmare devil, the devil rings a blasphemous variation on the singing of 'Hosanna' by the heavenly host. He tells Ivan:

> I was there when the Word who died on the cross was ascending to heaven carrying on His bosom the soul of the thief who was crucified to the right of Him. I heard the joyous shrieks of the cherubim singing and howling: 'Hosanna', and the thundering howls of ecstasy of the seraphim from which heaven and the whole universe shook! (XV, 82), (11, 9)

The devil retains the canonical elements here, except, in contradistinction to Trishatov's 'opera', the words he uses to describe the angels' singing—'shrieks' (*vzvizgi*), 'howls' (*vopli*) are also used to denote the 'squeals', 'yelps', 'screeches' of pigs, dogs, wolves and demons.[13] Thus, with his angels' 'shrieks' and 'howls', with their familiar associations to swine and demons, the devil mocks the most sublime Christian mystery. But mockery of divine things is no longer amusing to Ivan. He has just learned the truth about his role in his father's murder, partly through a song that debases and mocks him.

After the murder of Fyodor Karamazov, Dostoevsky subtly introduces a musical leitmotif, a song Ivan hears at three critical moments. The first instance occurs when Ivan, driven by tortuous doubts to find out the truth about his father's murder, sets out for the last time to Smerdyakov's lodging. Making his way there in the night, during a snowstorm, he comes across a little peasant stumbling along the road, 'muttering and cursing' and singing in 'a hoarse, drunken voice':

> Ach, Van'ka's gone to Piter,
> I won't wait for him. (XV, 57), (11, 8)

The befuddled peasant keeps breaking off after the second line, 'again begins to curse someone' and then starts the song again. An intense hatred towards the peasant, a strong urge to beat him, wells up in Ivan. When the peasant accidentally bumps against him, Ivan furiously shoves him aside, leaving him lying unconscious in the snow. 'He'll freeze to death', notes Ivan, but goes on his way. (XV, 57) Why this violent hatred, so out of proportion to the little peasant's offence? As Terras remarks, Ivan 'recognize[s] himself in the peasant's

---

[13] As Victor Terras notes, 'the noun *vzvizg* is decidedly deprecatory', Victor Terras, *A Karamazov Companion: Commentary on the Genesis, Language and Style of Dostoevsky's Novel* (Madison, Wisconsin: University of Wisconsin Press, 1981), p. 394.

song'.[14] Indeed, 'himself' and another; the peasant is singing about 'I' and 'Van'ka', the pejorative diminutive for Ivan, thus indicating a certain contempt and implying they are on familiar terms, which Ivan could only find deeply insulting. The 'Ach' is a fine touch in that here it expresses a knowing expletive over 'Van'ka's' departure to 'Piter' (a popular nickname for St Petersburg). The peasant knows, and 'Van'ka' doesn't want to know, why he won't be waiting for him. And he cannot get past the song's second line, but keeps repeating it, and so Ivan keeps hearing it, as though insinuating some important but only hinted at meaning. And is the 'someone' the peasant is cursing 'Van'ka', and is it for his having gone to 'Piter'? If so, he has unwittingly hit a raw nerve in Ivan, who, as he was absconding on the train to Moscow, cursed himself as 'a scoundrel'. (XIV, 255), (5, 7) And whom does the peasant remind Ivan of? Earlier in the novel, the narrator recalls a painting which depicts 'in the forest...a peasant standing all alone' in the snow, 'as if he were lost in thought, but he is not thinking, rather he is "contemplating" something...storing up his impressions.' Such a one 'was Smerdyakov...greedily storing up his impressions...still not knowing why himself.' (XIV, 116-17), (3, 6) In this foreshadowing of Smerdyakov's potential criminality, the narrator uses the same pejorative diminutive (*muzhichonko*) for the peasant in the painting as for the one Ivan encounters in the snowstorm on his way to Smerdyakov.[15]

Shortly thereafter, at the climax of their last conversation, Smerdyakov openly accuses Ivan of what he has long been accusing himself, but struggling to suppress:

> 'You killed him, you're the main murderer, I was just your minion...and according to your word I performed the deed.'
> 'Performed? Was it really you that killed him?' Ivan went cold. Something shook, as it were, in his brain, he began shivering all over with cold little shivers...
> 'You mean you really didn't know anything?', murmured [Smerdyakov] mistrustfully looking him in the eye with a crooked grin.
> Ivan kept staring at him, he seemed to have lost his tongue.
> > Ach, Van'ka's gone to Piter,
> > I won't wait for him—
> suddenly rang out in his head. (XV, 59), (11, 8)

The voice and image of Smerdyakov, with his mocking 'grin', coalesce with the image and song of the peasant who is singing almost exactly what Smerdyakov could have said when Ivan ran off to distant Moscow, thereby abandoning his

---

[14] Terras, p. 381.

[15] Smerdyakov himself sings a song to an admiring young woman in 'Smerdyakov with a guitar'. For a superb analysis of this passage and of Smerdyakov, see Lee B Johnson, 'Struggle for Theosis: Smerdyakov as Would Be Saint', in *A New Word on 'The Brothers Karamazov'*, ed. Robert Louis Jackson (Evanston, Illinois: Northwestern University Press, 2004), pp. 74-89 (pp. 78-80).

father to his death. Smerdyakov took Ivan's departure as his consent to the murder; indeed, he knew he did not have to wait for him. It was precisely Ivan's indirect but critical collusion with Smerdyakov to desert his father, when he knew that a murder could take place, which constitutes his crime.[16] The peasant's short musical refrain, then, expresses the essence and extent of Ivan's complicity. This master stroke of innuendo obliquely but insistently reminds him of 'his guilt' in running off to Moscow.[17] Ivan projects onto the peasant his hatred of Smerdyakov, or rather, his hatred of that part of his divided soul that succumbed to the Smerdyakov in himself, which he now desperately tries to expunge.[18] So, when he 'furiously pushed the peasant away', consciously abandoning him to his death, he was subconsciously pushing away Smerdyakov and wishing for his death, just as he did with his father. The song, coming from the voice of a surrogate Smerdyakov, is psychologically a perfect vehicle because it impinges involuntarily on Ivan's consciousness, beyond the control of his intellect, struggling to deny the truth. The 'Ach' has become a sigh of dismay or despair, the nagging refrain, now lodged in his brain, analogous to the nagging pangs of conscience.[19] In Dostoevsky's artistic world, conscience is not only a psychological phenomenon, but a manifestation of the voice of God, which has been acting on Ivan all along.

The Van'ka song resurfaces once more when Ivan, in a state of total mental breakdown after the last visit of his nightmare devil, gives his catastrophic evidence at his brother's trial. Coming to the end of his mad ramblings about the devil's visits, he exclaims, and these are among his last words in the novel: 'It's just the same as if some drunken lout started bawling "Van'ka went to Piter"'. (XV, 117), (12, 5) General agitation ensues among the spectators. Ivan 'violently knock[s]' a court attendant to the floor. And then, Ivan 'began to howl with a furious howl *(zavopil neistovym voplem)*', a phrase reminiscent of the cry of the demonically possessed in the New Testament; and 'all the while he was being led' out of the courtroom, 'he kept howling and screaming out something inco-

---

[16] As Dostoevsky said in a letter, Ivan 'refrained (intentionally) [...] from expressing to [Smerdyakov] clearly and categorically his revulsion towards his planned villainy which he saw and had a presentiment of, and thus, *as it were, allowed* [Dostoevsky's emphasis] Smerdyakov to commit the villainous act. This *permission* [Dostoevsky's emphasis] was indispensable for Smerdyakov? (XXX: 1, 129).

[17] Ralph E Matlaw remarks that the song 'is a reminder to him...of his guilt in going to Moscow', in *'The Brothers Karamazov': Novelistic Technique* (The Hague: Mouton Press, 1957), p. 17.

[18] See Vladimir Kantor's discussion of this idea in 'Pavel Smerdyakov and Ivan Karamazov: The problem of temptation', in *Dostoevsky and the Christian Tradition*, ed. George Pattison and Diane Oenning Thompson (Cambridge: Cambridge University Press, 2001), pp. 189-225, especially pp. 213-220.

[19] Dostoevsky used this musical analogy in *Notes from Underground* (1864), where the Underground man decides to write his confession because he is 'especially oppressed by a memory [of a base deed], which 'is like an annoying musical tune that refuses to go away'. (V, 123)

herent', the same 'howl' and 'howling' the devil used to describe the singing of the cherubim and seraphim. (XV, 118)[20]

Concluding Remarks

Dostoevsky's musical motifs never serve as mere atmospheric background, but as events in his characters' consciousnesses, bearing a symbolic or metaphorical relation to the critical events in his fiction, joining up with his major themes and ideological preoccupations. Dostoevsky thought in terms of oppositions and transformations, and this can be seen in his literary treatment of musical motifs. The passages we have examined are contrapuntal compositions marked by distinctive, opposing 'melodic' lines, contending with each other for dominance. He brought these oppositions close up against each other, forcing them to interact, to reveal their semantic essences and in the process, to undergo transformations. Thus, *Augustin* undermines the *Marseillaise*, and during his attack, both are transformed into a beast. Trishatov's opera represents a contest between *Dies irae* and *Dorinosima chinmi*, between Catholicism and Orthodoxy, with the latter triumphant and divinely transfiguring. Ivan is caught in an internal conflict between the two opposing voices, between denial and accusation, and exits the novel demonically transformed. Each of these musical motifs establishes resonances with the Logos, either eventually (*The Devils*), immediately (*The Adolescent*), or indirectly (*The Brothers Karamazov*).

Let us return to Bakhtin's metaphor of polyphony in Dostoevsky as an all-inclusive multiplicity of voices, each one individual, distinct, fully valid and all having equal rights. This follows from his idea that Dostoevsky created free people whose 'words possess extraordinary independence' and sound '*alongside the author's word*'.[21] But what holds the polyphony together? Why do the separate voices not simply go off in all directions, pulling the narrative apart? Is polyphony in Dostoevsky diversity without unity, are all the voices equal? In the art of counterpoint, one or more melodic lines are pointed against the notes of an original, given, principal melody, called plainsong or the *cantus firmus*. The original melody holds true, pure, there is no ornamentation, or parodic improvisation, but the counter-pointed melodies, whilst having distinct, varied identities and considerable freedom to develop, are all responses to the *cantus firmus*, whether they enhance, debase or oppose it. And they are all equal in that none renders the others mute. Amongst the many clashing voices he hears, Dostoevsky,

---

[20] Vetlovskaia similarly remarks that Ivan's furious howl is that of 'a possessed man in whom, according to old religious beliefs, a demon has taken root'. V E Vetlovskaia, *Poetika romana 'Brat'ia Karamazovy'* (Leningrad: Nauka, 1977), p. 99.

[21] Bakhtin, p. 7. David S Cunningham, in his chapter 'Polyphony', in *These Three are One* (Oxford: Blackwell, 1998), pp. 127-164, argues for 'a polyphonic understanding of God'. He finds in polyphony an ideal expression of Trinitarian theology, in that it simultaneously embodies 'oneness and difference' without exclusions, p. 127. Ware writes: 'The mystery of the Trinity is a mystery of unity in diversity', p. 237.

said Bakhtin, 'seeks the highest, most authoritative' voice which 'he perceives' in 'the image of Christ, who 'represents for him, the resolution of ideological quests. This image or highest voice must crown the world of voices, must organize and subdue it'.[22] We may fairly call this voice the *cantus firmus* of Dostoevsky's polyphonic art. In this perspective, Gretchen's salvation is achieved when her plainsong prayer, 'in the highest degree medieval', and thus purged of sensuous lyricism and flamboyant ornament, naïve and pure, most closely approaches the purity and perfect fullness of the *cantus firmus*. Lyamshin's Franco-Prussian War receives its higher significance when the novel's events are read as an enactment of demonic infestation related in the Gospel text. For Dostoevsky, the healing of the demoniac by Christ, the *cantus firmus*, indicates the way out of a spiritually infected world. In *The Devils*, it is realized only in Stepan Trofimovich Verkhovensky's deathbed illumination. In *The Brothers Karamazov*, it is the voice of Ivan's conscience, the *cantus firmus* within, which makes him suffer guilt, and thus opens his way to salvation. For Dostoevsky, it is by the *cantus firmus* that we know that murder is a crime.[23]

In a letter written from Tegel prison in 1944, Dietrich Bonhoeffer speaks of God's love as:

> a kind of *cantus firmus* to which the other melodies of life provide the counterpoint...Where the *cantus firmus* is clear and plain, the counterpoint can be developed to its limits. The two are 'undivided and yet distinct'...like Christ in his divine and human natures. May not the attraction and importance of polyphony in music consist in its being a musical reflection of this Christological fact?...if the *cantus firmus* is full and perfect...the counterpoint has a firm support and can't come adrift or get out of tune.

In Dostoevsky's works, many go adrift, get out of tune with the *cantus firmus*, but even at the very periphery, the *cantus firmus* keeps pulling them in to itself, it never totally dies out. This is why Dostoevsky can develop his dissonant counterpoints to their limits, without breaking the aesthetic and moral integrity of his artistic works. To quote Bonhoeffer again, 'only a polyphony of this kind can give life a wholeness and at the same time assure us that nothing calamitous can happen as long as the *cantus firmus* is kept going.'[24] The struggle to keep the *cantus firmus* going, despite the many calamities depicted in his fiction, may serve as that aim to which Dostoevsky's works bear powerful witness.

---

[22] Bakhtin, p. 97.

[23] In his *Notebooks* for 1880-1881, Dostoevsky remarked: 'I have one moral model and ideal, Christ. I ask, would He have burned heretics—no. Well, that means burning heretics is an immoral act!' (XXVII, 56)

[24] Dietrich Bonhoeffer, *Letters and Papers from Prison*, ed. Eberhard Bethy (London, 1971), p. 303.

BUDDHISM IN DOSTOEVSKY: PRINCE MYSHKIN AND THE TRUE LIGHT OF BEING

Sarah Young

PRINCE Myshkin, Dostoevsky's attempt to create a 'perfectly beautiful human being',[1] is usually interpreted within the Christian tradition.[2] However, there are aspects of this character which do not fit easily into the Christian context in which the author was undoubtedly writing. In particular, while it is plain in *The Idiot* that the hero's epileptic aura can be categorized as a type of religious experience which is personally convincing and informs his world view and actions, the connection between the experience and the resultant effects is not obvious, and it is unclear how this relates to any specifically Christian ideas, specifically as it is not a numinous experience (there is no direct apprehension of God), but is rather *nirvanic*, relating to an awareness of the fleeting states of consciousness as the essence of selfhood.[3] Because of this latter feature, I want to show, by looking at the issues from a Buddhist perspective, how Myshkin's experience is related to his world view. This is in no way to suggest that Dostoevsky was in any sense a Buddhist; it is rather a recognition of the fact that although he was clearly writing within the Christian tradition, some aspects of his work do not correlate with Christianity in any coherent way, but can be elucidated with reference to other traditions, reflecting his originality, and the complexity and depth of his artistic world. He is never a writer who can be captured within a single framework.

Lev Tolstoy once commented to Maxim Gorky that an acquaintance with the teachings of Buddhism would have calmed Dostoevsky down,[4] and the assumption has always been that Dostoevsky, unlike his fellow giant of nineteenth-

---

[1] *PSS*, XXVIII: 2, 241, 251.
[2] See, for example, R Guardini, 'Dostoevsky's Idiot: A Symbol of Christ', *Cross Currents*, 6, 1956, 451-462; G G Ermilova, *Taina kniazia Myshkina: O romane Dostoevskogo 'Idiot'* (Ivanovo: Ivanovo State University, 1993); Liza Knapp, 'Myshkin Through a Murky Glass, Guessingly', in Liza Knapp, ed., *Dostoevsky's 'The Idiot': A Critical Companion* (Evanston, IL: Northwestern University Press, 1998), pp. 191-215; A E Kunil'skii, 'O khristianskom kontekste v romane F M Dostoevskogo *Idiot*', in V N Zakharov, ed., *Evangel'skii tekst v russkoi literature XVIII-XX vekov*, II (Petrozavodsk: Petrozavodsk University Press, 1998), pp. 391-408.
[3] Keith Yandell, *The Epistemology of Religious Experience* (Cambridge: Cambridge University Press), pp. 21-22.
[4] George Steiner, *Tolstoy or Dostoevsky: An Essay in Contrast* (London: Faber, 1960), p. 229.

century Russian prose, had no knowledge of Buddhism whatsoever.[5] While we have no evidence that this was not the case while he was writing *The Idiot*, towards the end of his life Dostoevsky in fact had a book in his library by A Gusev, *The Moral Ideal of Buddhism in its Relation to Christianity (Nravstvennyi ideal buddizma v ego otnoshenii k khristianstvu)*, published in Petersburg in 1874.[6] In the light of the ideas I am about to suggest, it would be interesting to speculate what Dostoevsky made of this book, and whether he saw any of the connections I have made. It is generally recognized that the Orthodox church has retained more Buddhist influence than Western branches of Christianity,[7] so it is perhaps not so strange that Buddhistic patterns of thought should emerge in Dostoevsky. How or whether this relates to later upsurges in Buddhism in Russia and their reflection in Russian literature would be another topic for debate. Notably, the fact that the Russian symbolists were both heavily influenced by Dostoevsky and interested in Eastern religions suggests that there may be more points of contact between the nineteenth-century author and Buddhist ideas than has previously been imagined. The indirect juxtaposition of Dostoevskian and Buddhist motifs in Russian literature recurs most powerfully in Evgeny Zamyatin's anti-utopian novel *We*, and has recently reasserted itself in the works of Victor Pelevin, in particular his 1996 novel *Chapaev and Pustota*.

Suggestions of a connection between Dostoevsky and Buddhism were first raised by Hermann Hesse, himself profoundly interested in oriental mysticism, who saw in the Russian author's novels 'a turning back to Asia'.[8] More recently Grigory Pomerants compared Prince Myshkin's vision at the waterfall to Zen art and poetry,[9] a fascinating idea on which the philosopher unfortunately does not expand. Two articles have been dedicated specifically to Buddhist motifs in Dostoevsky: Michael Futrell examines Alyosha Karamazov in relation to the Bodhisattva ideal of compassion,[10] and Irina Kirk compares Prince Myshkin to the Buddha, Siddharta Gautama.[11] She presents quite a persuasive argument, but the similarities she notes are largely on a superficial level, relating to the story of the Buddha's life and certain aspects of Buddhist symbolism, and she does not

---

[5] It has indeed become almost *de rigueur* to preface any discussion of Buddhism in Dostoevsky by quoting this remark of Tolstoy's.

[6] L P Grossman, *Seminarii po Dostoevskomu* (Letchworth: Prideaux Press, 1972), p. 43, entry 182 in the catalogue of Dostoevsky's library. I am extremely grateful to Malcolm Jones, among so many other things, for providing me with this information, which gave me a concrete starting point for the present article.

[7] As Irina Kirk states, 'Buddhistic Elements in *The Idiot*', *Studia Slavica Academiae Scientiarum Hungaricae*, 18.1-2 (1972), 77-84 (pp. 77, 84).

[8] Hermann Hesse, *In Sight of Chaos* (Zurich: Verlag Seldwyla, 1932), p. 1.

[9] G Pomerants, 'Knjaz' Myshkin', *Sintaksis*, 9 (1981), 112-166 (p. 153).

[10] Michael Futrell, 'Buddhism and *The Brothers Karamazov*', *Dostoevsky Studies*, 2 (1981), 155-162.

[11] Kirk, 'Buddhistic Elements', pp. 77-84.

attempt to equate any of Buddhism's teachings about time, impermanence and death, to Dostoevsky's themes of faith, morality and mortality.

Echoes of Buddhist teaching in *The Idiot* emerge most strongly in relation to the two most striking aspects of the figure of Prince Myshkin and his discourse: his story of the condemned man and his epileptic aura, both of which are central to shaping his world view and the image he presents to other characters and the reader. The two experiences described in the novel are linked by the altered concept of time they suggest, and by the direct apprehension of death as the source of true knowledge about life, and understanding of time.[12] Both areas—time and death—feature very strongly in Buddhist thought.

Similarities between approaches to the latter subject, death, are evident in their relation to Near Death Experiences. Although neither the epileptic aura nor the moments before execution fits into the traditional definition of a Near Death Experience, there are strong grounds for considering them to be analogous. In the first place, Near Death Experience has been linked to temporal lobe dysfunction and is therefore closely related to epilepsy.[13] Secondly, the characteristic falling and loss of consciousness associated with the fit signify an *imitatio mori*, suggesting that in his attacks, Myshkin—like his creator—has repeatedly undergone a pre-death-like experience,[14] and been 'reprieved' from this death in order to reflect on the changes to his consciousness and perception, and incorporate them into his philosophy of life, just as Near Death Experiences generally lead people to a spiritual awakening and a new, more positive, relation to life and to other people based on compassion, as a result of the insight they gain into suffering and responsibility.[15]

---

[12] For further details of the connections between Myshkin's experiences and ideas, see Sarah Young, *Dostoevsky's 'The Idiot' and the Ethical Foundations of Narrative: Reading, Narrating, Scripting* (London: Anthem, 2004), especially pp. 75-110.

[13] See M A Persinger, 'Religious and Mystical Experiences as Artifacts of Temporal Lobe Function: A General Hypothesis', *Perceptual and Motor Skills*, 57 (1983), 1255-1262; M Roth and M Harper, 'Temporal Lobe Epilepsy and the phobic anxiety-depersonalization syndrome, Part II: Practical and theoretical considerations', *Comprehensive Psychiatry*, 3 (1962), 215-226, or Susan Blackmore, *Dying to Live*, (Buffalo, NY: Prometheus Books, 1993); William James, *The Varieties of Religious Experience* (New York: Penguin, 1982), also notes the links between illness and religious experience in general, pp. 15, 384 and *passim*.

[14] Sigmund Freud, 'Dostoevsky and Parricide', in R Wellek, ed., *Dostoevsky: A Collection of Critical Essays* (Englewood Cliffs, NJ: Prentice Hall, 1962), pp. 98-111, states that such attacks 'signify an identification with a dead person' (p. 102).

[15] Near Death Experience typically results in 'a heightened appreciation of life, a sense of personal renewal and search for purpose, increasing confidence, compassion, empathy, tolerance and understanding'; 'Introduction', in Lee W Bailey and Jenny Yates, eds., *The Near-Death Experience: A Reader* (New York & London: Routledge, 1996), p. 10; one survivor reports: 'Above all, I was shown that love is supreme. I saw that truly without love we are nothing. We are here to help each other, to understand, forgive, and serve one another', Betty Eadie, 'Embraced by the Light', Bailey and Yates, *The Near-Death Experience*, pp. 53-62 (p. 59).

The condemned man's knowledge of the absolute certainty of death, and even of its precise timing, is seen in the novel to have a similar effect, and Dostoevsky's own experience of the death sentence and reprieve suggests that he himself saw its significance in these terms; his letter to his brother describing his feelings on his reprieve shows that he also saw it as a moment of regeneration, full of possibilities and new life. (XXVIII: 2, 88)[16] Whatever Dostoevsky thought, Myshkin certainly sees analogies between the two experiences; it is his epileptic aura which allows him to identify with the thoughts of the condemned man who 'knows everything'.

Finally, Dostoevsky's later story 'The Dream of a Ridiculous Man' describes the typical elements of a Near Death Experience with an accuracy that can hardly be coincidental; whether Dostoevsky actually underwent an experience of this sort through his epilepsy or his death sentence, or whether the understanding he gained from these two experiences simply allowed him to imagine the mind's journey in the moment before death, we have to say that the author showed remarkable insight into the process of death, which became fundamental to his creativity and the development of his 'fantastic realism'.[17]

Near Death Experience is not of course an exclusively Buddhist phenomenon; in Western literature the first mention of it is probably Plato's Myth of Er,[18] in which Er is refused permission to drink from the waters of Lethe and has to return to life to tell others about the other world and what happens during and after death.[19] There is also a popular tradition of Near Death Experience in Russian folk culture.[20] However, there are a number of crucial links between Near Death Experience and Buddhist teaching, arising out of the general importance attached within Buddhism to the understanding of impermanence and our own mortality; as the Buddha said in the Mahaparinibbana sutta,

> Of all the mindfulness meditations
> That on death is supreme.[21]

This has led different Buddhist sects to approach death and the moment before death in different ways, and in the Mahayana tradition, these are often linked to

---

[16] Michael Grosso suggests that 'Near-death imagery is oriented around the process of becoming a Self', 'The Archetype of Death and Enlightenment', in Bailey and Yates, *The Near-Death Experience*, pp. 127-144 (p. 140).

[17] See Liza Knapp, ed. and trans., *Dostoevsky as Reformer: The Petrashevsky Case* (Ann Arbor, MI: Ardis, 1987), pp. 23-24.

[18] Plato, *The Republic*, trans. Desmond Lee, 2nd edn. (Harmondsworth: Penguin, 1987), pp. 447-455.

[19] See Carol Zeleski, *Otherworld Journeys: Accounts of Near-Death Experience in Medieval and Modern Times* (New York and Oxford: Oxford University Press, 1987), p. 79.

[20] As Faith Wigzell demonstrated in a fascinating paper given at a workshop on Russian religious and spiritual culture at the University of Surrey in March 2003.

[21] Quoted in Sogyal Rinpoche, *The Tibetan Book of Living and Dying*, 2nd edn., ed. P Gaffney and A Harvey (London: Rider, 1998), p. 26.

Near Death Experiences. For example, the Pure Land sect places emphasis on understanding the experience of death, and practitioners strive to cultivate knowledge of death by accessing Near Death-type Experiences through meditation.[22]

Parallels have also been noted between Near Death Experiences and *The Great Liberation Through Hearing*, or what is known in the West as *The Tibetan Book of the Dead*. This text, which is read to the dying person and their corpse in the days after death, and is intended to give them insight into the nature of mind and death, and the chances of a more favourable rebirth, has many features in common with reports of Near Death Experiences (encounters with bodies of light, time shifts and travel to unearthly realms, insight into suffering and responsibility, and true awareness of being). The concept of *Rigpa* described by Sogyal Rinpoche in relation to *The Tibetan Book of the Dead* is particularly important, as here it is made clear that the visions associated with the death-like experience originate in the nature of mind, and precisely in the individual's understanding of this fact. *Rigpa*, or the True Light of Being, is described as the awareness of one's own self-radiance, or perception of the Buddha nature within us.[23] For the unenlightened person, the moment of witnessing one's true mortality as an imminent fact is the best chance of seeing and comprehending this true nature of our being.

A similar state is described in the prelude to Myshkin's fit, in which the 'highest synthesis' of 'beauty and prayer' is directly associated with a feeling of self-awareness and the full consciousness of one's own existence:

> The sensation of life and self-awareness increased almost ten-fold in those moments which passed like lightning. His mind and heart were illuminated with an extraordinary light; all his agitation, all his doubts, all his anxieties seemed to be instantly pacified, resolved in a sort of lofty tranquillity, full of pure, harmonious joy and hope, full of reason and knowledge of the ultimate cause of things [...] But that this truly was 'beauty and prayer', that it truly was 'the highest synthesis of life', he could not doubt, or even admit the possibility of doubt [...] *These moments were purely and simply an intense heightening of self-awareness* [...] and at the same time *the most immediate sense of one's own existence*. (VIII, 188; my emphasis)

Thus in *The Idiot*, as in Buddhism, a clear and direct apprehension of death is crucial to having the right relationship to life, the other, and one's own consciousness. And in coming to this insight, a correct understanding of time is essential, because of the fundamental connection between temporality and mortality. This is most evident in *The Idiot* in the thoughts of the condemned man:

> It worked out that he had five minutes left, no more. He used to say that those five minutes seemed to him like an eternity, like immense wealth; he

---

[22] See 'Introduction,' in Bailey and Yates, *The Near-Death Experience*, p. 21.

[23] Sogyal, pp. 260, 277 and *passim*.

felt that in those five minutes he could live through so many lives, that there could be no thinking now of the last instant. (VIII, 52)

The intensity with which the condemned man experiences his remaining minutes, and feels his mortality as a physical rather than simply an intellectual truth, suggests both that this is life at its most real, and that there is a possibility of spiritual regeneration. When the precise moment of death is calculated and contemplated beforehand, all the delusions of everyday life are forcibly stripped away, as the past and future cease to have any significance, and all that remains is the intensified present. In the idea of 'liv[ing] through so many lives' there are also echoes of the teaching that the Buddha, in achieving enlightenment, saw and re-experienced all his past lives.

The idea of counting every second and living precisely in the present is illustrated in the prisoner's journey to the scaffold, as his perception of time becomes more intense and elongated in inverse proportion to the amount of time he has left to live:

> I think he would still imagine he has an eternity left to live while they're taking him. I imagine he probably thought on the way, 'There's still a long time, three streets still to live; there's this street, then the next one, then the one after with the bakers' on the right...it'll be ages before we reach the bakers'!' (VIII, 55)

Perception is sharpened with the nearness of the moment of death: 'the brain is terribly alive and active, it must be working, working, working really hard, like a machine'. (VIII, 56) Again Myshkin suggests that this is a moment of absolute truth, with no room for delusions about the nature of reality and mortality; the prisoner at this point *'knows everything'*. (VIII, 56, author's emphasis) The fact that the prince sees the significance of the fully conscious realization of the instant before death as the experience of true reality, free from all delusions, is evinced in his comment, 'me, if I was lying there, I would deliberately listen for it to hear the sound'. (VIII, 56) The most terrifying moment, of hearing the guillotine blade as it descends, is also for Myshkin the moment of maximal awareness of the reality of life, and is therefore the most valid experience, even if—or precisely because—it is followed immediately by annihilation.

Prince Myshkin's understanding of the importance of time in relation to death is evident when he states that the reprieved man believed he would never waste another minute, and would count every second ('I would turn every minute into a whole century, nothing would be lost, every minute would be accounted for, nothing would be wasted!' (VIII, 52)) Although he then admits that the man 'didn't live like that at all and wasted very many minutes', the prince is convinced there is some truth in the man's words. When Alexandra rejects the idea, 'So it follows from your example that you can't really live your life "counting every minute"', he will not completely deny it: 'Yes, for some reason it's impossible [...] I thought so myself [...] But somehow I can't quite believe it all the same'. (VIII, 53) Slattery suggests that clinging to the notion that every second of life can be counted is one of the hero's major faults, as it is a denial of the temporal reality of human life: 'to be enmeshed in human life is to be in human time', and to place oneself outside human time is to cease participation in human life.[24]

However, in his descriptions of men awaiting execution, Myshkin is in fact describing in its most clarified and shocking form the inevitable conclusion of all human life. Therefore this access to a different temporal perception from that which we normally experience, which Slattery calls 'a violation of human temporality', formulated in order to evade the terrible certainty of the future,[25] is in fact a *reassessment* of human temporality designed specifically to confront that certainty. The prince is asserting that by fully realizing and understanding one's true, mortal nature, we can appreciate the essential value of life, which gives rise to the aspiration to count every minute.[26] The hero's final comments show his awareness of the difficulty, or perhaps impossibility, of this task, but the idea of examining one's relation to time with respect to the inevitability of death, far from fleeing reality, directly addresses the problem of perceiving the reality of the 'world as it is given'.[27]

As with his understanding of death, the altered concept of time described by Myshkin is related directly to his epileptic experience:

> At that moment I seem to understand the extraordinary phrase *'there shall be time no longer'*. [...] It was probably the same second in which the epileptic Muhammad managed to behold all Allah's mansions before his overturned water-jug spilled a single drop. (VIII, 189, author's emphasis)

In the infinitesimal moment of light before his fit, Myshkin understands as a physical reality the concept of the eternal, absolute present. Boethius, who wrote *The Consolation of Philosophy* while facing the death sentence, described eternity in similar terms, not as an endless life, but as 'that which embraces and possesses simultaneously the whole fullness of everlasting life, which lacks nothing of the future and has lost nothing of the past, that is what may properly be said to be eternal'.[28] The space—or *Bardo*—between life and death, here between Myshkin's moment of light and the darkness of the fit which follows, is the moment with the greatest potential for self-awareness—the moment of absolute presentness.

---

[24] Dennis Slattery, 'The Frame Tale: Temporality, Fantasy and Innocence in *The Idiot*', *IDS Bulletin*, 9 (1979), 6-25 (pp. 15-16).

[25] Slattery, 'Frame Tale', p. 15.

[26] As stated in V N Belopol'skii, *Dostoevskii i filosofskaia mysl' ego epokhi. Kontseptsiia cheloveka* (Rostov: Izd. Rostovskogo universiteta, 1987), p. 164.

[27] Slattery, 'Frame Tale', p. 16.

[28] Boethius, *The Consolation of Philosophy*, trans. V E Watts (Harmondsworth: Penguin, 1969), p. 168.

The concept of presentness is central to Buddhist thought, because of the belief that everything is in a constant state of change, every instant is different, and nothing is permanent. This has a fundamental impact on our view of the self. As everything is *anicca*, impermanent, not only do we die, but we are never precisely the same person we were from one moment to the next; our body cells die and are replaced by new ones, our thoughts change, and our external environment is equally in constant flux.[29] We rarely coincide with ourselves, as Dostoevsky once commented (XIII, 370), because we are never exactly the same person, we are essentially the aggregate of all the changes taking place within what we call 'I'. (The deconstructive conception of the human personality in Buddhism has been linked recently to questions of identity in postmodern thought,[30] and connections with Bakhtinian ideas may also be perceived here.) This view of human identity not only undermines the concept of the Ego, because there is no unchanging core of our being (the concept of anatta, or not-self), but it also leads to the conclusion that the only means we have of truly understanding, or coinciding with, ourselves, is to focus on what we truly are, what we are experiencing, and how we are relating to the other in the present.[31]

For these reasons, *vipassana* or 'insight' meditation in its various forms focuses on the cultivation of awareness or mindfulness of the present moment; in Therevada Buddhism the basic meditation technique involves watching one's breath and observe the passing phenomena one experiences—physical sensations, feelings, thoughts—as they arise and disappear.[32] (In Mahayana sects a similar idea is expressed in different terms, such as meditating on the moments between moments.) In everyday life as well, the ideal is full awareness of what you are doing at the present moment.[33]

This is the first step to enlightenment, in which complete and sustained awareness of the present is achieved; as Dudjom Rinpoche states, 'pure awareness of nowness is the real buddha'.[34] In this state, the notion of the Ego is understood to be illusory, and as one discovers that there is no absolute self, one also rejects the concept of dualism which separates us from the other. Reality is seen to be interdependent, as all beings and their suffering are interconnected.

---

[29] See Peter Harvey, *An Introduction to Buddhism: Teachings, History and Practices* (Cambridge: Cambridge University Press, 1990), or Walpola Rahula, *What the Buddha Taught* (Bangkok: Hawtrai Foundation, 1990) (first publ. 1959).

[30] See, for example, John Pickering, 'Selfhood is a Process', in *The Authority of Experience: Essays on Buddhism and Psychology*, ed J Pickering (Richmond: Curzon, 1997), pp 149-169 (pp. 158, 163).

[31] See, for example, Padmasiri de Silva, 'Exploring the Vicissitudes of Affect and Working with Emotions: An Early Buddhist Perspective', in *The Authority of Experience*, pp. 123-145 (p. 132).

[32] See the *Satipatthana sutta*, <http://www.accesstoinsight.org/canon/majjhima/index.html> 'Access to Insight: Readings in Theravada Buddhism', compiled by John Bullitt (accessed December 2004).

[33] See Thich Nhat Hanh, *The Miracle of Mindfulness: A Manual on Meditation*, trans. Mobi Ho (London: Rider, 1991).

[34] Dudjom Rinpoche, *Calling the Lama from Afar* (London: Rigpa, 1980), quoted in Sogyal, p. 44.

This understanding leads to all-embracing compassion and a sense of universal responsibility. We see this in general terms in Myshkin's self-effacement for the sake of the other and to alleviate their suffering, particularly early in the novel. More specifically, in the chapter leading up to Myshkin's fit, as his thoughts shift from the nature of his experience to the suffering of Nastasya Filippovna and Rogozhin, the need of both for compassion to restore them to life, and Myshkin's own acknowledgement of his shared responsibility for their situation and their (wrong) actions, we see the connection between his religious/near-death experience and his philosophy and actions.

Thus by relating the dissolution of the ego to the concept of presentness—a crucial theme and structuring principle in *The Idiot* as it is in no other work of Dostoevsky's—the depiction of the hero comes very close to Buddhist thought.

We must also, however, account for the dark side of Myshkin's epilepsy and the less positive aspects of his personality and actions. Myshkin undergoes a severe decline in the novel after his initial appearance as a source of moral values. This decline begins with his loss of a sense of detachment from the material world and from other people (in Buddhism, attachment coupled with the fact of impermanence, is the source of all *dukkha* or suffering), leading to the gradual loss of the acute sense of the importance of the present moment with which he begins the novel.[35] As a result of these factors, the hero's ego begins to re-assert itself, in, for example, his relationship with Aglaya, which jeopardizes his ability to save Nastasya Filippovna, or in the change in his attitude towards General Ivolgin, which plays no small part in the latter's death, as the distinction between self and other is reinforced rather than being erased. This in turn leads to a shift from the self-less compassion he exhibited at the beginning of the novel to a dualistic pity which leaves him incapable of a fully compassionate response, and at the very least contributes to the final catastrophe. Thus through his moral decline we see both the ideal and the implications of its absence.

Certain negative consequences of the prince's epilepsy can also be linked to his decline: his new-found tendency to judge others, evident notably in the build-up to his first fit in Part II and intermittently present thereafter, in comparison with his previous refusal to do so, denotes a dualistic separation of the self from the other, and an assumption of superiority over the other; his growing paranoia, arising at the same stage, equally signifies a loss of trust in the other.

But what of the ambivalence of his epileptic experience itself? Should the fact that Myshkin's True Light of Being is inseparable from spiritual horror and chaos ('stupor, spiritual darkness, idiocy stood before him as the graphic consequences of those "highest moments"' (VIII, 188)) signify that his fit in its entirety must be interpreted as wholly negative? Perhaps not; if in his moment

---

[35]This also has far-reaching consequences for the narrative and the narrator's relationship to Myshkin; see Young, *Ethical Foundations*, especially pp. 156-182.

of 'higher synthesis' he discovers the reality of the interconnection of all beings, then it is in the torment which follows that he achieves true understanding of the nature of suffering, which cements his compassion and gives him the impulse to action in order to assuage the suffering of others. However, the signs are ambiguous: in his final return to idiocy, the hero succumbs to the pressure of the knowledge he has gained, a knowledge he, paradoxically, does not, because of his illness, have the strength to bear.

I would suggest that Dostoevsky, who experimented throughout his life with the deconstruction of the human personality, was, in *The Idiot*, focusing—in truly Buddhist fashion—on the mind and mental processes as the ultimate (spiritual) basis of existence. Here the pathology which elsewhere in his *oeuvre* produces doubles, devils and underground men is stripped down to its bare, clinical essentials, as a means of exploring not only its bleaker manifestations, but also for the first time in any sustained and coherent manner its postive potential, suggesting that as beauty and harmony originate in the same source as moral chaos and destruction, redemption and new life remain a possibility even for the most desperate criminal or tormented soul. The polarities of the epileptic experience as depicted in *The Idiot* represent a harrowing pathological version of Mitya Karamazov's later, and somehow more acceptable, expression of the coexistence in his heart of the 'ideal of the Madonna' and the 'ideal of Sodom'; while one might imagine that the conscious expression of the idea of the extremes of human nature would be more repulsive, in fact the idea of these extremes in the uncontrollable form of an illness is far more shocking and grotesque,[36] perhaps because it is precisely here that the full and inescapable implications, and origins, of the 'broadness' of human nature are most graphically evident.

That the novel sabotages the idea of depicting a 'perfectly beautiful human being' by grounding Myshkin's perfection in a neurological dysfunction—and repels many readers into the bargain—does not necessarily signify that Dostoevsky rejects it altogether, only that the medium he used to crystallize it proves sustainable neither in itself nor as a source of lasting values. But in the diseased consciousness of Myshkin, Dostoevsky's distinctly *im*-perfectly beautiful man, we see the seeds not only of the moral ambivalence of Mitya Karamazov, but also, and more importantly, of the determinedly normal and healthy-minded spirituality of Alyosha Karamazov and the Elder Zosima, and of the doctrine of compassion, Active Love and universal responsibility as the only responses to the inevitable fact of the suffering of humanity.

---

[36]One should not forget how relatively recently epilepsy, inspiring in witnesses 'an unbearable horror, which even has something mystical about it' (VIII, 195), was popularly believed to be a manifestation of demonic possession.

'THE HERO'S MISTAKE' AS A SPECIAL DEVICE IN DOSTOEVSKY'S WORKS

Tatiana Kasatkina

IN his memoirs, Anatoly Naiman cites the following episode,[1] in which Anna Akhmatova boasted that she had discovered a mistake by Dostoevsky: the hero of *The Adolescent*, Arkady Dolgoruky, wishing to give Lambert an example from history in which the gratification of sexual passion quickly entails aversion for the object of desire, exclaims, 'Do you know the story of Abishag?' Dostoevsky, Akhmatova said, had confused the story of Abishag with the story of Tamar. (II Samuel 13) Naiman, however, suggests in a footnote that it is not the author who is mistaken, but his hero. Naiman is obviously absolutely correct, but nevertheless 'Akhmatova's mistake' is not accidental, and it discloses something in Dostoevsky's works which is in no way characteristic of other literary texts, for Akhmatova was, after all, a professional writer, an expert of the highest order, who knew (and felt) the secrets of her craft well enough.

This 'something', uncharacteristic of literary technique in Akhmatova's experience (and technique always serves as a reflection and expression—and perhaps in the most profound and coincident manner—of the outlook and attitude of the writer working with it), and appearing, apparently for the first time (?) in Dostoevsky, is the assumption of an *uncorrected mistake by the hero*, that is, a mistake conceived by the author precisely as a mistake, and which is moreover not only not corrected, but not even noticed as such by the run-of-the-mill reader.[2]

Anna Akhmatova was not boasting for nothing: in the thirty-volume Academy Edition (XVII, 391),[3] the hero's mistake is not registered at all, and the footnote appended to the name 'Abishag' refers precisely to the episode from the First Book of Kings which mentions Abishag. (I Kings 1: 1-4) But, however, when

---

[1] See *Novyi mir*, 1, 1989.

[2] In essence, one can say that we have before us a particular and more formalized instance of what Malcolm Jones is talking about in the following extract: 'Dostoyevsky might indeed be thought of as the novelist of "deviations" and "false developments" *par excellence*. Deviations and false developments do not however imply a dialectic movement in which they are recuperated on a higher level', Malcolm Jones, *Dostoyevsky after Bakhtin: Readings in Dostoyevsky's Fantastic Realism* (Cambridge: Cambridge University Press, 1990), p. 7. But this instance, precisely by virtue of its maximal formalization, shows that in Dostoevsky's works there is always a level—textual, subtextual or supratextual—in relation to which 'deviations' and 'false developments', uncorrected, are defined precisely as distortions and mistakes.

[3] *PSS*, as cited throughout.

I came to write a commentary for *The Adolescent*,[4] I immediately spotted the mistake in the notes, knowing nothing at that point of Akhmatova's corresponding observation.[5] I say this not in order to brag, but only to verify that this mistake is noticed by the reader, and to suggest that the ranks of readers who have noticed do not end with Akhmatova and myself.

In the history of commentary-writing on Dostoevsky's works, there is at minimum one extract which is widely known as a 'hero's mistake'. This is the point in *The Brothers Karamazov* when Ivan, citing the text of Psalm 118 (widely used in the liturgy), mercilessly—and corresponding to his ideological purposes—misinterprets it. 'And for how many centuries had mankind prayed with faith and ardour: "God our Lord, reveal thyself to us", for so many centuries they had been calling out to him, that he in his immeasurable compassion desired to descend to those who were pleading?' (XIV, 226)

Ivan presents here as an appeal and entreaty of a humankind abandoned by God this famous verse, which was sung in the Liturgy, and conceived as a *rejoicing* at the appearance and *eternal co-presence of God to man:* 'God our Lord is revealed to us'. (Ps. 118: 27)[6] The whole of Psalm 118 is, incidentally, dedicated to this rejoicing, and reads in its own way as an anti-poem to the Grand Inquisitor, as it praises the blessedness and grace of the Lord, asserts His immediate active help in response to the appeal from the crowded multitude, and speaks of the vanity of placing confidence in man or in princes. (Ps. 118: 8-9)

On the subject of distortions of the Gospels from ignorance or misunderstanding, Dostoevsky writes in his notebooks to the novel: 'THE MOST IMPORTANT THING. The landowner quotes from the Gospels and makes a gross mistake. *Miusov* corrects him and makes an even worse mistake. Even the Scholar makes a mistake. Nobody knows the Gospels. "Blessed is the womb which bore thee", said Christ. It was not Christ who said this, etc. The *Elder* says, "There was a learned professor (Wagner)". From the Gospels: "The Lord praised the cunning of the robber-steward". "How can this be? I don't understand"'. (XV, 206; author's emphasis) I would suggest that it was precisely this preparatory note which became the reason for the confident verification of the 'hero's mistake' in the commentaries to the thirty-volume Academy Complete Works. That is, commentators have based everything on authorial testimony of the necessity of a mistake being present (although loaned from the notebooks).

---

[4]See F M Dostoevskii, *Sobranie sochinenii v deviati tomakh* (Moscow: Astrel' AST: 2003-2004) (Preparation of the text, compilation, notes, introductory articles, commentary by the Chair of the Commission for the study of Dostoevsky's works at IMLI RAN, Tat'iana Aleksandrovna Kasatkina) VI, 688-689.

[5]I am grateful to my research student Anna Gumerova for pointing out this observation by Akhmatova.

[6]A more literal translation, closer to the Russian, 'Bog Gospod', i iavisia nam'; the Authorized Version, used for other quotations from the Bible, has 'God is the Lord, which hath shewed us light'. (*Translator's note.*)

What is more, as far as I am aware, nowhere, in pointing out inaccuracies and distortions in the cited texts (the most obvious example of a mistake in the text), do commentators notice the presence of a 'hero's mistake'. On the contrary, scholars stubbornly continue to insist that the position of Dostoevsky's heroes is difficult to distinguish from the author's position, even in those cases when the writer, outside the bounds of his artistic work, clearly expressed his disagreement with one or other opinion in direct utterances from the first person.

Meanwhile, under conditions of so-called 'polyphony', that is, the presence in the text of the fully-fledged *voices* of the heroes, which are *not reducible to the direct evaluations of the author* (and which are maintained by Dostoevsky even when the hero is directly and unambiguously evaluated by a harmonious chorus of characters, as in the case, for example, of Rakitin or Luzhin), and are outside the 'consummated' authorial word (in general outside the presence of the voice of the omniscient author in at least four of the five great novels, and in the presence of an embodied narrator, who is frequently *declared* in Dostoevsky to be less competent than the protagonists; it is characteristic that it is precisely to this figure that all *evaluations* are handed, whereas the *depiction* of the series of scenes is given, as has been noted more than once, through the vision of the omniscient author),[7] thus, in the aforementioned conditions, the 'hero's mistake' becomes an exceptionally significant device, which allows the author not only to show the falsity of his protagonist, but also to demonstrate *the means of distorting the truth* characteristic of his understanding of the world. As I have already said, and as I attempted to show in my latest book,[8] Dostoevsky's hero always speaks 'against a background'—in general, against the background of the fully signifying word—and of course, the most obvious distortions introduced by him must be on the level of quotations, which are presumed to be well known to the reader.

Dostoevsky begins to work on the device of the 'hero's mistake' whilst working on *The Devils*, but, apparently, all the planned 'hero's mistakes' in that novel remain in the notebooks (in this sense, it is particularly essential to focus attention on the substituted 'fantastic pages'). This novel, however, and the structure of the existence of this device within it, demands separate study. However, it can help us a little even now.

---

[7]That is, the omniscient author knows everything that is going on, sees everything that is going on, and *shows* what is going on, but does not *tell* us about it (this is linked to the cinematographic quality of Dostoevsky's texts, which has been noted more than once, and accordingly, does not evaluate the hero and does not polemicize with him. This is precisely why the authorial position of Dostoevsky has not been discovered in the realm of the voice, but is expressed by other means (including, and with the help of, the 'hero's mistake', but above all with the help of the visual field, to which, however, one must also in a sense attribute the device of the 'hero's mistake', for this distortion is *visible against the background* of the true text).

[8]Tat'iana Kasatkina, *O tvoriashchei prirode slova: Ontologichnost' slova v tvorchestve F M Dostoevskogo kak osnova 'realizma v vysshem smysle'* (Moscow: IMLI RAN, 2004).

Commenting on the only instance of the 'hero's mistake' noted thus far, Valentina Vetlovskaia writes, 'Possibly, Ivan's mistake acts as *a means of characterizing this hero*, pointing to his uncertain knowledge of that which he is attempting to refute'. (XV, 557; my emphasis) *The Devils*, in my opinion, shows with the utmost clarity that *Dostoevsky does not introduce into his text any essential devices with the aim of characterizing any of his protagonists*. That is the prerogative of the sort of realism which, according to Dostoevsky, 'lacks depth'. In Dostoevsky's works, on the contrary, so to speak, the *characteristics of a protagonist* (his social status, educational qualifications etc.) act as *justification* for the introduction of this or that device, with quite a different aim, on another level. An example of this distinction is the role of French speech in the construction of the image of Stepan Trofimovich. I would suggest that Stepan Trofimovich speaks French in situations (or at least, it is thanks to these situations that his obtrusive French language exists in the text) when the Russian text, and Russian words, cannot express exactly the ideas hidden behind the everyday dialogue which it is necessary for the author to convey.

Here, in my view, is an incontrovertible example. In the chapter 'Stepan Trofimovich's final journey', he encounters Anisim, who pesters him with importunate questions: 'You're not going to Spasov, are you?' 'Yes, to Spasov. *Il me semble que tout le monde va à Spassof...?*' (X, 487) The translation offered by the Academy Edition is, 'It seems everybody's heading for Spasov'. However, a literal translation of the French phrase would be, 'the whole world is going to Spasov', which not only much more graphically presents the idea developed by the character (and the author) in the final pages of the novel, that the whole world is moving towards salvation and the embrace of the Saviour, but also as a direct quotation relates to a point in the Gospel of John which is exceptionally important in this chapter: 'The world is gone after him'. (John 12: 19)

In order to show that this is not an isolated example, let us examine a phrase from the preceding page, which literally anticipates the establishment of the procession of the world towards salvation. Sofya Matveevna addresses Stepan Trofimovich: 'Would you care to buy, sir?' offering him books engraved with a cross on the covers. Seeing the cross on the cover, Stepan Trofimovich replies, '*Eh...mais je crois que c'est l'Evangile*; with the greatest of pleasure'. (X, 486) The translation given (which is perfectly correct, however, as in the previous case), is: 'Oh...it seems to be the Gospels'. However, the literal meaning of the phrase is, '...but I believe that it is the Gospel' (or, to be even more literal, 'but I believe that it is the Good News'). The meaning of the episode, in this way, lies in the confession by the hero of the Cross as the Good News.

Thus the introduction by Dostoevsky of any device always has a more essential aim than that of characterizing his protagonists. Moreover, as it seems to me at present, in the two novels where the device of the 'hero's mistake' is presented quite widely, *The Adolescent* and *The Brothers Karamazov*, these aims are not identical.

In *The Adolescent*, this device is used to demonstrate a quite complex idea: the hero invariably makes a mistake when he has just accused others of a blunder. Thus he muddles the story of Abishag with the story of Tamar immediately after he has accused Lambert of ignorance. In the novel there is a particularly telling incident (where, incidentally, the reader is directly prompted; the device, so to speak, is demonstrated graphically, for the mistake is corrected *before it is committed* by the hero himself). Arkady points out to Liza that she has used the pronoun 'them' rather than 'him' when speaking of a single person: 'Is it about Vasin you're speaking when you say *them*, Liza? You must say *him*, not *them*. Forgive me, sister, for correcting you, but I'm grieved that your education seems to have been completely neglected'. (XIII, 84; author's emphasis) And later, on his very next appearance at his mother's home, he makes the same mistake himself, when he comes in with Olya, whom Versilov has been seeking: '"I didn't come about this", I hurried to wave her aside and stood a little apart, "I just met this individual by the gate; she was looking for you, but no-one could tell her where you were. I'm here on my own business, which I will have the pleasure to explain after them..."' (XIII, 131; my emphasis)

Thus in *The Adolescent* the aim of the device is to demonstrate something that has the most immediate relation to the idea of the double and doubling, which is one of the most fundamental ideas in the novel: characters generally notice and criticize others precisely for their own blunders (faults, *sins*; 'sin' in Greek is αμαρτία, from αμαρτανω, to make a mistake (*oshibat'sia*), or blunder (*promakhivat'sia*), to miss or fail).[9]

The aim of introducing the device in *The Brothers Karamazov*, as it appears to me at this stage of my research, is to fix the distortion of the truth in the hero's speech and show the direction of his distortion; that is, accordingly, to define the *true aims* of the hero's speech.

The most essential operation which Ivan carries out with the phrase under examination, 'God our Lord is revealed to us', is the alteration in its modality. The action moves from the category of the real to the category of the conditional, the desirable.[10] And this alteration in modality, fixed and shown to the reader of the 'hero's mistake', point to the operation logically carried out by Ivan in his speech, in relation to the facts of the presence of God in the world:

---

[9] 'A double is one whose acts, desires, dreams you view with fundamental loathing, whose life principles arouse irritation and resistance in you, one upon whom you look arrogantly and condescendingly, until you finally notice that it is you', Kasatkina, *O tvoriashchei prirode slova*, p. 428.

[10] I would suggest that archbishop Ioann (Shakhovskii) of San Francisco had just this in mind when he said that one of the main means of action of spiritual evil in the world in general, and in the world of the 'Grand Inquisitor' in particular, is 'falsehood, the assertion that Christ's truth is "impractical", "unreal", and can only in the best case be admired, but cannot be lived', Arkhiepiscop San-Frantsisskii Ioann (Shakhovskii), 'Velikii inkvisitor Dostoevskogo', in *K istorii russkoi intelligentsii* (Moscow, 2003), p. 440. Ivan later states this directly, calling Christ 'a great idealist, dreaming of his harmony'. (XIV, 238)

Fifteen centuries have passed since *he gave the promise to come in his Kingdom*, fifteen centuries since his prophet wrote 'Behold, I come quickly'. Of that day and that hour knoweth not even the Son, but only my heavenly Father, as he himself declared while still on earth. But mankind awaits him with the same faith and the same tender emotion. Oh, *with even greater faith, for fifteen centuries have passed since man ceased to receive pledges from heaven:*
> Believe what the heart tells you,
> For heaven offers no pledge.

And only faith in what the heart tells you! True, there were many miracles then. There were saints who performed miracle healings; to some righteous men, according to their biographies, the Queen of Heaven herself came down. But the devil never rests, *and in mankind there had already arisen some doubt about the authenticity of these miracles*. Just then in the north, in Germany, a terrible new heresy appeared. A great star, 'like a lamp' (that is, the Church) 'fell upon the fountains of waters, and they were made bitter'. These heretics began blasphemously denying miracles. But those who still had faith became all the more ardent in their *faith*. The tears of mankind rose up to him as before, they *waited* for him, loved him, hoped in him, thirsted to suffer and die for him as before...And for how many centuries had mankind prayed with faith and ardour: 'God our Lord, reveal thyself to us', they had been calling out to him for so many centuries that he in his immeasurable compassion *desired* to descend to those who were pleading. He had descended even before then, he had visited some righteous men, martyrs and holy hermits while they were still on earth, as is written in their 'lives'. Our poet Tiutchev, who *deeply believed* in the truth of his words, proclaimed that:
> Bent under the burden of the cross
> The King of Heaven in the form of a slave
> Walked the length and breadth of you,
> Blessing you, my native land.

It must have been so, let me tell you. And so he *desired* to appear to people, if only for a moment—to his tormented, suffering people, stinking of sin but loving him like children. (XIV, 225-6; my emphasis)[11]

As a consequence of such alterations, as a consequence of the constant introduction of an irreal modality, almost unnoticed by the reader, the presence of God in the world becomes gradually in Ivan's speech not simply problematic, but already no more than a fantastic assumption—and this just when the hero, so to speak, insists on the verity of everything to which he has referred. But every time after emphasizing its verity ('True', 'It must have been so') he immediately moves on not simply to establishing doubt (everybody doubts something), but also to the *expectation* and *belief* of the faithful and of the *desire* of the Lord to

---

[11] The translation of this and further quotations from *The Brothers Karamazov* are based on Fyodor Dostoevsky, *The Brothers Karamazov*, trans. Richard Pevear and Larissa Volokhonsky (London: Vintage, 1992), pp. 247-248, with some alterations. (*Translator's note.*)

come, which with skilful manoeuvring begins to be perceived as *only* expectation (without presence), only faith (without certainty), and even only *desire* (without action). (I will not analyse Ivan's other distortions in this extract at this point.)

In the end, the action of the Lord itself turns out to be unreal. In this sense, another distortion of a Gospel text in Ivan's poem is characteristic: the inquisitor attributes to Christ the words: 'I want to make you free'. (XIV, 229) As has been noted in the commentary to the Academy Edition, this relates above all to the following words of Christ:

> If ye continue in my word, then ye are my disciples indeed; and ye shall know the truth, and the truth shall make you free. They answered him, We be Abraham's seed, and were never in bondage to any man; how sayest thou, Ye shall be made free? Jesus answered them, 'Verily, verily I say unto you, Whosoever committeth sin is the servant of sin. And the servant abideth not in the house for ever: but the Son abideth ever. If the Son therefore shall make you free, ye shall be free indeed'. (John 8: 31-36)

In spite of the formal presence of the conditional modality in the Gospel text, it resides entirely in the realm of real modality, as Christ is showing the conditions in the presence of which the action will take place *without fail*. That is, Christ *has already made* man free (for his part, he has completed the necessary action for man's liberation), and now all that is needed is the necessary (necessary precisely insofar as it is free) counter action.

It is precisely on this foundation of the action already carried out by Christ that the Elder Zosima (following his brother Markel) will assert the possibility at every moment, or rather the presence already, of heaven on earth (heaven is the kingdom of freedom above all, deliverance from the yoke of natural necessity, including the necessity of death and decay, which will not end until man carries out an action in response to Christ's action and appeal; this is exactly why Zosima says: 'Man, do not raise yourself above the animals: they are sinless, and you with your grandeur *corrupt* the earth with your appearance on it, and *leave your festering trace* behind you—alas, almost every one of us does!' (XIV, 289; my emphasis) Heaven has not been fulfilled only because man *has not perceived* it. Markel begs forgiveness from the birds thus:

> Birds of God, joyful birds, you too must forgive me, for I have also sinned before you. [...] There was so much of God's glory around me: the birds, the trees, the meadows, the sky, and I alone lived in shame, I alone dishonoured everything, and *did not notice* the beauty and glory of it all. (XIV, 263; my emphasis)

This *lack of perception* is also an active action by man, a manifestation of his freedom, guaranteed by Christ. It is, so to speak, the other side, the wrong side of freedom. Heaven is already there, and man is free to enter it, but heaven will remain unfulfilled, unperceived, until man *desires* to see it. A S Khomyakov explains the ascension of Christ and the descent of the Holy Spirit on the Pentecost exactly in terms of this protection of human freedom:

The mystery of Christ, saving creation, is the mystery of the unity and freedom of mankind in the incarnate word. Cognition of this mystery was entrusted to the unity of the faithful and their freedom, for the law of Christ is freedom...Christ *beheld* would be a truth thrust upon man, incontrovertible, but it was pleasing to God that the truth should be assimilated *freely*. Christ beheld would be an external truth, but it was pleasing to God that it became internal for us, by the grace of the Son, sent down by the spirit of God. This is the meaning of the Pentecost. Hence the truth must be for us ourselves in the depths of our conscience. No visible sign will limit our freedom, will gives us criteria for our self-condemnation against our will.[12]

Christ withdrew so as not to become an importunate fact, so as not to encroach on freedom with an external image—and is revealed to anyone who is ready. In *The Brothers Karamazov*, the miracle at Zosima's tomb is related to this action by Christ. The people are expecting a miracle which is visible to all, which would place before them an incontrovertible fact, securing their weak faith with external evidence and the authority of witnessed event. But such miracles do not occur, and what is more, Zosima meekly withdraws into the realm of the action of the laws of nature in the fallen world, the laws of decay (he 'stinks'), so as not to encroach on the freedom of *those who do not wish to perceive heaven*. And miracles do take place at the tomb, addressed, however, not *to all*, but *to each one* who urgently and vitally needs them, and who in addition is able to and wishes to see. Above all, this is of course the miracle in the chapter 'Cana of Galilee', the vision of the eternal feast revealed to Alyosha, which turns him into the most steadfast warrior of Christ, but it is also the miracle of the 'radiant spirit' which appears to prevent Mitenka committing parricide.[13] It is also the miracle of the resurrection of the dog Zhuchka by the sickbed of Ilyushechka, repeated as a travesty by Kolya Krasotkin, who demonstrates that the dog fulfils his command 'die!' and is then 'resurrected', only and exclusively at his command. The miracle, as distinct from the *laws* of nature, is also the realm of freedom: the freedom of God, man and the universe.

Ivan, in spite of the reality of the world of the novel and the world of God, in his poem again translates the very action of Christ into the realm of irreal modality: 'I *want* to make you free'.

Thus, in *The Brothers Karamazov*, the 'hero's mistake' defines the vector of deviation in the position of the hero from the truth and, in principle, in this case allows the reader, long before it is formulated in Alyosha's exclamation, to guess that everything consists in the fact that Ivan, like the Grand Inquisitor, 'does not

---

[12]Cited in Nikolai Berdyaev, *Sobranie sochinenii, V: Aleksei Stepanovich Khomiakov; Mirosozertsanie Dostoevskogo; Konstantin Leont'ev* (Paris: YMCA Press; Khristianskoe izdatel'stvo, 1997), p. 79.

[13]'In my opinion, sir, in my opinion this is how it was', says Mitya to the investigator and the procurator. 'Whether it was someone's tears, or my mother's prayers to God, or a bright spirit kissing me at that moment, I don't know, but the devil was overcome'. (XIV, 425-426)

believe in God' or, in any case, does not acknowledge his *real, constant existence in the world*, on which the whole of Christianity is based. The distorted quotation from Psalm 118 shows that Ivan, like the hero of his poem, is one of those builders who has refused the stone,[14] which remains of paramount importance: this is probably the most famous verse from this Psalm, repeated by Jesus in all the Synoptic Gospels. (Matt. 21: 42; Mark 12: 10; Luke 20: 17) And this means that Ivan's entire construction is fantastic and groundless.

However, the device of the 'hero's mistake' is evidently indebted for its existence in Dostoevsky's works not only to the logical consequences of the polyphonic principle—or perhaps it is more accurate to say that it is precisely *to the full and final logical* consequences of the polyphonic principle—but also to the fact that it is not confined to the limits of the work, but also includes the reader. Our Western colleagues (above all, Robin Feuer Miller)[15] have long since formulated another principle of Dostoevsky's 'literary technique', relating to the role of the reader. This consists in the fact that the reader is given no—above all no moral—advantage over the hero, who makes mistakes and is too quick to rush to judgement. The device of the 'hero's mistake' shows that the reader of Dostoevsky is similarly given no advantage—not only in intellectual terms, but also relating to information—over the hero who makes mistakes; that is, he or she is not given it as a gift, as a 'prompt' thrust upon him or her, as 'help' from the author, but turns out to be in intellectual dialogue with the hero, face to face as an equal. The reader of Dostoevsky is given the possibility (when whether out of ignorance or for another reason—for example, ideological—he is mistaken along with the hero), and the *freedom not to perceive* the mistakes, to experience a delusion as the truth, to be struck down by a delusion in the framework of the novel; and this is akin to a vaccination against a terrible illness—not without danger, but to the highest degree an effective preventative method. The author in Dostoevsky's novels acts as Christ acted in the Ascension and the Pentecost; he does not allow any obtrusively obvious signs to limit our freedom. He neither gives us criteria nor forces them upon us, either for the unthinking and easy, but utter condemnation of the hero, or 'for our own self-condemnation against our will'.

Translated by Sarah Young

---

[14] See Psalm 118: 22. The stone is in general the central image of *The Brothers Karamazov*, and namely the rejected stone, Ilyusha's solitary stone in the field, where he wishes to be buried. It seems in a strange way that his burial in Church grounds does not contradict his wishes. It is as if the two places are combined, united as Ilyusha's grave (it is no accident that it is precisely at the stone that Alesha delivers his speech about Ilyusha and resurrection). This stone *is* the foundation of the Church but, called upon to be the foundation of the world, it is still rejected, even while it is still expected to act as a cornerstone. On it is constructed the world, but humankind always rebels against this obvious fact.

[15] See Robin Feuer Miller, *'The Brothers Karamazov': Worlds of the Novel* (Boston: Twayne, 1992).

DOSTOEVSKY'S FANTASTIC PAGES

Vladimir Nikolaevich Zakharov

IN his monograph *Dostoyevsky after Bakhtin: Readings in Dostoyevsky's Fantastic Realism*, Malcolm Jones correctly notes, 'I am not sure that Dostoyevsky ever actually used the expression "fantastic realism" but his statements about his style fully justify its use as a shorthand term'.[1] In fact, in spite of the continued existence of this delusion, Dostoevsky did not call his realism 'fantastic'. At the same time, the epithet attracts many scholars, and this is not a coincidence.

'Fantastic' is a favourite word of Dostoevsky's. In some cases it has a single meaning; in others, its meanings are multiple. It has a single meaning as a concept (a *poetic category*, or 'form of art', in Dostoevsky's expression). It has multiple meanings in its role as an *attribute* (its basic meanings are *fictitious, imaginary, invented, far-fetched; illusory, imagined, groundless; improbable, unlikely, unthinkable, inconceivable, implausible, unusual, uncommon*, and so on). These synonyms are appreciably inferior to the epithet *fantastic* in the richness of the 'internal form' of the word: they are limited, clear, they hold no semantic mystery, they are not so attractive.[2] In any case the word *fantastic* is an adjective, formed from the noun *fantasy*, and it defines its presence in phenomena belonging exclusively to the fantasy of man, but not to reality itself.

Dostoevsky had an original conception of the fantastic and his own rules for the fantastic in art. The fantastic is an essential property of art, a 'form of art', 'boundless fantasy', a fantastic work is a 'purely poetic (the most poetic) work'. His rule is that 'the fantastic must be so closely connected to the real that you almost have to believe in it'. In the fantastic man has contact with other worlds, the essence becomes the phenomenon.

---

[1] Malcolm V Jones, *Dostoyevsky after Bakhtin* (Cambridge: Cambridge University Press, 1990), p. 1. Indeed, the present article arose from Malcolm Jones's amiable invitation to dialogue in the introduction to the Russian translation of this work, *Dostoevskii posle Bakhtina: Issledovanie fantasticheskogo realizma Dostoevskogo* (St Petersburg: Akademicheskii proekt, 1999), p. 6.

[2] For further details see V N Zakharov, 1) 'Kontseptsiia fantasticheskogo v estetike F M Dostoevskogo', in *Khudozhestvennyi obraz i istoricheskoe soznaniie* (Petrozavodsk, 1974), pp. 98-125; 2) 'Fantasticheskoe v estetike i tvorchestve F M Dostoevskogo', Avtoref. dis. kand. filol. nauk., Petrozavodsk, 1975; 3) 'Fantasticheskoe kak kategoriia poetiki romanov F M Dostoevskogo *Prestuplenie i nakazanie* i *Idiot*', in *Zhanr i kompozitsiia literaturnogo proizvedeniia* (Petrozavodsk, 1978), pp. 55-87; 4) 'Fantasticheskoe kak kategoriia poetiki Dostoevskogo', in *Zhanr i kompozitsiia literaturnogo proizvedeniia* (Petrozavodsk, 1978), pp. 41-54; 5) 'Fantasticheskoe', in *Dostoevskii: Estetika i poetika* (Cheliabinsk, 1997), pp. 53-56.

In critical literature the collection of citations of Dostoevsky's pronouncements containing the word *fantastic* has long been defined. I will cite some lesser known ones.

In the October issue of *Time (Vremia)* (1862), an article was published with the title 'A vote for the Petersburg Don Quixote. Apropos of Mr Teatrin's article', signed with the pseudonym 'Ch Komitetsky'.[3] The article is an analysis of the polemic between two critics, concealing themselves behind the pseudonyms 'S'—the Petersburg Don Quixote (D D Minaev)—and a certain 'Mr Teatrin'. It was hardly necessary for the author of *Time* to participate in this polemic, but his interest in it is symptomatic.

The grounds for the polemic were that 'A certain Petersburg Don Quixote (whom we have never actually seen) has attacked some *fantastic committee*'.[4] This criticism of the literary-theatrical committee and the repertoire of Petersburg theatres offended one particular reader: 'A certain Mr Teatrin stood up for *the honour of his fantastic colleagues* [...] and cried out, "Don't don-quixotize Mr Don Quixote!"' (V, 214) The author of *Time* is playing up the conflict created by them themselves. The fantastic committee was not in fact fantastic at all:

Because Mr Teatrin, we are sure, *as a person is not at all fantastic (Mr Kraevsky has nothing fantastic about him,* that is, he doesn't allow anything inessential into his newspaper), *his character is not only not fantastic, but even lacks any element of fantasy*, then it's very possible that the *committee* as well, which is subjecting dramatic works to analysis, is *likewise not fantastic* (V, 214);

And that leads us to say: were the committee *truly fantastic*, what would be the point of the real Mr Teatrin standing up to it! (V, 214);

[...] he attributes this article to offended self-esteem...They say he gave some fantastic committee some drama or other, *Russia in 1862, or The Real National State*, but the members of the committee, having read the play, did not approve it, because they understand something about dramatic art (V, 214);

But Don Quixote probably didn't even write this drama, but *simply invented it*, so as to have the opportunity to *slip on to the fantastic committee*; it was on his part an act of military cunning, such as was once committed by knights (V, 214);

We have heard that the *fantastic committee* in accordance with the times is laying the blame on the censorship [...] (V, 216);

But a great deal depends on the *fantastic committee* (V, 216);

---

[3] On the attribution of this and other pseudonymous and anonymous articles in *Time* and *The Epoch*, see V N Zakharov, 'Triumf anonimnogo avtora', in F M Dostoevskii, *Polnoe sobranie sochinenii v 18-i tomakh* (Moscow: Voskresen'e, 2004), V, 521-539.

[4] F M Dostoevskii, *Polnoe sobranie sochinenii v 18-i tomakh* (Moscow: Voskresen'e, 2004), V, 214. (Emphasis in the text is mine—VZ). Further references to Dostoevsky's work cited in the text are to this edition, with the roman numeral indicating the volume number.

> *Thank God that singers aren't chosen by a fantastic committee—what an opera we'd have then!* (V, 217)
> Let the members of the fantastic committee meet like gods on Parnassus, and crown their faithful and grateful worshippers, but let them remember that openness, real, sacred, implacable openness, is not far off. (V, 217);

In Russian literature there has only been one author who could enjoy such skilful command over the epithet *fantastic*, and that is Dostoevsky.

Behind this fantastic duel of the pseudonyms there lies the authentic name of a literary hero:

> It is obvious that *Don Quixote looks on everything from his own point of view, and sees in everything some sort of magic or sorcery—this is quite in his character.* Moreover, *this wandering knight is fully convinced that all untruths, all abuses are committed not by people, but by spirits; that even bribes are not taken by people, but all by some wizard or enchantress or other. Oh, what lofty, noble madness! From what depths of belief in the honour of humanity you spring!* (V, 214)

This ironical interpretation of the image corresponds with the conception of the character of Don Quixote, about which Dostoevsky wrote more than once. The author of the feuilleton notes paid his due to the word play of Mr Teatrin, who 'even lacks any element of fantasy': 'Don't don-quixotize Mr Don Quixote!' (V, 214)

> Consequently, *Don Quixote began to don-quixotize* against the committee not for the sake of offended self-esteem, but simply because he *was indignant*, and because he was a Don Quixote of Petersburg, and not La Mancha, he hid his indignation.
> Seeing all this, Mr Teatrin *advised Don Quixote not to don-quixotify*, and assures us, the readers, that the role of a Don Quixote is the most pitiful and shameful. (V, 214-215)

Dostoevsky objects:

> No, Mr Teatrin, it's not quite like this.
> Perhaps it is because of this that we have seen so much of every kind of untruth and abuse, seen so many ignoramuses, bribe-takers and embezzlers of public funds, that there seems to be little else, alas! *Holy Rus' brings into the world very few Don Quixotes.* Indeed Don Quixote (Cervantes's creation, we will add), *is an ideal of integrity, incorruptibility and fearlessness.*
> *Don Quixote of La Mancha opened the lion's cage* and challenged the king of the beasts to battle. The Don Quixote of Petersburg will not challenge the lion, but he will more and more *open the doors on sessions of some committee or other*, have a look and see what the enchanters or the Mr Teatrins are doing.
> The lion once challenged by *Don Quixote of La Mancha* only yawned and turned its tail on him, not feeling any kind of guilt; and you, Mr Teatrin, would have done much better if in response to the challenge of the Petersburg

Don Quixote you have also yawned, but you couldn't do that: *the truth*, although it was in a mask, *taunted you*, you took fright and cried out: 'Don't don-quixotize Mr Don Quixote!'
We are moving now *from fantasy to reality*. (V, 215)

Dostoevsky does not declare either Don Quixote of La Mancha or St Petersburg to be fantastic characters. They are inspired by the ideal, and he is *quixotically* defending the higher values of poetry, Ostrovsky, Gogol, talented writers, the opera singers, Lablash and Mario, opera—art and culture in general.

The epithet *fantastic* is a chameleon-like word in Dostoevsky's language: its essence remaining undefined, the word conceals his most cherished ideas, enthusiasm and advocacy, it hides the prophetic illumination of the author and simultaneously attracts many meanings, it opens to each person their own personal meaning. It gives birth to a mystery and to the temptation to understand the mystery.

Another of Dostoevsky's enigmatic statements: 'In Russia the truth almost always has an entirely fantastic character'. (XI, 110)

This assertion is in the treatise 'Something about lying', and is the conclusion drawn from the opposition of two syllogisms. The thesis:

> We, Russians, are most of all afraid of the truth, that is, if you like we're not afraid, but constantly consider the truth to be somehow too boring and prosaic for us, insufficiently poetic, too ordinary, and thereby, avoiding it constantly, we have finally made it into one of the most unusual and rare things in our Russian world.

The antithesis:

> In this way we have completely lost the axiom that the truth is the most poetic thing there is on earth, especially in its purest condition; moreover, the most fantastic thing of all is that even the human mind can lie and show itself to be accustomed to lying.

Dostoevsky's paradox reveals the spiritual woe of the Russian people, in which the lie is more comprehensible than the truth, and the truth is fantastic. The epithet *fantastic* combines and unites in the tension of a single word the meaning of the antinomy: truth and falsehood, poetry and prose, reality and fantasy; the fantastic truth is more real than vulgar reality, the truth defeats the lie. The subtext flickers with cynical question of Pontius Pilate, unspoken but memorable to the reader: 'What is truth'? (John 18: 38) The answer is in the silence of Christ and in the miracle of His being.

In the preparatory materials for the novel *The Devils*, there is a body of notes which Dostoevsky isolated thematically and called the 'Fantastic pages'.[5] Anna Grigorievna Dostoevskaya understood their exceptional significance: indeed it

---

[5]The text of the 'Fantastic pages' is cited from the MS: RGB, f. 93.I.1.4, pp. 27-40, 124-125, 127-129.

was these very notes that she chose for publication in the eighth volume of the anniversary edition of the complete collected works of 1906.

The 'Fantastic pages' express the innermost thoughts of Dostoevsky. In them all the fundamental themes which constitute the essence of Dostoevsky's work are concentrated: his characters have conversations about the meaning of life and history, the past and the future, God and Christ, faith and unbelief, Truth and Russia, they argue about words and interpret the Gospels. Many of these words, phrases and episodes do not appear in the novel, but remain in the working notebooks. Dostoevsky was conscious of their intimate nature. They are what Katkov would not permit to be discussed in *The Russian Messenger (Russkii vestnik)*, and what the author would not risk discussing in *The Devils*.

In these scenes the characters often do not argue, but discuss problems, persuade each other, develop alien ideas as their own. Persuading others, they persuade themselves. These are distinctive dialogues by Dostoevsky, in which the final characters of the heroes are not yet elucidated, and their roles are not determined, but which ask the most pressing eternal questions: What is to be done? Is faith possible? Wherein lies happiness?

In one dialogue a character tells another, 'There are a huge number of such conversations going on in Russia'. (p. 33)

The 'Fantastic pages' embody a particular element of the novelistic life of the heroes. From one scene:

> Sh[atov]: What must I do?
> Pr[ince]: Repent, build yourself up, build up the Kingdom of Christ. [...]
> [...]
> Sh[atov]: so we have to take monastic vows if it is so?
> Pr[ince]: What for? Proclaim Christ on Russian soil, and proclaim yourself. Great feats of heroism are needed. Is it necessary to perform great feats? It is necessary to be great in order to go against common sense. [...]
> The prince. A great feat is needed. Let Russian strength show what it can do. With a great feat you will conquer the world.
> Shatov became strangely pensive: you know this is all simply fantasy, he said, also books or—or religious lunacy. Can you attract everyone to great feats?
> Pr[ince]: Why everyone. Do you know how powerful one man can be. Only one has to appear and everyone will follow. We need self-accusation and great feats, this idea is necessary, otherwise we won't find Orthodoxy and there will be nothing. (p. 27)

From Stavrogin's lips a sermon is issued:

> Strength is in the moral idea.
> The moral idea is in Christ.
> In the West Christ has been perverted and exhausted. The kingdom of the Antichrist. We have the Orthodox faith.
> This means that we are the bearers of the clear understanding of Christ and of the new idea for the resurrection of the world.

Do you believe in the eternal presence of Christ in the world?
And in order to declare the Orthodox faith a great feat is needed. (p. 27)

However, Stavrogin is not a prophet. In the notebooks to the novel he is still prepared to perform a heroic deed, he says that which in the novel will be preached by Shatov, who in the notebooks pronounces his doubt—in the novel he has no such instability in his opinions.

The 'Fantastic pages' communicate the typical condition of the soul of Dostoevsky's heroes, combining unbelief and the need for faith.

This conflict is artistically presented in a vivid manner in *The Brothers Karamazov*. In the chapter 'Over the Cognac', Fyodor Pavlovich asks his interlocutors in a very biased way whether God exists. Ivan firmly answers: no. Alyosha no less firmly says, God exists. Fyodor Pavlovich ponders and decides that Ivan is 'probably' right, and Ivan, in his turn, confesses to Alyosha in the 'Capital City' inn: 'Yesterday over dinner at the old man's I was teasing you on purpose about this, and I saw how your eyes flared up'. (XIII, 194) In the debate 'Over the Cognac' Alesha is adamant, but he also in spiritual confusion confesses to Lise the night before his meeting with his brother Ivan:

> 'But perhaps I also don't believe in God.' 'You don't believe, what's wrong with you?', quietly and cautiously uttered Lise. But Alyosha did not reply. There was, in these too sudden words of his, something too mysterious and too subjective, something that was perhaps not clear to him himself, but his torment was not in doubt. (XIII, 182)

This very doubt constitutes an element of the 'Fantastic pages':

> Pr[ince]: Be convinced.
> Sh[atov]: In the Orthodox faith and Russia?
> Pr[ince]: Yes.
> Sh[atov]: Yes of course then there would be salvation. I—I think I believe. Why have you gone quiet?
> Pr[ince]: That means you don't believe.
> Sh[atov]: And what about you?
> Pr[ince]: Again, what have I got to do with it?
> Sh[atov]: Can we really understand each other from two words? (p. 33)

Recognizing the need for faith, the heroes fearlessly test faith. Shatov in raptures generalizes their speeches:

> So everything's in the Orthodox faith!
> The essence of the question is in no way in this, it's in whether it's possible to believe in the Orthodox faith?
> Pr[ince]: The whole question therefore is whether one can believe.
> Sh[atov]: Do you really not believe?
> Look, either everything is in the faith, or nothing! We acknowledge the importance of saving the world through the Orthodox faith. And so the whole question is: Is it possible to believe in the Orthodox faith, casting off every

> philosophy that we've digested. If it's possible, then everything will be saved, if not, then it's better to burn.
> Is it possible that you don't believe?
> What have I got to do with it? I'm asking you: I wanted to come only to ask you whether you believe, I'm curious to know.
> I...I believe, I think.
> That means you don't believe? (p. 33)

However, this is not the final word.

> Is it possible to believe? And if it's impossible then why shout about the strength in the Orthodox faith of the Russian people? It's therefore only a question of time. Over there demoralization, atheism began earlier, with us later, but it will begin without fail with the establishment of atheism. And if that is even inevitable, then we even have to want it to happen, and the sooner the better'. (p. 28)

In the 'Fantastic pages' the heroes speak out about morality and Christianity, religion and science—themes that are inescapable in their plenitude. The characters not infrequently formulate their opinions in paradoxes.

> The prince goes to Sh[atov]. (For the first time after the slap in the face). I've not come about that. I noticed one of your ideas: An atheist cannot love Russia and Russian life—and I was surprised at it.
> Sh[atov] (smirking): There's nothing for me to explain to you about that.
> Pr[ince]: You don't have to. I know myself that an atheist can't love Russia. It's my idea. I've never come across it anywhere else. And suddenly you say the same thing. I'd like to know what are you looking at more, Orthodoxy or Lutheranism'. (p. 127)

Or:

> 'Moral foundations are given by revelation. Just destroy something in faith and the moral foundation of Christianity will all come crashing down, for everything is connected. (p. 28)

In the 'Fantastic pages' the prince expounds an original economic theory:

> There they petition for credit, for the restoration of the Credit rouble. A terrible question. And in fact they will not understand that there is only one cure: in the firm idea of national origin. They'd even laugh if it were explained to them. (p. 28)

It is as if he were speaking today:

> The majority of our capital is gained by conjuring tricks. It's pretty often no wonder to hear that the heirs have joined the gentry, given up work and gone into the hussars or squandered everything. It means that everything is a conjuring trick, to the extent that there is no understanding of how capital is formed. And that there cannot be large capital where there is no small capital, an enormous majority of small capital, in its rightful natural proportion to the

large. Large capital exists only because there is small capital. The whole of credit and the whole fall of the rouble depends only on the stability of small capital. Without it not even conjuring tricks will be able to repair or restore anything. (pp. 127-128)

Dostoevsky expresses similar ideas in the January issue of *Diary of a Writer* for 1881, in which he wrote about finances: about the devaluation of the rouble, the deficit, debts to foreign creditors, about the crisis in agriculture and trade, 'nobody's buying anything', 'factories are reducing production to the minimum', 'they've all got their eyes greedily fixed on the treasury and public funds'. Dostoevsky's advice is paradoxical. He could hardly be called an expert in macroeconomics: 'restore the roots'—and everything will settle down; restore the spirit—and the rouble will climb, the budget deficit will disappear, trade and production will improve.

In raising critical problems Dostoevsky's heroes courageously discuss the Scriptures. The prince formulates his understanding of Christianity:

> They all (Renan, Ge) take Christ for an ordinary man and criticize his teaching as bankrupt for our time. But there is no teaching there, only fortuitous words, and the main thing is the image of Christ, from which all the teaching comes forth. On the other hand, look at the vanity and moral condition of these critics. Well, can they criticize Christ? From Christ came the idea that the main gain and aim of humanity is the result of the morality that is acquired. Just imagine that all these Christs—well, would they be possible in today's instability, bewilderment, pauperism? Whoever doesn't understand that doesn't understand anything about Christ or Christianity. (p. 124)

Truth is not afraid of tests, contradictions, trials of the idea. From the unbelief and doubt of the heroes grows faith or the need for faith.

***

The author and his characters frequently express their doubt in the form of paradox. Paradox is not the truth, but a means of manifesting the truth, its rhetorical reinforcement.

In his fantasy apropos of a ball, 'The Golden Age in Your Pocket' (*Diary of a Writer*, January 1876), Dostoevsky assures the reader: 'You are beautiful!' and concludes

> You are laughing, you don't believe it? I'm glad I've made you laugh, and yet my whole outburst right now is not a paradox, but the absolute truth? And your whole trouble is that you don't believe it. (XI, 285)

In evaluating a paradox it is always necessary to take into account its generic nature. If we endow a paradox with a straightforward meaning, an insoluble contradiction, an absurdism, arises. In a paradox the idea which stands behind the words being pronounced is important.

Dostoevsky did not hide the rhetorical nature of such devices; cf.: 'I purposely placed the idea on its side and brought my wishes to the ideal of the almost impossible. I thought that having begun precisely from the absurd I will become more comprehensible'. (XI, 361) The writer recognized that there is an unwritten rule of literature:

> Set up some pleasing paradox, but don't see it through to the end, and it will come out wittily, subtly and *comme il faut* for you; but see another risky word to the end, say, for example, 'There he is—that's the Messiah', directly and not in hints, and nobody will believe you precisely for your naivety, precisely because you saw it through to the end, you said your very final word. And, however, on the other hand, if many of the most famous wits, Voltaire, for example, had instead of jibes, hints, half words and innuendo suddenly decided to state everything they believed in, to show their whole secret at once, their essence, be assured, they wouldn't have achieved a tenth part of the previous effect. Moreover, they would only have been laughed at. For man in general does not in any way like the final word, the 'uttered' thought, as: 'The thought uttered is a lie'. (XVI. 2, 308)

Instead of the spirit of the sermon, Dostoevsky more often proposed a paradox which aroused incomprehension and almost unreserved criticism from contemporaries and heirs.

Negation and affirmation in paradox have different provenance. One of the sources (nihilism) Dostoevsky revealed apropos of Voltaire. About the other he passed over in silence, but it is evident to everyone who perceives the Christian spirit of the work of the Russian genius—the Gospels, which illuminate with the light of truth his artistic realism.

In explaining the obvious, Dostoevsky not infrequently began from the 'absurd' in order to become more understandable and convincing to the reader. His crowning genre is the 'paradox within a paradox'. This is how Dostoevsky himself defined the style of his discussion of Russia in the June issue of *Diary of a Writer* for 1876. He wrote about this to the critic and writer Vsevolod Solovev, who enthusiastically responded to Dostoevsky's 'paradoxes' about George Sand, about Russia and Europe, the 'eastern question', about the 'dear girl' and the author's relations with her. In the June issue of *Diary of a Writer*, Dostoevsky for the first time stating directly and frankly his cherished convictions: 'I have never yet allowed myself, in my writing, to see some of my convictions through to the end, to say the *very last word*'. (XVI. 1, 308) Dostoevsky resolved to do this, in many ways meeting the expectations of readers and in spite of his own authorial bias.

What, then, did Dostoevsky write, revealing the paradox behind the paradox?

> We Russians have two homelands, our own Russia and Europe [...] (XI, 423);
> The greatest of all the great missions, which has already been recognized by Russians for their future, is the common human mission, service to humanity

as a whole, not just to Russia, not just to the Slavs, but to humanity as a whole (XI, 423);

George Sand was one of the most absolute confessors of Christ, without herself even knowing it (XI, 429);

[...] our most ardent Westernizers, precisely those who fight for reform, are on the extreme left and have become at the same time opponents of Europe' (XI, 432);

[...] if Belinsky had lived longer, he would certainly have joined the Slavophiles (XI, 434);

the essence of Russia consists in:

the idea of the universal regeneration of humanity, manifested in the form of God's truth, in the form of Christ's truth, which will one day exist on earth itself and which remains completely intact in Orthodoxy (XI, 432);

Pre-Petrine Russia [...] understood that she carried within herself a precious thing that no longer existed anywhere else—Orthodoxy, and that it was for her to preserve Christ's truth, for the read truth, the genuine image of Christ, has been obscured by all other faiths and in all other nations (XI, 437);

[...] through Peter's reforms there occurred a broadening of our *former* idea, the Russian Muscovite idea? (XI, 438);

Russia's destiny *in its ideal form* [is] to become the servant of all or the sake of universal reconciliation? (XI, 439);

and Russia must be at the helm of the unified Orthodox Church: 'Constantinople must be ours'. (XI, 439)

The majority of critics who have cited these words understand the idea as a call to geopolitical aggression. The paradox consist in the fact that for the sake of the coming into being of the idea it is not necessary to wage war. This is not political unification, political seizure or violence, but 'something special and unheard-of':

it will be a true exaltation of Christ's truth, which has been preserved in the East, a true, new exaltation of the cross of Christ and the ultimate word of Orthodoxy, at the head of which Russia has long stood (XI, 441);

[...] believe in human brotherhood, in the universal reconciliation of nations, in a union founded on the principles of universal service to humanity and finally in the utmost regeneration of people through the true principles of Christ. And if believing in this 'new word', which Russia at the head of a unified Orthodoxy can utter to the world, is 'utopian', worthy only of ridicule, then you may count me among the utopians, and I will keep the ridicule for myself. (XI, 441)

These are the same fantastic pages in which are manifested the essence of 'realism in a higher sense', but in the author's voice. There is no fantasy in them, but there is a conflict: for the author the fantastic is real, utopia is attainable, the ideal is vitally important; in received opinion, the sermon is fantastic, striving towards the ideal, towards Christ's commandment.

Dostoevsky entered world literature with a new word about the world and about man. This word is dialogic. It always takes into consideration the 'alien word' of another and is oriented towards the reader. It is deprived of the authority of 'omniscience' and does not exhaust the complexity, completeness and depth of phenomena. The author consciously articulates to himself the reader's right to 'guess and...make mistakes'. Who among contemporary and living writers needs this right? What writer today would trust his cherished word to an unauthoritative hero? In Dostoevsky this is the privilege not only of the authoritative and clever, but also of the lowly and stupid. In his works a stupid person is in principle impossible (precisely a 'stupid person' *(glupets)*; I do not use the word 'fool' *(durak)*: in Russian fairytales the fool is sometimes cleverer than the wise man, and the Russian fool always has his wits about him). Shakespeare trusted the wise knowledge of the world to jokes, but their lofty intellectual reputation was sanctified by the popular tradition of the Middle Ages. In Dostoevsky a different ethical situation arose; in his works a liar can speak and tell the truth, a 'fool' can utter a wise word, a scoundrel can yearn for a conscience, a cynic for the ideal, a sinner for sanctity. Man in Dostoevsky is complex and profound. Dostoevsky has no little people, everyone is boundless and significant, everyone has his own Face. With other writers the hero is frequently less than the author, whereas Dostoevsky was able to reveal the greatness of the simple man. In his artistic world, the Word creates the world, man, and connects him to God. In his soul 'all contradictions live together', 'God is fighting with the devil', 'the ideal of the Madonna' and 'the ideal of Sodom' come together, but the Faces of his heroes all shine, as in Rembrandt portraits, from the 'darkness' with the light of conscience, which is the harmony of man not only with people, but above all with Christ.

Dostoevsky's hero is sometimes unknown to himself, unpredictable not only for the reader, but also for the author. He always has his cherished 'suddenly', the unexpected 'about face' in opinions and actions, the 'rebirth of convictions', the transformation of the personality. Dostoevsky's artistic anthropology is based on the Christian conception of man.

In Dostoevsky's library there was a translation of Thomas à Kempis's book *The Imitation of Christ*, published with an introduction and notes by the translator Konstantin Pobedonostsev in 1869. The title of the book reveals one of the fundamental commandments of Christianity: everyone can repeat Christ's redemptive path, everyone can transform his own image, transfigure himself, sanctify himself, everyone can reveal in himself his divine and human essence. And in Dostoevsky 'dead souls' are resurrected, but the 'immortal' soul which has forgotten God perishes. In his works the 'great sinner' can be resurrected, but the 'true underground type' whose confession does not allow the 'rebirth of convictions', repentance and redemption, will not be reformed.

Dostoevsky had his own transfiguration (his death sentence and pardon on Semyonovsky square) and a 'rebirth of [his] convictions' in the stockade at Omsk (incarceration in the 'House of the Dead' and 'resurrection from the dead').

In world literature there have been quite a few writers who have had superlative knowledge of the Scriptures, who have studied them and have used their ideas and images in their own work. But we would struggle to find another writer who, like Dostoevsky, not only for four years read nothing but the Gospel, but who also experienced and lived it as his own fate—the suffering, death and resurrection of Christ as his own death in the House of the Dead and his resurrection to new life.

The Gospel for Dostoevsky was verily the Good News, the ancient and eternal new revelation of man, the world, and Christ's truth.

Dostoevsky had an almost religious conception of artistic creation. Like a priest at confession, the writer was confessor to his heroes. Their sins became his sins, increasing the burden of his cross. This idea was later expressed in the services and homilies of the Elder Zosima: to take on oneself the responsibility for another person's sins. All are guilty. This guilt of the heroes and their author is permitted by the very act of creation: by the confession, repentance and redemption of one's own and the other's sins. Everyone has their measure of guilt. Some are guilty for what they have done, others for what they have not done. Appearing innocent is only an illusion: each person answers for evil in the world. The spiritual resurrection and salvation of *any* person is possible (the conversion of Saul into Paul). This redemptive path of man is the metaphor of Christ's sacrifice and resurrection to save mankind.

The Gospel gives more to the understanding of Dostoevsky than any research about him, including Bakhtin's work of genius. The aesthetic principle of multiple points of view in the four Gospels anticipates the 'polyphonic novel' and the dialogism of poetics, the Christian conception of man and the world in many ways explains Dostoevsky's anthropological discoveries. Dostoevsky's originality lies not in his exceptional novelty, but in his consistent and uncompromising movement towards the Gospel truth, his proclamation of the hosanna, having passed 'through the crucible of doubt'.

***

The definition *fantastic* gives a form of realism to Dostoevsky. It is most fully revealed in Malcolm Jones's book, in which the scholar comes closest of all to a solution to 'realism in a higher sense'. There remains only to find an adequate synonymous substitution for the word *fantastic*. In my opinion, that which many people call 'fantastic realism' is in fact *Christian realism*.

It was not Dostoevsky who discovered this aesthetic principle of poetry and prose. It is present in the Gospels and appears in the living details of life. In it is uncovered not only historical reality, but also the mystical meaning of the events that are occurring, which are accomplished as it were before the eyes of the reader. This Gospel realism presents events in their fortuitous manifestation and their divine destiny. It is not afraid to show doubt in the Messiah, it gives sinners the possibility to become Christ's apostles. It is sufficient to remember how the Evangelists told the story of the birth, service, passion and resurrection of the Saviour. Their story contains such incidental and unexpected details which would be superfluous in a fictitious work, but in the Good News they are the historical testimony of eyewitnesses.

As an aesthetic principle, Christian realism appeared long before the discovery of realism in the arts. It is manifested in the New Testament conception of the world, man, and the dual (human and divine) nature of the Messiah. It is inevitable in hagiography, in which first the hero, then the author of the life followed the aesthetic canon of the Gospels. It is expressed in the highest artistic achievements of Christian painting—in the canvases of the titans of the Renaissance (and how can we not recall here the wondrous effect on Dostoevsky of Raphael's Madonna), in Rembrandt's pictures of stories from the Gospels, in the Russian painter Alexander Ivanov's picture 'The Coming of the Messiah'.

In its ethical and social significance Christian realism was realized by the Russian philosopher S L Frank, who set forth his ethical teachings in the work *The Light in the Darkness*,[6] tuning to the spiritual experience of Russian literature and particularly of Dostoevsky. Russian literature took possession of the aesthetic principle of Christian realism in the nineteenth century. And Dostoevsky, like no-one else, assimilated the whole fullness of the content of the New Testament.

The author arrived at the revelation of Christian realism in the hard labour camp in Omsk, when in his life there occurred a difficult and agonizing rebirth of his convictions. This new aesthetic quality of realism is clearly expressed in *Notes from the House of the Dead* and in the ethical purpose of *The Insulted and Injured*, it is present in the ideas of *Notes from Underground*, but it is indisputably displayed in the first of the celebrated 'five novels'.

Recalling Pushkin ('Again Pushkin, dear Pushkin sketched the plots of our future novels in *Onegin*...'), Dostoevsky wrote in his notebooks to the novel *The Adolescent*:

> Well, if I am to be a novelist, I can be in the highest degree a realist. I do not at all have to conceal that my characters are quite often the most ordinary people, that among them are the most ridiculous people, old men at their clubs, Moscow gossips. I can show even the ugliest cripple, like Silvio and the Hero of our time.[7]

Thus it was also with Dostoevsky. 'With full realism' the drunkard Marmeladov appeals to Christ to judge his guilt, Milkolka wants to suffer without guilt, Lizaveta gave the cypress-wood cross and Bible to Sonia, and she in turn gave them to the 'poor murderer', the murderer and the whore read aloud the story of the resurrection of Lazarus and interpret the Gospels, Sonya directs

---

[6] S L Frank, *Svet vo t'me: Opyt khristianskoi i sotsial'noi filosofii* (Paris, 1949). Compare I A Il'in, *Osnovy khristianskoi kul'tury* (Geneva, 1937).

[7] RGB, f. 93.1.8/21, p. 1.

Raskolnikov to the crossroads to bow down before the people, kiss the earth and confess, 'I am a murderer!', the people call the convicts 'unfortunates'. Raskolnikov places the Bible that has passed from Lizaveta to Sonya under his pillow, just as, at one time in Omsk, during his own hard labour, Dostoevsky also looked after this book; and the novel concludes with the apotheosis of Christian love ('love resurrected them, the heart of one contained an infinite source of life for the heart of the other') and the promise of the future resurrection of Raskolnikov. 'With full realism' Prince Lev Nikolaevich Myshkin fulfils and propagates Christ's commandments.

Dostoevsky's heroes, and this includes 'ridiculous people', 'underground paradoxicalists', 'faint-hearted' heroes, vulgar people and great sinners, robbers and whores, wait and appeal to the Messiah. It is in order to save them that Christ appeared in the world and will return again.

The presence of Christ in *The Devils* is manifest in the epigraph from the Gospels and in the plot of the novel. Whether the researcher sees His presence is conditional upon the spectrum of the interpretation of the novel. In *The Adolescent*, the 'Notes of a Young Man', in the literal sense the Lenten work of Arkady Dolgoruky, Raskolnikov's question who to be is transformed into the living problem of *how to live*. *The Brothers Karamazov*, not only continues the gallery of images of virtuous and earnest Christians (Sonya Marmeladova, Myshkin, Makar Dolgoruky, the Elder Zosima, Alyosha Karamazov), but also presents the Church as a positive social ideal.

The 'Christian idea' is presented by Dostoevsky as 'the fundamental idea of art of the nineteenth century', and is revealed by him in the introduction to the translation of Victor Hugo's novel *Notre Dame de Paris*: 'This is a Christian and to the highest degree a moral idea; its formula is the renewal of the dead man, who has been crushed unjustly by the yoke of circumstances, centuries of stagnation, and social prejudice. This idea is a justification of the insulted and of the pariahs of society who have been rejected by everyone'.[8] Of course, the sources of this idea lie in Dostoevsky's early work, beginning with translation of *Eugénie Grandet*, but it was revealed in all its fullness in the writer's post-exile works, from *Notes from the House of the Dead* and *The Insulted and Injured* onwards.

This 'Christian idea' sheds true light on the meaning of 'realism in a higher sense'. On this subject Dostoevsky wrote in his final notebook:

> With full realism to find the man in man. This is a Russian trait for the most part and in that sense I am of course of the people (for my direction flows from the depths of the Christian spirit of the people)—although the Russian people of today do not know this, those to come will.—

---

[8] *Vremia*, 9, 1862, 44-45.

They call me a psychologist: this is not true, I am only a realist in a higher sense, that is, I depict all the depths of the human soul'.[9]

These words have been quoted by many, by almost all critics. They have been used to explain the humanistic spirit of Dostoevsky's work: 'to find the man in man'. They have been seen as a prophecy, like that uttered at the Pushkin memorial: 'although the Russian people of today do not know this, those to come will'. They have been used to investigate the writer's psychological approach: 'They call me a psychologist: this is not true, I am only a realist in a higher sense, that is, I depict all the depths of the human soul'. The range of opinions is wide, right up to Bakhtin's categorical disagreement: Dostoevsky is not a psychologist.[10] Various questions remain unanswered: what is 'full' realism? Why is 'finding the man in man' a 'Russian trait for the most part'? Surely the same spirit of seeking 'the man in man' inspired Balzac and Hugo, about whom Dostoevsky wrote, proclaiming the 'restoration of man' as the fundamental idea of all art of the nineteenth century? Why is this 'a Russian trait for the most part and in that sense I am of course of the people (for my direction flows from the depths of the Christian spirit of the people)'? What does the expression 'realism in a higher sense' mean? What are the 'depths of the human soul'—and what does 'all' mean here? Why does Dostoevsky's direction 'flow from the depths of the Christian spirit of the people?'

Dostoevsky was the first of those who in their work expressed the idea of Christian realism. His 'realism in a higher sense' is realism in which *God is alive, the presence of Christ is visible, and the revelation of the Word is manifested*. Dostoevsky gave a new understanding of art as service to Christ, the meaning of which he saw in its apostolic vocation (the propagation of the Holy Spirit).

The route of Russian literature in its highest achievements of the last centuries is the route of finding with Russian realism the Truth, which is manifested by Christ and 'became the Word'. Fantastic and Christian are two epithets, two sides of the same coin, two images of Dostoevsky's 'realism in a higher sense': the obverse flickers with the enigmatic word 'fantastic', on the reverse we have the revelatory expression of its essence: *Christian*.

Translated by Sarah Young

---

[9] RGALI, f. 121.I.17, p. 29. First published in F M Dostoevskii, *Polnoe sobranie sochinenii*, t. 1: Biografiia, pis'ma, i zapisnye tetradi (St Petersburg, 1883), p. 73 (second pagination).

[10] M M Bakhtin, *Problemy poetiki Dostoevskogo* (Moscow, 1979), p. 71.

AFTERWORD

Lesley Milne

MALCOLM Jones is a scholar with an international reputation whose name is firmly linked with Nottingham. This *Festschrift* in his honour offers the University an opportunity to express pride in this long-standing association.

All but two years of Malcolm's distinguished career were spent at Nottingham, where he was a student 1958-1962, a postgraduate 1962-1965, and a member of academic staff from 1967. From 1965 to 1967 he was an Assistant Lecturer in Russian, in the School of European Studies, University of Sussex, a period that he recalls with great fondness, and regards in some sense as formative, declaring that he was in his element when he was teaching there on 'The Modern European Mind' course (European literature, philosophy, psychology, sociology, religion, theory). Although Malcolm has worked on many topics in the field of Russian—and indeed European—literature and thought, the most consistent focus of his work has been Dostoevsky, which is why it was chosen as the theme of this collection in his honour. Looking back, however, we can see that the inter-disciplinary discourse of his teaching at Sussex in the mid sixties encompasses areas in which Dostoevsky provides an ever-fascinating, constantly self-renewing case for academic study and dialogue. The mid-sixties themselves have gone down in cultural history as one of those eras symbolizing the excitement of discovery, a characteristic that has run through all Malcolm's research ever since.

In a retirement speech in 1997 he recalled the world events around 1958 when he entered Nottingham University. 'Prime Minister MacMillan flew to Moscow wearing a stylish fur hat; Pasternak was awarded and turned down the Nobel prize for Literature and the Russians were about to beat the US in the race to film the dark side of the moon.' This was still very much a post-war Britain, a time when buses hurtled along, 'driven by retired Second World War RAF pilots'. Other excitements seem to have been frowned upon. Landladies regarded themselves as responsible for their students' morals, 'men were not allowed in women's halls of residence after 7.30pm without a chaperone, and after 10.00pm not at all. There were terrifying rumours (some of them more or less true) about [the Warden of a women's hall] taking a shotgun to male students who were in the wrong place at the wrong time'. Nottingham students of the late 1950s navigated these restrictions with the resourcefulness shown by the student body world-wide in all times and places. Malcolm met his future wife, Jenny, and embarked upon a path strewn with accolades and prizes. He graduated in 1962 with a First Class Honours degree in Russian Studies and was awarded the Elizabeth and J D Marsden Prize for outstanding achievement. As a postgraduate he was awarded an Arts Research Scholarship and the Heymann Scholarship, completing his PhD on Dostoevsky and German Idealist Philosophy in 1966. After returning to Nottingham in 1967 as a Lecturer, he was promoted to Senior Lecturer in 1973, and in 1980 was appointed to the Chair of Slavonic Studies, a post that he held until his retirement. Currently he holds the position of Emeritus Professor in Residence, in which role he has, at last, been able to devote himself wholly to research.

Until his retirement Malcolm devoted himself unstintingly to the University of Nottingham. Throughout his academic career he has commanded respect not only as a scholar but also as a sagacious and astute manager, at every administrative level. In his time at Nottingham he has served on all the major committees of the University and held every major administrative post: Head of Department 1980-1989, 1992-1995; Dean of the Faculty of Arts 1982-1985; Pro-Vice Chancellor 1987-1991; Head of School of Modern Languages 1992-1994; Chair of the Institute of Russian, Soviet and Central and East European Studies 1994-1996. To all these posts he brought strategic foresight, managerial flair, and absolute integrity that inspired trust.

He also put his administrative talents to the service of many national bodies, too numerous to list in full. A short résumé will give indication of the scope of his activities. President of the Association of Teachers of Russian from 1985 to 1986, he then became President of the British Universities' Association of Slavists (BUAS) 1986-1988. In this post he used his consummate diplomatic skills to lead BUAS into what was for many a contentious merger with the National Association for Soviet and East European Studies (NASEES) to form the British Association for Soviet and East European Studies (BASEES), of which he was Vice-President from 1988 to 1990. BASEES flourishes to this day, which testifies to the success of the merger. The 1980s and 1990s saw a war of attrition between the government and the universities, with so-called 'minority subjects' under constant threat, and at this point Malcolm vigorously promoted Slavonic Studies locally and nationally, as a member of major governmental enquiries, such as the 'Wooding Report' of 1988-1989, the HEFCE Review into Former Soviet and East European Studies of 1995-1996, and the HEFCE Advisory group on Former Soviet and East European Studies 1996-2000. The support Malcolm gave to the subject in the UK at these times of instability and crisis made a huge positive difference. At the same time, 1989-1995, he was acting first as Vice-chairman, then Chairman, then member (as former Chair) of the Co-ordinating Council of Area Studies Associations. This period also saw the first of the Research Assessment Exercises, and Malcolm served on the Russian and other Slavonic languages panels in 1989, 1992 and 1996. In addition, from 1994 to 1997 he was a member of the Humanities Research Board of the British Academy. As that rare bird, a distinguished scholar who was also an efficient high-level administrator, Malcolm found himself elected, co-opted or invited onto every conceivable national committee, each with its own acronym. This phase in his career is recorded in Catriona Kelly's brilliantly updated version of Mayakovsky's 'Prozasedavishiesia':

Over-Committeed
After Mayakovsky

> Each morning, on the dot of 5 a.m.,
> I look through my window, just as the sky turns grey, and see them rushing: to their HEF,
> their CE,
> their Well, their Come, their MRC,
> their TQA or RAE,
> to their committees and their quangos.
> [...]
> Try calling round:
> 'I've an appointment with Professor Jones,
> Five times, you know, it's been postponed'—
> 'Professor Jones is out right now:
> BA, I think, or HRB.'
> [...]
> Without a lift (it's bust) you climb,
> mocked by a skinny, grey-faced moon,
> to the Arts Tower, fifteenth Floor:
> 'Where can I find Professor Jones?'
> 'Sorry! He has to chair
> the Sub-Committee under Section 1
> Para 11 Roman Figure iv.'[11]

Despite the Oxford reference to the fifteenth floor of the Arts Tower, this Professor Jones is clearly our Nottingham man, a legend in his lifetime for his ability to cope with all these meetings and sub-committees and paragraphs and small roman numerals, and, what's more, make sense of them. There must have been many times when he indeed felt 'over-committeed', and his UK and Nottingham colleagues owe him a debt of gratitude not least because he spared and protected others from that fate.

The wonder is that he had, at the same time as all the above activities, also been operating at the level of international research for over three decades. This commitment found expression not only in the books and articles listed in the Bibliography in this *Festschrift*, but also in the activities of the International Dostoevsky Society, of which Malcolm was a founding member in 1971. Vice-

---

[11] Publisherd in *Oxford Magazine* for Second Week, Trinity Term, 2001 and quoted here by kind permission of Catriona Kelly as her contribution to this *Festschrift*.

president from 1980 to 1986, he convened and organized the VI International Dostoevsky Symposium in Nottingham in 1986, and was President from 1995 to 1998. From 1995 to the present he has been honorary member of the Academic Advisory Council of the Dostoevsky Museum, St Petersburg.

On his retirement in 1997, Malcolm gave several speeches, in one of which he mischievously suggested that Dostoevsky, in particular the International Dostoevsky Society, had given him insights for his other administrative roles:

> The IDS is a sort of scaled-down version of what the world would have been like if it had been created by Dostoevsky. The most important qualification for membership, apart from having published research on Dostoevsky, is the ability to create limitless embarrassment. To be an officer, one needs in addition to know how to intervene at such moments in such a way as to make matters worse.

The world according to Dostoevsky functions here as an 'anti-model' of administration. To find Malcolm's model, one might turn to cricket, another of his special subjects. (And was it perhaps the international cricket ground at Trent Bridge that brought him back from Sussex and kept him in Nottingham thereafter?) Cricket, with its matches that are played out over several days, with civilized breaks for meals, and its elaborately complex rules that are none the less fully understood, provides the British metaphor for 'fair play'. Dostoevsky, however, illumines the dark and contradictory side of humankind, making us realise that people are always stranger than we might ever imagine. An intuitive grasp of these opposites—Dostoevsky's fantastic realism and cricket's decorum—might explain Malcolm's success as a member or chair of committees.

Despite his increasingly heavy administrative roles at Nottingham, Malcolm never gave up undergraduate teaching, communicating the excitement and intellectual rigour he remembered from his own mentors, in particular Frank Seeley. In the year of his retirement the students doing his Tolstoy option treated him to a 'Tolstoy party' (Tolstoy food, Tolstoy party games), a fitting celebration of the sheer intellectual fun that they were having behind the austere front of theoretical discourse. After his retirement, Malcolm was able to take on the supervision of postgraduate students, who blossomed under his tutelage and embarked on academic careers themselves, carrying on the tradition. They are represented in this volume, along with other colleagues, across continents and generations, who have benefited from his constant readiness to engage in their scholarly endeavours.

This *Festschrift* is an international recognition of the enormous respect in which Malcolm is held throughout the community of Dostoevsky scholars. It is also a tribute of thanks, on behalf of all those members of the world-wide academic community whose lives and works have been enhanced by contact with Malcolm's intellect, sagacity, generosity and subtly elegant wit.

BIBLIOGRAPHY OF MALCOLM JONES'S PUBLICATIONS

BOOKS

Dostoyevsky: The Novel of Discord (London: Paul Elek; New York: Barnes and Noble, 1976)
New Essays on Tolstoy, ed. (Cambridge: Cambridge University Press, 1978)
New Essays on Dostoyevsky, ed., with G M Terry (Cambridge: Cambridge University Press, 1983)
Résumés of Papers Given at the VI International Dostoevsky Symposium, ed. (Nottingham, 1986)
Dostoyevsky after Bakhtin: Readings in Dostoyevsky's Fantastic Realism (Cambridge: Cambridge University Press, 1990)
Dostoevsky and the Twentieth Century: The Ljubljana Papers, ed. (Nottingham: Astra Press, 1993)
The Cambridge Companion to the Classic Russian Novel, ed., with Robin Feuer Miller (Cambridge: Cambridge University Press, 1998) (reprinted 1999)
Dostoevskii posle Bakhtina, trans. A V Skidan (St Petersburg: Academic Project Agency, 1998)
Dostoevsky after Bakhtin (Chinese edition) (Beijing: Ji Lin Renmin Press, 2004)

Forthcoming

Dostoyevsky after Bakhtin: Readings in Dostoyevsky's Fantastic Realism (Cambridge: Cambridge University Press, 2005) (paperback edition)
Dostoevsky and the Dynamics of Religious Experience (London: Anthem, 2005)

ARTICLES AND CONTRIBUTIONS TO BOOKS

'Dostoyevsky's Conception of the Idea,' *Renaissance and Modern Studies*, 13 (1969), 106-131
'Some Echoes of Hegel in Dostoyevsky', *The Slavonic and East European Review*, 49 (October 1971), 500-520
'Dostoievskii's Notebooks', *Journal of European Studies*, 2.3 (1972) 277-284
'Dostoevsky, Tolstoy, Leskov and Redstokizm', *Journal of Russian Studies*, 23 (1972), 3-20
'The Sad and Curious Story of Karass: a Scottish Mission in the Caucasus, 1803-33', *Newsletter of the Study Group on Eighteenth-Century Russia*, 1 (1973), 23-26
'An Aspect of Romanticism in Dostoyevsky: *Netochka Nezvanova* and Eugène Sue's *Mathilde*', *Renaissance and Modern Studies*, 17 (1973), 38-61 (summary in Russian in *VII Miedzynarodowy kongres slawistow w Warszawie 1973, Streszenia referatow i komunikatow* (Warsaw, 1973), pp. 471-472)

'Dostoyevsky and an Aspect of Schiller's Psychology', *The Slavonic and East European Review*, 52 (July 1974), 337-354

'Raskolnikov's Humanitarianism', *Canadian-American Slavic Studies*, 8.3 (Fall 1974), 370-380

'The Sad and Curious Story of Karass, 1802-35', *Oxford Slavonic Papers*, n.s., 8 (1975), 53-81

'A Note on Mr J G Blissmer and the Society for the Encouragement of Spiritual Reading', *The Slavonic and East European Review*, 53.130 (January 1975), 92-96

'Comrade Dostoevsky' (a survey of recent Soviet scholarship with particular reference to Leonid Grossman's *Dostoevsky*, trans. Mary Mackler, London, 1974), *The Times Literary Supplement*, February 21, 1975, p. 198

'*Notes from Underground*', *Exeter Tapes*, 1976

'K ponimaniu obraza kniazia Myshkina', in *Dostoevskii: materialy i issledovaniia*, ii, ed. G M Fridlender (Leningrad: Nauka, 1976), pp. 106-112

'An Aspect of Tolstoy's Impact on Modern English Fiction: "The Kreutzer Sonata" and Joyce Cary's *The Moonlight*', *The Slavonic and East European Review*, 56 (January 1978), 97-105 (summary in Serbo-Croat in *VIII Medunarodni slavisticki kongres. Knjiga referata*, 1 (Zagreb, 1978), p. 385)

'Problems of Communication in *Anna Karenina*', in *New Essays on Tolstoy*, pp. 85-108 (see 'Books')

'Dostoevskii, Fedor Mikhailovich (1821-1881)', *Modern Encyclopedia of Russian and Soviet History*, ix (Academic International Press, 1978), pp. 235-238

'Winter notes on Autumn reading: five recent books on Dostoevsky', *Journal of Russian Studies*, 37 (1979), 32-39

'Karass Scottish Colony in Russia', *Modern Encyclopedia of Russian and Soviet History*, xvi (Academic International Press, 1980), pp. 13-15

'Dostoevsky and Europe: Travels in the Mind', *Renaissance and Modern Studies*, 24 (1980), 38-57

'Andrew Hay and the Griboedov Affair', *Journal of Russian Studies*, 42 (1981), 16-21

(with J Y Muckle), 'Three Letters from V D Bonch-Bruevich in the Pashkov Papers', *The Slavonic and East European Review*, 60 (January 1982), 75-84

(with W J Leatherbarrow), Guest Editor; Introductory Note, 'Dostoevsky Centenary Conference at the University of Nottingham' [being the proceedings of the Dostoevsky Centenary Conference, October 30-31 1981], *Dostoevsky Studies*, 3 (1982), 3-78

'Pashkovism', *Modern Encyclopedia of Russian and Soviet History* (Academic International Press, 1982), pp. 42-44

'Radstockist Movement', *Modern Encyclopedia of Russian and Soviet History* (Academic International Press, 1982), pp. 152-153

'Dostoevsky and European Philosophy', in Nina Kauchtschischwili, ed., *Actualité de Dostoevskij* (Genova: La Quercia Edizioni, 1982), pp. 103-118

'Introduction', in *New Essays on Dostoyevsky*, pp. 1-18 (see 'Books')

'Dostoevsky, Rousseau and Others', *Dostoevsky Studies*, 4 (1983 [1985]), 81-93

'British Protestantism as a Factor in the Development of Nineteenth-Century Russian Literature', in Roger Bartlett, ed., *Russian Thought and Society 1800-1917*, (Keele, 1984), pp. 128-152

'Dostoevsky's *Notes from Underground*', in Roger Cockrell and David Richards, eds., *The Voice of a Giant* (Exeter, 1985), pp. 55-65

'*Der Sandmann* and the Uncanny: a Sketch for an Alternative Approach', *Paragraph*, 7 (1986), 77-101

'*A Raw Youth*: A Novel of Disorder', Robin Feuer Miller, ed., *Critical Essays on Dostoevsky* (G K Hall, Boston, 1986) pp. 158-170 (reprint of edited extract from *Dostoyevsky: The Novel of Discord*)

'The Legend of the Grand Inquisitor: the Suppression of the Second Temptation and the Dialogue with God', *Dostoevsky Studies*, 7 (1986), 123-134

'Dostoevsky: Driving the Reader Crazy', *Essays in poetics*, 12.1 (1987), 57-80

'Bakhtin's Metalinguistics', in Christopher S Butler, Richard A Cardwell and Joanna Channell, eds., *Language and Literature—Theory and Practice: A Tribute to Walter Grauberg* (Nottingham: University of Nottingham, 1989), pp. 101-115

'How E J Dillon Left a Chair at Kharkov University and Joined *The Daily Telegraph*: a Biographical Note', in Peter Herrity, ed., *The Bell of Freedom, Essays presented to Monica Partridge on the Occasion of her 75th Birthday*, (Nottingham: Astra Press, 1990), pp. 77-84

'Introduction' to Fedor Dostoevsky, *Notes from Underground and The Gambler*, trans. Jane Kentish, (Oxford: Oxford University Press, 1991), pp. vii-xxv

'Mikhail Bulgakov: Beyond Modernism', in Cynthia Marsh and Wendy Rosslyn, eds., *Russian and Yugoslav Culture in the Age of Modernism* (Nottingham: Astra Press, 1991), pp. 101-109.

'Introduction' to Fyodor Dostoevsky, *The Brothers Karamazov*, trans. Richard Pevear and Larissa Volokhonsky (New York, 1992), pp. v-xxix

'The Creation of a Prosaics: Morson and Emerson on Mikhail Bakhtin', *Comparative Criticism*, 15 (1993), 243-260

'*Der Sandmann* and the Uncanny', in *Short Story Criticism*, 13 (Detroit: Gale Research Inc. 1993) pp. 236-246 (reprint)

'Shestov on Chekhov', in Faith Wigzell, ed., *Russian Writers on Russian Writers* (Oxford and New York, 1994), pp. 39-50

'Dostoevsky, Zasetskaya, and Radstockism', *Oxford Slavonic Papers*, n.s., 27 (1994), 106-120

'Dostoevskii and Radstockism', in W J Leatherbarrow, ed., *Dostoevskii and Britain* (Oxford and Providence: Berg, 1995), pp. 159-175 (reprint)

'*The Eternal Husband*: Discourse with a Noose', *Essays in Poetics*, 20 (1995), 46-59

'The Gospel According to Woland and the Tradition of the Wandering Jew', in Lesley Milne, ed., *Bulgakov: The Novelist-Playwright* (Luxembourg: Harwood Academic Publishers, 1995), pp. 115-124

'La tradition de la littérature comparée dans la slavistique britannique du XX siècle (le cas de Janko Lavrine)', in Irina Fougeron, ed., *Etudes russes—Mélanges offerts au Professeur Louis Allain* (Lille, 1996), pp. 37-43

'A Bachtinian Approach to the Gospels: The Problem of Authority', *Scandoslavica*, 42 (1996), 58-76

'The Evolution of Fantastic Realism in Russian Literature,' in Knut Andreas Grimstad and Ingunn Lunde, eds., *Celebrating Creativity, Essays in Honour of Jostein Børtnes* (Bergen: University of Bergen, 1997), pp. 58-69

'Silence in The Brothers Karamazov', in Horst-Jürgen Gerigk, ed., *Die Brüder Karamasow, Dostojewskijs letzter Roman in heutiger Sicht* (Dresden: Dresden University Press, 1997), pp. 29-45

'The Death and Resurrection of Orthodoxy in the Works of Dostoevskii' in Ingunn Lunde, ed., *Cultural Discontinuity and Reconstruction: the Byzanto-Slav Heritage and the Creation of a Russian National Literature in the Nineteenth Century* (Oslo: Solum forlag A/S, 1997), pp. 143-167

'*Notes from the Underground* Presents a Romanticized View of Freedom', in Tamara Johnson, ed., *Readings on Fyodor Dostoyevsky, Literary Companions to World Authors* (San Diego: Greenhaven Press, 1998), pp. 103-110 (reprint of edited extract from *Dostoyevsky: The Novel of Discord*)

'*The Idiot*' in Neil Cornwell and Nicole Christian, eds., *Reference Guide to Russian Literature* (London: Fitzroy Dearborn, 1998), pp. 257-258

'*The Devils*' in Neil Cornwell and Nicole Christian, eds., *Reference Guide to Russian Literature* (London: Fitzroy Dearborn, 1998), pp. 258-259

(with Robin Feuer Miller) 'Editors' Preface' to *The Cambridge Companion to the Classic Russian Novel*, ed., with Robin Feuer Miller (Cambridge: Cambridge University Press, 1998), pp. xi-xv

'Introduction' to *The Cambridge Companion to the Classic Russian Novel*, ed., with Robin Feuer Miller (Cambridge: Cambridge, University Press, 1998), pp. 1-17

'Sisters and Rivals: Variations on a Theme in Dostoevskii's Fiction', in Carsten Dutt, ed., *Die Wirklichkeit der Kunst und das Abenteur der Interpretation* (Dresden: Dresden University Press, 1998), pp. 159-169

'Preface' to F F Seeley, *Saviour or Superman* (Nottingham: Astra Press, 1998), pp. vii-viii

'Georgii M Fridlender, 1915-1995: Obituary', *Dostoevsky Studies*, 2.2 (1998), 199-200

'Fedor Dostoevskii,' in Paul Schellinger, ed., *Encyclopedia of the Novel* (Chicago: Fitzroy Dearborn, 1999)

'Predislovie k russkomu izdaniiu', in Malcolm V Jones, *Dostoevskii posle Bakhtina*, trans. A V Skidan (St Petersburg: Academic Project Agency, 1998), pp. 5-8.

'Introduction' to Fyodor Dostoevsky, *Notes from Underground* and *The Gambler*, trans. Jane Kentish (Oxford: Oxford University Press, 1999), pp. vii-xxv (reprint)

'Fyodor Mikhailovich Dostoyevsky', in Haim Gordon, ed., *Dictionary of Existentialism* (Westport, CT: Greenwood Press, 1999), pp. 109-114

'The Narrator and Narrative Technique in Dostoevsky's *The Devils*', in W J Leatherbarrow, ed., *AATSEEL Critical Companions: Dostoevsky's 'The Devils'* (Evanston, IL: Northwestern University Press, 1999), pp. 100-118

'Dostoevsky's *Notes from Underground*', in *Short Story Criticism*, 33 (Detroit: Gale Research Inc., 1999), pp. 207-211 (reprint)

'Roman-Nevaliashka: Further Thoughts on the Structure of Dostoevsky's *Idiot*', in G Kjetsaa, L Lönngren and G Opeide, eds., *Translating Culture, Essays in Honour of Erik Egeberg* (Tromso: Solum Forlag, 2001), pp. 129-139

'Janko Lavrin, Promoter of Modernism and the Avant-garde—a Footnote', in Horst-Jürgen Gerigk, ed., *Literarische Avantgarde. Festshrift für Rudolf Neuhäuser* (Heidelberg: Mattes Verlag, 2001), pp. 73-80

'Frank Friedeberg Seeley, an Obituary', *Dostoevsky Studies*, n.s., 5 (2001), 225-230

'Flirting her Way Round the Court of St Petersburg: Some Thoughts on Vigée-Le Brun's Russian Period and her Portrait of Varvara Nikolaevna Golovina', in Marie-Aude Albert, ed., *Diagonales Dostoïevskiennes. Mélanges en l'honneur de Jacques Catteau* (Paris, 2002), pp. 273-289

'Dostoevskii and Religion', in W J Leatherbarrow, ed., *The Cambridge Companion to Dostoevskii* (Cambridge: Cambridge University Press), 2002, pp. 148-174

'The Enigma of Mr Astley', *Dostoevsky Studies*, n.s., 6 (2002), 39-47

'Malcolm V Jones on "The Grand Inquisitor"', in Harold Bloom, ed., *Fyodor Dostoevsky*, (Broomall, PA: Chelsea House Publishers, 2003), pp. 81-83 (reprint of extract from *Dostoyevsky: The Novel of Discord*)

'Modelling the Religious Dimension of Dostoevsky's Fiction', *New Zealand Slavonic Journal* (2003), 41-53

'Raskolnikov's Humanitarianism', in Harold Bloom, ed., *Raskolnikov and Svidrigaylov* (Broomall, PA: Chelsea House Publishers, 2004), pp. 37-49 (reprint)

Forthcoming

'Slavonic Studies in the United Kingdom since 1945—a Personal View', in Giovanna Brogi Bercoff, ed., *Beiträge zur Geschichte der Slawistik in nicht-slawischen Ländern*, ii (Paris: Austrian Academy of Sciences, 2004)

'Dostoevskii, Zasetskaia i uchenie Lorda Redstoka', trans. T A Kasatkina, in T A Kasatkina, ed., *Dopolneniia k kommentariiu proizvedenii F M Dostoevskogo* (Moscow: Nauka, 2004)

'Romantizm v tvorchestve Dostoevskogo: *Netochka Nezvanova* i *Matil'da Ehzena Siu*', trans. Tatiana Kasatkina, in Tatiana Kasatkina, ed., *Dopolneniia k kommentariiu proizvedenii F M Dostoevskogo* (Moscow: Nauka, 2004)

'Spirituality in Literature: The Great Russian Novelists', in Jonathan Hill, ed., *The History of Christianity* (Lion)

Translations

Yury Nagibin, 'The Winter Oak', in *Modern Russian Short Stories*, i, ed. C G Bearne (London: McGibbon and Kee, 1968)

Il'f and Petrov, 'How they Wrote Robinson Crusoe', in *Modern Russian Short Stories*, ii, ed., C G Bearne (London: McGibbon and Kee, 1969)

F M Dostoyevsky, 'A Strange Man's Dream' in *The Penguin Book of Russian Short Stories*, ed. David Richards (Harmondsworth: Penguin, 1981), pp. 98-121.

Publications on Professional Matters

'Wanted: a New Rush to Learn Russian', *The Times Higher Education Supplement*, 10 September 1976, p. 8

ed., *Modern Languages, School and Higher Education*, Faculty of Education, University of Nottingham, Nottingham, 1977

'The Fascination of Russian Culture', in J Y Muckle, ed., *Russian in Schools. A Handbook of Information for Head Teachers, Advisers, Inspectors and Curriculum Planners* (Nottingham, 1982), pp. 92-94

Evidence to the House of Commons Foreign Affairs Committee, Second Report from the Foreign Affairs Committee, Session, 1985-86, UK-Soviet Relations, 2, 1986, pp. 141-51 *passim*.

'Concentrating Russian Studies', letter to the Editor, *The Times Higher Education Supplement*, 12 September 1986, p. 2

(with Martin McCauley), 'Talking with a Glasnostershire accent' [sic], *The Times Higher Education Supplement*, 22 May 1987, p. 13

(with Norman Wooding and Bryan Cartledge), *Review of Soviet and East European Studies*, Report to UFC and PCFC, July 1989

'Russian at Sussex'. *BASEES Newsletter*, n.s., 9.2 (November 2003), pp. 8 and 10.

Miscellaneous

'Soviet Ignorance of the West Most Disturbing Feature of Life in Russia', *Bristol Evening Post*, Tuesday September 1 1959, p. 8

'Independency Past and Present', *Breakthrough*, 2 May 1960, pp. 2-3

'Dostoevsky's *Notes from the House of the Dead*' in *Janacek, From the House of the Dead*, (programme of the Welsh Opera Company, November-December 1982), pp. 18-21

F M Dostoevsky, a touring exhibition from the USSR (catalogue with short articles on 'Dostoevsky's life and work', 'Biographical notes' and 'Dostoevsky in Britain'), University of Nottingham, 1983, 33pp.

'Dostoyevsky's *Notes from the House of the Dead*' in *Janacek, From the House of the Dead* (programme of the Scottish Opera Company, 1987, reprint)

The History of St Andrew's with Castle Gate United Reformed Church, St Andrew's with Castle Gate United Reformed Church, Nottingham, 1992, 32pp.

(with Rosemary Fasey and Alexandra Harrington), '"Pushing Forward the Frontiers": an Interview with Malcolm Jones on his Retirement', *Fontan*, 2 (May 1997), 8-17

'The origins of the Viney Family', in Viney Family Members, *The Viney Family History* (Viney Book Committee, Devonport, Tasmania, 2000), pp. iv-ix

(with Hinrich Siefken), *Fear Not, a Study Outline*, St Andrew's with Castle Gate United Reformed Church, Nottingham, 2001, 32pp.

(with Jennifer Jones), 'The Vineys of Somerset and Tasmania—an Update', *The Greenwood Tree*, 26, 3 (2001), p. 110

ACADEMIC REVIEWS

Robert Lord, *Dostoevsky. Essays and Perspectives* (London, 1970), in *The Slavonic and East European Review*, 49 (October 1971), 616-618

H Eichstadt, *Zukovskij als Übersetzer, Forum Slavicum*, 29 (Munich, 1970), in *The Slavonic and East European Review*, 1 (October 1972), 637-638

N M Lary, *Dostoevsky and Dickens: A Study of Literary Influence* (London, 1973), in *The Journal of European Studies*, 4 (1974), p. 98

Annelore Engel Braunschmidt, *Deutsche Dichter in Russland, Forum Slavicum*, 36 (Munich, 1973), in *The Slavonic and East European Review*, 53 (January 1975), pp. 154-155

Problemy poetiki i istorii (sbornik statei) k 75-letiiu so dnia rozhdeniia i 50-letiiu nauchno-pedagogicheskoideiatel'nosti Mikhaila Mikhailovicha Bakhtina (Saransk, 1973), in *The Times Literary Supplement*, July 25 1975, p. 857

Alex de Jonge, *Dostoevsky and the Age of Intensity* (London, 1975), in *The Times Higher Education Supplement*, 22 August 1975, p. 13 (correction, 12 September 1975, p. 16)

Vladimir Seduro, *Dostoevski's Image in Russia Today* (Belmont, Massachusetts, 1975), in *The Times Literary Supplement*, April 1976, p. 460

Wolf Schmid, *Der Textaufbau in den Erzählungen Dostoevskijs* (Munich, 1973), in *The Slavonic and East European Review*, 54 (April 1976), 280-281

Angus Calder, *Russia Discovered: 19th Century Fiction from Pushkin to Chekhov* (London, 1976), in *The Times Higher Education Supplement*, 3 December 1976, p. 17

Sven Linner, *Starets Zosima in The Brothers Karamazov: A Study in the Mimesis of Virtue* (Stockholm, 1975), in The *Journal of Russian Studies*, 32 (1976), 49-50

Alexandra H Lyngstad, *Dostoevskij and Schiller* (The Hague, 1975), in *The Slavonic and East European Review*, 55 (1977), 240-241

Joseph Frank, *Dostoevsky: The Seeds of Revolt, 1821-1849* (Princeton, NJ, and London, 1977) in *The Slavonic and East European Review*, 56 (1978), 121-122

Georgi M Fridlender, *Ästhetik und Literaturgeschichte, Aufsätze 1940-1972* (Berlin and Weimar), in *The Journal of European Studies*, 8.2 (1978), 148-149

Joseph Frank, *Dostoevsky: The Seeds of Revolt, 1821-1949* (Princeton, NJ, and London, 1977), in *The Times Higher Education Supplement*, July 21, 1978

Edward Wasiolek, *Tolstoy's Major Fiction* (Chicago and London, 1978), in *The Modern Language Review* (July 1979), 766-767

Michael Holquist, *Dostoevsky and the Novel* (Princeton, NJ, 1977), in *The Journal of European Studies*, 10 (1980), 220-221

Jacques Catteau, *La Création littéraire chez Dostoïevski* (Paris, 1978), in *The Slavonic and East European Review*, lviii) 1980, 115-117

o. S Gakkel' (S Hackel), *Mat' Mariya* (Paris, 1980), in *Sobornost'*, 3. 2 (1981), 243-246

Robin Feuer Miller, *Dostoevsky and 'The Idiot': Author, Narrator, and Reader* (Cambridge MA, and London, 1981), in The *Journal of Russian Studies*, 45 (1983), 54-55

Robin Feuer Miller, *Dostoevsky and 'The Idiot': Author, Narrator, and Reader* (Cambridge, MA, and London, 1981), and Robert Louis Jackson, *The Art of Dostoevsky: Deliriums and Nocturnes* (Princeton, NJ, 1981), in *The Times Literary Supplement*, 4 June 1982, p. 621

G M Fridlender, ed., Dostoevskii: materialy i issledovaniia, iv (Leningrad, 1980), in *Dostoevsky Studies*, 3 (1982), 199-200

Dostoevskij européen, Revue de littérature comparée, 219-220 (1981), pp. 265-518, in *The Modern Language Review* (October 1983), 996-997

Peter Henry, *A Hamlet of his Time. Vsevolod Garshin, the Man, his Works and his Milieu* (Oxford, 1983), in *Scottish Slavonic Studies* (Autumn 1984), 169-170

Neil Cornwell, *The Life, Times and Milieu of V F Odoevsky, 1804-69* (London, 1986), in *Irish Slavonic Studies*, 7 (1986), 180-181

Louis Allain, *Dostoïevski et l'autre* (Lille/Paris, 1984), in *Scottish Slavonic Studies* (1986)

Louis Allain, *Dostoïevski et l'autre* (Lille/Paris, 1984), in *The Slavonic and East European Review*, 44 (1986), 594-595

Ludolf Muller, *Dostojewskij, Sein Leben. Sein Werk. Sein Vermächtnis* (Munich, 1982), in *Zeitschrift für slavische Philologie*, 47.1 (1987), 215-217

W J Leatherbarrow and D C Offord, trans. and eds, *A Documentary History of Russian Thought from the Enlightenment to Marxism* (Ann Arbor, Michigan, 1987), in *The Modern Language Review*, 83.3 (1988) 805-807

Barbara Heldt, *Terrible Perfection: Women and Russian Literature* (Bloomington and Indianapolis, 1987), in *The Modern Language Review*, 84.2 (1989), 541-542

Gary Saul Morson and Caryl Emerson, eds., *Rethinking Bakhtin: Extensions and Challenges* (Evanston, IL, 1989); Catriona Kelly, Michael Makin and David Shepherd, eds., *Discontinuous Discourses in Modern Russian Literature* (London, 1989); and Tsvetan Todorov, *Literature and Its*

Theorists: A Personal View of Twentieth-Century Criticism, trans. Catherine Porter (Ithaca and New York, 1987), in *The Slavonic and East European Review*, 68.3 (1990), 543-545

W J Leatherbarrow, *Fedor Dostoevsky: A Reference Guide* (Boston, MA, 1990), in *The Modern Language Review*, 87.1 (1992), 269-270

Robert Belknap, *The Genesis of 'The Brothers Karamazov'* (Evanston, IL, 1990), in *The Scottish Slavonic Review*, 18 (1992), 134-135

Rita H Pitman, *The Writer's Divided Self in Bulgakov's 'The Master and Margarita'* (Basingstoke and London), in *The Slavonic and East European Review*, 71 (1993), 744-745

Robert Louis Jackson, *Dialogues with Dostoevsky: The Overwhelming Questions* (Stanford, CA, 1993), in *The Slavonic and East European Review*, 72.3 (1994), 510-511

David Shepherd, ed., *Bakhtin, Carnival and Other Subjects* (Amsterdam, Atlanta, 1993), in *The Slavonic and East European Review*, 73.2 (1995), 301-303

Frank F Seeley, *From the Heyday of the Superfluous Man to Chekhov* (Nottingham, 1994), in *The Slavonic and East European Review*, 73.1 (1995), 120-121

Nikolai Leskov, *Schism in High Society*, trans. and ed. James Muckle (Bramcote Press, 1995), in *Rusistika*, 13 (June 1996), 52-53

Bakhtin Around the World: The Bakhtin Newsletter, no. 5, ed. Scott Lee and Clive Thomson, (University of Sheffield, 1996), in *The Slavonic and East European Review*, 75.3 (1997), 719-720

Caryl Emerson, *The First Hundred Years of Mikhail Bakhtin* (Princeton, NJ, 1997), in *The Slavonic and East European Review*, 76.4 (1998), 727-728

Neil Cornwell, ed., *The Gothic-Fantastic in Nineteenth-Century Russian Literature* (Amsterdam and Atlanta, GA, 1999), in *The Slavonic and East European Review*, 78.3 (2000), 570-572

Victor Terras, *Reading Dostoevsky* (Madison, Wisconsin, 1998), in *The Slavic Review*, 58.4 (1999), 936-937

Bruce French, *Dostoevsky's 'Idiot': Dialogue and the Spiritually Good Life* (Evanston, IL, 2001), in *The Slavonic and East European Review*, 80.3, (July 2002), 516-517

Russell Scott Valentino, *Vicissitudes of Genre in the Russian Novel* (New York, 2001), in *The Slavonic and East European Review*, 80.4 (2002), 721-723

Laurence Kelly, *Diplomacy and Murder in Tehran: Alexander Griboedov and Imperial Russia's Mission to the Shah of Persia* (London and New York, 2002), in *The Slavonic and East European Review*, 80.4 (2002), 748-750

CAMBRIDGE STUDIES IN RUSSIAN LITERATURE (GENERAL EDITOR 1985-1996)

Simon Karlinsky, *Marina Tsvetaeva: The Woman, her World and her Poetry* (Cambridge University Press, 1985)

J A E Curtis, *Bulgakov's Last Decade: The Writer as Hero* (Cambridge University Press, 1987)

Raymond Cooke, *Velimir Khlebnikov: A Critical Study* (Cambridge University Press, 1987)

Pamela Davidson, *The Poetic Imagination of Vyacheslav Ivanov: A Russian Symbolist's Perception of Dante* (Cambridge University Press, 1989)

Jacques Catteau, *Dostoyevsky and the Process of Literary Creation*, trans. Audrey Littlewood (Cambridge University Press, 1989)

Valentina Polukhina, *Joseph Brodsky: A Poet for our Time* (Cambridge University Press, 1989)

Catriona Kelly, *Petrushka: The Russian Carnival Puppet Theatre* (Cambridge University Press, 1990)

Frank Friedeberg Seeley, *Turgenev: A Reading of his Fiction* (Cambridge University Press, 1991)

Gitta Hammarberg, *From the Idyll to the Novel: Karamzin's Sentimentalist Prose* (Cambridge University Press, 1991)

Diane Oenning Thompson, *'The Brothers Karamazov' and the Poetics of Memory* (Cambridge University Press, 1992)

Thomas Seifrid, *Andrei Platonov* (Cambridge University Press, 1992)

Julian W Connolly, *Nabokov's Early Fiction* (Cambridge University Press, 1992)

David Gillespie, *Iurii Trifonov* (Cambridge University Press, 1992)

Linda Hart Scatton, *Mikhail Zoshchenko: Evolution of a Writer* (Cambridge University Press, 1993)

Ellen Chances, *Andrei Bitov: The Ecology of Inspiration* (Cambridge University Press, 1993)

Darra Goldstein, *Nikolai Zabolotsky: Play for Mortal Stakes* (Cambridge University Press, 1993)

Bernice Glatzer Rosenthal, ed., *Nietzsche and Soviet Culture* (Cambridge University Press, 1994)

Susan Layton, *Russian Literature and Empire* (Cambridge University Press, 1994)

Rosamund Bartlett, *Wagner and Russia* (Cambridge University Press, 1995)

Efraim Sicher, *Jews in Russian Literature after the October Revolution* (Cambridge University Press, 1995)

Karen L Ryan-Hayes, *Contemporary Russian Satire: A Genre Study* (Cambridge University Press, 1995)

Rosalind Marsh, ed., *Gender and Russian Literature* (Cambridge University Press, 1996)

Graham Roberts, *The Last Soviet Avant-Garde, OBERIU: Fact, Fiction, Metafiction* (Cambridge University Press, 1997)

INDEX

Abaza, Iulia Fyodorovna, 68, 70
Abraham, Gerald, 137
Akhmatova, Anna, 46-63, 138n., 230-231;
  'Northern Elegies', 47, 52-54;
  Poem without a Hero, 47-63
Aksakov, Alexander, 90
Aleksiev, Vassily Alekseievich, 65
Alexander I, 81
Alfred of Great Britain, Prince, 102
Allah, 39, 226
Alov, Alexander: *A Nasty Story* (1966), 137
Amert, Susan, 47, 53, 54, 55n.
Andersen, Hans Christian: *The Little Match Girl*, 144n.
Arnold, Thomas, 99, 101-102, 105-106, 108
Artaud, Antonin, 126
Asafiev, Boris (Igor Glebov): *Nastasya Filippovna* (1964), 147
Augustine, St: *Confessions*, 169
Avdotia, Tsarista, 49, 51

Bakhtin, Mikhail, xiii, xvii, xviii, 48-49, 51, 58n., 84, 97, 123, 139, 150, 159n., 205, 207, 218-219, 227, 230n., 249-250, 253;
  'Author and Hero in Aesthetic Activity', 159n.;
  Problems of Dostoevsky's Poetics, 84, 97, 207, 253
Bakunin, M A, 125
Balmont, K D, 144
Balzac, Honoré de, 252, 253;
  Eugenie Grandet, 252
Batiuko, A I, 190
Beckett, Samuel, 126
Beethoven, Ludwig van, 150n.
Belinsky, Vissarion, 24, 32n., 76, 94

Belknap, Robert, xix, 161, 162, 163n., 184n.
Bely, Andrei, 49, 51-52;
  Petersburg, 51-52
Bem, A L, 21-22, 25
Berdiaev, Nikolai, 237n.
Berlin, Sir Isaiah, 46-47, 112n.
The Bible, 101, 135, 233, 250, 251, 252;
  Genesis, 11, 54, 158;
  II Samuel, 230;
  I Kings, 230;
  Psalms, 231, 238;
  Lamentations, 159;
  Matthew, 45, 191-193, 198, 200-202, 214, 238;
  Mark, 33n., 122, 211, 191-193, 198-202, 238;
  Luke, 238;
  John, 71, 178, 205, 233, 236, 237, 242, 251;
  Acts, 190;
  I Thess., 190;
  Revelation, 192, 193, 196
Bismarck, Otto von, 207-208
Blok, Alexander, 47, 49, 55, 58, 141, 146n.;
  'One Day', 146n.;
  'Slowly Streaming', 146n.;
  The Twelve, 146n.
Boborykin, Pyotr, xix, 84-97;
  For Half a Century, 86n., 89n., 95;
  'New Birds, New Songs', 94;
  On the Road, 86, 92;
  The Smallholder, 85;
  Victim of the Evening, 91-92
Boethius: *The Consolation of Philosophy*, 226
Bogdanov-Berezovsky, Valerian: *Nastasya Filippovna* (1964), 147

Bonhoeffer, Dietrich, 219
Bortko, Vladimir: *The Idiot* (2003), xv
Brahms, Johannes: First Piano Concerto, 138
Briusov, V, 22, 32n., 33n., 35n., 37n., 144, 145;
The Fiery Angel, 145
Brooks, Richard: *The Brothers Karamazov* (1958), xiv
Brunetière, Ferdinand, 96
Buckle, Henry Thomas, 166
Buddha, 221-222, 223, 225, 227
Bulgakov, Mikhail, 130
Bulgakov, S N, 191n., 192-193
Burenin, V P, 87-88, 91
Butsko, Iuri: *White Nights* (1968), 146-147
Byron, Lord, 99, 107

Calderón de la Barca, 67
Camden, William, 104
Camus, Albert, 162n.
Carroll, Lewis, 125
Catherine the Great, 31n., 82
Catteau, Jacques, xviii, xix, 56, 150n., 207n.
Cervantes, Miguel de, 82, 241
Chekhov, Anton, 129, 136;
The Cherry Orchard, 129-130
Chernyshevsky, Nikolai, 7, 76, 85, 174
Chertkova, A K, 115
Christ, xvii, 9, 65, 171, 189-206, 214, 219, 231, 233, 234n., 235-238, 242-244, 246-251, 253
Christa, Boris, xix, 173
Chukovskaia, Lidia, 46, 47, 48
Chukovsky, Kornei, 54n.
The Citizen (Grazhdanin), 65, 91, 92, 93, 98-109
Claudian, 76
Coetzee, J M, xiv, 163n.;
The Master of Petersburg, xiv
Coleridge, Samuel Taylor, 104
Comte, Auguste, 91
The Contemporary (Sovremennik), 76, 86

Copland, Aaron, 142n.

Dal, Vladimir, 51
Dargomyzhsky, Alexander Sergeevich: *The Stone Guest* (1860s), 144
Darwin, Charles, 100
Descartes, René, 123, 132-134
de Vogüé, Eugène Melchior, 96
Diaghilev, Serge, 145-146
Dickens, Charles, 154, 182n.;
Hard Times, 182n.
Dolgopolov, L K, 47, 50, 51
Dolinin, A S, 68n., 123
Don Quixote, 82, 129, 240-241
Dostoevskaia, Anna Grigorievna (Snitkina), xiv, 40, 64, 90, 150n., 242-243
Dostoevskaia, Maria Dimitrevna (Isaeva), 87, 195
Dostoevsky, Fyodor Mikhailovich:
The Adolescent, 4, 5, 6, 25, 39, 46-63, 64, 65, 103, 195n., 199, 200n., 202-203, 211-215, 218, 230-231, 233-234, 251, 252;
'Bobok', 8, 12, 93, 189;
The Brothers Karamazov, 5, 11, 13, 40, 64-71, 82-83, 107, 119, 124, 126, 127, 132, 138n., 143, 149-150, 171, 172, 177, 184, 195n., 199, 204-205, 215-218, 229, 231-232, 233, 234-238, 244, 249, 250, 252;
Crime and Punishment, xiv, xviii, xix, 3, 5, 7, 9, 14-20, 21-39, 83, 90, 95, 110, 111-114, 119, 153-156, 170-174, 175-186, 192n., 193-194, 199-201, 251-252;
'The Crocodile', 7, 12;
The Devils, xiii, 5, 6, 50, 58n., 64-65, 83, 85-86, 92, 93, 95, 123, 125, 127, 129-130, 137, 138, 139-141, 143, 150, 172, 200n., 203n., 207-211, 212, 213n., 218-219, 232-233, 242-246, 252;
The Diary of a Writer, xvi, 8-12, 38, 64, 68, 70, 91, 93, 103, 110, 114-119, 181, 189-206, 246-248;

270

The Double, 8, 70;
'Dreams and Reveries', 13, 103n.;
'The Dream of a Ridiculous Man', 10, 11, 12, 13, 58n., 189, 223;
'Environment', 103, 115, 117;
'The Eternal Husband', 10, 12;
'The Fantastic Pages', 232, 242-248;
The Gambler, xiv, xix, 3, 7, 9, 10, 11, 12, 40-45, 143-145;
'A Gentle Creature', 10, 11, 12, 138n.;
'The Golden Age in Your Pocket', 246;
The Idiot, xiv, xv, 5, 82, 124, 138n., 139, 143, 146, 147-148, 162, 172, 192n., 220-229, 252;
The Insulted and Injured, 3, 8, 251, 252;
'The Little Boy at Christ's Christmas Tree', 9, 143, 144;
'Masha is Lying on the Table...', 195;
'A Nasty Story', 7, 12, 137, 139, 150;
Netochka Nezvanovna, 3, 138;
Notes from the House of the Dead, xv, 7, 11, 44-45, 85, 100, 111, 118, 119, 249, 251, 252;
Notes from Underground, 8, 10, 11, 12, 87, 157-169, 251;
'The Peasant Marei', 9, 12;
Poor Folk, 3, 40, 118, 143, 148-149;
Speech at the Pushkin Memorial, 22, 66-68, 71, 95, 196, 253;
The Village of Stepanchikovo and its Inhabitants, 40;
'A Weak Heart', 50n.;
'White Nights', 138, 143, 146-147;
Winter Notes on Summer Impressions, 4, 11, 104n., 192n.
Dostoevsky, Mikhail Mihkailovich, 86, 87, 89
Druzhinin, A V, 105n., 108
Dubelt, L V, 79
Dudjom Rinpoche, 227

Durov, S F, 85

Efimov, Igor, 116
Egeberg, Erik, xix
Eisenstein, Sergei, 82, 139n.
Elgar, Edward, 150
Eliade, Mircea, 54-55
Emerson, Caryl, 84n., 141-143, 159n., 207n.
Engelhardt, M A, 114-115
The Epoch (Epokha), 64, 86, 87, 89-90, 240n.;
Ermler, Fridrikh: *The Great Citizen*, 138

Falconet, Etienne, 30-31, 33n., 51
Favre, Jules, 208
Fedorov, N F, 65
Flaubert, Gustav, 121
Forster, E M, 182n., 185;
  Aspects of the Novel, 185;
  Maurice, 182n.
Fourier, Charles, 10
Frank, Joseph, xvii n., 45n., 86n., 177, 178n., 210n.
Frank, S L, 251
Freeborn, Richard, 39n., 50n., 67n., 183n.
Freud, Sigmund, 9, 222n.
Fridlender, G M, 21, 58n., 92n., 123
Frye, Northrop, 180n.
Futrell, Michael, 221

Gaidenko, P, 121
Galen: Theory of Humours, 159
Garibaldi, Giuseppe, 78-79
Ge, N N, 246
Gerigk, Horst-Jurgen, xix, 4-6, 13, 171n.
Glazunov, A K, 139
Glinka, Fyodor, 139, 150n.
Goethe, Johann Wolfgang von, 212-215;
  Faust, 25, 211-215
Gogol, Nikolai, 49, 70, 130, 139, 142n., 145n., 146, 148, 240;
  Dead Souls, 130;
  The Government Inspector, 130;

'The Nose', 145n., 149;
'Notes of a Madman', 146
Goncharov, Ivan, 4n., 75
Gorky, Maxim, 173, 220
Gounod, Charles François: *Faust*, 212n.
Gozenpud, Abram, 137, 140n., 207n., 210n., 212n., 213n.
Gradovsky, G, 196-197
Griboedov, Alexander, 4;
Woe from Wit, 4-5, 6-7
Grieg, Edvard, 144
Grigoriev, Nikolai Petrovich, 84-85, 95
Grushin, Boris, 122
Gruv, DJ, 139
Gumilev, Nikolai, 53
Gusev, A, 221
Gusev, N N, 115

Harrington, Alexandra, xviii, xix
Hauptmann, Gerhart: *Hannele*, 144n.
Hegel, Georg Wilhelm Friedrich, 8
Hennequin, Emile, 96
Hesse, Hermann, 221
Huckleberry Finn, 183
Hudspith, Sarah, xvii n., xix
Hughes, Thomas: *Tom Brown's Schooldays*, 99-101, 107-108
Hugo, Victor, 81, 154, 252, 253;
Le Châtiment, 81;
Notre Dame de Paris, 252
Hus, Jan, 75, 78, 82

Ilenkov, Evald, 122
Irenaeus, St, 197
Iuriev, S A, 66
Ivan IV, 79-82
Ivanov, Alexander, 251
Ivanov, Vyacheslav, 177, 178n.

Jackson, Robert Louis, xvii n., 56, 61, 110, 119n.
James, William, 184n.
John Chrysostom, St, 213
Jones, Malcolm, xv, xvii n., xviii, 21, 58, 63 98, 137, 150n., 171,
175, 177, 185, 221n., 230n., 239, 250, 255-258, 259-268
John the Divine, St, 192-194

Kabalevsky, Dmitry, 138
Kachanov, Roman: *Down House* (2001), 139
Kafka, Franz, 126, 135
Kairova, Mlle, 90
Kant, Immanuel, 123, 131-132, 133, 134
Karatygin, V G, 144
Karetnikov, Nikolai, 137, 139, 150;
A Nasty Story (1966), 137, 139
Kariakin, Iuri Fyodorovich, 122, 124-125
Kasatkina, Tatiana, xvi, xvii n., xix, xx
Katkov, Mikhail, 68, 90, 99, 108, 179, 243
Kelly, Catriona, 257
Kempis, Thomas à: *The Imitation of Christ*, 249
Kharms, Daniil, 126
Khentova, Sofia, 141
Khodasevich, Vladislav, 143n.;
Solitude, 146n.
Kholminov, Alexander: *The Brothers Karamazov*, 149-150
Khomiakov, A S, 101, 107, 236-237;
'The Island', 101
Kirk, Irina, 221
Kirov, Sergei, 138
Kirpotin, V, 123, 193n.
Kogan, G F, 30
Korvin-Krukovskaia, Anna, 40n.
Kraevsky, A A, 240
Kronenberg, S L, 198
Kupreianova, E N, 26n., 33
Kurasawa, Akira: *Hakuchi (The Idiot*, 1951), xiv
Kurbsky, Prince A M, 97, 81
Kuzmin, Mikhail: *The Trout Breaks the Ice*, 28

Lamb, Charles, 104
Lantz, Kenneth, 110n., 190n.

Leatherbarrow, Willliam, xvii n., 56, 98n., 100n.
Lenin, Vladimir Ilych, 80, 125, 141
Leontiev, Konstantin, 237n.
Leontiev, P M, 108
Lermontov, Mikhail, 8;
  Hero of our Time, 8, 251
Leskov, Nikolai, 46, 89, 150;
  'Lady Macbeth of Mtsensk', 149;
  Nowhere to Go, 89
Levaia, Tamara, 143
Likhachev, D S, 189
Lim, Antonin, 122
Lipovetsky, Mark, 54, 59
Littré, Emile, 91
Loseff, Lev, 48
Lotman, Iuri, 3-4
Lyotard, Jean-Francois, 63
Liubimov, Iuri, 137, 139-140;
  The Possessed (1985), 137
Liubimov, N A, 66, 180n.
Lycurgus, 172

MacDonald, Malcolm, 141-142
McDuff, David, xiv, 22n., 113n.
MacMillan, Harold, 255
McMillin, Arnold, xiv, xviii, xix
McNair, John, xix, 85n., 88n., 89n., 92n., 95n., 96n.
Mack, Maynard, 185
Maikov, Apollon, 75-83;
  'At the Tomb of Ivan the Terrible', 80-81;
  'The Coach', 79;
  'EPM', 78;
  'Fishing', 78;
  'Haymaking', 76-78;
  'In Gorodets in 1263', 80;
  'It is airless or is it again the Sirocco', 78;
  'It is Spring! The first widow pane is out', 76;
  'Harlequin', 79;
  'Landscape', 76;
  'On Lord! Yesterday was bad weather', 76;
  'Meditation', 76;
  'Peter the Great in Ostrogozhsk', 79;
  Savonarola, 82;
  The Sentence, 75, 78, 82;
  'Thought', 76;
  'We have Grown up in a Harsh School', 82;
  'Who is He?', 79, 81
Maikov, Leonid, 75
Maikov, Valerian, 75
Maikov, Vladimir, 75
Makk, Karoly: *The Gambler* (1997), xiv
Mamardashvili, Merab, 120-136
Mandelshtam, Nadezhda, 61
Mandelshtam, Osip, 46, 49, 52, 53, 133, 136, 138n.;
  'Ariost', 52
Maria Alexandrovna, Grand Duchess, 102
Marseillaise, The, 208-211, 218
Martinsen, Deborah, xvii n., xix, 160n., 179n.
Mayakovsky, Vladimir, 257
Meerson, Olga, 153, 159, 160n.
Mein lieber Augustin, 208-211, 212, 218
Merimée, Prosper: 'Carmen', 150
Mertens, Bram, 174
Meshchersky, V P, 91, 98, 99, 100, 109n.
Michelangelo Buonarotti, 140
Mickiewicz, Adam: 'The Memorial of Peter the Great', 36-38
Mikhailovsky, N K, 93, 94
Mill, John Stuart, 100
Miller, Robin Feuer, xiv, xv, xviii, xix, 58n., 157n., 163n., 238, 259
Minaev, D D, 240
Mints, Zinaida, 58
Mirsky, D S, 76, 78, 82
Mochulsky, Konstantin, 44, 177-180, 183
Mombelli, N A, 85
Moscow News (Moskovskie vedomosti), 99, 102, 105n.
Muhammad, 172, 226

Musil, Robert: *The Man without Qualities*, 126
Mussorgsky, Modest, 143-144;
 Boris Godunov, 143n.;
 The Marriage, 144
Myaskovsky, Nikolai, 146

Naiman, Anatoly, 46, 50n., 230
Napoleon Bonaparte, xiii, 19, 81, 172, 185
Naumov, Vladimir: *A Nasty Story* (1966), 137, 139
Nechaev, Sergei, 125
Neuhäuser, Rudolf, xix, 8n.
Nekrasov, Nikolai, 76, 79;
 'On Maikov', 79
Nevsky, Alexander, 80, 81-82
Nicholas I, 53, 79, 85
Nikolai, Tsarevich, 109n.
Notes of the Fatherland (Otechestvennye zapiski), 60, 86
Novikova, E G, 192-193, 194n.
Nussbaum, Martha, 181-182

Orff, Carl: *Carmina Burana*, 140
Orwell, George, 126, 130;
 Nineteen Eighty-Four, 130
Ostrovsky, Alexander, 242
Ozmidov, Nikolai Lukich, 65

Palmerston, Lord, 18, 99
Palm, Alexander, 85
Parini, Jay, 180
Pasternak, Boris, 47, 133, 136, 138n., 255
Paul, Saint, 250
Paz, Octavio, 183
Peace, Richard, xvii n., xix, 16-17
Peel, Robert, 99
Pelevin, Victor, xiv, 221;
 Chapaev and Pustota, 221
Peter the Great, 22-25, 30-39, 51-53, 79-80, 81-82, 248
Peterson, Nikolai Pavlovich, 65
Petravshevsky circle, 52, 75, 84
Pevear, Richard, xiv, 205n., 207n., 214n., 235n.

Philosophical Questions (Voprosy filosofii), 122
Pilate, Pontius, 242
Pisarev, Dmitry, 7
Pisemsky, A F, 85
Plaksin, I, 144
Plato, 170-171, 223;
 The Myth of Er, 223;
 The Sophist, 171
Platonov, Andrei, 126, 130, 136;
 The Foundation Pit, 126
Plimak, E, 125
Pobedonostsev, K P, 64, 249
Poe, Edgar Allan: *Imp of the Perverse*, 171
Pogodin, M P, 100
Polivanova, M A, 67, 70
Pomerants, Grigory, 221
Pope, Alexander: 'Ode to Solitude', 76
Pound, Ezra, 171-172;
 The Cantos, 172n.
Pravda, 122
Pride and Prejudice, 183
Pritchett, V S, 183
Problems of the World and Socialism (Problemy mira i sotsializma), 122
Prokofiev, Sergei, 139n., 144-146;
 The Fiery Angel (1927), 145;
 The Gambler (1917, 1929), 144-145;
 Love of Three Oranges (1919), 145;
 Magdalen (1911-1913), 144, 145
Proust, Marcel, 123-124, 133;
 The Captive, 123-124
Pugachev, Emilian, 34
Pushkin, Alexander, xix, 21-39, 49-52, 56, 65-71, 75-80, 83, 86, 133, 136, 138n., 251;
 Boris Godunov, 22;
 The Bronze Horseman, 21-24, 28-39, 51, 80;
 Evgeny Onegin, 22, 251;
 The Miserly Knight, 86;
 'The Queen of Spades', 21, 23-28, 39, 50, 67-71;

'Stanzas', 51-52
Pyrev, Ivan, 138;
  The Brothers Karamazov (1967-1968), 138n.;
  The Idiot, 138n. (1958);
  White Nights (1959), 138-139
Pyzhov, Boris, 122

Rachmaninov, Sergei, 139
Radstock, Lord, 98
Raphael, 251
The Reading Library (Biblioteka dlia chteniia), 85-90, 92, 102, 105n., 106, 108
Rebikov, Vladimir: *The Christmas Tree* (1902-1903), 143-144
Redepenning, Dorothea, 141
Rembrandt Harmensz van Rijn, 124, 249, 251;
  The Night Watch, 124
Renan, Ernest, 65, 246
Rimsky-Korsakov, N A, 144
Roberts, Gareth, 13
Roshal, Grigory: *Petersburg Night* (1934), 138
Rossini, Gioacchino Antonio, 150n.
Rothschild, Baron de, xiii
Rousseau, Jean-Jacques, 157n., 163, 185
Rozhdestvennsky, Gennady, 140, 146
Rumiantsev, Aleksei Matveevich, 122
Rusanov, G A, 110
The Russian Messenger, (Russkii vestnik), 66, 98, 100-101, 106, 243
Russian Thought (Russkaia mysl'), 68
Ryleev, K F: 'Thoughts', 79

Saint Clair, Miss, 90
Saint Petersburg News (Sankt Peterburgskie vedomosti), 90-91, 94
Saltykov-Shchedrin, Mikhail, 7, 91
Sand, George, 154, 247
Scanlan, James, xvii n., 158n., 166n.

Schmidt, Rob: *Crime & Punishment in Suburbia* (2000), xiv
Schnittke, Alfred, 137, 139-140, 146n.;
  Music to an Imagined Play, 139-140
Schnitzler, Arthur, 9
Sedelnikov, Gleb: *Poor Folk* (1974), 148-149
Seleznev, Iu, 123
Shakespeare, William, 128, 177, 194n., 249;
  Hamlet, 128;
  King Lear, 138n., 142n., 185;
  The Merchant of Venice, 182
Shatner, William, xiv
Shcherbachev, Vladimir, 141
Shcherbina, N, 79
Sheinberg, Esti, 141, 142n.
Shostakovich, Dmitry, 137-138, 140-143, 145n., 146-147, 148, 149;
  Babi Yar (Symphony No. 13, 1962), 142n.;
  Four Verses of Captain Lebyadkin (1975), 137, 140-143, 146, 150;
  King Lear (1970), 138n.;
  Lady Macbeth of Mtsensk (1934), 141-142, 149;
  New Babylon, (1928-1929), 138n.;
  The Nose (1927-1928), 145n., 149;
  Suite on Verses of Michelangelo Buonarotti (1974), 140
Shteinberg, Maximilian, 141
Siddharta Gautama (Buddha), 221, 223
Skriabin, A N, 139
Slattery, Dennis, 225-226
Slavophiles, 17-18, 75, 86, 94, 95-96, 101
The Snowdrop (Podsnezhnik), 75
Socrates, 170
Sogyal Rinpoche, 223n., 224, 227n.
Solon, 172
Solovev, Vsevolod, 247
Sorokin, Boris, 116
Spasovich, V D, 198

Spencer, Herbert: *The Study of Sociology*, 99-100
Spinoza, Benedict de: Ethics, 157
Stalin, Iosef Vissarionovich, xiii, 53, 80-81, 138n.
Stanley, Arthur Penrhyn, 102n., 106
Star Trek, xiv
Steiner, George, 111, 220n.
Stellovsky, F T, xiv, 9, 40, 90
Stradella, Alessandro, 212
Strakhov, N N, 44n., 86-87, 100, 119n.
Surkov, Andrei, 61
Suslova, Appolinaria, 45, 86

Tacitus, 31
Taine, Hyppolyte, 96
Talankin, Igor and Dmitry: *The Devils (Nikolai Stavrogin)* (1992), 139
Tchaikovsky, Pyotr Ilych, 139, 144; *The Nutcracker Suite,* 144
Terras, Victor, 41n., 45n., 141n., 215, 216n.
Thompson, Diane Oenning, xvii n., xviii, xix, xx, 217n.
Tikhomirov, Boris, xvi n., xix, x, 196n., 204n.
Time (Vremia), 12, 64, 85, 240, 252n;
Timenchik, Roman, 48, 54
Tishchenko, Boris, 141
Tiutchev, Fyodor, 171, 235, 247; 'Silentium', 171, 247
Tolstoy, Aleksei, 81
Tolstoy, Lev, 46-47, 100n., 110-119, 128, 133, 220, 258;
Anna Karenina, 46, 110, 114-115, 116n.;
Resurrection, 110-119;
War and Peace, 82, 112, 119;
'Why do Men Stupefy Themselves?', 111-112
Transhel, A, 108
Trotsky, Lev Davidovich, 81
Trubetskoi, Evgeny: *The Meaning of Life*, 135
Tsevtaev, Mikhail, 146, 148;

White Nights (1933), 146
Tsypkin, Leonid: *Summer in B Baden*, xiv
Tunimanov, Vladimir, xv, xix
Turgenev, Ivan, 46, 60, 67, 11
A Nest of Gentlefolk, 46

Vainberg, Maisei (Mieczyslaw Weinberg): *The Idiot* (1980) 147-148
Varets, M I, 118
Velleman, J David, 159n., 16! 168
Vetlovskaia, V E, xviii, xix, 2 233
The Voice (Golos), 13n., 90, 1
Volokhonsky, Larissa, xiv, 2(207n., 214n., 235n.
Voltaire, 247
Voskoboinikov, Nikolai, 86, 90

Wagner, Richard, 15, 150n.; *Parsifal*, 150n.
Wasiolek, Edward, 41n., 56n., 141n.
Weihl, Renier, 4
Westernizers, 18, 91, 94
Whitman, Walt, 182n.
Wittgenstein, Ludwig: *Tractatus Logico-Philosophicus*, 121
Woody Woodpecker, 150
Wordsworth, William, 78
Wright, Richard, *Native Son*, 182n.

Young, Sarah, xvii n., xx, 39, 71, 136, 206, 222n., 228n., 238, 253

Zabolotsky, N A, 130
Zagladin, Vadim, 122
Zaitsev, V A, 7
Zakharov, Vladimir, xvi, xviii, xx, 47n., 100n, 220n., 239n., 240n..
Zamyatin, Evgeny, 126, 221; *We*, 221
Zhdanov, Andrei, 62, 124
Zohrab, Irene, xviii, xix, 100n., 102n., 103n., 107n., 109n.
Zola, Emile, 91
Zoshchenko, Mikhail, 130